LINCOLN AND THE MUSIC
OF THE CIVIL WAR

ABRAHAM LINCOLN

January 8, 1864. Reproduced from a glass-plate negative in the Truman H.
Bartlett Collection, Boston University, Boston.

PLATE I

Lincoln and the Music of the Civil War

By

KENNETH A. BERNARD
Professor of History
Boston University

ILLUSTRATED WITH PHOTOGRAPHS

The CAXTON PRINTERS, Ltd.
CALDWELL, IDAHO
1966

Printed, lithographed, and bound in the United States of America by
THE CAXTON PRINTERS, LTD.
CALDWELL, IDAHO   83605
105128

To my wife
Dorothy

whose love of music provided the inspiration
for this book, and whose interest, enthusiasm,
and companionship made possible its completion

A NOTE CONCERNING QUOTATIONS

IN THE MID-NINETEENTH CENTURY, WRITERS, ESPECIALLY newspaper reporters, were rather casual about such things as grammar, punctuation, and spelling. Thus variations, inconsistencies, and errors were frequent. Rather than make corrections which would necessitate the insertion of brackets [ ] and of [*sic*] many times, I have followed the policy of quoting exactly without corrections except in a few instances where emendation made for clarity. Thus the interruption of passages has been avoided and the flavor of the language of the times better preserved. This policy has been followed for musical programs, musical titles and verses of songs and poems as well as for straight narrative.

THE AUTHOR

ACKNOWLEDGMENTS

THIS BOOK HAS BEEN SOME TWELVE YEARS IN THE MAKING. During this time I have used the resources of many libraries and have received help from many people. For the privilege of spending profitable and exciting hours in the libraries visited I am grateful; to those librarians and Lincolnians whose assistance I received I shall always be indebted.

I especially wish to express my great gratitude to these good people who generously gave help and counsel on many occasions:

Mrs. Emmett L. Avery, Washington State University Library, Pullman, Washington.

Miss Josephine Cobb, The National Archives, Washington, D.C.

Frank E. Edgington, Washington, D.C.

Miss Margaret A. Flint, Illinois State Historical Library, Springfield, Illinois.

Miss Margaret Hackett, The Boston Athenaeum, Boston, Massachusetts.

Carl Haverlin, Northridge, California.

David A. Jonah, The Library, Brown University, Providence, Rhode Island.

R. Gerald McMurtry, Lincoln National Life Foundation, Fort Wayne, Indiana.

David C. Mearns, Library of Congress, Washington, D.C.

C. Percy Powell, formerly of the Library of Congress, Washington, D.C.

Wayne C. Temple, Illinois State Archives, Springfield, Illinois.

In addition, I wish to express my appreciation to the following who gave help on specific and often difficult problems:

Miss Constance E. Adams, Washington, D.C.

Rev. Charles A. Anderson, Presbyterian Historical Society, Philadelphia, Pennsylvania.

Mrs. Margaret B. Andrews, University of Rochester Library, Rochester, New York.

Mrs. Elden E. Billings, Columbia Historical Society, Washington, D.C.

Mrs. Joyce Bonk, The Clements Library, University of Michigan, Ann Arbor, Michigan.

Mrs. Emma E. Built, formerly of The Library, Brown University, Providence, Rhode Island.

George Calvin Carter, Manchester, New Hampshire.

M. W. Clay, McLeod County Historical Society, Hutchinson, Minnesota.

Miss Sarah Corcoran, Public Library, Walla Walla, Washington.

Miss Norma Cuthbert, formerly of the Henry E. Huntington Library, San Marino, California.

Deane Edwards, The Hymn Society of America, New York, New York.

Arnold Gates, Garden City, New York.

Joseph George, Jr., Villanova University, Villanova, Pennsylvania.

Mrs. Elizabeth S. Gilbert, Public Library, Spokane, Washington.

Col. Paul R. Goode, Washington, D.C.

Cornelius W. Heine, National Capitol Region, Washington, D.C.

James J. Heslin, The New-York Historical Society, New York, New York.

Miss Barbara D. Hobson, The Library, Brown University, Providence, Rhode Island.

Mrs. Alice P. Hook, The Historical and Philosophical Society of Ohio, Cincinnati, Ohio.

Andrew H. Horn, The Library, Occidental College, Los Angeles, California.

L. K. Jones, Walla Walla, Washington.

John H. Knickerbocker, The Library, Gettysburg College, Gettysburg, Pennsylvania.

Mrs. Dorothy Meserve Kunhardt, Morristown, New Jersey.

Mrs. Bernice B. Larrabee, The Free Library of Philadelphia, Philadelphia, Pennsylvania.

Lester S. Levy, Pikesville, Maryland.

Hugh C. McIlhenny, Gettysburg, Pennsylvania.

Mrs. E. R. Millar, Alexander, Arkansas.

Miss Amy Nyholm, The Newberry Library, Chicago, Illinois.

Weldon Petz, Birmingham, Michigan.

Mrs. Eleanor C. Pyne, Public Library, Providence, Rhode Island.

Paul L. Roy, Gettysburg, Pennsylvania.

Kenneth M. Scollon, Washington, D.C.

Mrs. Emma Sheffer, Gettysburg, Pennsylvania.

Bert Sheldon, Washington, D.C.

Mrs. Herbert Shive, Indiana University Library, Bloomington, Indiana.

Miss Jean W. Steele, The Westminster Press, Philadelphia, Pennsylvania.

Louis A. Warren, formerly of the Lincoln National Life Foundation, Fort Wayne, Indiana.

Dr. John E. Washington, Washington, D.C.

Arthur Weaver, Gettysburg, Pennsylvania.

Mrs. Earl T. Weaver, Spokane, Washington.

This list would not be complete without acknowledgment of help from these persons now deceased: Mary Bowditch Forbes, Robert L. Kincaid, Harry E. Pratt, Marion D. Pratt.

My thanks also go to Mrs. Alice Tonra, Chenery Library, Boston University, for continuous help in the search for materials, to Arthur J. Moscatel, Photographic Service, Boston University, for skilful work in photographic reproduction, and to Miss Ednamae Storti, Washington, D.C., for secretarial assistance.

Special thanks are due to Mrs. Raymond N. Heron, Lexington, Massachusetts, for her generous cooperation, patience, and skill in the arduous task of preparing the final manuscript. I gratefully acknowledge her invaluable assistance.

For financial help toward the expenses of research I express my thanks and appreciation to the Graduate School of Boston University.

During the Civil War Centennial Years, 1961-1965, the chapters in this book appeared quarterly in the *Lincoln Herald,* published by Lincoln Memorial University, Harrogate, Tennessee. I wish to express my deep appreciation to President H. LaMarr Rice of Lincoln Memorial University and to Wayne C. Temple, then editor of the *Lincoln Herald,* for their continued interest in "Lincoln and the Music of the Civil War."

TABLE OF CONTENTS

LIST OF ILLUSTRATIONS

FOREWORD

ABRAHAM LINCOLN WAS ONE OF OUR MOST "UNMUSICAL" Presidents. He never studied music, never had any training in it, and knew nothing of its technical aspects; he could not play any instrument (except possibly the harmonica), could not read music, nor could he really sing. Lincoln, the rail-splitter, the circuit lawyer, the saver of the Union and the Emancipator, was, in short, no musician.

Yet two significant facts are clearly evident when one thinks of Lincoln and music. He was extremely fond of music and, as President, he probably heard more music than any other occupant of the White House.

Just as the ax and the plow (implements which he did not particularly enjoy) were important in Lincoln's frontier days in Indiana and Illinois, so also were the songs, ballads, and play parties (which he did enjoy). "John Anderson's Lamentation," "Weevily Wheat," and the *Missouri Harmony* songbook helped to make life on the frontier happy and merry.

Springfield, Illinois, enjoyed a goodly amount of musical activity which Lincoln shared, but it was on the circuit that Lincoln experienced his greatest musical satisfaction. There many an hour was lightened by music, sometimes the jolly, boisterous singing of Ward Lamon, or, again, the genteel but highly popular concert programs of traveling musicians whose paths chanced to cross those of the lawyers on circuit.

Lincoln's musical taste extended, as did his taste in poetry, from the nonsensical and ludicrous to the sad and mournful—from "Hoosen Johnny" and the "Blue-

Tail Fly" to "He Doeth All Things Well" and "Twenty
Years Ago." He enjoyed such songs as "The Sword of
Bunker Hill" and "The Ship on Fire," and he was especially fond of sentimental songs and Scotch ballads
like "Auld Robin Gray" and "Mary of Argyle." "Annie
Laurie" was one of his favorites. He laughed heartily at
minstrels and appreciated the comforting solace of "Rock
of Ages."

The Civil War was, in a sense, a "musical war." Par-
ticipation in musical activity had been widespread during
the years preceding the conflict. The singing school, the
"musical institute," the piano and the band were popular
everywhere. When the war came this interest in music
was carried over and became an important component
of the war effort. The old music, ranging from "Yankee
Doodle" to "Home, Sweet Home" continued to be popular,
but to it was added a tremendous quantity of new music
inspired by the war.

Thus, during the first year alone, an estimated two
thousand compositions were produced, and by the end of
the war more music had been created, played, and sung
than during all our other wars combined. More of the
music of the era has endured than from any other period
in our history.

As President, Lincoln heard this music constantly and
continually, from his first serenade on February 28, 1861,
to the final notes of "Hail to the Chief!" on the evening of
April 14, 1865. He heard the old popular and patriotic
tunes and the new songs of the war; he listened to the
bands and to choruses and soloists. He came to know the
songs and the singers, the bands and their leaders. No
President, before or since, has been sung to and played to
as much as was Lincoln. No President enjoyed the sound
and sentiment of music any more than did Lincoln.

This volume tells the story of Lincoln's association with
the music of the Civil War—the music that he heard and
the occasions when it was played and sung; the musicians
and bands that he came to know and appreciate; the selections that he especially liked and enjoyed. Against a
background of specific events it shows how the music

of the war was inspired, how it in turn inspired the soldiers and the folk back home, and, finally, how it often inspired Lincoln himself.

It is hoped that to our already rich fund of knowledge of the Civil War this work will add something of value and significance.

LINCOLN AND THE MUSIC
OF THE CIVIL WAR

CHAPTER I

HAIL TO THE CHIEF!

IT WAS NEARLY ELEVEN O'CLOCK ON THE EVENING OF March 4, 1861. For some time the forty-five-piece band under the direction of Professor L. F. Weber had been playing popular dance tunes—Quadrille "Schaffer," Lancers "Fashion," a waltz and polka by Strauss. Some of the guests in the brilliantly lighted hall were dancing, some were promenading, some were just looking on.[1] The room was comfortably filled, but not crowded, for although there were perhaps fifteen hundred or two thousand people present, the hall was a large one. Adjacent to Washington's City Hall, where dressing rooms for ladies and gentlemen—the latter complete with a punch bowl—were provided, a building had been especially constructed for the occasion. Measuring two hundred and fifty by sixty feet, it had been carefully planned and attractively decorated.[2]

Around the entire room there was a carpeted platform with seats for those who wished to chat and observe the dancing. On one side a movable partition the full length of the hall separated the dance floor from the supper room, and opposite the entrance the band was stationed. Flags, shields, and bunting, with blue and white the predominating colors, helped to cover the bare walls and ceiling, while light from bracket clusters and from five elegant chandeliers (each containing one hundred burners) gave an effective brilliance to the entire scene. Even the exits were adequate and well planned.

With the chandeliers valued at $5,000, the catered

[1] Washington *Evening Star,* **Mar. 5,** 1861; **N.Y.** *Herald,* **Mar. 6,** 1861. The program for the Inaugural Ball included twenty-three numbers beginning with an inaugural march and concluding with a waltz and galop.

[2] **N.Y.** *Herald,* Mar. 3, 6, 1861; Washington *National Intelligencer,* Feb. 20, 1861.

supper costing over $4,000, the entire expense of the affair amounted to almost $17,000. The New York *Herald* reporter wrote with approval of the excellent taste in decorations and arrangements, while the New York *Tribune* commented enthusiastically: "It is the finest hall for the purpose ever built here, in design, decoration and accommodation." The committee in charge had done its work well.[3]

A few experienced observers, however, thought that in spite of the brilliant lights and attractive decorations, the affair lacked sparkle and gaiety, that it seemed apathetic and gloomy. To be sure, these experienced critics noted, there were in attendance many attractive young ladies in white and pink and blue, but the number of elderly dames in somber autumnal colors was very noticeable; there were a few members of the diplomatic corps present, but not many men in army and navy uniforms were in evidence (because, as one young lady remarked, "so many have resigned, you know").[4]

Cold formality prevailed, and the guests, even the dancers, seemed to be in a quiet and serious mood, showing none of the vivacity, exuberance, or joy that might be expected at the first big social event of a new administration in Washington. Thus, concluded the critics, the Union Ball was not turning out to be a great success.[5]

In their reasoning, these critics were, perhaps, partly right and partly in error. In contrast to previous social events in the capital, the Union Ball did lack in sparkle and gaiety, for the guests were mostly from the North; the old elite, that is to say, Southerners, especially Southern belles, were not present. They made it a point not to be. Instead, these were ladies and gentlemen from the cities and towns of New England and the prairie villages and

---

[3] N.Y. *Herald,* Mar. 3, 1861; N.Y. *Tribune,* Mar. 4, 1861.

[4] N.Y. *Herald,* Mar. 6, 1861.

[5] The affair was "about as happy as Horace Greeley in the presence of Thurlow Weed," observed a reporter. N.Y. *Herald,* Mar. 6, 1861. Robert C. Ogden thought it an apathetic affair and the guests ill-at-ease. Philip Whitwell Wilson, *An Unofficial Statesman—Robert C. Ogden* (Garden City, 1924), p. 60. Another observer labeled it "not grand, but gloomy and peculiar." G. B. Wallis, "Honest Abe and the Little Giant," *The Outlook,* CXXVII (Feb. 9, 1921), 217-18. Still another critic thought it the dullest of all balls. Mrs. Eugene McLean, "When the States Seceded. From the Diary of Mrs. Eugene McLean," *Harper's Monthly,* CXXVIII (Jan., 1914), 286.

towns of the West, and they were not so accustomed to elaborate social events as were the ladies and gentlemen who, up until now, had dominated the social scene.

Perhaps, also, they were aware of the antipathy of Washington society to Northerners, especially Republicans, and undoubtedly they sensed the tenseness of the dramatic day which was now coming to a close. Not only had armed men in uniform been much in evidence during the day, but even now soldiers stood on guard outside the hall. Times were changing in Washington, and the "different" atmosphere of the ballroom was an impressive instance of the change.

One critic commented, "The *haut ton* did not come out, because 'the Lincolns are not yet the fashion,' "[6] while another lamented:

> It was an extraordinary occasion . . . it was an extraordinary assemblage . . . in its prevailing elements. They told a story of dispossession and occupation of the Government, strange and portentous, the dispossession of the South and the forces of King Cotton, and an occupation by the "outside barbarians" of the Northwest. Oh, the fearful change! There was nothing like this in the inauguration ball of any President from the beginning to this day.[7]

But to assume that all observers were of the same mind, or that the dancers and promenaders did not consider the party a success, was scarcely correct. *Harper's Weekly* considered the ball a great success; the New York *Times* gave its approval, and this was echoed in an extended account in the Sacramento *Daily Union* in far-off California. Thus, the prophecy of the New York *Tribune* was, at least to some, fulfilled:

---

[6] Mrs. McLean who commented thusly, although the daughter of a Massachusetts colonel, E. V. Sumner, was married to an officer who went over to the Confederacy. Staying at Willard's "in the full odor of Black Republican sanctity," she was definitely out of sympathy with Northerners. In speaking of Northern women, she characterized them as "refreshing, wide-awake people who never go to sleep mentally and never allow anyone else to. I find it exhilarating, but as a friend from the modern Athens says, 'In the long run it is fatiguing.' " Mrs. Eugene McLean, *Harper's Monthly*, CXXVIII (Jan., 1914), 285-86.

[7] So wrote Wallis, *The Outlook*, CXXVII, 217-18; a writer on social affairs summed up the "anti" viewpoint: "This was called 'The Union Ball'; but, alas! with the true Union severed, many sad associations were called up. The South was unrepresented, and many citizens of Washington were absent." Mrs. E. F. Ellet, *The Court Circles of the Republic* (Hartford, 1869), p. 535; also N.Y. *Herald*, Mar. 6, 1861, and *Leslie's Illus. News*, Mar. 23, 1861.

The Inauguration ball tonight will be an immense success. It has been the fashion within the last two days, and will exceed in numbers and character the most sanguine expectation.

John G. Nicolay, writing to his fiancée three days afterward, said that the ball was really a very successful and brilliant affair, and Dr. William Jayne, many years later, recalled that it was a grand affair, and that the ladies' gowns were not only sensible and becoming—they were handsome.[8]

And now, toward eleven o'clock, the big event of the evening was about to take place. There was a feeling of expectancy as a group of dignitaries appeared at the entrance doorway. The band struck up a familiar tune, the guests arranged themselves in two groups, and into the hall came the presidential party.

To the stirring strains of "Hail to the Chief!" the President, in somber black, Mrs. Lincoln in an attractive blue gown, "the color which fits her fair complexion best," and their escorts, together with young Robert Lincoln and numerous relatives and dignitaries who made up the official party, all promenaded slowly through the aisle made by the guests to the raised platform at the other end of the hall.[9]

This was not the first inaugural ball that Mr. Lincoln had attended. Twelve years before, retiring Congressman Abraham Lincoln, as a spectator and one of the "managers," had gone to the ball for President Taylor, for whom he had campaigned and from whom he hoped to obtain a government position. On that occasion, too, a building had been especially constructed and decorated with flags

---

[8] *Harper's Weekly*, Mar. 16, 1861; N.Y. *Times*, Mar. 5, 1861; Sacramento *Daily Union*, Mar. 27, 1861; N.Y. *Tribune*, Mar. 5, 1861; John G. Nicolay to Therena Bates, Mar. 7, 1861, Nicolay Papers, Library of Congress; Dr. William Jayne, in *Illinois State Journal*, Mar. 5, 1911. Another sympathetic account was given by Mary A. Dodge, H. Augusta Dodge, ed., *Gail Hamilton's Life in Letters* (Boston, 1901), I, 314-15. Financially, the ball was a success also, last-minute efforts of the committee having brought results. Washington *Evening Star*, Mar. 2, 5, 1861.

[9] N.Y. *Herald*, Mar. 6, 1861. Other accounts vary in regard to details, particularly on two points (1) who actually escorted President Lincoln, and (2) whether the band played "Hail to the Chief!" or "Hail, Columbia." In regard to the latter point, the preponderance of evidence favors "Hail to the Chief!" Cf. Washington *Evening Star*, Mar. 5, 1861; N.Y. *Times*, Mar. 5, 1861; Philadelphia *Evening Bulletin*, Mar. 5, 1861; Sacramento *Daily Union*, Mar. 27, 1861; *Harper's Weekly*, Mar. 16, 1861; *Leslie's Illus. News*, Mar. 23, 1861; Wallis, *The Outlook*, CXXVII, 217-18; Dodge, ed., *Gail Hamilton's Letters*, I, 314-15.

and other insignia. President Taylor entered the ballroom at eleven o'clock. Inasmuch as Mrs. Taylor did not
participate in social functions, her place was taken by
their daughter, "Miss Betty." Her entrance to the ballroom was, according to one account, somewhat of a sensation:

> The throng pressed back, and . . . the young and handsome
> wife of the Russian Minister, enveloped in a cloud of crim-
> son satin and glistening with diamonds, supported by two
> ambassadors emblazoned in gold lace and orders, came for-
> ward—just behind were two "Louisiana beauties," a blonde
> and a brunette, whose brilliant charms subsequently divided
> the gentlemen in perplexity as to which should be acceded the
> palm of the belle of the evening. "Which is Miss Betty?"
> whispered the throng as these queenly creatures, by their
> native charms, without the aid of dress, eclipsed the more
> glowing splendor of the Russian court. Then behind these
> came "Miss Betty," plainly dressed in white, a simple flower
> in her hair. . . . The expectations of the vast crowd were for
> the moment realized, and then followed expressions of en-
> thusiasm that were overwhelming.[10]

It was no wonder that the ball was considered a very
brilliant affair, the like of which ex-Congressman Lincoln
had never seen before, and in which he was so much interested that he did not leave until about four in the
morning![11]

Did President Lincoln, as he moved slowly through the
aisle on this fourth of March, 1861, recall this earlier
occasion? It is unlikely, for he had been up since very
early and was now somewhat tired and worn. (One lady

---

[10] Laura C. Holloway, *The Ladies of the White House* (Phila., 1881), pp. 447-48.

[11] William E. Baringer, *Lincoln Day by Day: A Chronology 1809-1865* (Washington, 1960), II, 5, 6, 9; E. B. Washburne in Allen Thorndike Rice, ed., *Reminiscences of Abraham Lincoln* (N.Y., 1886), pp. 19-20.

    The ball was a tremendous affair and a great success. A long description in the
N.Y. *Tribune*, Mar. 8, 1849, carried the heading "The Grand Ball at Washington—
Great Blaze of Beauty—and High Times Generally." Some four thousand people,
many more than the capacity of the hall, crowded into the ballroom, thus resulting
in "a sweaty, seething, sweltering jam—a crush of duped foregatherers from all
creation," said another dispatch in the same paper.

    The music was provided by Josef Gungel's celebrated band, and the program
included twenty-six numbers—quadrilles, waltzes, polkas—plus an extra "grand
march" dedicated to the President. Interestingly enough, two of the pieces on the
program were also on the program for Mar. 4, 1861! They were "Dream on the
Ocean Waltz" (composed by Gungel for the ball in 1849 and dedicated to Mrs.
Col. W. B. Bliss [Miss Betty]), and a quadrille, "Martha," by Strauss. Cf. Washington *National Intelligencer*, Mar. 3, 5, 8, 1849.

thought that he was tipsy, but she was mistaken, not realizing how tired he might be.)

Scarcely had the party reached the platform when there was a general movement in that direction; these men and their ladies from the North and the West wanted to greet the new President, to shake his hand, and to offer congratulations.

"Hail to the Chief!" This was not the only time when the well-known piece had been played in Mr. Lincoln's honor. As the President-elect had entered his carriage that morning and started toward the Capitol for the inaugural ceremony, a band had struck up the tune, and on an earlier occasion, an occasion which proved to be one of the most pleasant occurrences of the hectic ten days that began with the President-elect's arrival in the capital city on February 23, the Marine Band had played it for his benefit.

From early morning till late at night since he had stepped off the train at six o'clock that Saturday morning (greeted only by an old Illinois friend, Elihu B. Washburne), Mr. Lincoln had been exceedingly busy. He had met with congressional delegations and with congressmen and senators individually, he had conferred with his Cabinet members and with General Scott, he had dined with prominent and influential Republicans and diplomats, he had called on President Buchanan, visited the Senate and House, and had paid his respect to the members of the Supreme Court. The retiring President and his Cabinet made a courtesy call at Willard's Hotel, as had also the mayor of the city and the city council. The members of the Peace Convention called and with some of them Mr. Lincoln talked at length.

In addition, Mr. and Mrs. Lincoln held numerous receptions, and after one general levee to which several hundred people came—loyal, curious, hostile—Mr. Lincoln was admonished to leave off the backwoodsman. He had introduced himself and Mrs. Lincoln as "the long and the short of the Presidency."[12]

---

[12] N.Y. *Herald*, Feb. 27, 1861. Later the same reporter wrote: "As he said 'the long,' he bowed; as he said 'the short,' he looked down at Mrs. Lincoln and

The pressures and demands upon the President-elect had been severe in Springfield since November; here in Washington they were much more concentrated and intense. In the midst of these political and social activities, important and petty, but necessary, came the event which afforded a moment of relief and pleasure, an occasion when a group of supporters gathered, not to ask for favors or to try to influence the President, but merely to show their loyalty and to receive only a greeting in reply.

It was Thursday, February 28. In the early evening, Mr. Lincoln attended a big dinner at the National Hotel ("very elegant and highly intellectual") given by Hon. Elbridge G. Spaulding, a New York congressman. Elsewhere, the Republican Association of the city was holding its regular meeting. New members were admitted, one prospective member was blackballed because of his color, and an appeal was made for all to turn out for the inaugural parade. Then the chairman announced that the serenade for Mr. Lincoln, originally planned for his arrival in Washington, but postponed at his request, would take place immediately after the meeting. The Marine Band was there and ready; but first it would have to be paid its fee of thirty dollars. A collection was taken, but it netted only twelve dollars; another was taken and five dollars more was received. After some debate it was voted to take the remainder from the treasury. The meeting adjourned and the members started for Willard's Hotel, headed by the well-known band.

Mr. Lincoln in the meantime had returned to Willard's from the dinner, there to be confronted, as usual, by a horde of guests—senators, representatives, army and navy officers, diplomats. About ten thirty the sound of music was heard in the street outside. The Republican Association, with numerous others who had joined the procession along the way, was approaching. The band

---

smiled. A shudder ran through the parlors. The ladies stared at the strange couple; the gentlemen bent their heads. That man the President of the United States! That woman the first lady of the land! All the etiquette of the republican court that had been established since the days of President Washington was violated." Stephen [R.] Fiske, "A Message that Made History," in Rufus Rockwell Wilson, ed., *Lincoln Among His Friends* (Caldwell, Idaho, 1942), p. 307.

played the popular "Ever of Thee I'm Fondly Dreaming," and when the hotel was reached a great cheer was raised. Then the band struck up "Hail to the Chief!," which was followed by more cheers.

Finally, after repeated calls, Mr. Lincoln went to the window and bowed. There was more music and more cheering. Mr. Lincoln then spoke briefly, assuring the throng which was more friendly than he had apparently expected in Washington, of his intention to treat everyone fairly and expressing the hope that they would become better friends. He closed by saying, "And now my friends . . . I again return my thanks for this compliment, and expressing my desire to hear a little more of your good music, I bid you good night."[13]

The crowd gave six hearty cheers, the band played "Yankee Doodle," and the throng went off. Mr. Lincoln, receiving his first complimentary serenade in Washington, had been saluted by the same stirring notes that had just echoed through the ballroom this inauguration day evening.

"Hail to the Chief!" Professor Weber's band resumed its playing, some of the guests danced and promenaded, but there was a constant crowding of well-wishers around the President. Once he remarked, "This handshaking is harder than rail-splitting." He might have added, "Especially at the end of an inauguration day," for not only had he been through the regular formalities, but, when he had arrived at the White House after the ceremonies at the Capitol, he had shaken hands with large numbers of people before having his lunch. Later in the day, as the family was eating its evening meal, some five hundred New Yorkers appeared and the meal was interrupted while he greeted them. And now, at eleven thirty in the evening, there were still more.

At length the presidential party was able to move into the supper room where an elaborate repast had been prepared by the well-known caterer, Gautier. On the tables decorated with a "pyramid motif" were stewed oysters, chicken salad, ice cream, champagne and Madeira.

---

[13] Washington *Evening Star*, Feb. 25, Mar. 1, 1861; N.Y. *Herald*, Mar. 1, 1861.

Returning to the ballroom after the supper, the President greeted more guests while some of his party made up a set for a quadrille—Mrs. Lincoln and Stephen Douglas; Mrs. Baker and Mr. Harrard; Mrs. Bergman, the wife of the Belgian minister, and Mr. Berret, the mayor of Washington; Miss Edwards, the belle of the ball, and the staid abolitionist Vice-President Hannibal Hamlin. There were eight quadrilles on the evening's program. Very likely the one in which this distinguished set participated was either "Martha" (Strauss) or "Handel's Elite" (Strauss). One is tempted to wonder what the comment would have been if some or all of them had danced one of the more lively numbers, such as the "Gallop—Atlantic Telegraph" or Lanner's "Gallop and Schottische!"

About twelve thirty the President left the ballroom to spend his first night—or what was left of it—in the White House. Some of the younger members of the party stayed for more dancing, which continued until four o'clock.[14]

It had been a strenuous day. It had also been a day filled with music. Bands and fife and drum corps had been busy everywhere giving forth national and patriotic melodies. As Mr. Buchanan and Mr. Lincoln had started from Willard's Hotel for the Capitol, bands played loudly; the inaugural ceremonies included the "Star-Spangled Banner," "Yankee Doodle," "God Save Our President," and an "Inaugural March" especially written for the occasion by Francis Scala, the leader of the Marine Band; later, when the new President arrived at the White House, he was serenaded by thirty-four young ladies who had represented the states in the procession; and finally, there was the Inaugural Ball with its six hours of music. Of all the selections played that day, one was of special significance. Mr. Lincoln had heard it twice—when he started toward the Capitol for the Inauguration in the

---

[14] N.Y. *Herald*, Mar. 5, 1861; N.Y. *Times*, Mar. 5, 1861; Washington *Evening Star*, Mar. 5, 1861; Washington *National Intelligencer*, Mar. 5, 1861; Sacramento *Daily Union*, Mar. 27, 1861; Ben: Perley Poore, *Perley's Reminiscences*. . . . (Phila., 1886), II, 80.

morning, and when he entered the ballroom that evening.[15] He was to hear it many times in the next four years on many different occasions—"Hail to the Chief!"

[15] N.Y. *Herald,* Mar. 5, 1861; N.Y. *Times,* Mar. 5, 1861; N.Y. *Tribune,* Mar. 5, 1861; Washington *Evening Star,* Mar. 4, 13, 1861.

CHAPTER II

"WHY DON'T THEY COME?"

NOT QUITE TWO MONTHS HAD PASSED SINCE THAT BUSY inauguration day when Abraham Lincoln had been greeted by the strains of "Hail to the Chief!" Now, waiting in suspense for a response from the nation to his call for seventy-five thousand militia to put down "combinations too formidable to be suppressed by the ordinary course of judicial proceedings," he uttered a question: "Why don't they come?"[1]

The city of Washington was isolated. Telegraph and railroad communication with the North had been cut off, and only a small Pennsylvania force, the Sixth Massachusetts Regiment and the District militia (of loyalty as yet untested) were available for the defense of the city.[2] Barricades were being prepared for the Capitol and the Treasury, barrels of cement and iron work intended for the new dome for the former and four-inch plank for the latter. Jim Lane, of Kansas, was on guard at the White House, and everywhere there were rumors—rumors of a battery on the Virginia shore overlooking the city, of a planned assassination directed against the President, of an impending attack on the city.[3]

The atmosphere was one of excitement, uncertainty, and uneasiness. Mrs. Lincoln became quite alarmed when Jean Davenport Lander appeared at the White House bringing the rumor of assassination, and John Hay had to do some "dexterous lying" to calm her fears. Benjamin

---

[1] Elizabeth Todd Grimsley, "Six Months in the White House," *Jour. Ill. State Hist. Soc.*, XIX (Oct.-Jan., 1926-27), 49-52.

[2] John G. Nicolay to Ozias M. Hatch, Apr. 26, 1861, O. M. Hatch Papers, Ill. State Hist. Library.

[3] N.Y. *Times*, Apr. 25, 1861; Tyler Dennett, ed., *Lincoln . . . in the Diaries . . . of John Hay* (N.Y., 1939), pp. 1, 5.

B. French, soon to become Commissioner of Public Buildings, concluded (after a long talk with the President) that Mr. Lincoln really knew little more than anyone else about what was going to happen.[4]

Apprehension among loyal citizens was heightened not only by the rumor-filled atmosphere, but also by the realization that secession sentiment and hostility to the new "Chief" were rampant. Gideon Welles thought the atmosphere thick with treason; Secretary Nicolay, writing to his fiancée, expressed the same feeling in graphic words:

> . . . with the city perfectly demoralized with secession feeling, no man could *know* whom of the residents to trust. We were not certain but that at the first moment when fate would seem to preponderate against us, we would have to look down the muzzles of our own guns. The feeling was not the most comfortable, I assure you. We were not only surrounded by the enemy, but in the midst of traitors. . . .[5]

Thus it was not surprising that Southern tunes and Southern songs were not infrequently heard in and about the city—especially "Dixie." Robert Lincoln, relaxing in the smoking room at Willard's one evening after dinner, was favored with "Dixie," played by two harpists at the urging of a "group of disunionists" after which, to even things up, the musicians played "Hail, Columbia" "with all the extras."[6] John W. Hutchinson, while waiting at the depot for the train to Baltimore (after the inauguration), heard "Dixie" and was disturbed. He wrote:

> I found [the depot] full of men who seemed completely possessed with a spirit of evil. They had had no chance to kill a "nigger" all day. They were "plug uglies" and as they swarmed about the station they kept up in a grim growling, nasal tone, the refrain of "Dixie."[7]

---

[4] Dennett, ed., *Lincoln . . . in the Diaries . . . of John Hay*, pp. 2, 3; John G. Nicolay to Therena Bates, Apr. 26, 1861, Nicolay Papers; Amos Tuck French, ed., *Diary of Benjamin Brown French* (N.Y., 1904), p. 113.

[5] John T. Morse, ed., *Diary of Gideon Welles* (Boston and New York, 1911), I, 10; John G. Nicolay to Therena Bates, Apr. 26, 1861, Nicolay Papers. The Morse edition of the *Diary of Gideon Welles* has been used in this work. For the passages in the *Diary* cited, the sense and meaning remain essentially the same in the carefully revised edition edited by Howard K. Beale.

[6] Washington *Evening Star*, Feb. 26, 1861.

[7] John Wallace Hutchinson, *Story of the Hutchinsons* (Boston, 1896), I, 375.

But then, Hutchinson was an abolitionist. Naturally he was disturbed.

In the streets hurdy-gurdies ground out "Dixie," to which they later added "Maryland," and "Bonnie Blue Flag," and from many a window came the notes of those same airs, played by young ladies from the South for the benefit of the "damned Yanks." A White House clerk called it "a perpetual tinkle of . . . favorite secession airs," noting that "Dixie" was the favorite.[8]

"Dixie!" They played it day and night. To the young clerk it had "a weird spell-like influence" and made him shudder. And while the Southern belles might have been gratified to know this, they might have been surprised had they known that "Dixie" had been a great favorite of Mr. Lincoln ever since he had heard it at a minstrel show in Chicago about a year before![9]

At the White House there had also been music, of quite a different kind, for even a divided Union did not interfere with some of the social functions which had begun with the Inaugural Ball. The first presidential levee, held on Friday evening of inaugural week, was a brilliant and crowded affair. When the doors were opened at eight o'clock, hundreds were waiting to get in, and soon the White House was filled to suffocation. Diplomats, army officers, congressmen and their ladies, and just plain people pushed, and were pushed, toward the place where the President stood.

Attorney General Bates thought it a motley crowd and a terrible squeeze, and Gideon Welles considered it the greatest jam he had ever witnessed. It took Welles one-half hour to get into the White House, and he was tempted to give up and go home, "but for the impropriety of ab-

---

[8] Harriet Riddle Davis, "Civil War Recollections of a Little Yankee." Typescript, Civil War Collection, Washington (D.C.) Public Library; William O. Stoddard, *Inside the White House in War Times* (N.Y., 1890), pp. 17-18; William O. Stoddard, Jr., ed., *Lincoln's Third Secretary* (N.Y., 1955), pp. 83-84; Katherine Helm, *Mary, Wife of Lincoln* (N.Y., 1928), p. 174. At the same time, there were expressions of Northern sentiment—men about the city were heard whistling "Yankee Doodle," the "Star-Spangled Banner," and other national melodies, and Negro bootblacks were manifesting an awareness of the new times by calling "Black your boots! Shine 'em up Old Abe fashion!" Ellet, *Court Circles of the Republic*, pp. 515-16; N.Y. *Evening Post*, Mar. 2, 1861.

[9] Henry Clay Whitney, *Life on the Circuit with Lincoln* (Caldwell, Idaho, 1940), pp. 102-3, 161.

sence." The reporter from the New York *Tribune* who estimated the attendance as the largest ever at such an affair was probably not exaggerating.[10]

Just before the levee began there was a minor crisis upstairs. Mrs. Lincoln and her numerous relatives were dressing for the occasion, but Mrs. Lincoln's dress was late in delivery! When the dressmaker finally arrived, Mary, tense and nervous, vowed that she couldn't get ready in time, that the others would have to go down without her. However, through the collective efforts of her relatives, the dressmaker, and Mr. Lincoln, who came in and complimented them all, Mrs. Lincoln was soon ready. Then, after her lace handkerchief, hidden by the mischievous Tad, had been retrieved, the presidential party went downstairs to greet the multitude.[11]

For two hours and a half, the President worked away at shaking hands, sometimes using both hands, and greeting his well-wishers. Mrs. Lincoln, in her rose-colored moire-antique dress, with pearl necklace, pearl earrings and bracelets, and with red flowers in her hair, carried herself well and was quite self-possessed.[12]

Throughout this gala evening there was music in the background, furnished by the Marine Band. This was but the first of many times when the "President's Own" would so perform. And though in the background for the entire evening on such occasions, taken for granted, or unnoticed, perhaps—in this instance, one reporter thought it worth mentioning that one of the band's selections was a "repeat" from the inaugural ceremonies, "God Save Our President"—there was one time during the evening when the band became of more than secondary importance. It gave the signal for the party to end by striking

---

[10] "It was a jam, it was a rush, it was a cram, it was a crush. . . ." reported the N.Y. *Herald,* Mar. 10, 1861; it was a "monster mass meeting," said a report from the Cincinnati *Commercial* carried in the Chicago *Tribune,* Mar. 12, 1861; Howard K. Beale, ed., *The Diary of Edward Bates* (Washington, 1933), p. 177; Gideon Welles to Mrs. Welles, Mar. 9, 1861, Gideon Welles Papers, Library of Congress; N.Y. *Tribune,* Mar. 9, 1861.

[11] Elizabeth Keckley, *Behind the Scenes* (N.Y., 1868), chap. 5.

[12] N.Y. *Herald,* Mar. 13, 1861; Keckley, *Behind the Scenes,* p. 88; *Illinois State Register,* Feb. 3, 1929. W. H. L. Wallace, writing to his wife on Mar. 9, commented: "Mr. Lincoln wore white kid gloves & worked away at shaking hands with the multitude, with much the same air & movements as if he were mauling rails." Harry E. Pratt, ed., *Concerning Mr. Lincoln. . . .* (Springfield, 1944), pp. 70-71.

up a march tune. At the signal, the President, with a partner on his arm, led the grand march or promenade around the room. At the first levee the march was begun at ten thirty with Elizabeth Grimsley, a cousin of Mrs. Lincoln, as the President's partner. Mrs. Grimsley recalled that the tune to which they promenaded was "Yankee Doodle."[13]

As the presidential party left the room to the strains of "Yankee Doodle," the guests, after a mad scramble for hats and coats, quickly departed. Even though one reporter saw political overtones in the gathering—he thought it terribly suggestive of a revolution, a new order of things with an antislavery flavor—and even though some hats and coats were lost in the exodus, the party was a success.[14]

It was a success, not merely because of the numbers who came, but because so many of the men were prominent and important in public life and were accompanied by so many charming ladies. An observer with an eye for such things thought that rarely had there been more beauty at a presidential levee, and he was impressed by the "many young and beautiful ladies present, whose sparkling eyes, lovely faces and genteel forms were the theme of conversation."[15]

Secretary Nicolay, writing to his fiancée two days afterward, summed it up more conservatively:

... the "Reception" on Friday night ... was voted by all the "oldest inhabitants" to have been the most successful one ever known here. . . . It was withal more "ton"-ish than such things usually are.

Then he added:

Of course in such a crowd crinoline suffered, and at least fifty men have been swearing worse than "our army in

---

[13] Washington *Evening Star,* Mar. 9, 1861; Grimsley, *Jour. Ill. State Hist. Soc.,* XIX, 49-50.

[14] N.Y. *Herald,* Mar. 10, 1861.

[15] N.Y. *Herald,* Mar. 13, 1861. An earlier dispatch had lamented that there were few Southerners present. ". . . the familiar Southern faces of distinguished men and beautiful and accomplished women we have been accustomed to meet on such occasions." *Ibid.,* Mar. 10, 1861.

Flanders," ever since they went home that evening, over the loss of new hats and valuable overcoats.[16]

For some time after this auspicious beginning the social calendar at the White House was a busy one—a formal reception for officers of the army, a second levee, again crowded and brilliant, a formal dinner for the Cabinet, and frequent afternoon receptions by Mrs. Lincoln. To add to the confusion, the two boys had an attack of the measles. The President, becoming weary and care-worn under the increasing pressure, had to curtail his own visiting hours.[17]

There was, however, one unusual interval of relaxation. Busy as he was on Saturday, the sixth of April, with the problem of relief for Fort Sumter uppermost in his mind, the President nevertheless appeared at the afternoon reception, where a pioneer from the far Northwest and an Indian songstress were among the guests.

John Beeson, originally from England, had for many years been interested in the Indians in Oregon. He had championed their cause against aggressive white settlers, had made trips East in their behalf, and had published a tract, *A Plea for the Indians,* calling attention to their plight. In late March, 1861, he had arrived in Washington to give a series of lectures, and his activities had received some notice in the newspapers.

Accompanying him, and assisting with his programs, was Larooqua, the Indian songstress. Known as the "aboriginal Jenny Lind," with a "mellifluous voice" and ". . . a richness of melody in her notes which flow out in perfect control and an ease and grace that would do credit to our best singers," she attracted much favorable attention by her singing. In a program a few days earlier, she not only sang most pleasingly in her "wood notes wild," but had recited (in excellent English) from Longfellow's "Hiawatha."

Consequently, it was not surprising that, when she

---

[16] John G. Nicolay to Therena Bates, Mar. 10, 1861, Nicolay Papers.

[17] N.Y. *Tribune,* Mar. 13, 18, 1861; N.Y. *Herald,* Mar. 16, 22, 23, 28, 29, 31, Apr. 2, 1861; Washington *Evening Star,* Mar. 30, 1861.

appeared at the Saturday reception, the suggestion was made that she sing. The President consented. Larooqua sang, but the report of her singing was somewhat restrained: ". . . the Indian songstress gave a specimen of her capabilities, showing a voice somewhat thin, but pleasant and of considerable cultivation."[18] What the President may have thought was not recorded, but very likely he was not over-critical.[19]

Then soon after came the crisis at Fort Sumter, the President's proclamation, and the waiting in the isolated, rumor-filled city. By April 24, morale had reached a low point. John Hay wrote: "This has been a day of gloom and doubt. Everybody seems filled with a vague distrust and recklessness." Even the President was dejected, and remarked, "I don't believe there is any North!"[20]

The next day, about noon, there was a great change. A train arrived at the station, full of soldiers—the New York Seventh Regiment, for whom everyone had been waiting. Amid cheers that seemed to echo throughout the city, the regiment quickly formed into line and started up Pennsylvania Avenue.

The city was now wild with excitement and relief. All the way to the White House people lined the avenue cheering and waving their handkerchiefs, and, reported the correspondent of the New York *Tribune*, "when, in place of the drums and fifes the full band struck up, the whole city danced with delight. A greater change never passed over a town, than that wrought in the space of one half hour, by the coming of the long looked for Seventh."[21]

---

[18] Washington *Sunday Morning Chronicle*, Mar. 31, Apr. 7, 14, 1861; Washington *National Intelligencer*, Apr. 3, 4, 6, 1861; Washington *Evening Star*, Apr. 6, 8, 1861. Thus Beeson and his Indian songstress received considerable publicity in the city. In one instance, he met with a rebuff. The Board of Managers of the Y.M.C.A. not only declined to help him, but also resolved "that we do not recommend Mr. Beeson to the confidence or assistance of the community." Washington *Evening Star*, Apr. 6, 1861. Beeson continued his efforts, however, both in the East and later in the West. A report from California in 1865 indicated that he had been "passing the hat" there. Sacramento *Daily Union*, Feb. 13, 1865.

[19] Indeed, the President seemed to enjoy Indian visitors. Shortly after Larooqua's visit, three Potawatomi Indians called at the White House and Lincoln "amused them immensely by airing the two or three Indian words he knew." Dennett, ed., *Lincoln . . . in the Diaries . . . of John Hay*, p. 14.

[20] Dennett, ed., *Lincoln . . . in the Diaries . . . of John Hay*, p. 11.

[21] Washington *National Intelligencer*, Apr. 26, 1861; N.Y. *Herald*, Apr. 30, 1861; N.Y. *Tribune*, Apr. 30, 1861; Sacramento *Daily Union*, May 14, 1861; Grimsley, *Jour. Ill. State Hist. Soc.*, XIX, 52-53; C. P. Stone, "Washington in March and April, 1861," *Mag. of Amer. Hist.*, XIV (July, 1885), 24.

With flags flying and the band playing, the regiment swung into the White House grounds where, surrounded by a throng of happy people, the President was waiting. He greeted the men with enthusiasm and congratulated the colonel for his successful march to defend the city. He would, in the next four years, hear many bands play on many occasions, but never again would he hear one with such a great sense of relief as now.

> Mr. Lincoln was the happiest looking man in town as the regiment was marching by him. . . . He smiled all over, and he certainly gave in his countenance clear expression to the feeling of relief born in all by this wished-for arrival.

The event had, indeed, as the *Tribune* correspondent remarked and as John Hay noted, gladdened the President's heart. With other regiments arriving constantly and the city resembling an armed camp, he no longer needed to repeat the question, "Why don't they come?"[22]

The New York Seventh received somewhat special attention from the President during its first short stay in the capital. The day after the regiment arrived it was mustered into the United States service and the President attended the ceremony; two days later he and Secretary Seward visited the regiment in its temporary quarters in the Capitol, and the same day they both went down to the wharf to welcome the regiment's supply ship. Even though it was raining, Lincoln insisted on shaking hands with all the crew, including the coal heaver from below.[23]

The President reviewed the Seventh on several occasions, and also witnessed a presentation ceremony at which the regiment received a flag from some New York ladies while the band played the "Star-Spangled Ban-

---

[22] Emmons Clark, *History of the Seventh Regiment of New York* (N.Y., 1890), II, 4-5; N.Y. *Tribune*, Apr. 27, 1861; Dennett, ed., *Lincoln . . . in the Diaries . . . of John Hay*, p. 11; French, ed., *Diary of B. B. French*, p. 14. A letter written by Elizabeth Grimsley a few days later reflected the changed feeling in the city. She wrote: "The intense excitement has blown over and with the exception of the presence of the troops Washington is very quiet and pleasant—We enjoy the beautiful drives around the city." Elizabeth Grimsley to Cousin Mary, Apr. 29, 1861, Elizabeth T. Grimsley Letters, Ill. State Hist. Library.

[23] Clark, *Seventh Regiment*, II, 6, 9; Egbert L. Viele, "The Seventh Regiment at the Capital, 1861," *Mag. of Amer. Hist.*, XIV (July, 1885), 69-77; Brooklyn *Daily Eagle*, Feb. 10, 1918.

ner," "Hail, Columbia," and several other national airs.[24]

By way of reciprocity the band of the Seventh gave two concerts on the White House lawn and serenaded the President at midnight just before it was mustered out. It was thus the first band to give a concert on the White House grounds for the Lincoln family.

Coming two days after the arrival of the regiment, the first concert attracted many people, including the President, Secretary Cameron, Carl Schurz, John Nicolay, John Hay, and several ladies. The President's party sat out on the portico for the whole program, which consisted of "a number of choice pieces including all the national airs." Even Tad and Willie were there with Union badges displayed on their jackets. John Hay, quite taken with the event, wrote in his *Diary*:

> The Seventh Regiment Band played gloriously on the shaven lawn at the south front of the Executive Mansion. The scene was very beautiful. Through the luxuriant grounds the gaily dressed crowd strolled idly, soldiers loafed in the promenades, the martial music filled the sweet air with vague suggestions of heroism, & Carl Schurz and the President talked war.[25]

The second concert was given four days later, on Wednesday, the first of May. Even though the Seventh had had an extremely busy day, its musicians appeared at the White House at five o'clock and played for two hours. The President came out, spoke briefly to the vast crowd (not many were able to hear him as a gusty wind was blowing), and then retired to the strains of "Hail, Columbia."[26]

The Seventh was mustered out on May 30 after a formal dress parade which the President attended. The preceding night the regiment had paid its respects to him by a torchlight procession to the White House and

---

[24] Clark, *Seventh Regiment*, II, 13, 23, 24; N.Y. *Times*, May 1, 16, 25, 1861; N.Y. *Herald*, May 24, 1861.

[25] Washington *Evening Star*, Apr. 29, 1861; Washington *Sunday Morning Chronicle*, Apr. 28, 1861; Dennett, ed., *Lincoln . . . in the Diaries . . . of John Hay*, pp. 12-13. Col. Lefferts, popular commander of the regiment, had offered the services of the band for music on the White House grounds whenever the President desired. N.Y. *Herald*, Apr. 29, 1861.

[26] Washington *Evening Star*, May 2, 1861; N.Y. *Tribune*, May 2, 1861.

a serenade by its band. The affair had pleased the President very much, and he and the family had sat in an open window and listened to the music. Now he was bidding good-bye to the men who had brought so much relief to him and to the city a month earlier, for the next day the regiment left for New York.[27]

---

[27] Clark, *Seventh Regiment*, II, 32 ; Washington *Evening Star*, May 30, 31, 1861 ; N.Y. *Tribune*, May 31, 1861. Not only was the New York Seventh considered the elite regiment of the North, but it had one of the half dozen best bands in the country. H. W. Swartz, *Bands in America* (Garden City, 1957), p. 79. Thus, early in the war, Lincoln heard the very best that could be offered of music for which he had a great liking—the music of a band.

CHAPTER III

"A LITTLE MORE OF YOUR EXCELLENT MUSIC"

THE PRESIDENT HAD BEEN TAKEN UNAWARES. A LARGE crowd in the mood for serenading had stopped before the White House on the evening of May 13 and amid cheers and music by an accompanying band had called for the Chief Executive. The President appeared and immediately there were requests for a speech. Having no speech to make, he was somewhat embarrassed. Nevertheless, he turned the request off rather adroitly. After a few apologetic remarks, he excused himself by saying: "I am one of those who believe that the best should come last; I should have made the speech first and had the music afterwards, and I therefore, again thanking you for this honor, will retire in order that I may hear a little more of your excellent music." The crowd cheered, the band played, and the serenaders moved off to pay their respects elsewhere.[1]

As a matter of fact on several occasions, in addition to those already noted, the President had heard much excellent music and was, certainly, in the next few weeks to hear much more. Just two days previous he and Carl Schurz, a frequent visitor during these early days of the war, had enjoyed the regularly scheduled Saturday afternoon concert by the Marine Band on the White House lawn. Later that same day, in the dusk of twilight, Schurz played the piano—with great skill and feeling, thought John Hay—until it was time for tea to be served.[2]

[1] Washington *Evening Star*, May 14, 1861; N.Y. *Times*, May 16, 1861. The serenade was primarily for the new postmaster, but the President and Secretary Blair were included as well.

[2] Dennett, ed., *Lincoln . . . in the Diaries . . . of John Hay*, p. 23; Gideon Welles to Col. John Harris, Apr. 29, 1861, Officers of the Marine Corps, No. 6. Navy Dept., Feb. 5, 1856 to Aug. 14, 1861, Letter Book, National Archives, 486; Washington *Sunday Morning Chronicle*, May 12, 1861; Washington *Evening Star*, May 13, 1861.

And on Thursday afternoon of the same week a program of concert music and cannon practice (which was quite to the President's liking) took place at the Navy Yard. It was a perfect spring day, clear and pleasant. At three o'clock the President and Mrs. Lincoln arrived at the Navy Yard, and as they entered the concert hall (a naval building specially decorated for the occasion), a thirty-four gun salute was fired. Some two or three hundred guests, including Cabinet members and their families who had gathered for the afternoon of music, rose and stood until the President and Mrs. Lincoln were seated.

The concert was given by members of the Seventy-First New York Regiment, then stationed at the Navy Yard. Harrison Millard, a well-known composer and singer (but currently a private in the regiment) conducted and Harvey Dodworth directed his famous band. Everyone was delighted with the program:

1. Quickstep, "Thou Art Far Away" .... Millard
   Dodworth's Band
2. Song, "Yes! Let Me Like a Soldier Fall" .... Wallace
   Mr. Millard
3. Quartet, "Come Where My Love Lies
   Dreaming" .... Foster
   Glee Club
4. Song, "The Monks of Old" .... Glover
   Mr. Camp
5. Finale of "La Traviata" .... Verdi
   Dodworth's Band
6. New National Ode, "The Flag of the
   Free" .... Millard
   Mr. Millard and Chorus
7. Trio, "Love's Young Dream" .... Moore
   Millard, Woodruff, and Camp
8. Fantasie on "Un Ballo in Maschera" .... Verdi
   Dodworth's Band
9. "Miserere" from "Il Trovatore" .... Verdi
   Mr. Millard, H. Dodworth and Chorus

10. Duetto, "I Would That My Love" .... Mendelssohn
     Dodworth's Band
11. Patriotic Song, "Viva L'America" .... Millard
     Millard
12. Full Chorus, "Star Spangled Banner" .... Key

The band did especially well on Millard's "Thou Art Far Away," the trio "Love's Young Dream" was repeatedly encored, Camp's singing of "The Monks of Old" was greeted with great applause as was also Millard's singing of his own patriotic composition "Viva L'America." As an encore Millard sang a humorous song that he had composed; it told the troubles of the New Yorkers as they went from Annapolis to Annapolis Junction, there to take the train for the defense of Washington:

Only Nine Miles to the Junction

The troops of Rhode Island were posted along
  On the road from Annapolis Station,
As the Seventy-first Regiment, one thousand strong,
  Went on in defence of the nation.
We'd been marching all day in the sun's scorching ray,
  With two biscuits each as a ration,
When we asked Gov. Sprague to show us the way,
  And "How many miles to the Junction?"

How many miles, how many miles,
  How many miles to the Junction?
When we asked Gov. Sprague to show us the way,
  And "How many miles to the Junction?"

The Rhode Island boys cheered us on out of sight,
  After giving the following injunction:
"Just keep up your courage—you'll get there tonight,
  For 'tis only nine miles to the Junction."

They gave us hot coffee, a grasp of the hand,
  Which cheered and refreshed our exhaustion,
We reached in six hours the long-promised land,
  For 'twas "only nine miles to the Junction."

How many miles, &c.

(Tune—The other side of Jordan.)

This, too, was "finely sung and warmly applauded."[3] The President enjoyed it all, but he wanted more, and he asked for one of his favorites, the "Marseillaise." Millard was generous—he sang the first verse and then repeated it, "interpolating nonchalantly 'Liberty or death' in place of 'Abreuve nos sillions,' which he had forgotten."

Then came the cannon practice. The President and his party went on board the *Pensacola* to watch the firing of the eleven-inch, smoothbore, Dahlgren cannon, and all were fascinated by the sight. Secretary Nicolay carefully described the process in a letter to his fiancée the next day, and John Hay commented in his diary:

> . . . we went down to the *Pensacola* and observed the shooting of the great Dahlgren gun Plymouth. Two ricochet shots

[3] Washington *Evening Star*, May 10, 1861; Washington *Sunday Morning Chronicle*, May 12, 1861; N.Y. *Herald*, May 10, 1861. In addition to the soloists, the chorus included some well-trained singers from such excellent choirs as those of Christ Church and Broadway Tabernacle. N.Y. *Evening Post*, May 9, 1861.

A Boston music editor who received a complimentary ticket regretted that he couldn't attend, printed the entire program, and commented that with Millard as conductor and with Dodworth's Band providing the instrumental music the concert would be well worth attending. John S. Dwight, ed., *Dwight's Journal of Music*, XIX (May 18, 1861), 55.

From the general reaction of enthusiastic appreciation for the program, there was, however, one note of restraint. "Perley" (Ben: Perley Poore) referred to the "charming instrumental music interspersed with amateur vocalism," and added that some of the songs of the chorus were "very well done." Boston *Journal*, May 13, 1861. "Perley" was also from Boston!

Dodworth's Band had since the 1830's been the leader in New York with the best musicians and the strictest training program. It played for weddings, balls, and military affairs. In 1860 Harvey B. Dodworth took over the direction of the band and continued as its director until 1890. This band contributed much to the music in Washington during the early months of the war. Later it played in Central Park during the summer months and for theatrical productions and on gala occasions such as the banquet for the Russian Naval officers in October, 1863. William Carter White, *A History of Military Music in America* (N.Y., 1944), pp. 49-51; Swartz, *Bands in America*, pp. 45, 78-79; James Grant Wilson and John Fiske, eds., *Appleton's Cyclopaedia of American Biography* (N.Y., 1888), II, 195; N.Y. *Herald*, Oct. 1, 3, 8, 20, 1863, June 4, 11, 18, July 3, 1864. Dodworth was also a composer. Among his compositions were the "Hymn of Columbia," "The Raw Recruit Quadrille," and "Leap Year Polka."

Harrison Millard, church and concert singer and composer, had studied abroad under the "most able masters of Europe." After his short stay with the Seventy-First New York Regiment he became a lieutenant in the United States Infantry (Nineteenth Regiment). While on the staff of General Rousseau, he was twice mentioned for his valuable work in battle (at Perryville and Murfreesboro). He was wounded at Chickamauga and soon thereafter resigned from the army. During the war and for years afterward he composed and produced a wide range of musical numbers. Among his patriotic pieces were "Viva L'America: Home of the Free," and "The Flag of the Free," both sung at the concert on May 9, 1861. His popular pieces included "All Alone," "Clouds of Summer Evening," and "Don't You Cry So, Norah Darling." *Dwight's Journal of Music*, XVIII (Mar. 23, 1861), 416; XIX (June 22, 1861), 96; *Appleton's Cyclopaedia of Amer. Biog.*, IV, 324; Francis B. Heitman, *Historical Register and Dictionary of the United States Army* (Washington, 1903), I, 709; *War of the Rebellion: Official Records of the Union and Confederate Armies* (Washington, 1880-1901) (hereafter cited as *O.R.*), Ser. I, Vol. XVI, Pt. 1, 1048; Vol. XX, Pt. 1, 381, 406. Cf. also, Sigmund Spaeth, *A History of Popular Music in America* (N.Y., 1948), *passim*.

were sent through the target and one plumper. The splendid course of the 11 inch shell flying through 1300 yds of air, the lighting, the quick rebound, & flight through the target with wild skips, throwing up a 30 ft. column of spray at every jump, the decreasing leaps and the steady roll into the waves were scenes as novel and pleasant to me as to all the rest of the party. The Prest was delighted.

Returning to the Yard, the President reviewed the Seventy-First in parade; then, about six o'clock, as the band played "Hail to the Chief!," he entered his carriage and departed for the White House.[4]

Having spent such a pleasant and relaxing afternoon, the President was in fine humor that evening at the reception for army officers at which Major Anderson, the hero of Fort Sumter, was an important guest. "Everybody was there," reported the New York *Tribune*. "The marine band played splendidly. The president looked well. The Madame looked better, and a more joyous, happy, patriotic gathering probably never convened before at the Presidential mansion."

Major Anderson, being a modest man, had stepped back into the crowd after paying his respects. But the President thought that he should not remain so inconspicuous. In the words of the *Star*: "The President seemed to think that a bird that can sing and won't sing, should be made to sing, for he hastened in quest of the Major, and leading him forward placed him by his side, where the eager crowd could have the opportunity of taking him by the hand." So for the rest of the evening the Major stood beside the President "dividing the honors."

Shortly after ten o'clock the Marine Band struck up "Yankee Doodle." Thus was the reception ended, and so likewise was the day, a day which had included not only the fine music of the Marine Band but an unusual afternoon musical treat as well.[5]

---

[4] Washington *Evening Star*, May 10, 1861; Washington *Sunday Morning Chronicle*, May 12, 1861; N.Y. *Herald*, May 10, 1861; *Dwight's Journal of Music*, XIX (May 18, 1861), 55; Dennett, ed., *Lincoln . . . in the Diaries . . . of John Hay*, pp. 21-22; John G. Nicolay to Therena Bates, May 10, 1861, Nicolay Papers.

[5] Washington *Evening Star*, May 10, 1861; Washington *Sunday Morning Chronicle*, May 12, 1861; N.Y. *Herald*, May 10, 1861; N.Y. *Tribune*, May 10, 1861. The

A week earlier the President had attended a significant flag-raising ceremony, one of two such events to be held in the same month. In the government service there were still numerous pro-Southern employees. Some had resigned and more would do so later. The loyal employees at the Patent Office had purchased a large flag, twenty-four by sixteen feet, and the ceremony of raising the flag was to be a demonstration of their loyalty.

At twelve o'clock on the second of May, a "dense mass of spectators" gathered at the Patent Office building. The Rhode Island troops, then quartered in the building, together with the Metropolitan Rifles, appeared and drew up in military formation. The President with Secretaries Seward and Smith and Governor Sprague took their places, and amid the cheers of the crowd the President raised the flag.

The Rhode Islanders' band played "choicest and most soul-stirring national airs," John T. Parsons, of Washington, sang "The Flag of Our Union," and the crowd cheered again. The Rhode Islanders demonstrated their proficiency in military formations and drills, and then reentered the building singing "Our Flag Still Waves." The ceremony was over and the crowd dispersed.[6]

Three weeks later another similar ceremony took place at the Post Office where the employees had also purchased a flag for the occasion. This time the crowd was even

---

correspondents of both the *Tribune* and the *Times* were favorably impressed with the President's appearance. They were also complimentary to Mrs. Lincoln, but whereas the *Tribune* correspondent, after observing that Mrs. Lincoln looked well, went on to describe her costume (". . . a very elegant blue silk, richly embroidered, and with a long train; also point lace cape, and a full set of pearl ornaments. . . ."), the *Times* reporter, after commenting in general terms on the "jewels and feathers of the ladies," said of the First Lady, "The beauty of her arms and shoulders attracted my attention. They were very white and polished as marble." N.Y. *Times*, May 13, 1861.

Major Anderson, ending the day in the pleasant gathering at the White House, had begun it under exciting circumstances. He was awakened about three o'clock in the morning by smoke and noise—a fire had broken out in the building next to Willard's Hotel and his room was adjacent to the burning building. The fire was extinguished by none other than the famous Fire Zouaves of Col. Elmer Ellsworth who, after putting out the fire, saluted the flag over the hotel and greeted the Major who had been watching them from his window. The grateful hotel proprietor, Mr. Willard, gave the Zouaves a free breakfast, and a purse of five hundred dollars was given to Ellsworth. Washington *Evening Star*, May 9, 1861; Washington *National Intelligencer*, May 9, 1861; N.Y. *Evening Post*, May 9, 1861; Garnett Laidlaw Eskew, *Willard's of Washington* (N.Y. 1954), pp. 55-56.

[6] Washington *National Intelligencer*, May 2, 3, 1861; Washington *Evening Star*, May 2, 1861; N.Y. *Herald*, May 3, 1861; N.Y. *Times*, May 3, 1861; N.Y. *Tribune*, May 2, 3, 1861; N.Y. *Evening Post*, May 2, 1861.

greater, numbering eight thousand according to one estimate. As the President appeared on the platform, the
Hartford Cornet Band played "Hail to the Chief!" General Skinner first spoke for the employees, and the President, after responding briefly, raised the flag to the top
of the pole as the band played the "Star-Spangled Banner."

The flag at first hung limp, then, caught by the breeze,
it unfurled and waved in most appropriate fashion. This
gave the President an idea. He stepped forward and said:

> I had not thought to say a word, but it has occurred to me
> that a few weeks ago the "Stars and Stripes" hung rather
> languidly about the staff all over the nation. So, too, with
> this flag, when it was elevated to its place. At first it hung
> rather languidly, but the glorious breeze came, and now it
> floats as it should. . . . And we hope that the same breeze is
> swelling the glorious flag throughout the whole nation.

This was the high point of the meeting, but the crowd
listened attentively to the short speeches of Secretaries
Blair, Seward, and Smith, and many joined in singing
as the band brought the meeting to an end by again playing the "Star-Spangled Banner" and "Yankee Doodle."[7]

Such enthusiastic demonstrations, although they con-
sumed the time and energy of the Chief Executive, were
much worthwhile; they helped to offset the effect of dis-
affection such as was evidenced in the recent refusal of
forty employees in another department to take an oath of
allegiance, and they aided in building up support for the
Union cause among government employees.[8]

In terms of popular appeal, however, nothing in the
musical line (except perhaps serenades) exceeded band
concerts. Whether regularly scheduled or for special occasions, whether at the White House or elsewhere, band
concerts never failed to attract large and enthusiastic
audiences. Thus, during the early months of the war, a
German band played in the business district each morning

---

[7] Washington *National Intelligencer*, May 23, 1861; Washington *Evening Star*,
May 22, 1861; N.Y. *Herald*, May 23, 1861; N.Y. *Times*, May 23, 1861; N.Y.
Evening Post, May 22, 1861.

[8] N.Y. *Evening Post*, May 22, 1861.

at eleven; Dodworth's famous band gave concerts every evening at the Navy Yard. These and other performances drew large crowds.[9]

But most popular of all were the concerts on the White House grounds, begun so auspiciously by the band of the Seventh New York Regiment on April 29 and May 1. The grounds to the rear of the Executive Mansion were an ideal spot for such events. The spacious, gently-sloping lawn, with shade trees here and there made an attractive place for people to gather and listen, converse, or promenade. More than one observer commented on the charm and the pleasant atmosphere to be found there on a Saturday afternoon during a band concert.[10]

To be sure, there was the unfinished Washington Monument in the distance, and there was the debris-littered landscape around it; and sometimes the odor from the stagnant creek became quite noticeable. But the people came, nevertheless, and when the President and his family appeared on the portico, they received an additional thrill of pleasure.

Each summer since the administration of President Tyler the Marine Band had given Saturday afternoon concerts at the White House. As the band had increased in numbers and proficiency under the leadership of Francis Scala, its programs had become more popular and its reputation more firmly established until the *Star* could say with utmost confidence ". . . we in Washington flatter ourselves that this favorite band is an institution not to be beat anywhere."[11]

This year the Marine Band concerts, although not beginning until May, had been anticipated some weeks ear-

[9] Washington *Evening Star*, June 6, 12, 1861.

[10] Allan Nevins and Milton Halsey Thomas, eds., *The Diary of George Templeton Strong* (N.Y., 1952), III, 153; N. P. Willis in *Home Journal*, June 29, 1861.

[11] Washington *Morning Times*, Jan. 19, 1896, Apr. 26, 1903; Halloway, *Ladies of the White House*, p. 393; Washington *Evening Star*, May 9, 1861. The Marine Band had been playing for presidential functions since the days of Thomas Jefferson, and its first appearance at inauguration ceremonies was on March 4, 1809, when James Madison took office. Yet it was not until Lincoln's administration that the band received full official status with thirty musicians, a drum major and a "principal musician" or leader. *The United States Marine Band* (n.d.); *Revised Statutes of the United States* (2nd ed., 1878), 272 (Act of July 25, 1861). Later writers did not consider the band to have been as outstanding as its leader and contemporary newspapers thought it was. Cf. White, *Military Music in America*, chap. 7, and Swartz, *Bands in America*, p. 80.

lier by the *Sunday Morning Chronicle* in a brief news
item that scarcely hinted at the seriousness of the times:
"Those delightful summer and spring entertainments,
the concerts of the Marine Band in the Capitol and the
President's grounds, will shortly be commenced for the
season."[12]

When occasionally something happened to mar the routine of pleasure at these concerts, it was news. On June
1, the concert was interrupted, if not disrupted, by the
sound of gunfire. John Nicolay, writing to his fiancée the
next day, described the incident in detail:

> We have music here in the Presidents grounds every Wed-
> nesday and Saturday evening, when the grounds are opened to
> everybody. Yesterday at about half after five, there was quite
> a large crowd here promenading in the grounds, when all at
> once a very brisk firing of musketry became heard on the
> other side of the river. There was almost an instantaneous
> excitement in the crowd and everybody rushed down to the
> edge of the grounds where they could see across the river.
> Several of us went on top of the house, and with a spy-glass
> could see that it was no battle, but only a detachment from one
> of the Regiments over there engaged in practice at loading
> and firing *"at will."* They kept it up for about half an hour,
> and we had a chance to hear what a small battle or skirmish
> would probably sound like, at a distance.[13]

The following Saturday there was a diversion of quite
a different sort. The weather was threatening, but the
concert had begun. A sprinkle of rain came down and
then ceased. The band made another attempt, but soon
the rain fell in torrents. Many people got thoroughly
drenched. Some sought shelter in the lower floor of the
White House and were forthwith invited up to the East
Room where they stayed until the storm was over![14]

In addition to the regular Saturday concerts, there were
frequently concerts during the week by bands from different regiments stationed in and about the city. On the
afternoon of May 15, a Rhode Island band gave a program
of opera selections on the lawn in front of the White

[12] Washington *Sunday Morning Chronicle*, Mar. 31, 1861.
[13] John G. Nicolay to Therena Bates, June 2, 1861, Nicolay Papers.
[14] Washington *Evening Star*, June 10, 1861.

House; a week later, between five and seven in the afternoon, a concert was given by the band of the First Michigan Regiment. When the program was half over, Mrs. Lincoln, just returned from New York, came out onto the South balcony for the rest of the music. Thousands were in attendance for the concert which was hailed in the press as a "rich treat."[15]

In the latter part of June, the band of the Seventy-Ninth New York Regiment played at the White House grounds. The event caused unusual comment, not only because of the music but because of the appearance of the men. The band was made up of professional musicians and the men of the Seventy-Ninth were justly proud of it. Its music on this occasion met with evident approval, being described by the *Star* as "delicious."

But it was the costumes of the regiment which drew more attention, for being otherwise known as the "Highlanders," the men of the Seventy-Ninth came to Washington appropriately clad. They were but one of many regiments that answered the call in the early days of the war in picturesque costumes, soon to be discarded as the war became more real. From the day they arrived in Washington and were reviewed by President Lincoln, the "Highlanders" naturally caught the eye of many. The *Star*, which had given its briefly-worded approval of the music of the Seventy-Ninth, had more to say of the men: "Many of the Highlanders were present in full dress— or rather undress—and attracted the attention of everybody, especially the ladies, who seemed rather taken with the abbreviated anti-friction skirt, or kilt, of the Gaels." The *Star* went on to suggest that the regiment should have a parade for the benefit of the ladies who were evidently partial to the "fine-limbed Highlanders" and their costumes.[16]

Some four months later the men of the Seventy-Ninth, who on this afternoon in June had made such a hit, re-

---

[15] N.Y. *Times,* May 17, 1861; Washington *Evening Star,* May 22, 23, 1861; Washington *Sunday Morning Chronicle,* May 26, 1861. On the day that the Michigan band played the President had heard the Hartford Cornet Band at the flag-raising at the Post Office.

[16] Washington *Evening Star,* June 21, 1861; William Todd, *The Seventy-Ninth Highlanders* (Albany, 1886), pp. 13, 185.

turned to the White House. Coming from the Virginia side of the Potomac where they had been stationed, they crossed the Long Bridge on a night march. Their band had played "O Carry Me Back to Old Virginny," and, more to the liking of the men, "We'll Gang Na Mair to Your Town." The men began to sing "John Brown's Body," and "such like" songs. As they reached the city they swung up toward the White House, there, at three o'clock in the morning, to serenade Mrs. Lincoln with "favorite Scotch airs!" This was a "Thank you" to the President for allowing them to go with their colonel on a new assignment.[17]

Of course, President Lincoln did not attend all the band concerts on the White House grounds. He was far too busy for that. But in spite of the great pressures of his office he did attend many of them, usually sitting on the South porch with members of the family, friends, and dignitaries.

Preceding the concert on June 29, a special ceremony was held to which General Scott and other prominent persons had been invited. A conical tent of blue and white canvas (cost, with accessories, $335.50) had been erected over the bandstand on the grounds. Through the top of the tent extended a twenty-five-foot flagpole. The tent was Mrs. Lincoln's project. Whether she thought of it after the concert three weeks before had been "rained out" by a torrential shower is not known, but at any rate the musicians and their instruments would be protected from the elements in the future.[18]

---

[17] Washington *National Intelligencer*, Oct. 21, 1861; Washington *Evening Star*, Oct. 21, 1861; Todd, *Seventy-Ninth Highlanders*, pp. 86-88. It may be noted that in August, 1861, the "Highlanders" demonstrated a degree of independence that was incompatible with military discipline; they had "mutinied," or in the more restrained language of one reporter, showed "symptoms of insubordination." Some forty or fifty were put in the guardhouse, the colors were taken from the regiment, and a score of ringleaders sent to Dry Tortugas. But a few weeks later, the colors were restored and all was forgiven. The men on Dry Tortugas returned to the ranks in February, 1862. President Lincoln was on the scene when the announcement was made that the colors were to be restored, and the Highlanders' Band played "Hail to the Chief!" Washington *National Intelligencer*, Aug. 15, Sept. 18, 19, 1861; N.Y. *Herald*, Sept. 11, 17, 1861; Frank Leslie's *Pictorial History of the Civil War* (N.Y., 1862), I, 128, 135, 146; Frank Moore, ed., *The Rebellion Record* (N.Y., 1862-1868), II, D.66, Doc. 527-28; III, D.29; Todd, *Seventy-Ninth Highlanders*, pp. 66, 73.

[18] Accessories for the tent included 508 yards of canvas, one tent pole and gilded ball, twelve side poles, iron hooks, rings and bolts, ropes and halliards. The tent was set up and taken down six times during July at a cost of thirty dollars

On this occasion the tent was to be used for the first time, and the President was to raise a flag to the top of the pole, an ensign which had already been under fire on the gunboat *Freeborn* at a minor engagement down the river at Mathias Point. The Twelfth New York Regiment and a special detachment of Regulars, together with Withers' Band and the Marine Band, stood at attention in a hollow square formation around the bandstand. At four o'clock the President and his party appeared and proceeded to the stand as the bands played and the crowd cheered. General Scott and his staff came out at the South portico of the White House amid a "tornado of cheers" to which the bands added "Hail, Columbia."

The ceremony began with an earnest prayer by Dr. Pyne of St. John's Episcopal Church. Then, to the accompaniment of a thirty-four-gun salute, music from both bands, and cheers from the multitude, the President seized the ropes and raised the flag. It stuck at the top opening of the tent, and the President gave an extra tug. Up the flag went to the top, albeit slightly torn in the process. Thus the ceremony ended. In spite of the mishap to the flag (it was mended later), the whole affair in the words of one reporter "went off with éclat." The Marine Band continued to play until sunset, offering several new selections in honor of the occasion.[19]

A sort of climax to all other such events that the President had thus far witnessed was the mammoth parade and review on July 4. At nine o'clock that hot Independence Day morning, with a band playing "Hail to the Chief!," the President, General Scott, and numerous dignitaries and officials made their way from the White House to the flag-decorated, covered platform out in front where two regiments were already drawn up, having moved into position an hour before. From the

---

each time. Harry E. Pratt and Ernest E. East, "Mrs. Lincoln Refurbishes the White House," *Lincoln Herald*, XLVII (Feb., 1945), 19.

[19] Washington *Evening Star*, June 28, July 1, 1861; W. S. Wood to Gideon Welles, June 27, 1861, Welles Papers; Chicago *Tribune*, July 6, 1861; N.Y. *Tribune*, June 30, 1861; N.Y. *Herald*, June 30, 1861; Washington *National Intelligencer*, July 1, 1861. Band leader William Withers, Jr., was in charge of the music on a fateful evening nearly four years later. He led the orchestra at Ford's Theatre, April 14, 1865.

immense crowd there arose tumultuous cheers, and soon the twenty or more regiments, approximately twenty thousand men, began to pass in review before the platform. For an hour and a half the dignitaries gave attention while the parade, four miles long, went by.

As each regiment reached the stand its band or drum corps went into action, filling the air with patriotic music. There were brass bands and cornet bands, spectacular bands like that of the "Highlanders," and famous bands like Dodworth's. When the Garibaldi Guards with their exciting music approached the stand, they all reached to their plumed "Rinaldo" hats, plucked therefrom sprigs of evergreen or small bouquets of flowers and tossed them toward the President and General Scott. The ground was soon quite covered by this "shower of field pieces" (flowers of the field pressed into military service, as one observer put it), but not for long as spectators who were souvenir-minded made a dash for them. A tall good-looking lady, as if acting on impulse, quickly moved up to the reviewing stand and made a curtsey to the President. He acknowledged her greeting by shaking her hand, and before the guards could intervene she had slipped back into the crowd and was gone.

When the parade ended, the crowd gathered around the platform and, of course, there were calls for the President. He rose, introduced half a dozen dignitaries (each of whom spoke briefly) but declined to make a speech himself, saying: "I appear at your call, not to make a speech. I have made a great many dry and dull ones. Now I must fall back and say that the dignity of my position does not permit me to expose myself any more. I can now take shelter and listen to others."

The crowd seemed satisfied, for it gave three cheers for him and for General Scott. Then there was a general movement toward the Treasury Building. There the morning exercises were finished off by the President raising another flag, while the Seventy-First New York Regiment stood as guard of honor and a band played the "Star-Spangled Banner."[20]

[20] Washington *Evening Star*, July 5, 1861; Washington *National Intelligencer*,

It had been a "grand and imposing sight." The spectators were excited, confident, exultant. But the President, as one who stood close to him observed, was pale, sad, and silent, as if oppressed by the weight of what it all might mean.[21]

What did it all mean? The country would soon know —Bull Run was but a few days away, and then Ball's Bluff, and the winter of preparation, and McClellan's campaign, and more. Perhaps the President already knew— it meant not only men marching, exultant crowds cheering, bands playing stirring patriotic airs. It meant men cold and silent and dead; it meant solemn and anxious crowds, and the music of church bells tolling, and muffled drums beating as bands played a funeral march. Yes, perhaps the President knew, for three times already he had participated in solemn services for men who were no more—young men, too, and one of whom he loved as a son and whose death had caused him to weep.[22] Please, "a little more of your excellent music."

July 6, 1861; Washington *Sunday Morning Chronicle*, July 7, 1861; N.Y. *Herald*, July 6, 1861; N.Y. *Tribune*, July 6, 1861; N.Y. *News*, July 6, 1861, in Moore, *Rebellion Record*, II, 84-85; N. P. Willis in *Home Journal*, July 27, 1861.

A minor controversy arose afterward due to a dispatch in the N.Y. *Times* on July 6 which stated that the parade was a failure and was ill-advised anyway. An officer who had been on the platform said that this statement was false. The parade, he said, was imposing, every regiment had participated except one, it was over by 9:30 and the men were not fatigued. Two men from the ranks took a different view and expressed their sentiments in the press; one called the idea of the parade obnoxious and tiring and claimed that the men would rather celebrate in their own way; the other complained about the heat, stating that many had succumbed on their way back to camp, that many had sore feet and that 120 from his regiment were on the sick list. N.Y. *Times*, July 6, 1861; N.Y. *Herald*, July 9, 10, 1861.

[21] A. G. Riddle in Francis Fisher Browne, *The Every-Day Life of Abraham Lincoln* (Chicago, 1913), II, 326.

[22] The services were for Col. A. S. Vosburgh of the Seventy-First New York Regiment, for Elmer Ellsworth, and for a private in the Garibaldi Regiment. The first two occurred during the same week in May. Col. Vosburgh was in his thirties. His funeral was held at the Navy Yard and during the service the regiment chanted a hymn "In Memoriam" composed by Harrison Millard who had taken a prominent part in the concert on May 9. Ellsworth was but twenty-four years of age. After this funeral at the White House the President rode in the solemn procession to the railroad depot while church bells tolled and the band played mournful music. Ellsworth's death inspired both poetry and music. Sometime later the President heard one of the musical compositions played in the White House. The service for the Hungarian private was held at the camp of the regiment during the latter part of June. Washington *Evening Star*, May 21, 25, 27, June 26, 1861; N.Y. *Times*, May 22, 28, 1861; N.Y. *Herald*, June 26, 1861.

CHAPTER IV

THE PRESIDENT SEES A
COMET AND A STAR

THAT FIRST WEEK IN JULY OF 1861, ALTHOUGH BUSY AND hectic with newly arrived troops to be greeted, the big review, and the opening of Congress, nevertheless brought moments of pleasure and relaxation for the President and Mrs. Lincoln. It also, according to one view, brought forth a warning sign in the heavens. Early on the morning of July 2, after a severe thunderstorm with high winds and torrential rains that flooded sewers, drains, and army encampments and covered many streets with mud, a comet was observed in the sky. It was very brilliant and had a long tail—longer than that of Donati's comet three years before—and for more than two weeks it was to attract much attention. Accounts of it or of previous comets appeared in the newspapers; it was referred to as the "War Comet of 1861" and as a mysterious harbinger of a terrible conflict.[1]

That evening the President saw the new comet and also a new star, a musical star who was about to start out on her career as a concert artist. Mrs. Lincoln was having an informal gathering at the White House and among the guests was Mrs. Meda Blanchard. As a girl in Washington, Mrs. Blanchard had sung at school, at concerts, and in churches. Then, in 1859, she had gone to study in Italy and now, after her two years abroad, had just returned to the city.

So popular was the singer that she had been invited and urged, in a public letter signed by twenty-two leading citizens including Seward, Blair, Chase, Welles, Governor Sprague, Thurlow Weed, and others, to give her first public concert in her native city. She had graciously

---

[1] Washington *Evening Star*, July 2, 16, 1861; N.Y. *Herald*, July 3, 4, 8, 1861.

agreed, and the concert was to take place on Saturday, July 6, at Willard's Hall. The esteem in which Mrs. Blanchard was held was reflected in the *Sunday Morning Chronicle:*

> Two years ago, Mrs. Blanchard left her native land, to cultivate her genius under the most famous masters in Europe; and the results of her industry, we are assured, are very manifest in a great accession of melody and power. She returns to America laden with the highest encomiums of the best judges in the Land of Song; and we are happy to see that she is to give her first concert in her native city.[2]

Mrs. Blanchard had called at the White House to thank Mrs. Lincoln for her interest in the coming concert. Urged to sing for Mrs. Lincoln's guests, she did so. Playing her own accompaniment, she sang in a manner that charmed everyone present. Just as she had finished and was about to leave, the President appeared. The music had reached his office upstairs, and he had now come down to listen. Mrs. Blanchard was recalled with the request that she sing for the President. She agreed, again went to the piano and, as one observer put it, ". . . having laid off the shawl from shoulders that no 'South' would ever have seceded from, (with its eyes open,)," sang "Casta Diva" and one or two ballads, and then, at the President's request, the "Marseillaise." The President was delighted and thanked her enthusiastically.

Shortly thereafter music was heard outside. A band

---

[2] Washington *Sunday Morning Chronicle,* June 30, 1861. The same issue contained the letter of invitation to Mrs. Blanchard and her reply. The letter of invitation follows:

WASHINGTON, D.C., 11th June, 1861

Mrs. Meda Blanchard,

DEAR MADAM: Learning that you have just finished a successful course of culture of your eminent musical gifts, under the most eminent masters of Italy, and that you are about to commence what we are sure will be a most brilliant professional career, we take this mode of making known to you that we would esteem it a great kindness, and a rare privilege, if you would favor the residents and strangers now in Washington by giving your opening concert in this your native city—

We remain, dear madam,
Your friends and servants,

Mrs. Blanchard replied:

WASHINGTON, D.C., 29th June, 1861

GENTLEMEN: I have the honor to acknowledge the receipt of your letter, requesting me to give my opening concert in this my native city. Fully appreciating the high compliment with which you thus honor me, I shall be most happy to comply with your request, and will give the concert at the public hall of Willard's Hotel on Saturday evening, the 6th of July.

Very respectfully,
MEDA BLANCHARD

and some singers from the Eighth New York Regiment had come to serenade the President. Mr. Lincoln came out, stood with his arms folded, and enjoyed the music. As the band reached a crescendo in a selection from *I Puritani,* the President looked up and saw the comet, millions of miles away. He put one hand on the shoulder of his companion and with the other pointed to the comet. One of the guests, just about to leave, profoundly impressed by the scene, recorded it vividly:

> As he stood for a moment in this attitude of self-forgetting wonder, his face upturned and his whole gigantic frame outstretched toward the sky, I really thought I had seen nothing in my life more like an historic apparition. The strong and picturesque features had an unconsciousness of earnest contemplation which formed a temporary look of prophetic meaning and dignity, and his extraordinary stature and bold freedom of attitude were marvellous heightenings of the effect! I looked on—the band played on—then the music ceased. The serenade had been exquisitely fine—but, while it was being played, it seemed to me, I had been privileged to watch a "writing on the sky"—to see the Chief Magistrate of a nation of millions, while, at his country's and his own most critical hour, he recognized the finger of God![3]

Four evenings later when Mrs. Blanchard gave her concert at Willard's Hall, the President and Mrs. Lincoln were present. The program was a varied one. Mr. Scherman, a pianist, played an aria from *Lucrezia Borgia* and for an encore favored the audience with the "Gold Fever Galop," "thus giving a touch of the eccentric." An agreeable tenor, Signor Lotti, made a good impression, and Professor McCoy read from Shakespeare. Mrs. Blanchard, reported the *Star,* gave a satisfactory performance, but her voice seemed tired, probably, the reporter observed, because of over practice and the oppressive weather. (Washington was in the throes of an extreme heat wave at the time.)

But while the reporter for the *Star* was not over-en-

---

[3] N. P. Willis in *Home Journal,* July 20, 1861; N.Y. *Tribune,* July 8, 1861. The N.Y. *Herald* reported that Mrs. Blanchard "astonished a select party at the President's a few evenings since by her great powers," and later commented caustically (and quite unfairly), "This court patronage is a new idea in this country." N.Y. *Herald,* July 6, 8, 1861.

thusiastic about the concert, another listener gave a glowing account in which he noted the President's reaction as well as his own. The elite were there, he said, ". . . and our Republican President seemed to have been oblivious to the cares of office, and wholly absorbed by the syren voice of the fair cantatrice," while Mrs. Lincoln appeared to ". . . vie with the songstress in getting the attention of Mr. Seward."

As for the singer, her operatic numbers were just right, but, he added, ". . . the *impressive naivete* with which Mrs. Blanchard sang her final song, . . . 'Good-bye, Sweetheart,' took all hearts by storm." Amid the applause she reappeared and sang the "Star-Spangled Banner" with such effectiveness that the enthusiasm of the audience became "rapturous and unbounded." Thus the concert ended on a strong, but sobering note of patriotic feeling.[4]

From an appreciative member of the audience whose enthusiasm was accurately reflected in this second account of the concert, Mrs. Blanchard received a bouquet of flowers. In acknowledging the tribute thus paid her, she wrote:

> Mrs. Blanchard cannot sufficiently express her sense of the high honor which the President has so graciously conferred upon her, in the presentation of these beautiful flowers.
>
> Unhappily their beauty and freshness will soon have passed away, but the impression produced by their reception will ever live in her memory.[5]

It was a nice note, and Mr. Lincoln was undoubtedly as pleased with it as he had been with the singing of its sender. The star would never reach great heights, but she had gladdened the heart of the harassed President whose love of music was something passionate.

---

[4] Washington *Evening Star*, July 8, 1861.

[5] Nicolay Papers. Mrs. Blanchard apparently went on with her career as a concert artist. Cf. George C. D. Odell, *Annals of the New York Stage* (N.Y., 1936), VII, 458 ; VIII, 682.

CHAPTER V

"YANKEE DOODLE" AND
THE "MARSEILLAISE"

BY AUGUST THE COUNTRY WAS RECOVERING FROM THE shock of Bull Run, and people were taking a sober second look at the war. In Washington a remarkable transformation had occurred. The untried soldiers who had started out toward Manassas singing "Yankee Doodle," "The Watch on the Rhine," the "Marseillaise," and even "Dixie," and who had returned on the run disorganized and demoralized, were rapidly becoming a real army. General McClellan had arrived and was hard at work, and the city was no longer the scene of target shooting and midnight junkets by officers and men. The New York *Evening Post* reported that Washington was as quiet as a country village. A congressman recalled that the change was really striking:

> McClellan's coming to the Capital was like the advent of a beneficent prince. We awoke one morning to find the streets, the city, serenely free of the wandering gangs of brass and blue. They had all disappeared in a night. In his presence order and quietude at once found themselves everywhere established.[1]

At the White House social activity had not been entirely curtailed during July. On three Tuesday evenings levees were held, and in spite of the heat the first two were crowded almost to suffocation. At the first levee generals and colonels were as thick as blackberries, at the second (on the evening of the day the troops started for Manassas) General Scott made a brief appearance, but at

---

[1] N.Y. *Evening Post*, July 12, Aug. 5, 10, 1861; N.Y. *Tribune*, July 18, 1861; Julia Taft Bayne, "Good Times in the White House," *The Dearborn Independent*, Feb. 12, 1927; N.Y. *Herald*, Aug. 3, 1861; Albert G. Riddle, *Recollections of War Times* (N.Y., 1895), p. 63

the third (July 30) fewer uniforms were in evidence, and the President, although in good spirits, seemed somewhat worn and harassed.

On the twenty-third there was no levee; the President had spent the day visiting the troops. Some of the men were gloomy and dejected, and his kindly sympathy as he went from one unit to another cheered them and did them much good.[2]

Early in August preparations were being made for a very important visitor—important not for himself, but because of his name—Prince Napoleon, second son of Jerome Bonaparte and cousin of Emperor Louis Napoleon, a monarch not too friendly disposed toward the North.

The Prince, fat, fair and forty, good-looking and strongly resembling the great Napoleon, and his Italian wife had arrived in New York on July 27 aboard a handsome steam yacht and had forthwith been invited to visit Washington and to be guests at the White House during their stay. The invitation was not accepted; the Princess remained in New York, but the Prince had come to the capital city (as the guest of the French Minister) for a week's stay, and the first big event on his busy schedule was to be a formal dinner at the White House.[3] It was set for seven o'clock on the evening of August 3. Twenty-seven persons were included—the secretaries, Nicolay and Hay, members of the Cabinet, Lord Lyons and M. Mercier, the Prince and his entourage. Mrs. Grimsley, the only lady other than Mrs. Lincoln to be present, rather dreaded it and wished it over before it began.[4]

The Prince had had a busy day. After being formally

[2] Washington *Evening Star*, July 10, 17, 24, 31, 1861; N.Y. *Herald*, July 11, 17, 1861; N.Y. *Tribune*, July 17, 31, 1861; Todd, *Seventy-Ninth Highlanders*, pp. 53-54. John Nicolay thought the heat in Washington very intense and much more oppressive than in Illinois. John G. Nicolay to Therena Bates, July 10, 1861, Nicolay Papers.

[3] Washington *National Intelligencer*, July 31, Aug. 2, 1861; N.Y. *Evening Post*, July 29, 1861; N.Y. *Tribune*, July 30, Aug. 2, 1861. The royal visitors attracted much attention in the press, and *Harper's Weekly* and *Leslie's Illustrated Newspaper* both published sketches of them and their activities. Cf. *Harper's Weekly*, Aug. 17, 24, Sept. 7, 1861, and *Leslie's*, Aug. 17, 1861. There was general agreement that the Prince bore a remarkable resemblance to the first Napoleon.

[4] Washington *Evening Star*, Aug. 5, 1861; N.Y. *Herald*, Aug. 5, 1861; Mrs. E. J. Grimsley to John T. Stuart, Aug. 3, 1861, Elizabeth T. Grimsley Letters. "The dinner is today," she wrote, "I wish it was over."

presented to the President and his Cabinet at noon, he had visited the Capitol with Secretary Seward. There he had "shaken hands with Senators like a gentleman" and talked with congressmen in an easy and pleasant manner. He and the other guests were at the White House shortly before seven o'clock.[5]

But the President? At six thirty he was sitting at an upstairs window reading and listening to the music of the Marine Band which was giving its regular Saturday afternoon concert on the south lawn. Would he be ready to meet his guests? An observer sitting on a settee during the concert looked up and saw a servant enter the room; quickly the presidential face was shaven, the official towel shaken out the window, and then:

> The long arms were busy about the tall head for a moment, probably with brush or comb—there was a stoop, probably for bi-forked disencumberment, and immediately after, a sudden gleam of white linen lighted aloft—a momentary extension of the elbows with the tying of a cravat, and a putting on of the black coat—and, then, the retiring figure of the dressed President was lost to our sight. The toilet of the sovereign of the great realm of the West . . . had occupied precisely twenty-two minutes. . . .

Ten minutes later the President, the Prince and other guests appeared on the portico. The Prince came forward, put his eyeglass on his nose, looked at the crowd gathered for the concert, smiled, and bowed. The band was playing its final number, "Yankee Doodle," and when it finished the dinner party moved inside. By the time the guests reached the dining room, the band, having made a quick change of location from the lawn to the front entrance of the White House, struck up its first evening selection, the popular "Partant pour la Syrie."[6]

---

[5] Washington *National Intelligencer*, Aug. 5, 1861; N.Y. *Evening Post*, Aug. 3, 1861; B. B. French to Mrs. Pamela French, Aug. 16, 1861, B. B. French Papers, Library of Congress. In general, the Prince made a favorable impression. The N.Y. *Evening Post* observed that in New York the Prince wore a summer suit of linen and a straw hat "like any other middle class gentleman," N.Y. *Evening Post*, July 29, 1861; the N.Y. *Herald* commented on his easy, gracious manner and modesty, and noted that people on the train from Philadelphia to Washington did not recognize him as the nephew of one emperor and the cousin of another. N.Y. *Herald*, Aug. 5, 1861.

[6] N. P. Willis in *Home Journal*, Aug. 17, 1861; Grimsley, *Jour. Ill. State Hist. Soc.*, XIX (Oct.-Jan., 1926-27), 69-70; Washington *Evening Star*, Aug. 5, 1861.

The dinner was a success—"elegant and recherché." The White House had been decorated with fresh flowers, and on the table the sparkling new crystal gleamed amid fragrant and tastefully arranged bouquets. Mrs. Lincoln's attractive white silk dress and Mrs. Grimsley's salmon tulle added color to the scene as did likewise the broad red ribbon which the Prince wore across his chest.

For two hours the guests enjoyed the delicious meal which, on Mrs. Lincoln's insistence, had been prepared in the White House kitchen instead of by a caterer. Earlier in the day Mrs. Grimsley had marvelled that things moved so smoothly one scarcely realized that meal preparations were under way for nearly thirty people. The tastefulness and completeness of the dinner had never been excelled, reported the New York *Herald,* and the credit went to Mrs. Lincoln for her planning and arrangements and her graceful courtesy and charming manners.[7]

As was the custom, the Marine Band played at intervals during the meal, offering national airs of France and the United States. In its effort to please the guests of honor the band committed what might have been considered a minor diplomatic blunder—it played the "Marseillaise," not once, but twice, and while it was quite appropriate when played for Lafayette many years before, and while it was a favorite of the President, that stirring piece was not exactly popular nor appropriate during the period of the Second Empire! But the Prince took it in good humor, remarking, "Mais, oui, je suis Républicain—en Amérique."[8]

An interesting repercussion resulted from Willis's intimate description of the President's toilet as here given. A few weeks later while Mrs. Lincoln was vacationing at Long Branch, New Jersey, an entertainment consisting of a series of tableaux was planned at one of the hotels. Some of the young ladies who were to take part feared that a reporter might spy on them as they were dressing and report what he saw just as President Lincoln's toilet had been reported when Prince Napoleon was a guest at the White House! Of course, the reporter reassured them that it would not happen. N.Y. *Herald,* Aug. 22, 1861.

[7] Washington *Evening Star,* Aug. 5, 1861; N.Y. *Herald,* Aug. 5, 1861; Mrs. E. J. Grimsley to John T. Stuart, Aug. 3, 1861, Elizabeth T. Grimsley Letters. Gideon Welles thought it a quiet and pleasant dinner. Welles Papers (1861). Gen. McClellan was bored. George B. McClellan, *McClellan's Own Story* (N.Y., 1887), p. 84.

One unhappy feature came to light later. In 1867 Thurlow Weed printed a statement indicating that Mrs. Lincoln had difficulty getting the bills paid for the dinner and that finally the amount ($900) was "covered up in a gardener's account." Pratt and East, *Lincoln Herald,* XLVII (Feb., 1945), 17.

[8] Washington *Evening Star,* Aug. 5, 1861; N.Y. *Herald,* Aug. 4, 5, 1861; Frederick W. Seward, *Reminiscences of a War-Time Statesman* (N.Y., 1916), p. 183.

During the ensuing week, the Prince followed an exhausting schedule in spite of the heat which he thought might be as bad as midsummer in India. He toured the fortifications around the city, he made a trip to Mount Vernon (and was so late in returning that there was speculation that he might have been waylaid by the Confederates), he attended other formal dinners and receptions, and he visited the Confederate headquarters at Manassas. But nowhere was he more handsomely treated than at the presidential dinner where he was greeted with the plebian tune of "Yankee Doodle," and then specially favored with the revolutionary notes of the "Marseillaise!"[9]

W. H. ("Bull Run") Russell was quick to note the "amusing blunder" concerning the "Marseillaise" and commented on it in his letter to the London *Times*. Cf. Washington *Evening Star*, Sept. 5, 6, 1861.

[9] N.Y. *Evening Post*, Aug. 6, 8, 1861; N.Y. *Times*, Aug. 5, 6, 7, 12, 1861; William Howard Russell, *My Diary North and South* (Boston, 1863), p. 243.

That there was some awareness of possible diplomatic ramifications connected with the visit of the Prince is fairly evident, especially when the Prince visited the Confederates at Manassas. The N.Y. *Herald* commented: "it hardly appears consistent with that friendship which we have a right to expect from our old ally, that the representative of the French dynasty should lend to the rebellious cabal sitting at Richmond the moral encouragement which his presence will afford." The reporter feared that recognition of the Confederacy might follow. N.Y. *Herald*, Aug. 10, 1861. But the next day he felt reassured and concluded that the Prince was too sensible a man to recommend that such lawless people as he saw there be recognized. N.Y. *Herald*, Aug. 11, 1861. *Harper's Weekly*, in publishing portraits of the Prince and his wife, commented frankly: "should any political complications grow out of the visit of the Prince—as seems not unlikely—they [the portraits] will possess Historic interest." *Harper's Weekly*, Sept. 7, 1861. At any rate, the President, Mrs. Lincoln, and Secretary Seward had done an excellent job in showing the Prince every possible courtesy and consideration.

CHAPTER VI

THE MUSIC AT BAILEY'S CROSS ROADS

DURING THE LATE SUMMER AND FALL OF 1861 THERE WERE many troop reviews in and about the city of Washington, so many in fact that they provoked criticism and protest. They were, it was alleged, a waste of time and were held merely for show. To these criticisms an editorial writer for the *Sunday Morning Chronicle* replied that, quite the contrary, reviews were of great value to both officers and men. Soldiers, by participating in reviews, obtained valuable experience in maneuvres and troop movements, and also got a sense of belonging to the larger whole—the army itself.[1]

If his actions were any indication, the President sided with the editorial writer, for he was frequently present at reviews and took a great interest in them. Here he saw the progress being made in the development of a real army, here he became better acquainted with the generals and learned to gauge the morale and appreciate the attitude of the men. Furthermore, when at reviews he got away temporarily from the atmosphere of state affairs (like the dinner for Prince Napoleon) and could, for a while, escape from difficult problems such as that created by General Frémont's mishandling of the critical situation in Missouri (and Jessie Frémont's sharp tongue when she came to the White House to plead her husband's cause) and the even more acute crisis brought on by the irresponsible Captain Charles Wilkes when he

---

[1] Washington *Sunday Morning Chronicle*, Oct. 13, 1861. In his characteristic manner, Gen. McClellan explained: "The frequent reviews I held at Washington were not at all for the benefit of the public, nor yet for the purpose of examining the individual condition of the men. . . . But they were to accustom the regiments to move together and see each other, to give the troops an idea of their own strength, to infuse *esprit de corps* and mutual emulation. . . . With new troops frequent reviews are of the greatest utility and produce the most excellent effect." McClellan, *McClellan's Own Story*, pp. 97-98.

removed Confederates Mason and Slidell from the *Trent*.

And a prominent feature of the reviews was the music that the President loved—the music of the bands. Thus it was that in the latter part of August, Mr. Lincoln witnessed no fewer than half a dozen reviews, some at the White House, others as far away as Tennallytown or across the river in Virginia. A carriage ride of several miles to and from a review did not deter the busy executive at all!

August 21 was a perfect summer day, sunny and clear, with a gentle breeze, and not too hot. At Tennallytown ten thousand troops were lined up for review. When all was ready, General McClellan galloped onto the field with his staff, accompanied by two companies of dragoons. In contrast, the President of the United States merely appeared in a carriage with Secretary Chase, but he was greeted by a salute from a battery of sixty-four pounders.

As each regiment passed in review, its band played "soul stirring and patriotic airs," then left the ranks and faced the troops as they marched on. When the review ended, nine hearty cheers, "which made the earth tremble," were given for the President. By this time it was three thirty in the afternoon, and the President was treated to a "princely collation" at the residence of F. P. Blair, Sr. After the refreshments there was a review of five thousand more troops![2]

The next day the President reviewed the regiment of his long-time friend, Colonel Edward D. Baker (whose funeral he was to attend two months later, almost to the day), and two days after this he and Secretary Seward appeared in a carriage at a review across the river in Virginia and heard once more the stirring strains of the "Star-Spangled Banner."

On Sunday, August 25, he and Secretaries Seward and Welles attended church services at the camp of a New Hampshire regiment, reviewed a brigade, and ended the day with another look at Colonel Baker's regiment. Dur-

---

[2] Washington *Sunday Morning Chronicle*, Aug. 25, 1861; N.Y. *Herald*, Aug. 22, 1861; N.Y. *Times*, Aug. 22, 1861.

ing the following week he was present at other reviews.[3]

Through most of September and October the weather was unusually pleasant, and conditions were ideal for outdoor activities. Large crowds continued to turn out for the music of the Marine Band on the White House grounds on Saturdays. Because of the popularity of these concerts, Secretary Welles ordered them extended until the first of November.[4]

Meanwhile, the President was constant in his attendance at reviews. On September 10 he again went out to Tennallytown where twelve Pennsylvania regiments were in line, each being presented by Governor Curtin. Following the review and refreshments at headquarters, Mr. Lincoln crossed the river to the camp of some New York regiments. Here he was greeted by "Hail to the Chief!," and then heard General McClellan inform the Seventy-Ninth ("Highlanders") Regiment that they would soon receive their colors back. After witnessing the parade of the Thirty-Third Pennsylvania Volunteers, he recrossed the river by ferry and arrived back at the White House at seven o'clock. It had been a long but satisfying day. Weary as he was that evening, he yet had to contend with a most difficult visitor, for who should appear but Mrs. Frémont![5]

On the afternoon of September 24, he and Mrs. Lincoln and Secretary Chase drove over to the grounds near the Capitol where a review of eight batteries of artillery and three regiments of cavalry was under way. Two full mounted bands supplied the music, and at four o'clock General McClellan rode onto the field to inspect the troops.

An even more imposing sight was the review two weeks later of 7,500 troops—1,500 artillerymen with more than one hundred cannon, and 6,000 cavalry with their standards flying in the breeze. European observers viewing

[3] Washington *Sunday Morning Chronicle,* Aug. 25, 1861; N.Y. *Herald,* Aug. 23, 25, 31, 1861; N.Y. *Times,* Aug. 23, 26, 1861.

[4] Washington *Sunday Morning Chronicle,* Sept. 15, 22, 1861; Gideon Welles to Col. J. L. Harris, Oct. 5, 1861, Officers of the Marine Corps, No. 7 (1861-1867), Letter Book, National Archives, p. 38.

[5] Washington *Evening Star,* Sept. 11, 1861; Washington *National Intelligencer,* Sept. 12, 1861; N.Y. *Herald,* Sept. 11, 1861. Concerning the withdrawal and restoration of the colors of the Seventy-Ninth (Highlanders) Regt., see Moore, *Rebellion Record,* II, D. 66, Doc. 527-528; III, D. 22, 29; Leslie's *Pictorial History,* I, 128, 135, and *supra,* chap. III. Gen. McClellan was quite severe with the Highlanders. Cf. *McClellan's Own Story,* pp. 86-87, 99-100.

this vast panorama were greatly impressed, and McClellan felt quite satisfied, commenting: "The review . . . passed off very well; it was a superb display, by far the finest ever seen on this continent, and rarely equalled anywhere."[6]

In addition, the President and Mrs. Lincoln had seen a flag presentation ceremony of the Seventh New Jersey Regiment and had gone with a distinguished party on a Sunday picnic visit to the camp of the Nineteenth New York Regiment sixteen miles from the city, leaving at ten in the morning and arriving back at eight in the evening.[7] On October 18 the President himself, at the request of Governor Sprague, of Rhode Island, presented a flag to the colonel of the Second Rhode Island Regiment in camp near Fort Slocum. On this occasion a serious address, a solemn prayer, and the singing of the Doxology concluded the ceremony.

But the climax, for men and officers, for the public and the President, came in a huge review on November 20 at Bailey's Cross Roads, eight miles on the way to Fairfax Court House, in Virginia. Toward this spot on a clear but windy morning upwards of 100,000 people converged—50,000 to 70,000 troops and 25,000 spectators. By nine o'clock the regiments, some of which were stationed so far off that they had been up and on the march since two in the morning, began to arrive and take their stations under the direction of a score of generals and a hundred staff officers. As far as the eye could see there stretched regiment after regiment moving into formation. Never before had there been such a spectacle.

Meanwhile, the thousands of spectators were crowding across the Long Bridge (no passes required) and up the highway to Bailey's Cross Roads. In the city, buggies and carriages of all sorts were at a premium and brought high prices, so great was the demand for transportation. The traffic on the Long Bridge and on the highway was

[6] *Leslie's Illus. News*, Oct. 5, 1861; Leslie's *Pictorial History*, I, 153, 176; Boston *Journal*, Sept. 25, 1861; N.Y. *Herald* Oct. 9, 1861; *Harper's Weekly*, Oct. 26, 1861; *McClellan's Own Story*, p. 169.

[7] N.Y. *Herald*, Oct. 6, 7, 19, 1861; Washington *Evening Star*, Oct. 19, 1861; Leslie's *Pictorial History*, I, 170. Several ladies were included in the Sunday picnic outing, among them Mrs. Frederick Seward and the two daughters of Secretary Cameron.

so dense that it took hours to reach the field where spectators crowded every vantage point.

Cheers "like the roaring of the sea" broke out when General McClellan, his staff, an escort of several cavalry regiments, and a band appeared on the scene. At 11:15 the President's party, Cabinet officers, diplomats, and other dignitaries, with their wives and families, arrived and took a position on a little knoll. The President, the Secretary of War, and the Assistant Secretary of War, left their carriage and joined General McClellan on horseback, and for an hour and a half inspected the lines, front and rear, sometimes proceeding at a gallop.

Then came the review itself, and for three hours the troops, regiment by regiment, wheeled into line and marched past the reviewing party. A reporter, watching it all, speculated:

> What strength was slumbering in that mighty host, and what death and carnage lay before it, when it should move on the foe. When the question of union and disunion was so glibly discussed by politicians on the stump, who ever dreamed he should live to behold such a sight as this?[8]

With the cheers of the soldiers and the shouts of the spectators and the salutes (and smoke) of the artillery was mingled the music of the bands—fifty of them! Never before had the President, nor likely the troops or spectators, heard such an outpouring of martial music. In some cases the bands of whole brigades were joined together, thus increasing the volume of music as the men marched on their way. The consolidated band of General Butterfield's brigade, totaling 120 pieces, played with excellent effect, and as it passed in review it played "The Standard Bearer Quickstep," which was dedicated to the general himself.

When the last regiment passed in review, the troops started back toward their camps and the spectators streamed down the road toward the Long Bridge. The confusion and congestion of traffic seemed even worse than in the morning, for now hundreds of soldiers mingled with the thousands of civilians hurrying back toward the

---

[8] N.Y. *Times*, Nov. 23, 1861.

city. Refreshment wagons along the route, selling fruit and pastries, did a big business.[9]

For such a tremendous crowd, accidents seemed to have been relatively few in number. A reporter for the New York *Herald* noted only that one soldier had a leg fractured when kicked by a horse, that there was a collision between a galloping officer and an infantryman, that General McDowell was thrown from his horse, and that President Lincoln was almost thrown when his horse became entangled in a wire fence.[10]

The review had been a success; it was impressive and spectacular, and, according to one reporter, "the most magnificent ever held." But it was also strenuous. One of the soldiers, who saw the event as a participant and not merely as a spectator, summed it up realistically in a letter to his sister:

> The grand review, which you of course have read of, was a truly grand affair, and must have been a splendid scene to look upon for those who took no part in the parade, for there is really hard work in such ceremonies. For instance, our regiment marched six miles to the reviewing ground with knapsacks, twenty rounds of ball cartridges, haversacks with dinner, and canteens with water. After arriving, we stood in the mud ankle deep for over two hours, waiting for the balance of the forces to take their positions. We stood at "attention" while the President and General McClellan and his staff made the rounds of the entire force, and it was no small task to ride past seventy thousand men in line of battle. After that we waited for about half the number to pass, before our turn came to march by the reviewing stand, from which we made a circuit of two miles, to reach the road which led to our camp; and when we reached it, all felt we had performed a hard day's work.[11]

Doubtless the officers, the reporters, the spectators, and even the President would have agreed—it had been a hard day's work.

---

[9] Washington *Sunday Morning Chronicle*, Nov. 24, 1861; Washington *National Intelligencer*, Nov. 21, 1861; Washington *Evening Star*, Nov. 20, 1861; N.Y. *Herald*, Nov. 20, 21, 1861; Sacramento *Daily Union*, Dec. 25, 1861; Moore, *Rebellion Record*, III, D. 85; *Harper's Weekly*, Dec. 7, 1861; *Leslie's Illus. News*, Dec. 14, 1861; Leslie's *Pictorial History*, I, 232-33.

[10] N.Y. *Herald*, Nov. 21, 1861. One reporter was surprised that there were not more accidents because of the mounted men's reckless dashings here and there over the rough ground. N.Y. *Times*, Nov. 23, 1861.

[11] Newton Martin Curtis, *From Bull Run to Chancellorsville* (N.Y., 1906), pp. 81-82.

Very likely, too, after such an exhausting day, most of those who were present at the review slept soundly that night. But one of the multitude of onlookers apparently did not sleep well—a little incident on the journey back to the city, a chance remark by a companion, kept coming back to mind. At last, as early morning drew near, the restless individual arose from bed, took up a pen and began to write. The writing continued without deliberation or hesitation until the task was completed. With relief, the pen was laid aside. The message was written, and thus, in the early hours of the twenty-first of November, 1861, the nation received what was to become the greatest song of the war.

For the person who could not sleep was Julia Ward Howe. She had come to Washington a few days before with her husband, Dr. Samuel Gridley Howe, in a small party that included Governor John A. Andrew, of Massachusetts, and the Reverend James Freeman Clarke. Not only had Mrs. Howe visited Lincoln at the White House, she had also seen the twinkling watch fires of a hundred circling camps, she had seen the burnished rows of steel, and she had talked with men who were to die in the cause of freedom—and freedom was a holy cause.

And so, when, on the return to the city from the troop review, their party heard the soldiers singing the "John Brown Song"—"John Brown's body lies a-mould'ring in the grave"—and when Mr. Clarke suggested that she write some words more fitting and worthy, Mrs. Howe could not forget. Nor could she rest until she had given expression to her thoughts and feelings:

> Mine eyes have seen the glory
> of the coming of the Lord. . . .
> - - - - - - - - - - - - -
> His truth is marching on.[12]

Bailey's Cross Roads was just another troop review, albeit a grand one, and President Lincoln witnessed many

---

[12] A detailed account of Mrs. Howe's trip to Washington is in Julia Ward Howe, *Reminiscences 1819-1899* (Boston, 1900), pp. 269-77. Some additional facts are given in Florence Howe Hall, *The Story of the Battle Hymn of the Republic* (N.Y., 1916). According to Mr. Clarke's account, the party left Boston on Nov. 12, 1861, and arrived home again on the twenty-fourth. James Freeman Clarke, *Autobiography* (Boston, 1891), p. 275.

such events. But out of the confused pageantry of the day came the inspiration for a song—a song which later would affect Lincoln deeply, stir the conscience of the whole North, and become not merely a song for the times but a hymn for the ages.[13]

Appropriately enough, there is in the Hotel Willard in Washington, D.C., a memorial tablet commemorating the writing of the hymn inspired by the incident at Bailey's Cross Roads. It reads:

In Honor of

JULIA • WARD • HOWE

who wrote the

"BATTLE HYMN OF THE REPUBLIC"

Here at the Old Willard Hotel

November 21, 1861

"In the beauty of the lillies Christ was born across the sea

With a glory in his bosom that transfigures you and me."

Presented by the

LADIES OF THE GRAND ARMY

OF THE REPUBLIC

January 24, 1930[14]

---

[13] Earlier in the year a contest had been held for a "National Hymn." The winner of the contest was to receive a prize of five hundred dollars. A committee of prominent New Yorkers laboriously went through the 1,200 songs that were submitted, while the idea of the contest was criticized and ridiculed from the start. Thus, *The Musical Review and Musical World* on May 25, 1861, doubted that a worthwhile hymn could be obtained from a contest—inspiration was necessary to produce a great work. It suggested that possibly the committee intended to give employment to unoccupied poets and musicians! In *The Orpheus C. Kerr Papers*, 1st ser. (N.Y., 1865), Letter VIII, Robert H. Newell humorously satirized "The Rejected 'National Hymns.'"

Even the judges were skeptical. George Templeton Strong, a member of the committee, noted on June 26, 1861, that the committee disposed of "bushels of rubbish," and added, "This committee is responsible for the production of an enormous bulk of commonplace, watery versification. . . . It's clear, I think, that we get no national hymn." Nevins and Halsey, eds., *Diary of George Templeton Strong*, III, 162. Strong was right. No prize was awarded as the judges thought no composition submitted was worthy of it.

The decision not to award a prize provoked further criticism, and finally Richard Grant White wrote a complete account in explanation and defense of the committee's work. Interestingly enough, White's book, entitled *National Hymns: How They Are Written, and How They Are Not Written*, was one of the more than 125 books drawn from the Library of Congress under the account of Abraham Lincoln!

As a final bit of irony, it may be noted that Mrs. Howe wrote a poem (for which a Boston musician composed music) for the National Hymn contest in which no one received the $500 prize, and that when "The Battle Hymn of the Republic" was accepted for publication in the *Atlantic Monthly* of February, 1862, she received four or five dollars.

[14] A photograph of the tablet is in Eskew, *Willard's of Washington*, following page 64, and a delightful account of the writing of the hymn is found on pages 90-97 of the same volume.

CHAPTER VII

"THE PRESIDENT LOOKED SOMEWHAT WORN"

THE EXECUTIVE MANSION WAS IN READINESS; ITS EXTErior gleamed with two coats of fresh paint, and its interior, thoroughly refurbished and redecorated, reflected an elegance that was fitting and proper for the house of the President. When, at eight o'clock on the evening of December 17, 1861, the waiting crowd surged in for the initial levee of the winter season that first year of the war, the President and Mrs. Lincoln were likewise ready. They stood in the Blue Room and greeted everyone cordially. Mrs. Lincoln wore a becoming gown of light flowered silk brocade and a wreath of flowers on her hair. Jewels sparkled on her fingers.

With the inspiring music of the Marine Band in the background, the guests moved from room to room admiring the new furnishings—wallpaper, draperies, curtains, and especially the famous new carpet. They made a colorful picture.

> Grave Senators and gallant Representatives; officers of the army and navy, with varied specimens of volunteers; city exquisites, arrayed regardless of expense, and hardy backwoodsmen in heavy boots; newspaper men after items, and fortune hunters after heiresses; commission seekers and heavy contractors. . . .

Interestingly enough, one reporter who gave unqualified endorsement to the refinishing job that had been done under Mrs. Lincoln's direction, was less enthusiastic about the brand new costumes of some of the ladies present. Concerning the White House, he wrote:

> President John Adams' wife Abigail, who used—so she wrote—to use the unfinished East-room to dry her clothes

in when it was stormy on washing days, never dreamed that the excellent taste of one of her successors, aided by Philadelphia furnishers, could give such an imperial appearance to the national drawing-room. It is alike creditable to the nation and to the lady whose good taste supervised its renovation.

But, as for the ladies' dresses, the reporter commented:

Varied, too, were their dresses, of almost every shade of color and quality of material, some high necked, some low necked; some with trains, some with flounces, some really very pretty, others dowdy enough.

Not very complimentary, considering the fact that many of the ladies, having "nothing to wear," and wanting to appear properly dressed at the first levee in the newly-decorated White House, had, for two days, kept the dry-goods and millinery shops quite busy.

As the reception drew to a close, the Marine Band struck up "Yankee Doodle." Mr. Lincoln, with his partner, Mrs. T. Bigelow Lawrence, wife of the consul general at Florence, and Mrs. Lincoln, escorted by former Governor Newell, of New Jersey, and by Congressman Colfax, of Indiana, led the final promenade.

During the evening, the President, it was observed, was pleasant, sociable, and in good spirits. And although he was not wearing the ruddy glow that he had when he first came to Washington, he looked quite healthy. Perhaps his good spirits and healthy looks were in part the result of his many visits to the soldiers those glorious autumn days before the winter season set in. The next few weeks were to bring a marked change.[1]

---

[1] Washington *Evening Star*, Dec. 16, 18, 1861; Washington *Sunday Morning Chronicle*, Dec. 22, 1861; N.Y. *Herald*, Dec. 18, 1861; N.Y. *Times*, Dec. 17, 1861; Sacramento *Daily Union*, Feb. 3, 1862; French, ed., *Diary of B. B. French*, pp. 117-18 (Dec. 18, 1861).

An unfortunate consequence of the refurnishing of the White House was that Mrs. Lincoln exceeded the amount appropriated for the work. Congress allowed $6,000 a year for painting and repairs and appropriated $20,000 for the refurbishing, but Mrs. Lincoln overspent by $6,700. In tears, she begged Commissioner French to use his influence with the President to get him to approve a bill for the amount of her overdraft. When French brought the matter up, the President was greatly upset and declined to approve, saying, ". . . it would stink in the nostrils of the American people to have it said that the President of the United States had approved a bill over running an appropriation of $20,000 for *flub-dubs* for this damned old house, when the soldiers cannot have blankets." He thought the house well enough furnished and better than any they had ever lived in. He would pay the bill out of his own pocket, he said. But eventually Congress passed deficiency bills to cover the excess. B. B. French to Pamela

The traditional New Year's Reception ushered in not only a new year but a very busy social month for the President. There were four Tuesday evening levees, each more brilliant than that which preceded it; in addition, the President listened to sharp criticism of his policies by Horace Greeley in a lecture at the Smithsonian; he and Mrs. Lincoln drove out to Tennallytown for a parade, dinner, entertainment, and speeches in observance of the victory at New Orleans (1815), and later in the month they went together to the opera where they saw scenes from *Il Trovatore* and heard the famous duet "Suona la Tromba" from Bellini's *I Puritani*.

Unlike much of the rest of the month, New Year's Day was clear and sunshiny, although the streets were cloudy with dust. The reception, beginning at eleven o'clock, was a three-hour ordeal. First came the Cabinet members and their families, then the diplomatic corps *en costume* (a gaudy show, remarked Attorney-General Bates), then the Justices of the Supreme Court, followed by army and navy officers (another gaudy show, said Bates), and at noon the doors were opened to the public.

In from the sidewalks where they had been gathering for hours streamed the thousands, kept in order by two lines of city police in new uniforms. There was a rush, a push, and a scramble as the crowd moved slowly toward the place where the President stood. After brief greetings were exchanged, the throng moved through the

French, Dec. 24, 1861, B. B. French Papers; French ed., *Diary of B. B. French*, p. 117 (Dec. 18, 1861); Pratt and East, *Lincoln Herald*, XLVII (Feb., 1945), 13.

Actually, the amount granted was hardly excessive in view of the size of the White House and the wear and tear to which it was subject. When the Lincolns took up residence there it was, thought Congressman Riddle, dilapidated, unattractive, bare, worn and soiled "not unlike the breaking up of a bad winter about a deserted farm." Riddle, *Recollections of War Times*, pp. 15, 17. Unfortunately, the bright new look of 1861-62 did not last long. An English visitor in 1864 commented on the plain furnishings and worn carpets. Robert Ferguson, in Henry S. Commager, ed., *The Blue and the Gray* (Indianapolis, 1950), II, 1081 ff. Toward the end of the war it was much worse. When some Illinois visitors became enthusiastic about the Mansion, its stately magnificence and its many interesting features, John Nicolay found their enthusiasm only slightly contagious—". . . almost enough to make me forget for the moment what an ill-kept, inconvenient, and dirty old rickety concern it really is, from top to bottom." "I wonder," he went on, "how much longer a great nation, as ours is, will compel its ruler to live in such a small and dilapidated old shanty and in such a shabby-genteel style." John G. Nicolay to Therena Bates, Mar. 26, 1865, Nicolay Papers. Of course, the worst depredations were committed by souvenir hunters who despoiled draperies, curtains, and furniture. Cf. Washington *Evening Star*, Nov. 29, 1864, and Margarita Spalding Gerry, ed., *Through Five Administrations: Reminiscences of Colonel William H. Crook* (N.Y., 1910), pp. 26-27.

East Room (on coverings specially laid to protect the new carpets), and made its way out through one of the large windows on a neat, carpeted platform.

Among the notables attending was Major W. F. M. Arny. Successor to Kit Carson as Indian agent in New Mexico, the major attracted considerable attention, dressed in his suit of buckskin embroidered with beads. He had made a gift, privately, to Mrs. Lincoln of a Navajo blanket, figured in red, white, and blue, and woven by a squaw who had worked on it for five months.

Everyone was good-natured, and although Senator Browning was relieved of between fifty and one hundred dollars by a pickpocket, the police, in general, did a good job in maintaining order in the huge crowd. Through it all, the Marine Band gave a magnificent performance of national and patriotic airs, lending "additional life to a scene already lively."[2]

The weather progressively worsened that month, but the Tuesday evening levees continued to be popular, crowded, and "brilliant." Of the first of these levees one reporter wrote approvingly:

> We have never seen the east room so crowded with dazzling beauty as on that occasion. The ladies did not seem any less refined and graceful because they were ladies of Northern birth, and the gentlemen, civilians and soldiers, statesmen and seamen, bore themselves with as much ease and dignity as those who, for many years, figured as the magnates and masters of metropolitan society.[3]

A week later, when, in spite of cold, disagreeable, sleety weather, a sizable crowd appeared at the levee, the fash-

[2] Washington *Evening Star*, Jan. 1, 1862; N.Y. *Herald*, Jan. 3, 1862; N.Y. *Times*, Jan. 3, 1862; *Leslie's Illus. News*, July 5, 1862; John G. Nicolay to Therena Bates, Jan. 3, 1862, Nicolay Papers; "Source Material of Iowa History: An Iowa Woman in Washington, D.C., 1861-1865," *Iowa Jour. of Hist.*, LII (Jan., 1954), 64; Beale, ed., *Diary of Edward Bates*, p. 221; T. C. Pease and J. G. Randall, eds., *The Diary of Orville Hickman Browning* (Springfield, 1927-1933), I, 521; Poore, *Perley's Reminiscences*, II, 106.

[3] Washington *Sunday Morning Chronicle*, Jan. 12, 1862. Northerners, it would seem, had a rather marked inferiority complex when it came to social amenities and social activities. Perhaps this feeling was fostered by the attitude of Southern society leaders and by comments in the press like the one here quoted—comments which expressed somewhat surprised gratification that Northerners were not entirely uncivilized! The reporter went on to say that all Washington needed to realize its possibilities was "an infusion of the indomitable energy, unceasing enterprise, and inexhaustible invention that have made the free cities of the North the finest in the world."

ion and beauty "exceeded that of the palmiest days of the regency of Harriet Lane." On the evening of the twenty-first, the streets were muddy and a snowstorm set in, but still the attendance was large, and the "many rich dresses of the ladies and uniforms of the military made a varied and beautiful scene."[4]

Following the reception on January 7, the Lincoln family and a few friends who had been invited to remain, experienced an unusual musical treat. The famous Hutchinson Singers from New Hampshire, known by the Lincolns as they were known over the country for their family concerts, were present at the levee and were requested to sing.

Interested in reform movements and politics as well as music, the Hutchinson family had taken an active singing part in the campaigns of 1856 and 1860, and during the latter campaign a songbook edited by John W. Hutchinson, *Hutchinson's Republican Songster, For 1860*, was used at rallies everywhere. When Lincoln, en route to Washington for his inauguration, was waiting at Jersey City for his train to be made ready, the Hutchinsons appeared on the balcony of the station and sang:

> Behold the day of promise comes—full of inspiration—
> The blessed day by prophets sung, for the healing of the
>   nation.
> Old midnight errors flee away: they soon will
>   all be gone;
> While heavenly angels seem to say, "The good
>   time's coming on."
>   Coming right along,
>   Coming right along,
> The blessed day of promise is coming right along.
>
> Already in the golden east the glorious light is
>   dawning,
> And watchmen from the mountain tops can see the
>   blessed morning.

---

[4] Washington *Evening Star*, Jan. 15, 22, 1862; N.Y. *Herald*, Jan. 16, 22, 1862. On the thirtieth of the month, John Nicolay, writing to his fiancée, said that the weather was rainy and bad underfoot as well, the same as it had been the past four or five weeks—wet, muddy, cold, nasty, slushy, slippery. He continued, "You may add all the other disagreeable adjectives you can remember and not overdraw the picture." John G. Nicolay to Therena Bates, Jan. 30, 1862, Nicolay Papers.

O'er all the land their voices ring, the harvest
    now we're reaping.
Awake, sad heart, now comes the morn; arouse, there's
    no more weeping.
            Coming right along,
            Coming right along,
Oh! I hear the angel voices; "we're coming right along."

The captive now begins to rise and burst his chains
    asunder,
While politicians stand aghast, in anxious fear and
    wonder.
No longer shall the bondman sigh beneath the galling
    fetters—
He sees the dawn of freedom nigh, and reads the golden
    letters.
            Coming right along,
            Coming right along,
Behold the day of freedom is coming right along!

As he heard the singing and recognized the singers, the President's face lighted up with pleasure. When the song was finished, he boarded his train and resumed his journey.

At the outbreak of the war, the Hutchinsons gave concerts at recruiting places, for Soldiers' Aid Societies, and at the camp at Lynnfield, Massachusetts. Wishing to continue their work, they had come to Washington for a series of concerts and to sing for the soldiers. During the first two weeks of January, they sang almost nightly at the Y.M.C.A. and elsewhere, but on the seventh they appeared at the White House to pay their respects to the President whom they had helped to elect.

Surrounded by the "choice party" of listeners in the Red Room, the Hutchinsons made ready to sing. But there was difficulty. The piano key could not be found. Then when it was discovered, the piano stool was not in evidence. John Hutchinson concluded that the decrepit piano was in too bad shape anyway, and they sang, without accompaniment, "The War Drums Are Beating—Up, Soldiers, and Fight."

The audience was pleased. The President had a request. He asked for a song that he had heard back in

Illinois, "The Ship on Fire." For this song, an accompaniment was necessary, so the melodeon that the Hutchinsons used at their concerts was brought in from their carriage. It was an emotional and exciting song and Hutchinson sang it well. The President relaxed and smiled. Other songs were sung, and when the impromptu concert was ended, Mr. Lincoln thanked the singers for the pleasure they had provided.

Before the end of the month, the President heard more of the Hutchinsons. Having obtained a permit from Secretary of War Cameron, they crossed the Potomac and gave one concert for some New Jersey soldiers at the chapel at Fairfax Seminary. The concert almost ended in a riot, for not all the men in the audience approved when the singers sang Whittier's abolitionist "Hymn of Liberty." Only the earnest efforts of two chaplains and the singing of "No Tear in Heaven" prevented a breakup of the concert.

As a result of the disorder of the evening, the Hutchinsons' permit to sing in the camps was cancelled. The Hutchinsons protested, and John Hutchinson was much upset because General Franklin charged that their singing would demoralize the army. How could their singing be considered "demoralizing" he wrote later, if compared with the usual type of entertainment of the soldiers in saloons where liquor was put before them by disreputable persons, ". . . while *lewd women dressed in tights, and without tights,* sang Bacchanalian songs and danced on an elevated stage to the amusement of the stranger."

So John Hutchinson appealed to Secretary Chase, and Secretary Chase brought the matter before the Cabinet. There the poem was read:

> We wait beneath the furnace-blast
> The pangs of transformation;
> Not painlessly doth God recast
> And mould anew the nation.
> Hot burns the fire
> Where wrongs expire;
> Nor spares the hand
> That from the land
> Uproots the ancient evil.

There were nine verses in the poem which was to be sung to the tune of Luther's "A Mighty Fortress Is Our God." President Lincoln did not disapprove; rather, it is claimed, he said: "I don't see anything very bad about that. If any of the commanders want the Hutchinsons to sing to their soldiers, and invite them, they can go."

They did go, and sang many times for the soldiers thereafter. It was not often that the Cabinet considered such a matter as the propriety of the singing of an abolitionist hymn before the soldiers![5]

John Nicolay, the President's secretary, made no mention of the Hutchinsons in his letters to his fiancée, but as for the receptions in general, he informed her that they were extremely boring. "I suppose," he wrote, "they are both novel and pleasant to the hundreds of mere passersby who linger a day or two to '*do*' Washington; but for us who have to suffer the infliction once a week they get to be intolerable bores." He preferred the opera, and in one week this month he managed to go three times.[6]

Mrs. Lincoln was far from bored by the levees. At each one she appeared to be in excellent spirits. Always attractively dressed, she made a charming hostess as she curtsied and offered the tips of her white kid gloves to her guests.[7] She enjoyed the Hutchinson Singers, too, and one of Viola Hutchinson's most pleasant memories in later years was of the flowers frequently sent by Mrs. Lincoln to the "little lady who had sung for them so sweetly." At the end of the month's busy social calendar—which included two operas in addition to the

---

[5] Hutchinson, *Story of the Hutchinsons*, I, 372 ff.; "Interview with Mrs. Viola (Hutchinson) Campbell," *Christian Science Monitor*, Feb. 12, 1930. N. P. Willis, in the *Home Journal*, commented that the Hutchinsons "doxologized" the guests as they departed from the levee at the White House. Earlier that same evening they had been scheduled to give a concert in Georgetown; if the concert was given, it was over in time for the singers to get to the presidential levee. Washington *Evening Star*, Jan. 7, 1862; N.Y. *Herald*, Jan. 8, 1862. Details concerning the Hutchinsons at the White House and concerning their singing are in John W. Hutchinson, *The Book of Brothers* (Boston, 1864), pp. 7-21; Asa B. Hutchinson, *Book of Words of the Hutchinson Family* (N.Y., 1851), pp. 19-20; Rice, ed., *Reminiscences of Abraham Lincoln*, pp. 239-40, 364; Charles Carleton Coffin, *Abraham Lincoln* (N.Y., 1902) pp. 294-95; Moore, *Rebellion Record*, I, P. 85; R. Gerald McMurtry, "Lincoln and the Hutchinson Family Singers," *Lincoln Herald*, XLVI (Dec., 1944), 10-22, 41.

[6] John G. Nicolay to Therena Bates, Jan. 15, 26, 1862, Nicolay Papers.

[7] French, ed., *Diary of B. B. French*, pp. 117-18 (Dec. 18, 1861).

levees—the *Evening Star* reported that Mrs. Lincoln looked extremely well.[8]

And the President? He was in fine spirits, too—occasionally. He was glad to talk with an old Illinois acquaintance, General Shields (with whom in times past he had nearly come to a duel), and was cheered by the news of General Burnside's success at Pamlico Sound and the victory of General Thomas at Mill Springs in Kentucky. But he was also profoundly disturbed, increasingly so as the month went on. The war was costing one million dollars and more a day, and what was being accomplished? Affairs in the West were not going well; in the East, General McClellan had not made a move, and the people were growing impatient. The General had been ill, and what is more, had not cooperated fully with the President.

In the hope of getting some action, the President had ordered a forward movement of the armies for February 22, and had even thought of taking to the field himself! If something wasn't done, he feared that "the bottom would be out of the whole affair," and it was at this time that he made his well-known remark that if General McClellan didn't want to use the army, he would like to borrow it.

Such were the problems that beset the President as, greeting the crowds at the levees, he "appeared to be in fine spirits."[9]

A really high spot of enjoyment for the President had been the visit of the Hutchinsons at the reception on January 7. How he enjoyed John Hutchinson's singing of "The Ship on Fire!" But by the end of the month so much had happened, and had *not* happened, that it was no wonder that, two days after the President issued General War Order No. 1 (for the forward movement of the troops), the reporter who commented on how well Mrs. Lincoln looked said of the Chief Executive, "The President looked somewhat worn with the cares of office."[10]

---

[8] "Interview with Mrs. Viola (Hutchinson) Campbell," *Christian Science Monitor*, Feb. 12, 1930; Washington *Evening Star*, Jan. 23, 24, 29, 1862.

[9] N.Y. *Herald*, Jan. 8, 22, 1862.

[10] Washington *Evening Star*, Jan. 29, 1862. A letter to the *Des Moines State Register* gave this graphic word picture: ". . . the wheels of society roll on. The President stands, gaunt and care-worn, receiving his friends in the gilded departments of the White House." *Iowa Jour. of Hist.*, LII (Jan., 1954), 65.

CHAPTER VIII

"WILL THE LEADER OF THE BAND PLEASE SEE MRS. LINCOLN?"

THE PRESIDENT DID NOT APPROVE OF THE PLAN AT ALL. It was contrary to White House tradition and would surely cause much comment and criticism. Mrs. Lincoln, on the other hand, maintained that it would be more sensible and economical and would enable them to show some special attention to many more people than was possible under the usual arrangements.

Mrs. Lincoln finally won the President's reluctant consent. Preparations were then begun, the date was set, and engraved cards were sent out. The first of three "receptions by invitation," to supplant the many costly formal dinners and to allow for more sociability than occurred at the huge public levees, was scheduled for February 5, 1862.[1]

Secretary Nicolay was dubious about the new venture. Writing to his fiancée on February 2, he commented:

> Mrs. Lincoln has determined to make an innovation in the social customs of the White House and accordingly has issued tickets for a party of six or seven hundred guests on Wednesday evening next. For years past dinners and receptions have been the only "Executive" social diversions or entertainments. But from what I can learn "La Reine" has determined to abrogate dinners and institute parties in their stead. How it will work remains to be seen.[2]

Inasmuch as this was a very special party, Mrs. Lincoln naturally considered it advisable to give personal atten-

---

[1] Keckley, *Behind the Scenes*, pp. 95-97. Ben: Perley Poore said that the party was given at the urging of Seward to generate more good feeling in Washington society. Poore, *Perley's Reminiscences*, II, 113. It is unlikely, however, that Mrs. Lincoln would have accepted any such suggestion from Seward for whom she had little friendly feeling.

[2] John G. Nicolay to Therena Bates, Feb. 2, 1862, Nicolay Papers.

tion not only to such questions as the decorations for the White House and the selection of a caterer but also to a matter ordinarily left entirely in other hands, the musical program for the evening. Thus it was that the day before the big event the President, as was his wont when he wished to send a brief message, took a small card and wrote a note:

> Will the leader of
> the Marine Band, please
> call and see Mrs. L.?
> to day —
> Feb. 4, 1862. A. LINCOLN[3]

The leader of the band was Francis Scala. Born in Italy, Scala had played his way to the United States, beginning as a third-class musician on an American war vessel. Once in America, Scala went to Washington where, in 1842, he joined the Marine Band. He became its leader in 1855 and continued as such until 1871.

When Scala joined the Marine Band, it consisted of only ten musicians. During the years in which he was a member, the band became increasingly active and important. Weekly concerts at the Capitol had begun in 1838, and in the 1840's the concerts at the White House were started. In 1854, extra pay, "White House Pay," of four dollars a month was allotted the musicians because of their many engagements at the Executive Mansion. By 1862, when the band had grown to thirty-two members and had received full status by act of Congress, it had become almost indispensable for social functions, particularly those held at the White House.[4]

Whenever called upon, Scala's musicians were ready, and in spite of the heavy demands upon them, they maintained a high reputation. Their musical selections were invariably well received by both listeners and critics. Presumably, in this instance, the program of "most enchanting operatic gems" arranged for the party on Feb-

---

[3] Lincoln to Francis Scala, Scala Collection, Music Division, Library of Congress.

[4] Washington *Morning Times*, Jan. 19, 1896, Apr. 26, 1903; Washington *Evening Star*, Aug. 15, 1937; *The United States Marine Band*, n.p. Cf., also *supra*, chap. III, n. 11.

ruary 5, was the outcome of the conference between Scala and Mrs. Lincoln, brought about by the President's brief message.[5]

The President was right about the comment and criticism that such a party would—and did—provoke. Indeed, observed a reporter for the New York *Herald*, it became the main point of conversation next to the British question!

The engraved cards of invitation caused a "decided sensation," and also much disappointment. "Half the city," wrote Secretary Nicolay, "is jubilant at being invited, while the other half is furious at being left out in the cold." Applications for invitations, it was said, could be "measured by the bushel," for if 550 received invitations, there were 5,500 who thought themselves entitled to receive them as well! Consequently, the number of cards sent out was doubled.[6]

Unused to presidential parties "by invitation," Washingtonians were further surprised when it was announced that the invitations must be presented at the door! One congressman, having sent his invitation home to his wife, had to request another at the last minute.[7]

Critics were quick to charge the President with inaugurating undemocratic and exclusive functions contrary to custom, and, what was worse, of sponsoring frivolous entertainment which was quite unnecessary and in very poor taste in wartime. The extravagant affair at the White House was contrasted to the lonely bivouac or cheerless hospital bed of the soldiers—didn't the President realize that there was a war?

As the rumor spread and persisted that there was to be dancing at the "ball," criticism became even stronger. The fact that both President and Mrs. Lincoln thought dancing inappropriate on this occasion, and that there

---

[5] Washington *Evening Star*, May 10, 1861; Sacramento *Daily Union*, Mar. 10, 1862.

[6] Washington *Sunday Morning Chronicle*, Feb. 9, 1862; N.Y. *Herald*, Feb. 3, 5, 1862; John G. Nicolay to Therena Bates, Feb. 2, 1862, Nicolay Papers.

[7] Washington *Evening Star*, Feb. 4, 1862; H. G. Blake to John G. Nicolay, Feb. 5, 1862, Nicolay Papers.

was *no* dancing, was obscured by the persistence of the rumor.

The reporter for the New York *Tribune* seemed disappointed that he could not report any dancing. In his dispatch on the evening of the party he mentioned that no dancing had occurred up to one o'clock, "but we are assured there will be"; soon after, he again brought up the subject by saying that we are told "no dancing."[8]

In addition, the *Tribune* objected to the elaborate outlay of refreshments arranged by a caterer from New York. It stated (erroneously) that the supper had cost "thousands of dollars," and to emphasize the point, itemized the entire menu even to such delicacies as "Patti-Giblets à la Eraisanz" and "Fillert de Beef."[9]

However, the usefulness, propriety, and right of the President to have such a party was just as ably upheld. It was pointed out, in support, that state dinners took care of diplomats and other high officials, the levees had become like nightmares because of the crowds, but these parties would enable the President to entertain and recognize distinguished people in business and the professions. As for the propriety of an invitation party during wartime, it was recalled that during the dark days of the Revolution, subscription parties were held, and that George Washington was the first subscriber![10]

A most vigorous defense of the "party by invitation" —the general tone of which the President himself would very likely *not* have approved—appeared in the editor-

---

[8] *Leslie's Illus. News*, Feb. 22, 1862; Poore, *Perley's Reminiscences*, II, 120; Browne, *Everyday Life of Lincoln*, II, 450; N.Y. *Tribune*, Feb. 6, 1862.
   As late as Feb. 27, 1862, the matter of dancing was in the news. The *Tribune* was taken to task by the *Herald* for printing as a joke, the following:
   "Why don't you dance?" blithely inquired an eminent functionary of a leading Senator, at a recent social festivity in Washington. "I never dance in a besieged city," was the quick and stern reply.
   The implication that the President had danced at the White House while the city was practically besieged was unfair, said the *Herald*. N.Y. *Herald*, Feb. 27, 1862.
   Even the humorist, Newell, made some sharp comments. Cf. Newell, *Orpheus C. Kerr Papers*, 1st ser., Letter XXX, "Description of the Gorgeous Fete at the White House . . . With Some Notes of the Toilettes, Confections, and Punch."
[9] N.Y. *Tribune*, Feb. 6, 1862. The actual cost of the party was $1,061.91, and the President paid for it out of his own pocket. B. B. French to H. H. F., Feb. 27, 1862, B. B. French Papers; Pratt and East, *Lincoln Herald*, XLVII (Feb., 1945), 22.
[10] *Leslie's Illus. News*, Feb. 22, Mar. 8, 1862; Washington *Evening Star*, Mar. 6, 1862; Washington *Sunday Morning Chronicle*, Feb. 9, 1862.

ial columns of the New York *Herald*."[11] The policy, said the *Herald*, was a wise one, and a return to the customs of earlier days. The gates had been opened by Jefferson, and especially by Jackson, and it was now time that the infiltration of the White House "by crowds of individuals, neither whose manner, habits nor antecedents entitle them to a place in respectable society," was ended.

Mrs. Lincoln was trying, on the one hand, to combat the hostile influence of pro-Southern ladies who were "doing their best to make the city a gloomy place," and, on the other hand, to rid the White House of "pestiferous and dangerous influences, . . . a swarm of long haired, tobacco chewing and tobacco spitting abolitionists, whose presence, both physically and morally, was contamination." In short, she was endeavoring to make conditions right for decent people. For this she should be commended, said the *Herald*.

But, if there was difference of opinion concerning the event set for February 5 itself, there was general agreement over the weather. For the first time in three weeks the sun had shone for more than two hours, and there was no rain or snow! Clear air and bright moonlight ushered in the evening.

At the White House all was in readiness—the East Room, newly furnished, the Red and Blue Rooms, and the Green Room "richly decorated with a profusion of natural flowers." Wreaths were hung from the chandeliers, flowers graced the tables, and in a side room a Japanese punch bowl containing ten gallons of champagne was available for thirsty guests.

At nine o'clock the guests began to arrive, and as carriage after carriage deposited its load of fortunate ticket holders, the rooms of the White House soon became crowded. The scene was described as "a huge kaleidoscope . . . a medley of bright jewels and bright eyes . . . silks and satins," and a spectacle of "elegant taste and loveliness," with the brilliant uniforms of the

---

[11] N.Y. *Herald*, Feb. 3, 4, 5, 1862.

men making a fine contrast to the "striking plumage" of the ladies.[12]

Mrs. Lincoln's gown was "simple and elegant"—white satin, deeply flounced, with black lace looped up at intervals with black and white ribbons, and a low corsage trimmed with black lace. On her hair was a floral wreath of black and white flowers with crape myrtle on the right side. A full set of pearls and a beautiful bouquet of crape myrtle completed her costume.

Earlier in the evening when the President, upon observing her low-cut dress remarked that "our cat has a long tail tonight," and suggested, with a glance at her bare arms and neck, that "if some of the tail was nearer the head, it would be in better style," she was slightly annoyed. She was fond of low-cut dresses, she wore them well, and, after all, Mr. Lincoln was not aware that they were very much in style.

The newspapers gave much space to detailed descriptions of the ladies' gowns, generally with approval, and one reporter proudly wrote: ". . . no European Court or capital can compare with the Presidential circle and the society of Washington, this winter, in the freshness and beauty of its women."[13]

At eleven o'clock, the President led the promenade around the East Room and to the dining room. Supper was about to be served.

A delay while the steward obtained the key led to some crowding at the doors, but the guests took it good-naturedly. "I am in favor of a forward movement," said one. Another observed, with obvious reference to the military stalemate then prevailing, "An advance to the

---

[12] Washington *Evening Star*, Feb. 6, 1862; Washington *Sunday Morning Chronicle*, Feb. 9, 1862; N. Y. *Herald*, Feb. 5, 1862; *Leslie's Illus. News*, Feb. 22, 1862; Sacramento *Daily Union*, Mar. 10, 13, 1862. After describing at length the kaleidoscopic scene, the reporter for the *Chronicle* concluded: "No language can describe that shifting mosaic beauty and gay colors, as uniforms and foreign stars—gems, laces, and illusion—like all the rainbows since the flood, were blended in confusion."

[13] Washington *Sunday Morning Chronicle*, Feb. 9, 1862; N.Y. *Herald*, Feb. 6, 1862; Keckley, *Behind the Scenes*, pp. 101-2; *Leslie's Illus. News*, Feb. 22, 1862. Mrs. Milton Hay, writing to her husband concerning her shopping attempts in Washington, said that the important thing was to have as little dress on as possible—it didn't matter what the dress was, so long as it was low in the neck and had short sleeves! Mrs. Milton Hay to her husband, [April] 6, 1862, Stuart-Hay Papers, Transcript, Ill. State Hist. Library.

front is only retarded by the imbecility of commanders."[14]

When the doors were finally opened, the guests were "struck with admiration" by the scene which met their eyes—a "coup d'oeil of dazzling splendor." On the long center table was a vase five feet high, full of exotic flowers, and flanked on either side by smaller vases also filled with flowers.

Decorations and ornaments included a representation of a steam frigate, the Hermitage, a warrior's helmet supported by cupids, and a Chinese pagoda. Then there were double cornucopias set on a shell supported by mermaids and surmounted by a star; likewise, a candelabrum held up by cupids, and a fountain of four bowls supported by water nymphs. Besides these, a reporter observed twenty or thirty ornaments of cake and candy "delicately conceived and exquisitely executed."

For the equally elaborate bill of fare, the caterer had provided nearly a ton of turkeys, ducks, venison, pheasants, partridges, hams, and delicacies, such as stewed and scalloped oysters, Charlotte Russe à la Parisienne, Orange glacé, fancy cakes, fruits, and grapes.[15]

Once the guests had entered the dining room so magnificently prepared, there began the "assault on the banquet" thus described in verse:

> In the parlor, in the parlor,
> Through the parlor onward,
> Into the banquet hall
> Crushed seven hundred.
> Good cheer to right of them,
> Good cheer to left of them,
> Good cheer in front of them.
> How the "Verdants" wondered.
> Stupid men trod on toes,
> Tore nice young ladies clothes,
> Into the banquet hall
> As if very hungry all
> Crushed seven hundred.

[14] Washington *Evening Star*, Feb. 6, 1862; Poore, *Perley's Reminiscences*, II, 115 f.

[15] Washington *Evening Star*, Feb. 6, 1862; Washington *Sunday Morning Chronicle*, Feb. 9, 1862; N.Y. *Herald*, Feb. 5, 6, 1862.

"Give me vanilla ice!"
"Here! I have called you twice,"
"Now champagne, and in a trice,"
"Waiter, you've blundered."
Flashing of spoons in air,
Eating of salad there—
Hungry men everywhere,
Scrambled and thundered;
Squeezed round by floating skirts;
Joked with by charming flirts;
Eating by rapid spirts;
There, in the banquet hall,
Lacking nothing at all,
Supped seven hundred.[16]

Meanwhile, as the guests visited, promenaded, supped, and flirted until three o'clock in the morning, the full Marine Band added to the gaiety of the evening with its program: a march for the President, a polka for Mrs. Lincoln—both by Scala—and a full schedule of operatic selections.[17]

President's March _____ Scala
Overture _____ Masaniello
Quartette _____ I Poliuto
Terzetto _____ Un Ballo in Maschera
Coro and Sestetto _____ Lucia di Lammermoor
Pot Pourri _____ Il Trovatore
Brindisi and Duetto _____ from La Traviata
Coro and Terzetto _____ from Joan of Arc
Quartette and Tarantella _____ Les Vêpres Siciliennes
Mrs. Lincoln's Polka _____ Scala

In spite of the critics, the party was a success. Even the domestic help, stimulated by the spirit of the occasion, finished off the evening in an exciting fashion. John Nicolay, in describing the evening's events for his fiancée, concluded confidentially: ". . . by way of an interesting *finale* the servants (a couple of them) much moved by wrath and wine had a jolly little knock-down in the kit-

---

[16] Washington *Sunday Morning Chronicle*, Feb. 9, 1862.
[17] Washington *Evening Star*, Feb. 6, 1862; Washington *Sunday Morning Chronicle*, Feb. 9, 1862.

chen damaging in its effect to sundry heads and champagne bottles."[18]

The *Evening Star* thus summed it all up:

> The entertainment, in the completeness of its arrangements, the distinguished character of the guests assembled, and the enjoyment afforded to those present by the avoidance (through the limit as to numbers) of the jam, heat and confusion of a crowd, will rank, we take it, as by far the most brilliant and successful affair of the kind ever experienced here.[19]

There was just one cloud over the evening. Upstairs in the White House, Willie Lincoln lay very ill. Both the President and Mrs. Lincoln were anxious and worried. At one time Mrs. Lincoln had even considered postponing the party, but then decided to go on with it. On the day of the event, Willie became somewhat worse, and during the evening both parents went upstairs several times to see their sick son.[20]

What had begun as a social function in fulfillment of obligations incumbent upon the occupants of the White House and had been hailed by the loyal press as a decided success, ended in personal tragedy. Willie Lincoln lingered between life and death until February 20, and then he was gone. The White House was full of sorrow, and there was no more music there for many months.[21]

---

[18] John G. Nicolay to Therena Bates, Feb. 6, 1862, Nicolay Papers.

[19] Washington *Evening Star*, Feb. 6, 1862.

[20] Keckley, *Behind the Scenes*, p. 97; Poore, *Perley's Reminiscences*, II, 120-21.

[21] "Today," wrote Mrs. J. A. Kasson, of Iowa, "it is thought the little fellow must die, and very heavy are the hearts in the house so recently the house of feasting, so soon, it may be, to turn to the house of mourning. . . ." This was on February 20, the day Willie died. *Iowa Jour. of Hist.*, LII (Jan., 1954), 68.

CHAPTER IX

"WE ARE COMING, FATHER ABRAAM"

IT WAS THE SUMMER OF 1862. CLEARLY, THE COUNTRY needed a morale booster. Events at the front had not been going well for the Union cause. To be sure, there had been some success in the West—at Mill Springs in January, at Forts Henry and Donelson in February, and at Pea Ridge in March—but those victories were months past, and then there had come Shiloh with its fearful casualties. And what of Halleck in the West, Buell in the center, and Farragut on the river?

Most devastating to Northern morale, however, was the failure of McClellan before Richmond. After months of preparation, weeks of struggle in which the Army of the Potomac got within sight of the church spires of the Confederate capital, and with constantly mounting casualties, the campaign was ended and the army back from whence it had started. It was not to be wondered at that many were discouraged.

Likewise, the President, hard-pressed from many directions, needed something to bolster his spirit and strengthen his determination. For, not only was he beset by military problems and attendant matters such as the growing sentiment for drastic and sweeping confiscation and the increasingly difficult task of financing the war, but his personal grief and Mrs. Lincoln's sorrow cast a gloom over the White House that was not easily dispelled.[1]

After the death of Willie Lincoln in February social activity at the presidential mansion almost ceased. No

---

[1] In addition to the loss of Willie, Mrs. Lincoln, during the dark months of 1862, learned of the death of two half brothers, Samuel B. Todd at Shiloh, and Alexander H. Todd at Baton Rouge. In 1863 another half brother was killed at Vicksburg and a brother-in-law, Ben H. Helm, lost his life at Chickamauga.

longer were there crowded receptions, lightened and brightened by the music of the Marine Band, at which Mr. Lincoln could give a hearty greeting and a warm handshake to supporters and admirers; and no longer, when the warm weather came, did people gather in crowds on the White House grounds for those afternoon concerts that were so popular.[2]

Perhaps Mr. Lincoln got a momentary lift from the music of the Marine Band and the sailors' cheers of *"Vive le Président"* when he visited the French warship *Gassendi* one afternoon in April,[3] or when he was serenaded at the summer White House in June by a group of Negroes singing to the "friends of freedom," or when, at a July assembly of schoolchildren he distributed prizes to the boys and heard the children sing "Carrie Lee."[4]

But mostly those trying weeks were without music; even on his several trips to the army he had little time for anything but military matters, and when, during his quick trip to West Point, he was serenaded at midnight by the Academy Band (in the rain) he was doubtless too exhausted to care![5]

It was no wonder that as he left the carriage at Secretary Chase's residence for the funeral service of General Lander his face was sad, and he seemed very weary.[6]

Senator Browning, a constant visitor at the White

[2] The Marine Band did give its regular concerts at the Capitol, however.

[3] Washington *Sunday Morning Chronicle*, Apr. 27, 1862; N.Y. *Herald*, Apr. 27, 1862; Washington *Evening Star*, Apr. 28, 1862; Washington *National Intelligencer*, Apr. 28, 1862. The visit was carried off with much ceremony. Upon the arrival of the President (he was rowed out to the *Gassendi* in a small boat), the Marine Band played and the French guns fired a salute which was answered by a shore battery. The French sailors and officers were all at their stations and the vessel was spic and span. After the visit there were more salutes as the President went ashore.
The visit had its diplomatic side also. This was the first visit of a French war vessel to our capital and the first time a President stepped on "foreign soil." The French officers were popular in the city and were entertained by several residents. Secretary Seward gave a select party for the French officers, thus doing his part to create pro-Union sentiment among Frenchmen. Washington *Sunday Morning Chronicle*, May 4, 1862.

[4] Washington *Evening Star*, July 1, 1862; Allen C. Clark, *Abraham Lincoln in the National Capital* (Washington, 1925), p. 41.

[5] Washington *Evening Star*, June 26, 1862; Washington *National Intelligencer*, June 26, 27, 1862; Sacramento *Daily Union*, Aug. 12, 1862.

[6] Washington *Evening Star*, Mar. 6, 1862; N.Y. *Herald*, Mar. 6, 1862; Brooklyn *Daily Eagle*, Dec. 23, 1886. The solemnity of the occasion was emphasized later by the dirge sung by the choir at the service at the Church of the Epiphany.

House in those depressing times, noted that the President was subject to headaches and passed sleepless nights. Only twice did Browning make reference to relaxing diversions during his visits—once when he and Lincoln spent an hour and a half reading Thomas Hood and again when Lincoln read with great pathos and enjoyment from Halleck's "Fanny" as they sat on the front steps at the Soldiers' Home one evening in June.[7]

By the first of July it was evident that more troops would be necessary to carry on the war. The public and the press had come to realize it; the governors of the loyal states urged it, and on July 2 Lincoln issued the call for three hundred thousand volunteers to serve for three years.[8]

Committees were organized, bounties were offered, and great war meetings were held to stimulate enlistments. On the twenty-eighth of July the President appealed to the governors, asking what progress was being made and how soon the new regiments would be on the way.[9]

Then on August 4 came the second call for three hundred thousand more men to serve for nine months. Soon the country began to respond and the President was reassured. That same day he wrote to Count de Gasparin:

The moral effect was the worst of the affair before Rich-

---

[7] Pease and Randall, eds., *Diary of O. H. Browning*, I (April 25, 1862), 542-43, (June 30, 1862), 555. Of his visit on April 25 Browning wrote: "I remained with [him] about an hour & a half, and left in high spirits, and a very genial mood; but as he said a crowd was buzzing about the door like bees, ready to pounce upon him as soon as I should take my departure, and bring him back to a realization of the annoyance and harrassments [*sic*] of his position." "Fanny" was a humorous poem of 175 stanzas and three "songs" in which social ambitions bring the chief characters to a sad end. It reminds one of the poems of Thomas Hood which Lincoln enjoyed so much on the evening of April 25.

[8] Lincoln had, of course, been badgered constantly by McClellan for more troops. The situation as Lincoln wrestled with it is indicated by telegrams which he dispatched that first week in July:
To McClellan, July 1, "It is impossible to re-inforce you. . . ."
To McClellan, July 2: ". . . the idea of sending you fifty thousand . . . is simply absurd."
To loyal governors, July 3: "If I had fifty thousand additional troops here *now*, I believe I could substantially close the war in two weeks."
To General Halleck, Juy 4: "You do not know how much you would oblige us, if . . . you could promptly send us even ten thousand infantry." Roy P. Basler, Marion Dolores Pratt, and Lloyd A. Dunlap, eds., *The Collected Works of Abraham Lincoln* (New Brunswick, N.J., 1953), V, 298, 301, 304, 305. (Hereafter cited as Lincoln, *Works*.)
As if to give emphasis to the problem, Lincoln, on the way to the Soldiers' Home that gloomy Independence Day, passed a train of ambulances bringing wounded men from the Peninsula campaign! N.Y. *Tribune*, July 8, 1862.

[9] Lincoln, *Works*, V, 347.

mond; and that has run its course downward; we are now at
a stand, and shall soon be rising again, as we hope. . . . We
shall easily obtain the new levy, however.[10]

On the sixth he received an encouraging telegram from
Amos A. Lawrence, of Massachusetts, and on the eighth
two more telegrams. From Pennsylvania came the message: "Our County has raised its quota of call for Volunteers. Have a surplus on hand and men still coming in."
From his loyal friends in Springfield came a message
that must have really gladdened his heart:

Springfield, Ill. Aug 8 1862

Mr. Lincoln. President
Washington D.C.
The Governor is absent. An immense number of people are
here. Many counties tender a regiment. Can we say that all
will be accepted under call for the war. An immediate answer
is very important

O. M. HATCH *Sec State*
J. K. DUBOIS *Auditor*
WM. BUTLER *Treasurer*
A. C. FULLER *Adgt. Genl.*[11]

To Baron de Stoeckl he observed that although enlistments were slow, two or three million men would respond if necessary. A record was being kept of the men
arriving, and later in the month he told Secretary Welles
that in one week over 18,000 had reached the city. Many
of the new regiments marched past the White House
singing, and the President often came out to greet them.[12]

In the meantime Washington, too, had a great war
meeting. At four o'clock on the afternoon of August 6,
bells rang all over the city and a thirty-four-gun salute
was fired. Government and business offices closed early,

---

[10] Lincoln, *Works*, V, 355.

[11] Lincoln, *Works*, V, 361, 362; O. M. Hatch Papers, Ill. State Hist. Library.
To Secretary Stanton Lincoln wrote: "I think we better take while we can get."
A message was promptly forwarded to Springfield: "All volunteers for the war
will be accepted until August 15. After that all that offer will be accepted for
filling up old regiments." Lincoln, *Works*, V, 365, and note.

[12] Albert A. Woldman, *Lincoln and the Russians* (Cleveland and New York,
1952), p. 196; Morse, ed., *Diary of Gideon Welles*, I, 89. Welles was also encouraged. He wrote: "There is wonderful and increasing enthusiasm and determination to put down this Rebellion and sustain the integrity of the Union";
Poore, *Perley's Reminiscences*, II, 130.

and people converged at the Capitol steps where the meeting was to take place. The Marine Band played. By five o'clock a huge crowd, estimated at 10,000, had gathered.

Called to stimulate enthusiasm and support for the latest war measures, the order for more troops, and for vigorous prosecution of the war, the vast assemblage was addressed and exhorted by a formidable array of speakers including George S. Boutwell, Leonard Swett, and L. E. Chittenden.

The program was under way when the President arrived. His appearance caused an interruption in the proceedings—cheers, applause, cannon fire—and music filled the air. When the President's turn came to speak, there were more cheers, and the band contributed "Hail to the Chief!"

Having no prepared speech to make, the President, after a rather witty introduction, took the occasion to minimize the alleged differences between General McClellan and Secretary Stanton. Both, he said, were good men, both were trying to do their duty, and if any one should be blamed it was he, the President, and not the Secretary of War.

The crowd was friendly and in good humor and wanted him to go on, but he finished and soon left the meeting. The program, however, continued well into the evening and was concluded in a blaze of fireworks, patriotic songs, and band music. The great war meeting was a success.[13]

The following day the Washington *Star* carried the words of a new song. It began—

> We are coming, Father Abraham
> Three hundred thousand more—[14]

---

[13] Washington *National Intelligencer*, Aug. 4, 6, 7, 1862; Washington *Evening Star*, Aug. 6, 7, 1862; N.Y. *Herald*, Aug. 7, 1862; N.Y. *Tribune*, Aug. 7, 1862; Lincoln, *Works*, V, 358-59.

[14] Washington *Evening Star*, Aug. 7, 1862. The paper spelled out "Abraham." In the press and in the various editions of sheet music a variety of spellings and title arrangements appeared. Cf. Boyd B. Stutler, "We Are Coming, Father Abra'am," *Lincoln Herald*, LIII (Summer, 1951), 2-13. The author himself wrote "Father Abraam" and gave his verses the title "Three hundred thousand more." Except in direct quotations from other sources the author's own spelling and punctuation are followed here. However, apart from the chapter title, "Abraham"

SCALA'S "UNION MARCH"

One of several selections played at Lincoln's inauguration and the only one composed especially for the occasion. Francis Scala, the composer, regularly directed the Marine Band for the music at the White House—the concerts in the summer and the receptions given during the winter.

PLATE II

DANCE PROGRAM FOR THE UNION BALL, MARCH 4, 1861
Outside covers
PLATE III

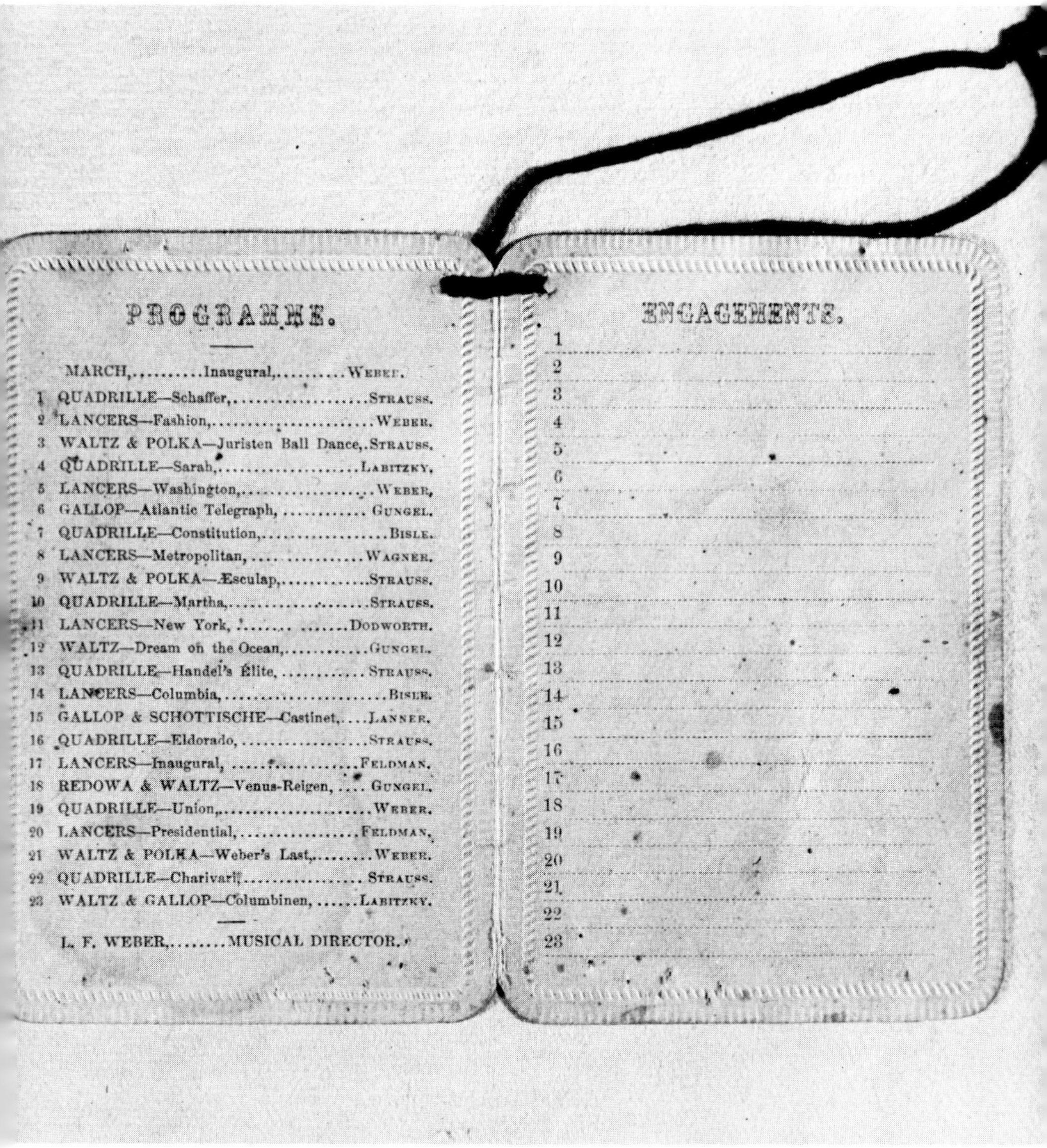

PROGRAMME.

MARCH,..........Inaugural,..........WEBER.
1 QUADRILLE—Schaffer,....................STRAUSS.
2 LANCERS—Fashion,.........................WEBER.
3 WALTZ & POLKA—Juristen Ball Dance,.STRAUSS.
4 QUADRILLE—Sarah,....................LABITZKY.
5 LANCERS—Washington,.....................WEBER.
6 GALLOP—Atlantic Telegraph,............GUNGEL.
7 QUADRILLE—Constitution,...................BISLE.
8 LANCERS—Metropolitan,..................WAGNER.
9 WALTZ & POLKA—Æsculap,...............STRAUSS.
10 QUADRILLE—Martha,........................STRAUSS.
11 LANCERS—New York,..............DODWORTH.
12 WALTZ—Dream on the Ocean,..............GUNGEL.
13 QUADRILLE—Handel's Élite,............STRAUSS.
14 LANCERS—Columbia,.........................BISLE.
15 GALLOP & SCHOTTISCHE—Castinet,.....LANNER.
16 QUADRILLE—Eldorado,....................STRAUSS.
17 LANCERS—Inaugural,....................FELDMAN.
18 REDOWA & WALTZ—Venus-Reigen,.....GUNGEL.
19 QUADRILLE—Union,..........................WEBER.
20 LANCERS—Presidential,..................FELDMAN.
21 WALTZ & POLKA—Weber's Last,..........WEBER.
22 QUADRILLE—Charivari,..................STRAUSS.
23 WALTZ & GALLOP—Columbinen,.......LABITZKY.

L. F. WEBER,.........MUSICAL DIRECTOR.

ENGAGEMENTS.

1
2
3
4
5
6
7
8
9
10
11
12
13
14
15
16
17
18
19
20
21
22
23

COURTESY NATIONAL PARK SERVICE — PHOTO BY ABBIE ROWE

DANCE PROGRAM FOR THE UNION BALL, MARCH 4, 1861
Inside pages
PLATE IV

THE UNION BALL, MARCH 4, 1861
(Frank Leslie's Illustrated Newspaper, March 23, 1861)
PLATE V

"VIVA L'AMERICA"

One of the selections heard by President Lincoln at the Navy Yard Concert, May 9, 1861.

"THE FLAG OF THE FREE"

Another of the selections heard by President Lincoln at the Navy Yard Concert, May 9, 1861.

PLATE VI

"CASTA DIVA"

During the first week of July, 1861, the President heard a wide variety of musical

LETTER OF MEDA BLANCHARD

After the concert at Willard's Hall on July 6, 1861, President

"GOOD BYE, SWEETHEART, GOOD BYE"

The President greatly enjoyed the concert given by Mrs. Blanchard in Willard's Hall on the evening of July 6, 1861. This selection brought forth much applause.

"GOLD FEVER GALOP DI BRAVURA"

At the concert given by Mrs. Blanchard on July 6, 1861, in Willard's Hall, which Mr. and Mrs. Lincoln enjoyed immensely, Scherman, the pianist, after playing an aria from *Lucrezia Borgia*, favored the audience with the "Gold Fever Galop."

PLATE VIII

THE SEVENTY-NINTH REGIMENT (HIGHLANDERS)
NEW YORK STATE MILITIA

These Highlanders, in their picturesque costumes, were popular everywhere. Their band gave a concert at the White House in June, 1861, and a few months later serenaded Mrs. Lincoln in the wee hours of the morning.
(*Harper's Weekly*, May 25, 1861)

VISIT OF PRINCE NAPOLEON

On August 3, 1861, Prince Napoleon visited the White House and heard the Marine Band give a concert. The band was stationed in the blue and white conical tent which had been one of Mrs. Lincoln's special projects.
(*Frank Leslie's Illustrated Newspaper*, August 17, 1861)

PLATE X

THE HUTCHINSON SINGERS

Henry, John, and Viola Hutchinson (with their friend, Frank Martin), made up the quartet which sang at the White House on the evening of January 7, 1862.

PLATE XI

"THE WAR DRUMS ARE BEATING"

This was the first song sung by the Hutchinsons at the White House on the evening of January 7, 1862. Although actually a temperance song, the words and music were so martial that the piece could readily be used as a war song.

"THE SHIP ON FIRE"

One of Lincoln's favorite songs. He had heard it in Illinois and, at his request, John W. Hutchinson sang it at the White House after the levee on January 7, 1862.

PLATE XII

HUTCHINSON'S

REPUBLICAN

SONGSTER,

FOR

1860.

EDITED BY

JOHN W. HUTCHINSON,

OF THE HUTCHINSON FAMILY OF SINGERS.

"Lincoln and Liberty!"

NEW YORK:

O. HUTCHINSON, PUBLISHER,

272 GREENWICH STREET.

1860.

Davies & Kent, Printers,   115 Nassau Street, N.Y.

"HUTCHINSON'S REPUBLICAN SONGSTER"

This campaign songster, edited by John W. Hutchinson, helped to elect
Lincoln in 1860.

PLATE XIII

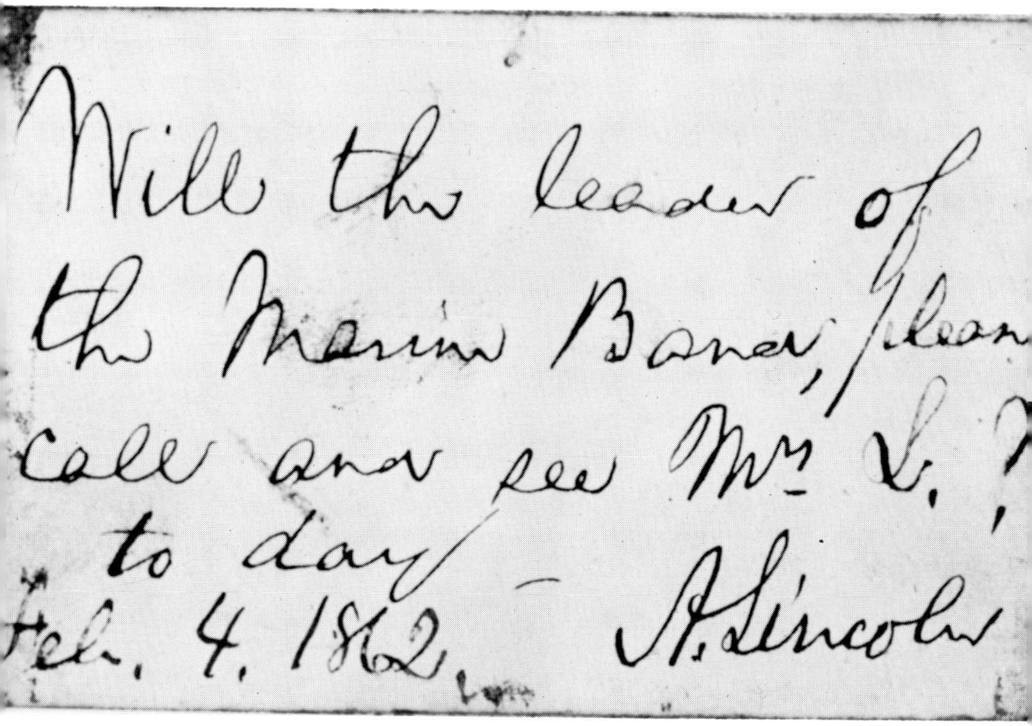

Will the leader of
the Marine Band, please
call and see Mrs. L. to
to day —
Feb. 4. 1862. A. Lincoln

LINCOLN'S NOTE TO BANDLEADER SCALA

Note sent by President Lincoln to Francis Scala the day before the party of February 5, 1862. Presumably Scala's conference with Mrs. Lincoln resulted in the choice of the numbers for the concert program that was performed at the party.

PLATE XIV

FRANCIS SCALA
Leader of the Marine Band during the war years
PLATE XV

THE GRAND PRESIDENTIAL PARTY, FEBRUARY 5, 1862
The Marine Band played a varied program during the evening. President and Mrs.
Lincoln were preoccupied, thinking of their sick son upstairs.
(*Frank Leslie's Illustrated Newspaper*, February 22, 1862)
PLATE XVI

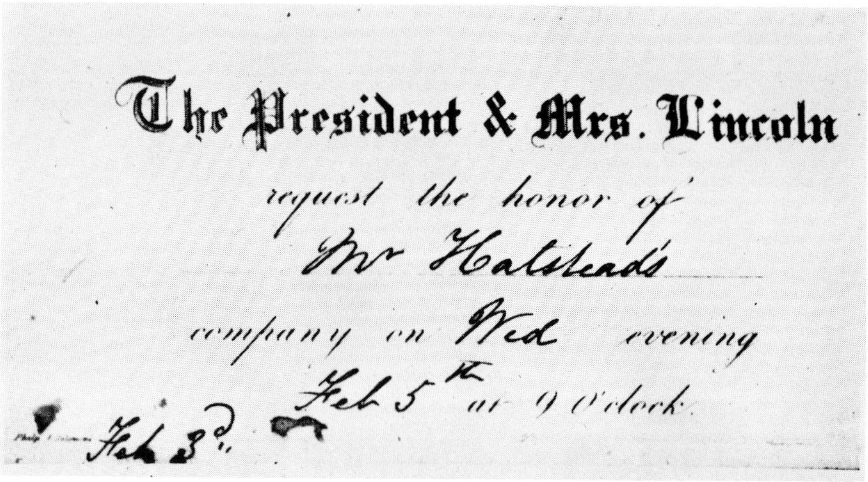
The President & Mrs. Lincoln
request the honor of
Mr Halstead's
company on Wed evening
Feb 5th at 9 O'clock.
Feb 3d.

COURTESY ILLINOIS STATE HISTORICAL LIBRARY

AN INVITATION TO THE WHITE HOUSE PARTY HELD FEBRUARY 5, 1862

The card had to be presented at the door

PLATE XVII

Two weeks earlier another song with stirring opening lines appeared in Chicago—

> Yes, we'll rally 'round the flag boys,
> We'll rally once again—[15]

Out of the excitement and activity prompted by the President's call had come the inspiration for two war songs that soon swept the country. "We Are Coming, Father Abraham" first appeared on the front page of the New York *Evening Post* on July 16, 1862, under the heading "Three Hundred Thousand More"; two days later it was printed in the Boston *Daily Journal;* the next day, Saturday, July 19, it was read at a war meeting on Boston Common in the afternoon, and at a rally in Chicago that same evening. By the time it was printed in the Washington *Star* it had already been put to music and published in sheet form, and by the end of 1862 some twenty or more issues were on sale! Two million copies were said to have been circulated in the lifetime of the composer.[16]

"Yes, We'll Rally 'Round the Flag Boys" ("The Battle-Cry of Freedom"), written about the same time, appeared in sheet form that fall, and, according to one estimate, fourteen printing presses could not meet the demand— between 500,000 and 700,000 copies were printed![17] Coming at just the right time, expressing just the sentiments that were needed, with music that was singable and words that were appropriate, these two war time songs played an immeasurably important part in restoring and sus-

---

is used instead of "Abraam." "Abraham" seems more natural today, and apparently did to many people then.

[15] The composer's spelling and punctuation are used except in direct quotations from sources other than the composer.

[16] N.Y. *Evening Post,* July 16, 1862; Boston *Journal,* July 18, 21, 1862; Chicago *Tribune,* July 20, 1862; Washington *Evening Star,* Aug. 7, 1862; *Dwight's Journal of Music,* XXI (Aug. 9, 1862), 152; Kansas City *Times,* Mar. 23, 1943. Stutler lists twenty editions of the song with publication data. *Lincoln Herald,* LIII, 12-13. It would appear that the first sheet-music edition was printed by Oliver Ditson & Company, with music by L. O. Emerson. The firm sent the poem to Emerson, a music teacher and composer, with the request: "Set these words to music instanter." Emerson complied, composed the music, and published copies were available by the first week in August. Newspaper clipping, unidentified, Lincoln Memorial University Collections.

[17] Lydia Avery Coonley, "George F. Root and His Songs," *The New England Magazine,* XIII (Sept., 1895-Feb., 1896), 564; Dena J. Epstein, "The Battle Cry of Freedom," *Civil War History,* IV (Sept., 1958), 307-18; and note 23, *infra.*

taining morale at home and at the front throughout the entire war.[18]

And what of the authors? No two men could have been of more different backgrounds than James S. Gibbons and George F. Root. Both were gentle, modest men. Both were patriotic with an intense love of the Union, and both were inspired in the same month by the President's call. But there the similarity ends.

James S. Gibbons was a New York economist, financier, and writer of weighty volumes on money, debt, and finance such as *The Banks of New York, Their Dealers, the Clearing House, and the Panic of 1857*.[19] Of Quaker background, brought up in the slave state of Delaware where his father was involved in the Underground Railroad, Gibbons was naturally opposed to slavery, and himself became active in the abolitionist movement.

It is well known that during the draft riots of 1863 his house was sacked from top to bottom and that he and some of his family narrowly escaped the irate mob. This Gibbons took quite philosophically, saying that it was their contribution to the war![20]

Moved by the President's call in July, 1862, disturbed by the plight of the country, and, one day, keeping step with a contingent of soldiers marching in the streets, he began to formulate ideas and phrases in his mind. The result—

---

[18] "We Are Coming, Father Abraham" not only inspired renewed zeal for the cause of the Union, it reflected the hold that Lincoln was coming to have on the people of the North. Cf. H. M. Savage, "A Momentous Paean," *Lincoln Herald*, LII (June, 1950), 22-23.
" 'The Battle-Cry of Freedom' ought to become our national air; it has animation, its harmonies are distinguished, it has tune, rhythm, and . . . a kind of epic colouring, something sadly heroic which a battle song should have." So said the virtuoso Gottschalk, who did not have a high opinion of most Civil War music. Louis Moreau Gottschalk, *Notes of a Pianist* (Philadelphia and London, 1881), p. 257.

[19] This book went to several editions, a tenth edition being published in 1873. In 1863 Gibbons produced the volume *The Organization of the Public Debt and a Plan for the Relief of the Treasury*. In view of the fact that in 1864 Gibbons recommended to President Lincoln that Horace Greeley be appointed Secretary of the Treasury, one wonders what kind of "Relief" there would have been! James S. Gibbons to Abraham Lincoln, Nov. 27, 1864, Robert Todd Lincoln Collection, Library of Congress, 38763-64.

[20] Sarah Hopper Emerson, *Life of Abby Hopper Gibbons* (N.Y., 1897), II, 43.

> We are coming Father Abraam
> Three hundred thousand more,
> From Mississippi's winding stream
> And from New England's shore;
>
> - - - - - - - - - - - - - -
>
> Six hundred thousand loyal men
> And true have gone before—
> We are coming Father Abraam
> Three hundred thousand more!

Inasmuch as his verses were printed anonymously, Gibbons received no credit in any of the sheet-music editions for this, his only song, but he did not seem to mind! Some years later the matter of the authorship was cleared up, and subsequently Gibbons was given due recognition.[21]

George F. Root was a teacher, composer, and publisher of music; music was his whole life from the time he began its study at the age of eighteen in Boston until the end of his career. Hundreds of young people received musical instruction in his classes and in his "Musical

---

[21] Brander Matthews, "The Songs of the War," *The Century Magazine*, XXXIV (Aug., 1887), 626-29; Emerson, *Life of Abby Hopper Gibbons*, II, 340; London *Daily Chronicle*, Nov. 12, 1914; Boston *Evening Transcript*, Nov. 24, 1917; Kansas City *Times*, Mar. 23, 1943.

Numerous parodies, favorable and unfavorable toward Father Abraham, were inspired by the piece. From his own state which responded well came "Illinois' Response":

> We're coming, and we know
> Your cheek will glow with honest pride,
> When you see our spangled banner
> Float our Sister States beside.
>
> We're coming, for we trace the lines
> Of care upon your brow,
> And silver hairs are twining fast
> Your "crown of glory" now.
>
> We know that near your burdened heart
> Our bleeding country lies,
> We come with freedom's stalwart arm
> To meet her enemies.

Willard A. and Porter W. Heaps, *The Singing Sixties* (Norman, Okla., 1960), pp. 90-92.

Exactly one month after the poem first appeared, *Punch* printed a critical parody in eight verses, with the comment that it hoped that Mr. Bryant did not write the verses and that "we don't like them." The parody began—

> To Abraham Lincoln
> On his Demand for 300,000 men.
> We're coming, Father ABRAAM, we're coming all along,
> But don't you think you're coming it yourself a little strong?
> Three hundred thousand might be called a pretty tidy figure,
> We've nearly sent you white enough, why don't you take the nigger?

Punch (London), XLIII (Aug. 16, 1862), 72. A month later, Sept. 20, 1862, *Leslie's Illus. News*, which until then had ignored the piece, reprinted the verses from *Punch!* For other parodies, see Stutler, *Lincoln Herald*, LIII, 9-12.

Institutes." He was associated with well-known musicians of his day—Lowell Mason, William B. Bradbury, and I. B. Woodbury. A prodigious worker, he compiled songbooks (*The Silver Lute* sold more than 100,000 copies), and composed dozens of songs including about thirty war songs of which four won wide popularity.[22] Of Root's war songs, by far the most popular and enduring was the one written in that dark month, July, 1862. Stirred by the call for more troops, Root, in his office at Root and Cady's in Chicago, one day hastily composed the piece, words and music together. It was sung on the evening of July 24 and again at a great war rally on July 26, with the popular singers, Jules and Frank Lumbard, leading the multitude:

> Yes, we'll rally 'round the flag boys,
> We'll rally once again,
> Shouting the Battle-cry of Freedom![23]

Writing some years later, Root modestly said:

> From there the song went into the army, and the testimony in regard to its use in the camp and on the march, and even on the field of battle, from soldiers and officers, up to generals, and even to the good President himself, made me thankful that if I could not shoulder a musket in defense of my country I could serve her in this way.[24]

---

[22] George F. Root, *The Story of a Musical Life* (Cincinnati, 1891), *passim*.

[23] The Chicago Board of Trade was very active in stimulating enlistments and in raising money. At its evening session on July 23, 1862, the Lumbard brothers sang the "Star-Spangled Banner" and a band played "Hail, Columbia," the "Star-Spangled Banner" and "John Brown." The next evening "The Battle-Cry of Freedom" was sung. Apparently Root composed it in the interval between the war meeting on Saturday, July 19, which he is said to have attended, and Thursday, July 24. It was at the huge rally on Saturday, July 26, that the song really "caught on." The rally began about 2:00 P.M. and continued into the evening. In the afternoon "The Battle-Cry of Freedom" was sung by a chorus with J. G. Lumbard "sustaining" the solo, and in the evening "they" sang it again "as they only can," amidst great applause and cheers. Chicago *Tribune*, July 20, 24, 25, 26, 27, 28, 1862. From the beginning, as was the case in the *Tribune*, the piece was referred to as either "The Battle-Cry of Freedom" or "Rally 'Round the Flag." Cf. also Root, *Story of a Musical Life*, pp. 132-33; Coonley, *The New England Magazine*, XIII, 555-70; Epstein, *Civil War History*, IV, 309-11.
Interestingly enough, at the meeting on July 19, Gibbons' poem was read "amid great enthusiasm!" J. G. Lumbard sang the "Marseillaise" and Frank sang "Red, White and Blue" and the "Star-Spangled Banner." Chicago *Tribune*, July 20, 1862.

[24] Root, *Story of a Musical Life*, p. 133. At a meeting in Root's honor in 1889 J. W. Fifer paid this tribute to the composer and the song: "Only those who were at the front, camping, marching, battling for the flag, can fully realize how often we were cheered, revived and inspired by the songs of him who sent forth the 'Battle-Cry of Freedom'." The true and correct history of the war for the maintenance of the Union will place George F. Root's name alongside of our

Yes, the song by Root and the song by Gibbons were sung, played, and heard all over the land. Soldiers in the streets of Washington responding to the President's call paraded by the White House singing "We are coming, Father Abraham"; strong men, thinking of their loved ones at home wept, and cheered and sang as they marched by a country schoolhouse in Maryland where the children had come out waving flags and singing "The Union forever, hurrah boys, hurrah!" A Union officer expressed surprise at the vigor of his Negro soldiers as they marched along singing "Yes, we'll rally 'round the flag, boys," and spectators in a small Georgia town stood in curiosity and wonder as a group of tired and bedraggled Union prisoners sang:

> Rally 'round the flag, boys;
> Down with the *traitor!*
> [Up with the star.][25]

The White House clerk, William O. Stoddard, related that one day during the bitter period after Fredericksburg a visitor announced that he wanted to sing for the President. It was James S. Gibbons. A procession of senators, officers and the secretaries paraded into the President's room, and with Lincoln's assent, Gibbons then sang:

> If you look up all our valleys
>   Where the growing harvests shine,
> You may see our sturdy farmer boys
>   Fast forming into line;
>
> - - - - - - - - - - - - -
>
> And a farewell group stands weeping
>   At every cottage door:
> We are coming, Father Abraham,
>   Three hundred thousand more!

great generals. While others led the boys in blue to final victory, it was his songs that nerved the men at the front and solaced the wives, mothers, sisters, and sweethearts at home, while more than a million voices joined in the chorus, " 'The Union Forever.' "
  Ibid., p. 211.
  [25] Poore, *Perley's Reminiscences*, II, 130; Louis Albert Banks, *Immortal Songs of Camp and Field* (Cleveland, 1898), pp. 126-28; Oliver Willcox Norton, *Army Letters, 1861-1865* (Chicago, 1903), p. 196; Root, *Story of a Musical Life*, p. 214; *Musical Rev. and World*, XIV (Sept. 26, 1863), 234.

Stoddard remarked: "We loved him as he sang."[26]

At a sedate gathering of socially prominent people in New York City the conversation centered on art and music. Louis M. Gottschalk played for the distinguished guests. An Englishman present made a deprecating remark about American music. Gottschalk was aroused. One of the listeners described what then happened:

> White as a sheet, and in his excited and overwhelming eloquence, he [Gottschalk] told them of a melody then being sung by regiment after regiment, marching down Broadway *en route* for the cars to Washington; of a melody they learned at home in the far West, and that they would carry with them, and sing it on the battle-field; of a melody that would sustain them in the thickest fight. And, on the spur of the moment, he sprang to the piano again, and gave such an astounding rhapsody on George F. Root's well-known "We'll Rally 'Round the Flag," as is entirely beyond description. I never heard any thing like it. . . . The effect was earthquakean almost. . . . The uproar could have been heard a mile.[27]

Far off in Mississippi the monotony in the lines before Vicksburg was relieved by the singing of the Lumbard brothers from Chicago. In camp and hospital they sang —sentimental songs and ballads, comic songs and patriotic numbers—"Home, Sweet Home," and "Listen to the Mocking Bird"; "Ole Shady," the "Star-Spangled Banner," and "The Battle-Cry of Freedom." The songs were "better than rations or medicine." An Iowa regiment after fearful losses in an assault closed ranks with flags

---

[26] Stoddard, *Lincoln's Third Secretary*, pp. 172-73. That not everyone was in accord with the sentiment in Gibbons' song is evidenced by the popularity of McClellan songs, especially among the soldiers. In August, 1862, *Harper's Weekly* contained a half-page sketch of soldiers in camp singing their favorite song:

M'Clellan is our man,
M'Clellan is our man,
We'll show our deeds,
    Where'er he leads,
M'Clellan is our man!

Harper's Weekly, Aug. 2, 1862.

After Fredericksburg, Septimus Winner's "Give Us Back Our Old Commander: Little Mac, the People's Pride" won immediate popularity. It also resulted in the arrest of the composer, who was a loyal Union man! He was released, however, on the promise that no more copies would be sold. Charles E. Claghorn, *The Mocking Bird, The Life and Diary of Its Author, Sep Winner* (Phila., 1937), pp. 32-35.

[27] Octavia Hensel [Mrs. Mary Alice Ives Seymour], *Life and Letters of Louis Moreau Gottschalk* (Boston, 1870), p. 209.

flying and sang: "Yes, we'll rally 'round the flag boys, we'll rally once again."[28]

Back in Washington on a Saturday afternoon in October, 1863, the President visited the Government Printing Office. He was much interested in all that went on in the plant. In the folding room he was greeted by 125 girl employees and presented some flowers. At the end of the tour a large group gathered in the composing room. The President was asked for a speech, but taken unawares, he declined, thanking the workers for the pleasant reception. Whereupon the assembly sang one song to close the event. A few days later up North in Brooklyn the same song "brought down the house" at a Union mass meeting. It was "The Battle-Cry of Freedom."[29]

Among the thousands that converged upon the little town of Gettysburg on that now famous day in November, 1863, was a well-trained chorus from Baltimore, the National Union Musical Association. During the train ride to Gettysburg and at station stops along the way the chorus whiled away the time by singing—"Yes, We'll Rally 'Round the Flag, Boys," and "We Are Coming, Father Abraham."

Although it was eleven o'clock in the evening (November 18) when they arrived at Gettysburg, the singers from Baltimore did not immediately go to bed. Instead, they paraded to the square and there, with the multitude around, serenaded the President. "We are coming, Father Abraham, three hundred thousand more," they sang.

Soon after, Father Abraham climbed into his bed in Judge Wills' house. It was after midnight. Outside, groups of singers still strolled in the streets. Between one and two o'clock a chorus could still be heard, and the song that floated on the early morning air was "We are coming, Father Abraham, three hundred thousand

---

[28] Benjamin P. Thomas, ed., *Three Years with Grant* (N.Y., 1955), pp. 96-97; Root, *Story of a Musical Life*, p. 133; *Musical Rev. and World*, XIV, 234.

[29] Washington *Evening Star*, Oct. 26, 1863; Washington *Sunday Morning Chronicle*, Oct. 25, 1863; N.Y. *Herald*, Oct. 28, 1863.

more."[30] One is tempted to wonder whether Father
Abraham noticed what was being sung and what he
thought as he lay there in bed with the important Day
of Dedication so near.

From Baltimore in April, 1864, a group of city officials
went to Washington to visit the Columbia Institute for
the Deaf, Dumb and Blind. Following the visit to the
Institute the party paid a call at the White House. After
the usual courtesies had been exchanged, the suggestion
was made that one of the guests who was an excellent
singer favor the group with a song. The singer obliged.
There was hearty applause, and Mr. Lincoln commented
that "the song contained an excellent sentiment and was
sung in a manner worthy of the sentiment." And the
song? It was "We Are Coming, Father Abraham!"[31]

The singer was Wilson G. Horner, a public-spirited citizen of Baltimore. He had given generously of his time
and talent singing for patriotic meetings and for soldiers
in hospital and camp. He was one of the leaders in the
party that had sung its way to Gettysburg the previous
November and had directed the Musical Association when
it sang at the exercises at the cemetery.

Two weeks and two days later after he had sung in the
White House, Horner again sang for the President, under very different circumstances. Standing beside Lincoln on the platform at the Sanitary Commission Fair in
Baltimore before a crowd estimated at three thousand
and with the assistance of the same chorus that had been
at Gettysburg, he sang "with fine effect" "We Are Coming, Father Abraham!"[32]

Shortly after this the President journeyed to Philadelphia to attend another fair. While his carriage tried
to get through the densely crowded streets of the city,
one of the bands blared forth "The Battle-Cry of Freedom"; and again, some months later on election eve
(November 8) crowds paraded in the rain and mud
of Washington's streets serenading and singing jubi-

---

[30] Cf. Chap. XIV, *infra*.
[31] Washington *Evening Star*, Apr. 4, 1864 ; Baltimore *American*, Apr. 2, 1864.
[32] Baltimore *American*, Apr. 19, 1864.

lantly "Yes, we'll rally 'round the flag boys, we'll rally once again."[33]

As the war came to its close the singing continued. Cheering soldiers at Petersburg made the air ring with "We Are Coming, Father Abraham" when Mr. Lincoln appeared there during his last visit to the army; joyous throngs in Washington's streets and at the White House raised their voices in "Yes, we'll rally 'round the flag boys, we'll rally once again" upon his return from City Point.[34]

Of all the times when the President heard those two songs of the war, no single occasion was so completely enjoyable and pleasant and thrilling as a memorable evening at Grover's Theatre. At the urging of Tad, who had seen the production before, they both went to Grover's for a performance of the "spectacular extravaganza," "The Seven Sisters."

The theatre was filled to capacity, for the play was very popular. Based upon the adventures and exploits of seven mythical sisters returned to earth from another world, the play really depended on the introduction of extemporaneous jokes and contemporary scenes for its appeal. The final scene, a tableau in which the entire cast appeared, was entitled "Rally 'Round the Flag."

The President seemed to forget the cares of office as he sat enjoying the performance. Tad, as was his wont, had wandered off.

Finally the whole company assembled on the stage for the last episode. John McDonough, the leader, began to sing, with the entire cast joining in the chorus—

> We will rally 'round the flag, boys,
> Rally once again—

McDonough noticed at the end of the line of singers a small boy dressed in a too large army blouse and cap, singing with the others. It was Tad Lincoln! He stepped over, handed Tad a flag, and the singing continued.

---

[33] Philadelphia *Inquirer*, June 17, 1864; Washington *Evening Star*, Nov. 9, 1864.

[34] Brooklyn *Daily Eagle*, Feb. 10, 1918; N.Y. *Herald*, Apr. 11, 1865; Horatio King, "My First and Last Sight of Abraham Lincoln," *Mag. of Amer. Hist.*, XVI (Sept., 1886), 254-57.

After the second verse the actor brought Tad to the center of the stage where the boy continued to wave the flag vigorously. Upon sudden inspiration McDonough repeated the chorus, combining the words of *two* songs:

> We are coming, Father Abraham,
> Three hundred thousand more,
> Shouting the battle-cry of freedom,
> We will rally 'round the flag, boys,
> Rally once again,
> Shouting the battle-cry of freedom.

Again, McDonough sang, the third and fourth stanzas. The crowd recognized the boy as Tad Lincoln, the President's son! The President was greatly amused and laughed heartily.

The time came for the final chorus. The whole house was in a state of excitement. All the players moved forward, the audience rose and everyone joined in the singing:

> We are coming, Father Abraham,
> Three hundred thousand more,
> Shouting the battle-cry of freedom,
> We will rally 'round the flag, boys,
> Rally once again,
> Shouting the battle-cry of freedom.

When the singing ended there were three cheers for "Father Abraham and his boy."

It was an incident packed with patriotic fervor and emotion. It was a high point of pleasure for Father Abraham.[35]

Perhaps no more conclusive evidence of the moving power and effect of these two songs, and others, is necessary than the words of a Confederate officer in Rich-

---

[35] Leonard Grover, "Lincoln's Interest in the Theatre," *The Century Magazine,* LXXVII (Apr., 1909), 943-50. Also printed in pamphlet form under the same title (n.d.). F. Lauriston Bullard, *Tad and His Father* (Boston, 1915), pp. 51-65. The play was billed for Grover's Theatre from March 14 to March 26, 1864, and returned in November for a two-weeks engagement at Ford's Theatre. Washington *Evening Star,* week of March 14 and 21, week of November 14 and 21, 1864. When Lincoln made his brief visit to Philadelphia in June for the Sanitary Commission Fair, "The Seven Sisters" was playing at Grover's Theatre just a short distance away. It was hailed as "the most successful play ever presented in the city," and the last scene "Rally 'Round the Flag, Boys!" was described as "the most gorgeous sight ever witnessed." Philadelphia *Inquirer,* June 16, 1864.

mond shortly after the fighting had ceased. A group of Union officers gathered after dinner one evening was passing the time in an informal "sing." Some Confederate officers in a house across the street asked if they could join the group and hear the singing. Their request was readily granted.

The Unionists continued their singing, and in deference to their guests chose glees and college songs. But the Confederates wanted to hear the songs of the war. The Unionists obliged with "the whole catalogue," including the "Battle Hymn of the Republic," "John Brown's Body," "Tramp, Tramp, Tramp," and "We Are Coming, Father Abraham." They ended with "Yes, We'll Rally 'Round the Flag."

One of the Confederate officers then spoke:

> Gentlemen, if we'd had your songs we'd have licked you out of your boots! Who couldn't have marched or fought with such songs? . . . every one of these Yankee songs is full of marching and fighting spirit.

He continued:

> I shall never forget the first time I heard "Rally Round the Flag." 'Twas a nasty night during the "Seven Days' Fight," and if I remember rightly it was raining. I was on picket, when, just before "taps," some fellow on the other side struck up that song and others joined in the chorus until it seemed to me the whole Yankee army was singing. Tom B——, who was with me, sung out, "Good heavens, Cap, what are those fellows made of, anyway? Here we've licked 'em six days running and now, on the eve of the seventh, they're singing 'Rally Round the Flag.'" I am not naturally superstitious, but I tell you that song sounded to me like the "knell of doom," and my heart went down to my boots; and though I've tried to do my duty, it has been an up-hill fight with me ever since that night.[36]

It seems safe to presume that countless men and women in the North, to the number of three hundred thousand and many more, including Father Abraham himself, would have understood.

---

[36] Richard Wentworth Browne, "Union War Songs and Confederate Officers," *The Century Magazine*, XXXV (Jan., 1888), 478; Root, *Story of a Musical Life*, pp. 134-35. The Confederate officer was evidently mistaken as to the time when the incident occurred, as "The Battle-Cry of Freedom" was not written until more than two weeks after the "Seven Days."

CHAPTER X

LINCOLN COMING WITH HIS CHARIOT
Let My People Go!

DURING THE DISCOURAGING AND DIFFICULT MONTHS OF 1862, Lincoln took one of the most significant steps of his entire presidency. This step—momentous in its implications and in its consequences—strengthened his position with an important segment of Northern opinion, encouraged friends of the North in Europe, and gave hope to lovers of freedom everywhere. It changed the nature of the war and gave it a moral basis previously lacking in the eyes of many, and it lifted the burden of servitude from upwards of four million human beings. It made Lincoln the Great Emancipator.

It was, as Lincoln himself said, the central act of his administration and the great event of the century. It was the issuing of the Proclamation of Emancipation.

Lincoln had pondered long and earnestly on the question of slavery and the war. He had listened to countless logical reasons and impassioned arguments, heated discussions, and quiet prayers for and against freeing the slaves. He was well aware of how divided the sentiments of the people were on the matter, and he knew how necessary public support would be should such a step be taken.

He had discussed Emancipation with Senator Sumner after breakfast and with Vice-President Hamlin after dinner; he had heard reports from Emancipation Societies which favored immediate action and from Border State delegates who were unmoved by his pleas for state action with compensation; he had discussed the question with the fiery Wendell Phillips and had listened to the quiet entreaty of sober Quakers; he had raised a storm by voiding General Hunter's famous order freeing slaves

in his Department and had quieted the concern of Marylanders about the enforcement of the Fugitive Slave Law
in the District of Columbia.[1]

From Boston, the abolitionist capital of the country,
he had been sent a communication from His Honor, Mayor
Joseph M. Wightman, which read:

> There may be small sections or towns where the doctrine of
> emancipation and arming the slaves is regarded with favor . . .
> but I assure Your Excellency that in Boston, and I believe
> in a large majority of the other cities and towns . . . the
> mingling of questions in relation to slavery with the crushing
> out of the present rebellion is viewed with the strongest feel-
> ings of disapprobation. . . .
>
> Trusting that you will continue to be firm and resolute in
> your endeavors for the restoration and welfare of our common
> country, and ignoring all other issues which tend to prevent
> the accomplishment of this great object, I have the honor
> to be. . . .[2]

And just previous to this, in a lecture in Washington
by the famous Dr. George B. Cheever, of New York, he
was compared to Pharaoh in ancient Egypt; with General
Frémont, the modern Moses; the rebellion, the river of
blood; and abolition, the means to *let God's people go!*
All topped off with a stirring antislavery hymn sung by
the Hutchinson Singers who had performed for the President earlier that same week![3]

Lincoln's position on slavery itself was clear. To a
friend from his own native state of Kentucky, he wrote:
"I am naturally anti-slavery. If slavery is not wrong,
nothing is wrong. I can not remember when I did not
so think, and feel."[4]

This position can be traced back to his first public statement on the question when, as a young legislator in Illi-

[1] Edward L. Pierce, *Memoir and Letters of Charles Sumner* (Boston, 1877-1893),
IV, 64; Charles E. Hamlin, *The Life and Times of Hannibal Hamlin* (Cambridge,
1899), pp. 428-29; Carl Schurz, *The Reminiscences of Carl Schurz* (N.Y., 1907), II,
329-30; Helen Nicolay, *Lincoln's Secretary* (N.Y., 1949), pp. 134-36; Irving H. Bartlett, *Wendell Phillips: Brahmin Radical* (Boston, 1961), p. 249; Rice, ed., *Reminiscences of Abraham Lincoln*, pp. 281-83; N.Y. *Tribune*, Mar. 19, 1862; Washington
Evening Star, June 21, 1862; Lincoln, *Works*, V, 278-79, 317-19.

[2] Washington *National Intelligencer*, June 19, 1862; N.Y. *Herald*, June 20, 1862.

[3] N. P. Willis in *Home Journal*, Jan. 25, 1862.

[4] Lincoln, *Works*, VII, 281.

nois, supported by only one other colleague, he went on
record that ". . . slavery is founded on both injustice and
bad policy. . . ."[5]

The depth of his feeling is manifest in his comment
to his close friend, Joshua Fry Speed, a few years later:

> In 1841 you and I had together a tedious low-water trip,
> on a Steam Boat from Louisville to St. Louis. You may re-
> member, as I well do, that from Louisville to the mouth of the
> Ohio there were, on board, ten or a dozen slaves, shackled
> together with irons. That sight was a continual torment to
> me. . . . [It is] a thing which has, and continually exercises,
> the power of making me miserable.[6]

When the war came, Lincoln's attitude and feelings
did not change. Rather, they were intensified. Slavery
was on his mind day and night, he said, and more so
than any other question.

But in this war to save the Union, the outcome of which
would determine whether government of the people, by
the people, and for the people would perish from the
earth, but which, nevertheless, had its roots in the long-
established institution of human slavery, Lincoln could
not act merely according to his own *feelings*. He could
only act in his capacity as Chief Executive and as Commander-in-Chief of the Army and Navy. He explained
it thus:

> . . . I have never understood that the Presidency conferred
> upon me an unrestricted right to act officially upon this judg-
> ment and feeling [that slavery is wrong]. . . . And I aver
> that, to this day, I have done no official act in mere deference
> to my abstract judgment and feeling on slavery.[7]

Lincoln, in spite of Dr. Cheever's likening him to the
Egyptian Pharaoh, wanted all men to be free. But under the circumstances, there must be a proper time for
him to act. In September, after Antietam, the right time
arrived, and the preliminary proclamation was issued.

Two evenings later, on the twenty-fourth of September,

[5] Lincoln, *Works*, I, 75.
[6] Lincoln, *Works*, II, 320.
[7] Lincoln, *Works*, VII, 281.

he was serenaded by a large assembly of people, gathered to honor the occasion. Headed by a band, the parade had formed at the National Hotel. By the time it reached the White House, it had become a small army.

The band played, the crowd cheered, and soon the President appeared. Surely, he was encouraged by the size and enthusiasm of the gathering. His remarks, while revealing something of his own burden, nevertheless, as so often was the case, turned to the soldiers at the front. He appealed for support for them as well as for the cause which he represented as he spoke:

> What I did, I did after very full deliberation, and under a very heavy and solemn sense of responsibility.
>
> -
>
> I can only trust in God I have made no mistake. . . . In my position I am environed with difficulties.
>
> -
>
> Yet they are scarcely so great as the difficulties of those who, upon the battlefield, are endeavoring to purchase with their blood and their lives the future happiness and prosperity of this country. . . . Let us never forget them. . . . I only ask you, at the conclusion of these few remarks, to give three hearty cheers to all good and brave officers and men who fought those successful battles.[8]

Kingdom Coming

As the days passed, more and more attention was focused on the big event to come on January 1—the final

---

[8] Washington *National Intelligencer*, Sept. 26, 1862; N.Y. *Times*, Sept. 25, 1862; Lincoln, *Works*, V, 438-39. It is of interest to note the reactions of three of the Cabinet members to the serenade. Secretary Chase, who was visited after the President, spoke in approval of the Proclamation, saying, ". . . it is, nevertheless, though baptized in blood, an act of humanity and justice which the latest generation will celebrate. Yes, the whole world will pay honor to the man who has performed it." He then appealed for unity in support of the President. Washington *Evening Star*, Sept. 25, 1862. In his *Diary* Chase wrote: ". . . a band of music, which had just serenaded the President by way of congratulation on the Proclamation, came to my house and demanded a speech—with which demand, I complied briefly." David Donald, ed., *Inside Lincoln's Cabinet: The Civil War Diaries of Salmon P. Chase* (N.Y., 1954), p. 157.

Attorney General Bates was surprised at the size of the gathering. He commented on the distress caused by the war in his own state. When asked to say something about the Proclamation, he refused, saying, "I will not. I shall not discuss the acts of the Cabinet of which I am a member, or of the President, who is my superior." Washington *Evening Star*, Sept. 25, 1862. He made no reference to the serenade in his *Diary*.

Secretary Welles heard the serenaders as he was writing in his *Diary*. He

proclamation. Visitors to the White House continued to express their opinions and to offer advice.

The day after the serenade one of the many religious delegations called with resolutions in favor of Emancipation; a few days later the military governor of North Carolina expressed his disapproval. A dozen Northern governors arrived to present their collective sentiments, and a memorial from prominent Tennesseans including Andrew Johnson urged that the proclamation be not applied in their state.[9]

The President listened, pondered, referred to the problem in his Annual Message, and conferred with his Cabinet. When December 31 arrived, he was ready.

Senator Browning, close confidant of the President, had grave doubts. In his *Diary,* he commented:

> The President was fatally bent upon his course, saying that if he should refuse to issue his proclamation there would be a rebellion in the north, and that a dictator would be placed over his head within a week. There is no hope. The proclamation will come—God grant it may not be productive of the mischief I fear.[10]

Perhaps Browning, and even the President himself, would have been reassured had they been able to read the anticipatory thoughts expressed by one soldier at the front:

> More than anything else—more than all the victories we can win in the field, however brilliant they may be, the first day of January next will affect for good the fate of our country.
>
> -
>
> Our only way out of this horror now blinding the nation, is by the door of Justice to the oppressed. We must "let the people go," at any rate. If it be through the Red Sea, still they must go.[11]

wrote: "The document [Proclamation] has been in the main well received, but there is some violent opposition, and the friends of the measure have made this demonstration to show their approval." Morse, ed., *Diary of Gideon Welles,* I, 147.

[9] C. Percy Powell, ed., *Lincoln Day by Day: A Chronology 1809-1865* (Washington, 1960), III, 141, 142, 158; Washington *Evening Star,* Sept. 26, 1862; Washington *National Intelligencer,* Sept. 26, 1862; Lincoln, *Works,* V, 441.

[10] Pease and Randall, eds., *Diary of O. H. Browning,* I, 607.

[11] Portland (Maine) *Press,* Jan. 14, 1863.

To Lincoln the Negro question was not wholly academic, for he had personal association with many colored people and knew their problems as individuals. One evening in June, 1862, he was serenaded by a group of Negroes who, honoring "the friends of freedom," had begun their parade at the Summer White House. In August he talked long and earnestly, albeit unsuccessfully, with a colored delegation, endeavoring to interest the delegates in a colonization project in Central America.[12]

He helped William Johnson, the colored boy who had come with him from Illinois to obtain employment as a messenger in the Treasury Department; he was fond of the colored servants in the White House, especially Peter Brown, the butler, and William Slade, his valet and messenger, and they thought highly of him.[13]

But it was Aunt Mary Dines who touched the President's heart and stirred his feelings most deeply. Aunt Mary was a rather unusual person. Sometime employee at the White House,[14] she was also active at the contraband camp on Seventh Street. She knew how to write and thus could be of help in composing letters for the many bewildered refugees at the camp; she knew how to sing and her capabilities as a leader brought a good response when the contrabands raised their voices in song.

Crowds of visitors went out to the camp, especially on Sundays, but Mr. Lincoln, according to Aunt Mary, often stopped there on his way to the Summer White House. He even made special visits to the camp.[15]

On one such occasion, the contrabands gathered and Uncle Ben, a "spirit preacher," opened the meeting with a prayer. Everyone, including the President, then sang

---

[12] Washington *Evening Star*, July 1, Aug. 15, 1862; Lincoln, *Works*, V, 370-75.

[13] Apparently Lincoln first found a place for Johnson at the White House, but the other servants did not accept him. This may have been because Johnson was very dark and was thus resented by the others. Lincoln three times wrote notes of recommendation for Johnson. In January, 1864, Johnson died, and then Lincoln recommended another boy, Solomon Johnson, for his place in the Treasury Department. Lincoln, *Works*, IV, 277, 288; V, 474; VI, 8-9; VII, 156-57; Ellet, *Court Circles of the Republic*, p. 529; John E. Washington, *They Knew Lincoln* (N.Y., 1942), pp. 105-17, 127-41.

[14] Cf. Lincoln, *Works*, V, 492.

[15] Mrs. Lincoln also took an interest in the camp and the people there.

"America." With her knees shaking, Aunt Mary led the singing. For an hour they sang—"Nobody Knows the Trouble I've Seen," and "Every Time I Feel the Spirit." The President wiped the tears from his face.

When they sang "I Thank God that I Am Free at Last," Lincoln bowed his head. On the last song, the President joined again. It was "John Brown's Body!"

Another time on a damp, dreary evening Lincoln appeared at the camp. He was feeling low and asked for more songs and another prayer from Uncle Ben.

Again the contrabands sang—"Swing Low, Sweet Chariot," "Didn't My God Deliver Daniel?", "Go Down Moses," "I Ain't Got Weary Yet," "I've Been in the Storm So Long," "Steal Away." They finished with the Doxology, "Praise God from Whom All Blessings Flow."

As Aunt Mary remembered it, the President, although sometimes choked with emotion, sang along with the rest. When he came to the camp, he was not the President—he was just like them—he stood and sang and prayed as they did. And, without doubt, he was grateful for the singing, and it made him feel better.[16]

Early in the war contrabands entering the Union lines began to awaken the people of the North to the problem of Negro refugees. Inevitably the refugees were attracted to the North, for there they might find freedom, and as they came in increasing numbers camps were hastily established to care for them.[17]

Down at Fort Monroe, where there were several thousands of them, the contrabands were accustomed to gather at their quarters at nightfall and sing their plantation songs. To Northerners stationed there it was striking and impressive to hear these homeless victims of the war singing—

---

[16] Washington, *They Knew Lincoln*, pp. 83-87. Strictly speaking, Lincoln could neither read music nor sing. It is doubtful whether he could carry a tune, even in group singing. If he "sang" on these occasions, it was probably in a monotone. But his limitations in no way detracted from his deep enjoyment of the music or the singing.

[17] Later on, the oft-criticized Freedmen's Bureau, our first attempt at dealing with a massive displaced persons problem, did some creditable work with whites as well as Negroes.

Could I but climb on Pisgah's top
And view the promised land,
My flesh itself would long to drop
At my dear Lord's command.

This living grace on Earth we owe,
To Jesus' dying love;
We would be only his below,
And reign with him above.[18]

The presence of the contrabands in Washington lent excitement and reality to the meaning and significance of the coming event. When the last day of the year 1862 arrived, the camp on Seventh Street was in a high fever of anticipation. As evening came the contrabands gathered to wait. Many speeches were given. A "Proclamation song" was sung, one verse of which went:

And blessed be Abraham Lincoln,
The Union army, too;
May the choicest of earth's blessings
Their pathway ever strew—

At 11:58 P.M. everybody knelt in prayer. At 12:02 A.M. an elderly leader offered a prayer. He prayed that the army might be successful and the rebellion crushed; he asked for the blessings of Heaven for the President, and he hoped that their friends left in Dixie might be saved.

Following the prayer a "Hallelujah song" was sung. Then came the handshaking and rejoicing. Around the camp the contrabands paraded, forming and re-forming as they marched, "frantic with joy, singing, dancing and shouting." Finally at one o'clock, after singing "I'm a Free Man," most of the jubilant participants went off to bed.[19]

Elsewhere at Negro churches throughout the land the members gathered that same night to sing, to pray, to praise, to watch and to wait.[20] At the Shiloh Presbyterian

---

[18] *Dwight's Journal of Music*, XIX (Sept. 7, 1861), 182.

[19] Washington *Evening Star*, Jan. 1, 1863; N.Y. *Tribune*, Jan. 5, 1863; *Vermont Watchman & State Journal* (Montpelier), Jan. 9, 1863.

[20] Washington, *They Knew Lincoln*, pp. 89-91; Henrietta Buckmaster, *Let My People Go* (Boston, 1959), pp. 303-4; Benjamin Quarles, *The Negro in the Civil War* (Boston, 1953), pp. 170, 174.

Church in New York it was announced that "The Great Jubilee," "Freedom's Watch-Night" would be held that evening. The announcement also said:

> At 9 o'clock we shall begin to dig the grave of American Slavery, and at 12 precisely we hope to bury the old Monster beyond the possibility of a resurrection.[21]

The time had come; a new day was about to dawn; colored people, whether contraband or not, who knew full well its meaning, would no longer need to pour out their hearts in "The Song of the Contrabands"—

> Oh! Let My People Go
> The Lord, by Moses, to Pharaoh Said: Oh!
> let my people go;
> If not, I'll smite your first-born dead—Oh!
> let my people go.
>
> Oh! go down, Moses,
> Away down to Egypt's land,
> And tell King Pharaoh
> To let my people go.[22]

Year of Jubilo

January 1, 1863, turned out to be a bright, balmy, almost springlike day. By eleven o'clock there was a long line of people outside the White House waiting for the President's New Year's Reception to begin. During the first hour only army and navy officers, diplomats, judges and other dignitaries were admitted. Then it was the ordinary citizens' turn. For two hours they pressed in, crowding as best they could to greet the President before the doors were closed.

A congressman had his coattails torn off, a young lady was reduced to tears because her hat was crushed, a tardy general was angry because he couldn't get in, a small Bostonian punched a Michigan gentleman in the stomach, and the latter was exceedingly annoyed because he was packed in so tightly that he could not retaliate!

---

[21] N.Y. *Tribune*, Dec. 31, 1862, Jan. 1, 1863.
[22] *The Continental Monthly*, II (July-Dec., 1862), 113.

The President suffered the usual swollen right hand, but no fatalities were reported.[23]

The reception over, the President went to his office and without ceremony signed the Proclamation of Emancipation. Soon the telegraph wires carried the news to all parts of the country. Later in the day, his work completed, Lincoln went over to the telegraph office to relax.[24]

Meantime the contrabands had again met to recognize the New Year of Jubilo. From noon until long after dark, except for a recess for the evening meal, they sang, prayed, testified, and listened to speeches. Many comparisons were made of their situation and the delivery of the Israelites from Pharaoh in Egypt.

During the afternoon service an elderly man began once again "I'm a Free Man Now," and the whole company joined in; an aged woman, keeping time with her head, hands and feet, started singing with great fervor "Go Down Moses"; another then took up "There will be no more taskmasters."

In the evening the singing was led by a venerable Negro of sixty years, erect and poised, named John the Baptist. He lined out the hymns, and the women kept time with the swaying motion as in a camp meeting. Prayers were offered, including one for the President:

> May thy will be done on earth as it is in heaven. Prosper the work to be done in this land and country, and aid us by thy invincible hand. Let thy blessing rest on everything belonging to the United States President who has bestowed such gifts upon us this night. We were bound as slaves—chains on our hands. We have seen our people bound in chains and carried away. . . . Bless the President, Jesus. Lay down with him this night, I pray God—rise in the morning with him. God give him a light of wisdom. God bless the Union army wherever it may be. God Almighty go with our people—lead us along in this dark, howling wilderness . . . make us willing to obey the United States President as much as do the soldiers as come down to break our chains. We were bruised and dragged about. Let us lay down our lives for those who break slavery's chains from our neck. Let the war be pushed

[23] N.Y. *Herald*, Jan. 3, 1863; Sacramento *Daily Union*, Jan. 29, 1863; Nicolay, *Lincoln's Secretary*, p. 164; F. B. Carpenter, *Six Months at the White House with Abraham Lincoln* (N.Y., 1866), p. 87.

[24] David Homer Bates, *Lincoln in the Telegraph Office* (N.Y., 1907), pp. 143-44.

on. Bless them who have just run away and come here, and bless all!

The superintendent of the camp read the President's Proclamation and explained it line by line so that all would understand it. Several leaders testified, recounting their hardships, trials and sufferings as slaves, and expressing their great gratification at being now free. One speaker ended his testimony by saying, "God put it in the heart of the President to make us free men, and I am now ready to fight for that freedom." Both sessions ended with "breaking songs," as they were called by the contrabands.[25]

And so it was in many places in the land—celebrations went on through the day. In Norfolk, Virginia, four thousand Negroes paraded though the streets with bands playing and flags flying, with such cheers for freedom "the likes of which doubtless never occurred in the 'Old Dominion' before." Colored citizens way up in Portland, Maine, held an "Emancipation Levee" at which many white people were in attendance "to meet with and congratulate their colored friends on the great event of the century—the proclamation of freedom to their oppressed brethren."[26]

More elaborate and extensive observances included two of rather special interest, one in South Carolina and one in Boston. At Port Royal, South Carolina, the abolitionist-minded General Saxton issued a proclamation of his own:

A Happy New-Year's Greeting to the Colored People in the Department of the South.

---

[25] *Vermont Watchman & State Journal* (Montpelier), Jan. 16, 1863; Portland (Maine) *Press*, Jan. 13, 1863.

[26] Moore, *Rebellion Record*, VI, D. 30; Bellows Falls (Vt.) *Times*, Jan. 9, 1863; Portland (Maine) *Press*, Jan. 2, 1863. In some cities observances and special services extended through the next week. Thus, on January 2 one hundred guns were fired in Haverhill, Massachusetts, and bells rang for an hour. That same evening one hundred guns were fired in Pittsburgh. Exercises were held in Bangor, Maine, and Buffalo, New York, on January 3, and at Rochester, New York, on January 4. A big meeting was held at the Cooper Institute on January 5. *Vermont Watchman & State Journal* (Montpelier), Jan. 9, 1863; Portland (Maine) *Press*, Jan. 7, 1863; N.Y. *Tribune*, Jan. 5, 7, 1863.

In England, most newspapers were critical of the Proclamation, but Lincoln's action received enthusiastic support in several large city gatherings held on the evening of Dec. 31, 1862.

In accordance, as I believe, with the will of our Heavenly Father, and by direction of your great and good friend, whose name you are all familiar with, Abraham Lincoln, President of the United States, and Commander-in-Chief of the Army and Navy, on the 1st day of January, 1863, you will be declared "forever free."

When in the course of human events there comes a day which is destined to be an everlasting beaconlight, marking a joyful era in the progress of a nation and the hopes of a people, it seems to be fitting the occasion that it should not pass unnoticed by those whose hopes it comes to brighten and to bless.

Such a day to you is January 1, 1863.

The proclamation then went on to urge the freedmen to raise their voices so that the "grand chorus of liberty" would reach every cabin in the land.

In accordance with the General's call, the Negroes began to assemble at ten o'clock from near and far. Boats had been provided to bring those coming from a distance. Many white visitors were also present for the occasion.

The exercises started at eleven thirty. After a prayer, the President's Proclamation was read. The high point of the meeting, at least to Thomas Wentworth Higginson, was the spontaneous singing of "America" by the freedmen during a flag presentation.

Not to be overlooked, however, was the great repast which came after the formal program. A dozen oxen, roasted slowly throughout the preceding night over open fires, turned regularly by willing volunteers so as to be properly done, provided the substance of a feast enjoyed by soldiers and civilians, colored and white.

When the day's end came, those who had come from afar boarded the boats for the return trip, and the last song was finished as taps was sounded.[27] Thus was Emancipation ushered in in South Carolina!

In Boston there were three significant gatherings on that memorable day. At Tremont Temple a continuous

---

[27] Moore, *Rebellion Record*, VI, D. 30; Thomas Wentworth Higginson, *Army Life in a Black Regiment* (Boston, 1870), pp. 39-42; Portland (Maine) *Press*, Jan. 7, 1863; N.Y. *Tribune*, Jan. 1, 1863; Quarles, *Negro in the Civil War*, pp. 178-79.

meeting was held throughout most of the day and evening under the auspices of the Union Progressive Association. Among the speakers were Anna Dickinson and Frederick Douglass. Douglass recalled that the great audience waited until late into the evening for the news that the Proclamation had been signed, and that after midnight the meeting adjourned to a nearby church and continued until dawn!

During the afternoon a great Jubilee Concert was given at the Music Hall. Admission was charged, the proceeds to go toward an educational fund for freedmen. The hall was full and excitement was high as the audience listened to the music of Beethoven and Mendelssohn, heard Ralph Waldo Emerson read his "Boston Hymn" —and waited. When the news finally arrived that the Proclamation had been signed, the dignified audience broke into hearty cheers.

That same evening a select group of abolitionists journeyed the half-dozen miles to Medford to the house of George Luther Stearns to witness the unveiling of a bust of John Brown.

At the appropriate time Wendell Phillips made a "graceful speech" and unveiled the bust. Later Emerson repeated his "Boston Hymn," and Mrs. Howe recited the "Battle Hymn of the Republic." It was nearly midnight when the guests departed—by special horsecars arranged for by Mr. Stearns. Emerson and Alcott remained overnight and stayed up late discussing philosophy.[28] Thus was the "Year of Jubilo" ushered in at Boston.

It was perhaps not inappropriate that both President and Mrs. Lincoln were well informed concerning the day's events in Boston. The President had been provided by Senator Sumner with a clipping from a Boston paper which told of the coming musical celebration, and Eliza S. Quincy reported to Mrs. Lincoln in a letter written on January 2. Miss Quincy ended her account of the meet-

[28] Portland (Maine) *Press*, Jan. 7, 1863; *Dwight's Journal of Music*, XXII (Jan. 10, 1863), 326-27; Boston *Evening Transcript*, Jan. 1, 1913; Frederick Douglass, *Life and Times of Frederick Douglass* (N.Y., 1962), pp. 352-54; Frank Preston Stearns, *The Life and Public Services of George Luther Stearns* (Philadelphia and London, 1907), pp. 274-76; Quarles, *Negro in the Civil War*, pp. 170-74.

ing: "It was a day & an occasion never to be forgotten. I wish you & the President could have enjoyed it with us here."[29]

Emancipation, of course, inspired its share of musical compositions, none of which ever attained great popularity. For the President, however, one such piece had a personal connection. A few days after he had affixed his name to the final Proclamation, Lincoln signed a letter addressed to a music teacher in a small town in Iowa. It read:

> EXECUTIVE MANSION, WASHINGTON, January 26 1863
> MY DEAR SIR Allow me to thank you cordially for your thoughtful courtesy in sending me a copy of your "Emancipation March"
>
> Your Obt Servt   A. LINCOLN[30]
> GEORGE E. FAWCETT ESQ
> MUSCATINE IOWA

The music teacher had sent to the President a copy of his composition "The President's Emancipation March" dedicated to him as "A Foe to Tyrants and my Country's Friend."

Whether Lincoln ever heard the march played is not known, but at least he appreciated the sentiment which inspired its writing and took the trouble to acknowledge it with thanks.

Two of the most widely sung pieces of the war which were associated in people's minds with the ending of slavery and the coming of freedom did not actually originate in the Emancipation controversy itself. In common use before the Proclamation, both, however, took on new meaning when Emancipation came.

"Kingdom Coming" ("Year of Jubilo") was the first of several war songs written by Henry Clay Work. Work, a Connecticut Yankee, was living in Illinois when the war broke. A printer by trade, a man of little formal education, Work had poetic interests and real musical

---

[29] Sarah Forbes Hughes, ed., *Letters . . . of John Murray Forbes* (Boston, 1899), I, 352; Eliza S. Quincy to Mrs. President Lincoln, Jan. 2, 1863, R. T. Lincoln Coll., 20924-5.

[30] Lincoln, *Works*, VI, 78.

talent. Moreover, he was a strong Unionist and an ardent abolitionist. His father had been jailed in Illinois in the 1840's for antislavery activity.

"Kingdom Coming" was published in the spring of 1862 by Root and Cady of Chicago. It was a success almost immediately. Soldiers sang it on the march and in camp; newsboys and the "folks back home" sang it; it was sung in the South as well as in the North, by both Negroes and whites. When the "Year of Jubilo" came, no other "freedom song" touched it in popularity.[31]

Why was "Kingdom Coming" so popular? Probably because of a happy combination of three things—its catchy tune, its relevant sentiments, and its all-pervading humor. As one writer commented: "It set the whole world laughing, but there was about it a vein of political wisdom as well as of poetic justice that commended it to strong men."[32]

> Say, darkies, have you seen the master,
>   With the mustache on his face,
> Go along the road some time this morning,
>   Like he's going to leave the place?
> He saw a smoke way up the river,
>   Where the Lincoln gunboats lay;
> He took his hat, and left very sudden,
>   And I expect he's run away!
>
> - - - - - - - - - - - - - -
>
> The master run, ha, ha!
> The darkey stay, ho, ho!
> It must be now the kingdom coming,
> And the year of Jubilo![33]

When the Twelfth Massachusetts Regiment marched down Broadway, New York, one day in July, 1861, singing a song recently put together at Fort Warren in Boston Harbor where the men had been previously stationed, it

---

[31] Boston *Evening Transcript*, Nov. 24, 1917; Banks, *Immortal Songs of Camp and Field*, pp. 138-45; Root, *Story of a Musical Life*, pp. 137-38; Heaps, *Singing Sixties*, pp. 268-70; Irwin Silber, *Songs of the Civil War* (N.Y., 1960), pp. 306, 317-19.

[32] Banks, *Immortal Songs of Camp and Field*, p. 140.

[33] It will be noted that in this and other songs mentioned in this chapter modern English is used for the most part.

gave the North the piece which, above all others, became the *musical symbol* of the slave set free.

No matter that the original subject of the song was an obscure sergeant in the regiment, that the music was an old camp-meeting tune, or that the words were first intended to poke fun at the lowly sergeant.

> John Brown's body lies a-mould'ring in the grave,
>   But his soul goes marching on.
> He's gone to be a soldier in the army of the Lord,
>   But his soul goes marching on.
> John Brown's knapsack is strapped upon his back
> (It is filled with leaden bullets and mouldy
>   hardtack),
>   But his soul goes marching on.

Soon Sergeant John Brown disappeared, and John Brown of Osawatomie and Harpers Ferry took his place—

> John Brown died that the slaves might be free
>   But his soul goes marching on.
> The stars above in Heaven now are looking
>   kindly down
> On the grave of old John Brown.

- - - - - - - - - - - - - - -

> Glory, glory, hallelujah,
> Glory, glory, hallelujah,
> Glory, glory, hallelujah,
> His soul goes marching on.

No matter that Julia Ward Howe's poem fitted the tune so well and that the "Battle Hymn of the Republic" became widely known and sung itself; no matter that John Brown of Osawatomie and Harpers Ferry was the subject of a poem, "The President's Proclamation," inspired by the events of January 1, 1863, to be used with the old tune. To the very end of the war—and after—nothing could take the place of the "John Brown Song."[34]

The precedent set by the Twelfth Massachusetts Regiment was continued, and other regiments sang "John

[34] Boston *Evening Transcript*, Nov. 24, 1917; Quincy (Mass.) *Patriot Ledger*, Dec. 2, 1959; Boston *Herald*, June 19, 1960; Boyd B. Stutler, "John Brown's Body," *Civil War History*, IV (Sept., 1958), 251-60; Silber, *Songs of the Civil War*, pp. 11-12, 23-26; Stutler, *Glory, Glory, Hallelujah!* (Cincinnati [1960]).

Brown's Body" as they marched through the streets of
New York; the "Highlanders" returning to Washington
from Virginia one night sang the "John Brown Song,"
and a correspondent heard the tune on a hand organ in
the capital streets; in the South, Negro children were
taught to sing the "John Brown Song" by an abolitionist
teacher, and Union prisoners in Memphis lightened their
spirits with music that included "John Brown"; as the
Army of the Potomac marched and remarched through
Virginia the song was heard—at Leesburg women onlookers scowled as a Yankee band struck up the piece,
while at Chancellorsville reinforcements went into battle
singing it.[35]

Sometimes it seemed as if the song fairly haunted Harpers Ferry and Charles Town. When the Twelfth Massachusetts reached that area in July, 1861, the men sang
"John Brown" with great fervor. That same autumn as
a train loaded to capacity with soldiers passed through
Harpers Ferry the air rang with "John Brown."

Months later a reporter passing by the engine house
where Brown made his final stand heard a boy whistling
the tune, and over at Charles Town, in the same jail where
Brown was lodged two years before, a Negro prisoner
brightened up and grinned as some Union soldiers passed
by singing "But his soul goes marching on." The Shenan-
doah Valley echoed with "John Brown" as troops marched
to and fro.[36]

It was all very impressive—the "Cromwellian touch"
when one thousand men sang "John Brown's Body" at
evening parade; the sound to disturb the deep when from
the vessels bearing General Banks' expedition to New
Orleans the men on board roared the "John Brown Song";
the echoes through a Virginia town when the army ended
a songfest of Irish, Scotch, and German songs with "John

[35] *Dwight's Journal of Music*, XX (Oct. 5, 1861), 216; Todd, *Seventy-Ninth Highlanders*, p. 88; N.Y. *Tribune*, July 22, 1862; Chicago *Times*, Oct. 20, 1862; Moore, *Rebellion Record*, IV, D. 82; Frank Rauscher, *Music on the March* (Phila., 1892), pp. 24-25; Harold Adams Small, ed., *The Road to Richmond: The Civil War Memoirs of Maj. Abner R. Small of the Sixteenth Maine Volunteers; with his Diary as a Prisoner of War* (Berkeley and Los Angeles, 1959), p. 86.

[36] Stutler, *Civil War History*, IV (Sept., 1958), 256; Emerson, *Life of Abby Hopper Gibbons*, I, 304; N.Y. *Commercial Advertiser*, Oct. 17, 1862; N.Y. *Tribune*, Oct. 18, Dec. 12, 1862.

Brown"; a thousand Negroes singing "But his soul goes marching on" as they worked on the defenses at Baltimore in 1863; Sherman's men leaving the ruined city of Atlanta on their march to the sea singing with great gusto "John Brown's Body."[37] There was something about the song.

Kingdom Coming

The Proclamation of Emancipation was but the beginning, the beginning of the end. To some who wanted everything at once, progress was too slow and Lincoln too deliberate.[38] There were hopeful signs and happy evidences of change which the critics of the President either failed to understand or to appreciate.

Negroes flocking to the Union lines in Kentucky during 1863 sang and shouted in joy. A Union soldier observed that "Massa Lincoln was a saviour that came after two hundred years of tribulation in the cotton fields and cane."[39]

Contrabands at the Washington camp celebrated their first Thanksgiving as free men with an extensive program of music by a brass band, speeches, and a fine dinner.[40]

When the constitutional convention in Louisiana took its stand for the abolition of slavery, a great celebration was in order. Thousands of Negroes assembled. General Banks, Governor Hahn, and other dignitaries were present. There were prayers and speeches and songs, followed by a procession through the streets. With banners and flags flying, the crowd paraded singing

[37] *Leslie's Illus. News*, Feb. 8, 1862; N.Y. *Tribune*, Dec. 29, 1862; George Alfred Townsend, *Campaigns of a Non-Combatant* (N.Y., 1866), pp. 248-49; Charles Carleton Coffin, *The Boys of '61* (Boston, 1887), p. 260; Commager, ed., *The Blue and the Gray*, II, 949.

[38] Moncure Daniel Conway, *Autobiography, Memories and Experiences* (Boston and New York, 1904), I, 377 ff.; Bartlett, *Wendell Phillips*, pp. 256-58; William M. Stewart to Lincoln, Mar. 20, 1864, R. T. Lincoln Coll., 31701-2.

[39] Commager, ed., *The Blue and the Gray*, I, 470.

[40] Stoddard, *Lincoln's Third Secretary*, p. 189.

Slavery's chain is bound to break,
And Master and I must part

- - - - - - - - - - - -

Our ransomed race is bound to take
The road that leads to light.

- - - - - - - - - - - -

Louisiana's star is shining bright,
And now we all are free.[41]

And in Washington, members of the Colored Odd Fellows Organization, with a band playing "Columbia, the Gem of the Ocean" and the "Star-Spangled Banner" paraded to the White House to honor the President; four colored men attended the New Year's Reception on the first anniversary of Emancipation, and two colored surgeons were present at a reception in February (unthinkable a year before, commented one newspaper); colored schoolchildren picnicked at the White House grounds on the Fourth of July and a month later Negroes gathered there to observe a day of humiliation and prayer; in September a group of Negroes from Baltimore called to present a handsome Bible to the President, and at election time in November he was again serenaded by Negro paraders with a band; on Inauguration Day, 1865, colored troops marched in the parade, and Frederick Douglass was greeted most cordially at the reception the same evening.[42]

In the meantime, a notable step forward had been taken in the Congress. The House, on January 31, 1865, finally approved the Thirteenth Amendment. This Lincoln had long wished for and worked for. It was, he said to a huge crowd of serenaders the next evening, an indispensable step forward and a "great moral victory."

But he also reminded his audience that the task was not completed—that only when the required number of

---

[41] N.Y. *Herald*, June 19, 1864.
[42] Washington *Evening Star*, Oct. 9, 1863, Feb. 24, 1864; Washington *Daily Morning Chronicle*, Jan. 1, 1864; Cincinnati *Gazette*, Jan. 4, July 6, 1864; Sacramento *Daily Union*, Dec. 2, 1864; Douglass, *Frederick Douglass*, pp. 365-66.

states had ratified the amendment would slavery be completely and forever eliminated from the land.[43]

Ratification, he was pleased to say, had already begun, and his own state of Illinois had been the first. It would only be a matter of time.

On December 18, 1865, the Thirteenth Amendment was officially proclaimed a part of the Constitution. *All slaves were now free.*

Lincoln was not there—or was he?

During the war a group of slaves had gathered alongside the fence of their plantation to watch the Union Army march by. An old Negro asked where Lincoln was. The soldiers said that Lincoln was way back at the rear. He would be along tomorrow in his chariot. Whereupon the Negroes began to sing—

> Don't you see them coming, coming, coming—
> Millions from the other shore?
> Glory! Glory! Hallelujah!
> Bless the Lord forevermore!
>
> Don't you see them going, going, going—
> Past old master's mansion door?
> Glory! Glory! Hallelujah!
> Bless the Lord forevermore!
>
> Jordan's stream is running, running, running—
> Million soldiers passing o'er;
> Lincoln coming with his chariot.
> Bless the Lord forevermore!
>
> Don't you hear him coming, coming?
> Yes, I do!
> With his robe and mighty army?
> Yes, I do!
> Want to march with him to glory?
> Yes, I do![44]

And so it was. The humble slaves by the roadside with their faith and hope could both see and hear—it was as clear as if written across the sky—

> Lincoln coming with his chariot—
> Bless the Lord forevermore!

---

[43] Lincoln, *Works*, VIII, 253-55.
[44] Small, ed., *Road to Richmond*, pp. 95-96.

CHAPTER XI

". . . THE LITTLE SAD SONG"

ON OCTOBER 1, 1862, THE PRESIDENT SET OUT ON WHAT proved to be his most strenuous trip since his inauguration. At six o'clock that morning (without having had any breakfast), together with several friends including Ward Lamon, John W. Garrett, and two prominent Illinoisans, General John A. McClernand and Ozias M. Hatch, he left Washington by train headed for Harpers Ferry and Antietam.

Arriving at Harpers Ferry about noon, the Chief Executive immediately began a series of inspections, reviews, observations, and interviews that occupied the better part of four days. Up and down hills, across fields and through woods, following rough bumpy roads or no roads at all, the party went, mostly on horseback, occasionally in an ambulance wagon.

That first afternoon, escorted by General Sumner and accompanied by General McClellan, who had ridden over from his headquarters, the party climbed to Bolivar Heights for a review. Then down again to Harpers Ferry they went, to inspect the somewhat battered town and there to spend the night.

The following day, after climbing Loudoun Heights, the visitors crossed the Potomac and ascended Maryland Heights, reviewing more troops at each place. General McClellan met the President and his friends during the day and conducted them to his headquarters. That night and the next, Lincoln slept in a tent beside that of "Little Mac."

On the third day, troop reviews again occupied most of the time, with considerable distances covered in getting from one camp to another.

Much of the time on Saturday, October 4, was spent in visiting wounded soldiers, Union and Confederate, and two wounded generals. Finally that afternoon the party boarded a train at Frederick and arrived back in Washington at ten o'clock in the evening.[1]

It had been an exhausting trip. In addition to the full schedule of reviews and consultations, the rugged terrain and the hours on horseback, weather conditions added to the physical discomfort. An extremely hot spell had settled over the region and the temperature was abnormally high; at times clouds of dust rose and covered the riders, and to make matters worse, the air was heavy, humid, and moist. The tent in which Lincoln slept may have been cool at night, but the days were quite the opposite.[2]

There were, however, some lighter moments and some gratifying compensations. At South Mountain an old farmer was selling cider. Here was a welcome chance to quench one's thirst! The President was invited to partake, but at first refused. When the old farmer avowed that it was "prime Union cider," Lincoln finally accepted some. But he did not care for it and made a wry face, such a wry face that the entire party was greatly amused and had a good laugh at the President's expense![3]

Less amusing, perhaps, but quite impressive to the staff officers who witnessed it, was the President's demonstration of horsemanship. He expressed interest in a fine black horse and wished to ride it. General Sumner had doubts and remarked that the animal was a bit high-

---

[1] Edward S. Delaplaine, "Lincoln's Companions on the Trip to Antietam," *Lincoln Herald*, LVI (Fall, 1954), 3-10; *Lincoln Lore*, No. 1277 (Sept. 28, 1953). The days of the week are incorrectly given in this otherwise useful summary of the trip.

[2] N.Y. *Times*, Oct. 5, 1862; N.Y. *World*, Oct. 7, 1862; N.Y. *Herald*, Oct. 7, 1862. The *Herald* reporter observed that the President left his pleasant summer home and went up to Antietam, thus subjecting himself to inconvenience and exhausting riding up and down mountains for three or four days in the broiling sun. On Friday, October 3, he had reviewed twelve divisions and ridden forty miles, and it was evening when he returned to headquarters. He would not do it, said the reporter, if he didn't consider it very important.

O. M. Hatch commented on the heat also. Cf. Browne, *Every-Day Life of Lincoln*, II, 417-18. The President himself mentioned the heat on Friday, October 3. Lincoln's own account of the Antietam visit, Ward Hill Lamon Papers, Huntington Library; Ward Hill Lamon, *Recollections of Abraham Lincoln, 1847-1865* (Chicago, 1895), chap. IX.

[3] London *Herald*, Nov. 11, 1862.

spirited. Some of the staff officers likewise anticipated that the Chief Executive might have trouble. But Lincoln laughingly said that a high-spirited horse would be more interesting and swung into the saddle. The horse started to prance and turn, but only for a moment. Under the firm and experienced rein of the President, the animal soon became quiet and amenable. The President had no trouble; both the horse and the officers who were watching knew who was the master of the situation.[4]

The reviews, although tedious, were spectacular and exciting—row after row of men drawn up in formation, some regiments badly depleted by losses in the recent battle, many uniforms showing the wear and tear of conflict, many flags torn by shot and shell.

As the presidential party appeared for each review, cannon roared in salute. The men were in good spirits, and as the cannon belched forth noise and smoke, the drums rolled and the troops gave cheer after cheer. One correspondent, catching the excitement of the occasion, wrote: "We had a grand review yesterday; the President paid us a visit, and such cheering when he and George B. came along, ain't been heard in a long time. . . ."[5]

A private in the ranks reported that even a long tiresome delay did not lessen the men's interest in the President's coming. His regiment had been in line all Thursday afternoon and had waited until dark, but the President did not appear; on Friday morning the men were again in formation, but still no President. It was three o'clock in the afternoon before Lincoln and General McClellan arrived to review the men! Nevertheless, in spite of the long wait, the soldiers cheered heartily as the President rode by, lifting his tall hat and smiling "a good honest homely smile."[6]

And from the confusion and pageantry rose the music that the President loved, the music of the bands. They played "Hail to the Chief!," "Hail, Columbia," "Columbia,

---

[4] Browne, *Every-Day Life of Lincoln*, II, 415-16; S. S. Sumner, "General Sumner and Lincoln," *The Magazine of History*, XXXIX (1929), 38 (Extra Number 153).
[5] N.Y. *Sunday Mercury*, Oct. 5, 1862.
[6] Chicago *Times*, Oct. 13, 1862.

the Gem of the Ocean," "Lo, the Conquering Hero Comes," and other well-known airs.

In addition, as the President's party entered McClellan's headquarters at the end of the second day, a band greeted him with "Hail to the Chief!," and that same evening the band of the Second Cavalry serenaded him "with some fine selections."[7]

In spite of the heat, dust, wind, and threatened shower, the people of Frederick turned out in large numbers to greet the President when he arrived there on Saturday afternoon. Houses were decorated, flags were flying, and the crowd cheered enthusiastically. Twice there were calls for a speech. The first time the President declined, but the second time, as his train was about ready to depart, he made a few remarks that were not only appropriate but which clearly showed his gratitude to the people of the state that earlier had given him some anxious moments. Perhaps he was surprised also, as was one newspaper reporter present, at the strong Union sentiment among the people.[8] He said:

FELLOW-CITIZENS: I see myself surrounded by soldiers, and a little further off I note the citizens of this good city of Frederick, anxious to hear something from me. I can only say, as I did five minutes ago, it is not proper for me to make speeches in my present position. I return thanks to our soldiers for the good service they have rendered, for the energies they have shown, the hardships they have endured, and the blood they have so nobly shed for this dear Union of ours; and I also return thanks not only to the soldiers, but to the good citizens of Maryland, and to all the good men and women in this land, for their devotion to our glorious cause. I say this without any malice in my heart to those who have done otherwise. May our children and our children's children to a thousand generations, continue to enjoy the benefits conferred upon us by a united country, and have cause yet to rejoice under those glorious institutions bequeathed us by Washington and his compeers. Now, my friends, soldiers and citizens, I can only say once more, farewell.[9]

---

[7] Washington *Evening Star*, Oct. 3, 4, 1862; N.Y. *Herald*, Oct. 7, 1862; N.Y. *Times*, Oct. 3, 5, 1862.

[8] N.Y. *Commercial Advertiser*, Oct. 5, 6, 1862; N.Y. *Herald*, Oct. 5, 6, 1862; N.Y. *Times*, Oct. 6, 1862; N.Y. *World*, Oct. 6, 7, 1862.

[9] Lincoln, *Works*, V, 450.

But all in all, this expedition, unlike most of Lincoln's visits to the army, did not really revive his spirit and restore his good humor. He did tell a few of his characteristic anecdotes, and one evening at dinner he kept the company in the best of humor by his apt remarks and amusing stories, but for the most part, he was sober and quiet, and seemed careworn, weary, and troubled, and he seldom smiled. How could he be otherwise after viewing such scenes as that described by a correspondent who accompanied the President's party.

> The battlefield was an object of particular interest to the President. Hundreds of dead horses, many of which had been burned, were lying on the field. Hundreds of human graves, where the dead of both armies lay buried, were seen at different points on the ground. The field was still strewn with the clothing of the wounded and dead. In one place there was a monster grave, over which there was this inscription— "Here lies the body of General Anderson and eighty rebels," and on another mound we could read by the early moonlight— "Here lie the bodies of sixty rebels. The wages of sin is death."[10]

How could he be otherwise after his visit to wounded Generals Hartsuff and Richardson and to the dozens of men, Union and Confederate, suffering and dying in the hospital camps?[11]

---

[10] O. O. Howard, Scrapbook, "General O. O. Howard's Personal Reminiscences of the War of the Rebellion," chap. XXI, Bowdoin College Library; N.Y. *Tribune*, Oct. 4, 1862; Sacramento *Daily Union*, Oct. 27, 1862; O. M. Hatch in Browne, *Every-Day Life of Lincoln*, II, 417; Albert Deane Richardson, *The Secret Service, the Field, the Dungeon, and the Escape* (Hartford, 1865), p. 291; N.Y. *Herald*, Oct. 7, 1862.

[11] Two of the most graphic accounts of the visit to the hospitals came from sources ordinarily very hostile to the President. Both, however, stressed Mr. Lincoln's attention to the *Confederate* wounded. His visit to them was at his own request. He shook hands with many, saying ". . . many on both sides must necessarily become victims; but although they (the wounded Confederates) were our enemies by circumstances that are now uncontrollable, he bore them no malice, and could take them by the hand with as much feeling and sympathy as if they were brothers." After all who could walk had come forward and shaken hands with the President and General McClellan, they then went to those who were in bed, and both ". . . *knelt down beside the unfortunate rebel sufferers, smoothed their aching temples, cheered them in their afflictions with words of comfort, bade them be of good cheer, and assured them that every possible care should be given them to ameliorate their condition*." There was not a dry eye, either Union or Confederate. Chicago *Times*, Oct. 10, 1862. One very sick Confederate soldier who was amazed to learn with whom he had just shaken hands said, "There should be no enemies in this place." London *Herald*, Nov. 11, 1862.
It is of interest that on Friday, October 3, Lincoln posed for the several group photographs that have since become so well known. Even though he was following a strenuous schedule and was under great strain, he appears relaxed, poised, calm and confident in the photographs. His inner strength is clearly evident.

Moreover, during the entire four-day excursion, the President seemed preoccupied—he had a number of things on his mind. There was the knotty question of whether parolees could be used to protect the people of Minnesota from the aroused Indians who were causing trouble there. Parolees were restless, especially at Camp Chase and Camp Douglas, and significant numbers of troops had to be detailed to keep them in order. And as with so many problems, Lincoln got little help from Halleck and others upon whom he depended in such matters.[12]

But in particular the condition of the Army of the Potomac bothered the Chief Executive. After Second Bull Run came the removal of Pope and restoration of McClellan. In September he was dismayed by the great number of deserters and stragglers.[13] While at Antie-

---

[12] Both the question of using paroled Union soldiers and the Indian uprising in Minnesota had been hanging fire for some time. Governor Ramsey of Minnesota had urged the use of parolees in August and Governor Tod of Ohio had suggested it in September, stressing the difficulty of preserving order at Camp Chase. Lincoln urged Stanton to do something about it, pointing out that four good regiments were necessary to guard the 20,000 parolees at Annapolis alone. These four regiments could be used for more active duty if the parolees were sent to Minnesota. Lincoln, *Works*, V, 432, and note.

Lincoln's often encountered difficulty in obtaining clear-cut advice from General Halleck is illustrated by the exchange of telegrams on this question on October 3 and 4, while Lincoln was at Antietam. At 8:00 A.M. on the third, Lincoln telegraphed Halleck asking his opinion concerning the use of parolees for fighting the Indians. Lincoln, *Works*, V, 449. Halleck replied that he resolved there was "nothing against" Lincoln's proposal. Later in the day he reversed himself and informed Lincoln that the cartel agreement for paroled prisoners prohibited *all* military duty. The following day (October 4) he again reversed himself and said that after consultation with Stanton and Holt he concluded that the cartel did *not* prohibit using parolees against the Indians. *O. R.*, Ser. II, Vol. IV, 593, 594, 598. Thus the matter was unsettled when the President returned to Washington. Finally, on October 14, Adjutant General Thomas gave his opinion that parolees could not be used against the Indians. *Ibid.*, 621; Lincoln, *Works*, V, 432, n. Four days later Attorney General Bates affirmed that the terms of the cartel were explicit—parolees could not be used for any military duty. *Ibid.*, 449.

As for the Indian problem in Minnesota, that dragged on until the year's end. The atrocities committed by the Indians were shocking and aroused much public indignation. Cf. *Leslie's Illus. News*, Oct. 25, 1862. In his annual message in December the President estimated that eight hundred persons had been killed by them. Three hundred captured Indians were condemned to death by a military commission. From time to time during the busy months of November and December the President gave attention to the problem and procrastinated on giving assent to the mass execution. Review of the commission findings reduced the number to 38. These were publicly hanged on December 26 at Manketo, Minnesota. A stone monument today marks the site of the execution. Lincoln, *Works*, V, 493 *et passim*; VI, 7, n.; *O. R.*, Ser. I, XXII, Pt. 2, 8801; *Lincoln Lore*, No. 1250 (Mar. 23, 1953). A report in a New Hampshire paper from the St. Paul *Press* described the execution in detail. As the Indians were being bound and made ready, they broke into their death song; as they went up the gallows they took it up again, and "the noise they made was truly hideous." Then there was silence; the scaffold fell; the onlookers gave one cheer of relief, and it was over. The *New Hampshire Sentinel* (Keene), Jan. 29, 1863.

[13] Hughes, ed., *John Murray Forbes*, I, 329.

tam he jotted down figures on the men in the army there,[14] and on Friday morning he arose very early and went for a walk to a nearby hill with his friend O. M. Hatch.

It was a beautiful morning. There was no sound except the singing of the birds and faint voices from distant farms. A private, writing later, described the scene:

> Friday morning the sun rose clear and bright, promising a warm but pleasant day. . . . The scene was very beautiful. Far as the eye could reach were stretched long lines of troops, their bayonets glittering and flashing in the golden sun. A few fleecy clouds were floating lazily across the sky, their shadows resting on the distant mountain sides, while a soft and gentle breeze dallied with the green and golden autumn leaves, and caused the battle-stained and tattered banners of our legions to stream out gaily and gallantly above us.[15]

Lincoln saw not the beauty of the morning, but waving his hand toward the scene of the camp spread out before them, said in a voice that was almost a whisper, "Hatch, Hatch, what is all this?"

Hatch replied, "Why, Mr. Lincoln, this is the Army of the Potomac."

Lincoln hesitated, straightened up, and said, more loudly than before, "No, Hatch, no. This is *General McClellan's bodyguard.*"

Nothing more was said, and the two men turned and walked back to the camp. The incident was an eloquent revelation of the depth of the President's concern for the Army of the Potomac and the cause for which it stood.[16]

As the day progressed Lincoln's mood did not change. While proceeding in an ambulance toward General Porter's camp after visiting General Burnside's corps, he said to Ward Lamon, "Lamon, sing one of your sad little songs."

Lamon had often sung for Lincoln. Back in Illinois many an hour on the circuit or in some local hostelry after a busy day in court had been enlivened by his "home-

---

[14] Lincoln, *Works*, V, 448.

[15] Chicago *Times*, Oct. 13, 1862.

[16] Browne, *Every-Day Life of Lincoln*, II, 417-18 ; John G. Nicolay and John Hay, *Abraham Lincoln: A History* (N.Y., 1914), VI, 174-75 ; *Lincoln Lore*, No. 1277 (Sept. 28, 1953).

ly renditions." Sometimes he sang jolly nonsense songs, and again in an instant he would change the mood of the entire company, judge and lawyers alike, with a sentimental ballad or a "little sad song."

During the tedious journey to Washington in February, 1861, Lamon with his banjo had brought relaxation to the anxious President-elect, and often at the White House when they were alone his singing was a welcome relief from the tensions of the war.[17]

Consequently, Lamon well knew what would please the President when this request was made, and he sang one of Lincoln's favorites—"Twenty Years Ago."

As Lamon finished the song, Lincoln's sadness deepened, and in order to bring him out of his melancholy, Lamon did what he had done many a time before—he sang snatches of a comic song or two.

This was all, and the party continued with what the President later called ". . . a very hard, hot, and dirty day's work."[18]

If the comic song cheered the President, it was only temporarily. The somber mood of concern, compassion and distress which gripped him during the trip carried over after his return. Two days later, on Sunday, October 5, a fellow-worshipper at the New York Avenue Presbyterian Church was profoundly impressed by Lincoln's appearance and attitude. He wrote:

> In all my experience I have never seen such an expression on a human face. The quiet solemnity of the service, the orderly dismission of the congregation—there was no gaping crowd watching the President—all tended to natural repose of feature, and the result was a pathos of sadness that had in it an expression more nearly the Christ ideal than I have ever seen in art or in any other person.[19]

As time went on, conditions did not improve. Difficulty piled upon difficulty for the President. He prodded Mc-

---

[17] Carl Sandburg, *Abraham Lincoln: The War Years* (N.Y., 1939), I, 63; Lamon, *Recollections of Lincoln*, pp. 146-48.

[18] From the accounts written by Lamon and by the President in 1864. Lamon Papers.

[19] Wilson, *An Unofficial Statesman*, pp. 60-61.

Clellan, he made another memorandum on the Army of the Potomac, but, as Gideon Welles wrote in his *Diary*, ". . . the army is quiet, reposing in camp. The country groans, but nothing is done."[20] Finally, McClellan was replaced by Burnside, and the result was the disastrous carnage at Fredericksburg (echoed, one might say, from Stone's River in Tennessee).

Added to the desperate military situation was the setback for the administration in the fall elections, and in mid-December came the Cabinet crisis which, according to Senator Browning, distressed the President more than any event of his life. In despair, Lincoln said to Browning, "We are now on the brink of destruction. It appears to me the Almighty is against us, and I can hardly see a ray of hope."[21]

This, it has been said, was Lincoln's "darkest hour," the climax of weeks of gloom and disappointment. There were in these weeks but two brief musical moments to lighten the picture. On October 22 the President went down to Alexandria by boat to review the troops commanded by General Sickles. Escorted by the Thirty-Fourth Massachusetts Infantry and accompanied by some two hundred mounted officers, he witnessed the imposing parade while drums rolled and bands played. Later he visited a convalescents' camp, a parolees' camp, and a stragglers' camp, returning to the White House at dusk.[22]

A few days earlier George Washington Morrison Nutt appeared at the White House, having been invited to call by the President.

"Commodore" Nutt, as he was popularly known, was a protégé of P. T. Barnum, and one of several midgets then being featured on the entertainment stage. He had been engaged by Barnum for three years for the sum of $30,000 and was dubbed "Barnum's $30,000 Nutt."

According to newspaper advertisements, two hundred

---

[20] Lincoln, *Works*, V, 469-70 ; Morse, ed., *Diary of Gideon Welles*, I, 176.

[21] Pease and Randall, eds., *Diary of O. H. Browning*, I, 600-601. Secretary Welles thought that the President had managed his own case in the Cabinet crisis admirably. Morse, ed., *Diary of Gideon Welles*, I, 197.

[22] Washington *Evening Star*, Oct. 25, 1862 ; N.Y. *Herald*, Oct. 23, 1862 ; William S. Lincoln, *Life with the Thirty-Fourth Massachusetts Infantry in the War of the Rebellion* (Worcester, 1879), p. 48.

thousand had seen him in New York and thought him the most bewitching and enchanting little man ever seen. He was said to be the smallest living man and a remarkable entertainer—

> The Songs, Dances, Drum Playing, Grecian Statues and Comic Performances of this King of the Pigmies, in Various Costumes, astonish and delight all who behold them.

Lincoln greeted the "Commodore" cordially and introduced him to the members of the Cabinet then in session. The Commodore was in the best of spirits and upon request demonstrated his talents for the audience by singing "Columbia, the Gem of the Ocean."

As the "manly little Commodore" was about to depart, Lincoln, according to Barnum, joked with him, saying: "Commodore, permit me to give you a parting word of advice. When you are in command of your fleet, if you find yourself in danger of being taken prisoner, I advise you to wade ashore."

Nutt replied, gazing upwards the length of Lincoln: "I guess, Mr. President, you could do that better than I could."[23]

It was Mrs. Lincoln, however, on a trip to New York and Boston in October and November, who was favored with more music than was her husband! On the evening of October 25, a crowd estimated at three thousand gathered outside the Metropolitan Hotel where she was staying. There were repeated cheers for Mrs. Lincoln and also for Generals Scott, McClellan, and Anderson (and

---

[23] Washington *Evening Star*, Oct. 17, 1862; N.Y. *World*, Oct. 18, 1862; *Struggles and Triumphs; or Forty Years' Recollections of P. T. Barnum, Written by Himself* (Buffalo, 1871), chap. 36. Some newspapers gave additional "details" on the visit, stating that Secretary Welles claimed jurisdiction over the "Commodore" as lord of the sea, Secretary Chase promised to recommend him as his successor in view of his ability to make money, but, even so, he doubted that Nutt could make it as fast as Secretary Stanton could spend it. N.Y. *Tribune*, Oct. 18, 1862; Chicago *Times*, Oct. 23, 1862.

There was considerable rivalry among the several midgets of the times. Nutt and "General Tom Thumb" had been suitors for the hand of Lavinia Warren. "The General" won, and he and Miss Warren were married in New York City on February 10, 1863. The newlyweds went the "Commodore" one better at the White House also, for they were guests there at a reception and stayed overnight. Washington *Daily Morning Chronicle*, Feb. 14, 1863; Washington *Evening Star*, Feb. 14, 1863. However, neither the "General" nor his bride was invited to sing for the President as the "Commodore" had done. Two other rivals, then playing at Nixon's Garden Circus, were "Those Men of Miniature, Samsons in Intellect! Commodore Foot with his Little Companion, Col. Small." Washington *Evening Star*, Oct. 24, 1862.

three groans for General Frémont). From 9:30 until 10:30 the band from the U.S.S. *North Carolina* gave a concert which included the "Star-Spangled Banner," "Hail, Columbia," two operatic selections, a galop, and "Yankee Doodle." Toward the end Mrs. Lincoln appeared and waved to the crowd, and a spokesman thanked the band for her.[24]

A few days later Mrs. Lincoln was the guest of honor at a party on the *North Carolina*, then at the Brooklyn Navy Yard. Her entourage, which included generals, judges, an admiral and an archbishop, went out to the vessel at one o'clock and climbed the long side ladders with the band playing vigorously "to enliven the tedious ascent."

During lunch the band provided more music, and the daughter of the ship's captain sang a "sweet song." Then, lunch finished, the party went to the poop deck there to be favored with a concert of operatic music. As some of the young people present wanted to dance, the band swung into waltzes, schottisches, and polkas. The sailors were fascinated by the dancers and the dancing, for the scene was somewhat novel on the decks of the good ship *North Carolina*.

At four o'clock, amid cheers from the sailors, music by the band, and the smoke and roar of a fifteen-gun salute, the party left. An hour's boat ride in the harbor and up the East River to see an ironclad under construction ended the day's outing. Mrs. Lincoln, subject to so much unjust criticism, had reason to be pleased with the attention given her on this very pleasant occasion."[25]

From New York Mrs. Lincoln went on to Boston to see her son Robert. During her stay she was visited by Governor Andrew, Senators Sumner and Wilson, Julia Ward Howe and Professor Agassiz, and on Monday eve-

---

[24] Washington *Evening Star*, Oct. 28, 1862; N.Y. *Herald*, Oct. 26, 1862; N. Y. *Tribune*, Oct. 26, 27, 1862; *Harper's Weekly*, Nov. 8, 1862.

[25] N.Y. *Herald*, Oct. 30, 1862; N.Y. *Tribune*, Oct. 30, 1862. The New York correspondent of the London *Herald*, always critical, wrote: "They say she rules Old Abe, and as he rules us, I do not known why Madame is not entitled to a salute." London *Herald*, Nov. 15, 1862.

ning, November 10, was serenaded by a band and a cheering crowd that gathered outside the Parker House.[26]

Upon her return to Washington, Mrs. Lincoln again gave her attention to the sick and wounded soldiers in the hospitals. Ever since the previous summer she had maintained an increasing interest in them, visiting the hospitals and providing fruits and delicacies for the sufferers. So effective were her ministrations in this work that a Boston merchant contributed one thousand dollars for her use, and other gifts were received from time to time.[27]

The Christmas season in the city that winter was anything but joyous, but the well-organized plan for providing Christmas dinners for all the hospitals, in which Mrs. Lincoln participated wholeheartedly, brought comfort and gratitude to many a suffering and homesick soldier.

Mrs. Caleb B. Smith, wife of the Secretary of the Interior, made the arrangements and supervised the entire project. One or two ladies had charge of each hospital. Through printed circulars and personal appeals donations of money and food were solicited.

Shipments of food arrived in large amounts, including an estimated seven thousand turkeys and chickens from as far away as Chicago. Three hundred turkeys from Albany were precooked and ready to serve when they arrived! Each hospital had prepared an estimate of its needs, and the supplies were distributed accordingly.

The dinners were a complete success, and every hospital was provided with ample food for the occasion. At the Judiciary Square Hospital, which President and Mrs. Lincoln visited during the festivities, the dining hall was

---

[26] Boston *Post*, Nov. 11, 1862; Detroit *Advertiser*, Nov. 25, 1862. A letter writer to one of the Boston newspapers complained that Mrs. Lincoln and her party had a railroad car all to themselves. This necessitated two trips for the ferry from Jersey City to New York, with the result that the train arrived in Boston at one o'clock in the morning, four hours late in a snowstorm! Thus to accommodate one person forty or fifty other passengers were greatly inconvenienced. She also had a private car on her return trip, the writer added. Boston *Courier*, Nov. 12, 1862.

[27] Sacramento *Daily Union*, Aug. 21, 1862; Washington *Evening Star*, Aug. 29, Oct. 4, 1862; *Weekly Oregonian* (Portland), Sept. 27, 1862; N.Y. *Herald*, Dec. 6, 1862; Lincoln, *Works*, V, 377-78; Stoddard, *Inside the White House*, pp. 87-88; Ruth Painter Randall, *Mary Lincoln: Biography of a Marriage* (Boston, 1953), pp. 299-301.

gaily decorated with evergreens, flowers, and red, white, and blue streamers. Five hundred sat down to the dinner. The menu included ". . . turkeys, chickens, roast beef, mutton, hams, oysters, side dishes, vegetables of all sorts, apples, raisins, grapes, pies, &c, &c, all of which were displayed on tables spread with neat white tablecloths, and shining dishes, knives, and forks."

Mrs. Lincoln had done more than her share to make the dinners a success. Early in the month she had begun making inquiries at the hospitals to ascertain what the soldiers most desired (chicken and turkey proved to be their favorites). She then set up a receiving and distributing center at the White House for the quantities of food that came in, and she contributed, not to one hospital, but to two, the Judiciary Square and Thirteenth Street Baptist Church hospitals. In addition, she donated generously to the special menu for the five hundred residents of the contraband camp.[28]

Thus, as the year 1862, with its disappointments and failures came to an end, Mary Lincoln's Yuletide activities had brought a warm glow of comfort and a revival of spirit to hospitalized soldiers and homeless Negroes in the capital city.

The President, at the depths of distress and despair earlier in the month, had a revival of spirit also. There had come to his attention a pamphlet, written by a loyal Unionist who had likewise been greatly discouraged by the events of the year. This loyal citizen, in his own discouragement, turning to history, to the struggle of the English forces in the Peninsula Campaign of the Na-

---

[28] N.Y. *Herald*, Dec. 9, 24, 25, 1862; Washington *Evening Star*, Dec. 26, 1862; N.Y. *Times*, Dec. 26, 1862; Washington *Daily Morning Chronicle*, Dec. 27, 1862; Lamon Papers, Box 13 (Aug. 15-Dec. 31, 1862) (Printed circular soliciting donations and letter, Mrs. C. B. Smith to Mrs. Ward Lamon asking for a contribution); Letters to the *Des Moines State Register*, Dec. 13, 28, 1862, in *Iowa Jour. of Hist.*, LII (Jan., 1954), 72-73. According to one report, Mrs. Lincoln distributed over three tons of poultry, several hundred bushels of apples and cranberries, and large amounts of butter, coffee and other supplies to the hospitals, all on Dec. 24! N.Y. *Tribune*, Dec. 25, 1862.

Where else but in America, one reporter philosophized, would there be such a scene—35,000 sick and wounded served Christmas dinner in gaily decorated halls, waited on by men and ladies of the first families, entertained by singers singing songs of home and country and by speeches from Congressmen and Cabinet officers. And there, among the visitors, was the Chief Executive himself. Wherever he went, he brought "excitement and sunshine . . . among the bandaged and becrutched revelers." *New Hampshire Sentinel* (Keene), Jan. 1, 1863.

poleonic War, had written an essay on the war which he entitled *How a Free People Conduct a Long War.*

It was this essay, a copy of which the author, Charles J. Stillé, of Philadelphia, sent to the President, that revived his spirit.[29] Impressed by Stillé's forceful demonstration of how the English people, in spite of the gloom and defeatism spread by carping critics, sustained their government and saw the campaign through to a successful conclusion, Lincoln wrote to the author:

EXECUTIVE MANSION
WASHINGTON, December 31, 1862
C. J. Stillé, Esq.
SIR:
Your letter of the 27th and pamphlet were duly received, and for which please accept my sincere thanks.

The pamphlet is far the best production upon the subject it treats which I have seen. The reading, and re-reading of it has afforded me great pleasure, and I believe also some profit. May I express the hope that you will not allow your pen to rest?

Your Obt Servt
A. LINCOLN[30]

That the carping critics of his own administration would continue their attacks, the President fully expected. But that they would descend to the level that was reached a year and a half later was scarcely anticipated.

Of all the attacks that would be made on Lincoln and his work during the campaign of 1864, the most unscrupulous, unfair, and distorted would stem back to an incident that took place during his visit to Antietam in October, 1862.

The nature of the attack was forecast in a newspaper item that appeared about a week after the President read Stillé's pamphlet. It said:

By the bye, it is a fact that President Lincoln, when he visited the battle-field of Antietam, before the corpses had

[29] Charles J. Stillé, *How a Free People Conduct a Long War: A Chapter from English History* (Philadelphia, 1862). The essay, in pamphlet form, was widely distributed; 250,000 copies of it were printed.

[30] A. Lincoln to C. J. Stillé, Dec. 31, 1862, Pennsylvania Historical Society. Cf. Joseph George, Jr., "Charles J. Stillé, 'Angel of Consolation,'" *Penn. Mag. of Hist. and Biog.*, LXXXV (July, 1961), 303-15, and Joseph George, Jr., "A Recently Discovered Lincoln Letter," *Lincoln Herald*, LXIV (Winter, 1962), 191-93.

been buried, called upon an officer, who had been reported to him as a good singer, to "step out and sing me a song," and then in an open plain, in hearing of the dying, and in sight of the sightless dead, the officer sung for the President of the United States "Jim along, Josey."

- -

What a splendid, but much abused, ruler old Nero was. His tyranny never slaughtered as many bodies as Lincoln's incompetency, and though he fiddled while Rome was burning, he never called out one of his officers to sing "Jim along, Josey."[31]

And this and much more because the war-burdened President, while riding in an ambulance at Antietam in October, 1862, made the simple request of Ward Lamon that he sing "the little sad song"—

I've wandered to the village Tom,
I've sat beneath the tree;
Upon the schoolhouse playing ground
Which sheltered you and me.
But none were there to greet me Tom;
And few were left to know,
That played with us upon the grass,
Some twenty years ago.

- - - - - - - - - - - - - - - -

Near by the spring, upon an elm,
You know I cut your name,
Your sweetheart's just beneath it, Tom,
And you did mine the same;
Some heartless wretch had peeled the bark
'Twas dying sure but slow,
Just as that one, whose name was cut,
Died twenty years ago.

- - - - - - - - - - - - - - - -

Some now are in the churchyard laid
Some sleep beneath the sea,
But few are left of our old class,
Excepting you and me;
And when our time shall come dear Tom,
And we are called to go,
I hope they'll lay us where we played
Just twenty years ago.

---

[31] This will be dealt with fully in a subsequent chapter.

CHAPTER XII

"TENTING ON THE OLD CAMP GROUND"

DURING THE WINTER OF 1862-63 THE WEATHER IN VIR-
ginia was miserable. It was cold and windy; it rained
and the rain changed to sleet; it snowed and the snow
changed to rain. And always—or almost always—there
was the mud, Virginia mud— ". . . waves and tides of
mud, sudden as the sea, and about as deep in spots."[1]

The Army of the Potomac, its morale and spirit at a
low ebb after the bitter defeat at Fredericksburg, set up
winter quarters in the old familiar area from Aquia Creek
to the Rappahannock. The soldiers' huts, half logs and
half canvas, with their chimneys of empty barrels which
sometimes caught fire, were reasonably comfortable, but
picket duty, reconnoitering expeditions, foraging and the
ever-necessary drilling, meant long hours and exposure to
the weather and to danger.[2]

The famous "mud march" was the end for General
Burnside, but not for the army.[3] It stayed, and although
the elements did not improve for many weeks, the army
did. It had a new commander, "Fighting Joe" Hooker.

"Hooker," said one officer, "took command of an unhappy army, defeated, despondent, ravaged by desertion,

---

[1] Adin B. Underwood, *The Three Years' Service of the Thirty-Third Massachusetts Infantry Regiment 1862-1865* (Boston, 1881), pp. 14-15. Another veteran of
the Army of the Potomac commented: "One great discomfort in camp was caused
by mud, the soil of Virginia seeming to be peculiarly adapted for making that
delicious compound." Benjamin W. Crowninshield, *A History of the First Regiment
of Massachusetts Cavalry Volunteers* (Boston and New York, 1891), p. 109.

[2] The experience of the Thirty-Third Massachusetts Regiment one day in February 1863, was quite typical. It was ordered out in zero weather, with the snow
falling. It marched six miles. By that time the snow had changed to rain. The
men bivouacked in slush and water, finished the hike in the mud, and proceeded
to build another camp. Underwood, *Thirty-Third Massachusetts Infantry*, pp. 17-18.

[3] "Our march was made over roads that were beaten into quagmires by the
passage of artillery, or over soggy fields and swampy meadows, or through drip-
ping woods. The rain fell now in a slow, exasperating drizzle, and now in drench-
ing torrents. The day went out in water. The night was a black flood." Small,
ed., *Road to Richmond*, p. 78.

unpaid, and stuck in the mud without hope of moving before spring." This army he transformed into a spirited fighting machine. The food service was improved, bakeries were put into operation and vegetables became plentiful. More and better clothing and supplies were made available. Sanitary conditions were improved, hospitals made neat and orderly, and sickness began to lessen.[4]

Discipline was tightened. Sunday observance was enforced, and foraging on the countryside was curbed. Desertion and absence without leave, which had reached alarming numbers (200 a day, and a total of 85,000 in all), began to decline sharply.[5]

Drill was conducted regularly and vigorously when the weather permitted and reviews were held frequently. And, more important, Hooker inaugurated a thorough system of inspection which provided rewards for work well done. Regiments which showed up well were granted more furloughs while regiments which were lax had furloughs and leaves cut sharply. Hooker, himself, appeared at reviews and inspections and saw to it that the new regulations were enforced.[6]

The men in the ranks appreciated the fact that here was a commander who cared for them and who really looked out for their interests. "Ah! the furloughs and vegetables he gave! How he did understand the road to the soldier's heart! How he made out of defeated, discouraged and demoralized men, a cheerful, plucky and defiant army, ready to follow him anywhere! That problem he had before him, and he did it well."[7]

---

[4] Small, ed., *Road to Richmond*, p. 80; Walter H. Hebert, *Fighting Joe Hooker* (Indianapolis and New York, 1944), p. 179.

[5] *O. R.*, Ser. I, Vol. XXV, Pt. II, 55, 78, 89.

[6] Small, ed., *Road to Richmond*, p. 80; Crowninshield, *First Regiment Massachusetts Cavalry*, p. 108; George A. Bruce, *The Twentieth Regiment of Massachusetts Volunteer Infantry 1861-1865* (Boston and New York, 1906), pp. 229-30; Abner Doubleday, *Chancellorsville and Gettysburg* (N.Y., 1882), p. 3; Hebert, *Hooker*, p. 179. On March 5 Headquarters announced that Inspection Reports showed that certain regiments were not up to "a proper state of discipline and efficiency." No more leaves of absence or furloughs were to be given in those regiments and all on leave were to be recalled. Twenty-five regiments plus several batteries from Pennsylvania, New York, Indiana, and Massachusetts were named. The order further singled out several regiments which had good Inspection Reports. These were allowed an increase of furloughs and leaves at the discretion of the Corps Commander. Philadelphia *Evening Bulletin*, Mar. 6, 1863.

[7] Underwood, *Thirty-Third Massachusetts Infantry*, p. 18; Hebert, *Hooker*, p. 179; Philadelphia *Evening Bulletin*, Mar. 3, 1863.

Even some of the officers (Hooker was not so popular with them as with the men) were surprised at the change. Abner R. Small, disturbed by the situation when he departed for two weeks leave in February, noted upon his return that the new spirit was already beginning to show itself! Charles Francis Adams, who had no great respect for Hooker as a man or as a soldier, grudgingly admitted that the commander had brought about considerable improvement in the army.[8]

The monotony of camp life—always a serious problem—was in part offset by such regular but supposedly forbidden activities as gambling and trading with the enemy through the picket lines, by band concerts and amateur theatricals, and by special observances on holidays.

Some regiments fared very well on Thanksgiving and Christmas with turkeys, chicken, and geese from home. Washington's Birthday was celebrated by a snowball fight, six inches of snow having fallen the night before. On Saint Patrick's Day there was activity from morning until night. The day began with religious services, with martial music, and then was given over to races, eating, drinking, and gambling. A "bountiful collation" was served at headquarters at which a number of ladies were present.[9]

A highly attractive and greatly appreciated feature of camp life this winter and spring was the constant influx of visitors. The camps took on an air of festivity whenever visitors appeared. And inevitably, some of the visitors and some of the festivities gave the army unpleasant notoriety which in turn led to strong criticism.

The irascible Count Gurowski who earlier had high

---

[8] Small, ed., *Road to Richmond*, p. 80. Charles Francis Adams' changing attitude is shown in his letters. On Jan. 26, 1863, he wrote to Henry Adams: ". . . Hooker never had their [the soldiers'] confidence." Four days later he reiterated this viewpoint in a letter to his father. By March, however, he felt differently. On the twenty-second of that month he wrote to his brother that the army was improving and that it was in better condition than ever. "And if Hooker continues we may be within sight of Richmond by June 1," he concluded. He thought that Hooker's running his head into a stone wall might do him some good. "Things might be worse," he wrote on May 8. Worthington Chauncey Ford, ed., *A Cycle of Adams Letters 1861-1865* (Boston and New York, 1920), I, 241, 250, 265, 295-96. Philadelphia *Evening Bulletin*, Mar. 20, 1863.

[9] Bruce, *Twentieth Regiment Massachusetts Volunteer Infantry*, pp. 232-33; Underwood, *Thirty-Third Massachusetts Infantry*, p. 16; Crowninshield, *First Regiment Massachusetts Cavalry*, pp. 100-101; Philadelphia *Evening Bulletin*, Mar. 18, 1863.

hopes and some commendation for Hooker wrote in his *Diary* in April:

> I wrote to Hooker imploring him for the sake of the coun-
> try, and for the sake of his good name, to put an end to the
> carousings in his camp, and to sweep out all kind of women,
> be they wives, sisters, sweethearts or the promiscuous rest
> of crinolines.[10]

Severe and sweeping criticism was recorded later by Charles Francis Adams.

> During the winter (1862-63), when Hooker was in com-
> mand, I can say from personal knowledge and experience, that
> the Headquarters of the Army of the Potomac was a place
> to which no self-respecting man liked to go, and no decent
> woman could go. It was a combination of bar-room and
> brothel.[11]

But these criticisms gave a somewhat distorted picture. There were genuine good times in camp, and there were many visitors to the army who had a real interest in the welfare of the men and whose presence, while it may have complicated army routine, did the men a world of good. An elaborate wedding with ten bridesmaids and ten groomsmen which ended with a banquet and a ball provided interest and excitement for some; serenades and receptions during the "ladies season," subject to interruption when regiments were suddenly ordered to duty, broke the routine for others.[12]

More serious—and arduous—was the visit of a Com-

---

[10] Adam Gurowski, *Diary, from March 18, 1862, to October 18, 1863* (N.Y., 1864), II, 170, 180, 199.

[11] Charles Francis Adams, *Charles Francis Adams 1835-1915: An Autobiography* (Boston and New York, 1920), p. 161.

Hooker made some effort, but it was not effective. In March citizens were forbidden within the lines. Philadelphia *Evening Bulletin*, Mar. 6, 1863. That month, the paper noted, most all the females had left the camps but that a few remained and some were still permitted to come. Philadelphia *Evening Bulletin*, Apr. 3, 1863. But in June, Stanton, exasperated, wrote to Hooker: "I have been trying hard to keep the women out of your camp, but finding that they were going in troops, under passes, as they said, from your provost-marshal and commanders, I have given up the job. I think no officer or soldier should have his wife in camp or with the army. In other military districts, the order of the Department excludes them. If you will order them away, and keep your provost-marshal and other officers from issuing passes, not one shall be issued here, and all that profess to come from the Department will be forgeries." *O. R.*, Ser. I, Vol. XXVII, Pt. III, 18.

[12] Allan Nevins, *The War for the Union: The War Becomes Revolution* (N.Y., 1960), II, 435; Underwood, *Thirty-Third Massachusetts Infantry*, p. 105.

mittee of Ladies for the Soldiers' Relief Association of Philadelphia. Early in March the committee arrived at Aquia Creek with forty boxes of gifts and supplies for men in the hospitals.

From Aquia the ladies traveled to Falmouth in a freight car—there was standing room only for the trip which took nearly two hours. That same night they managed to find shelter in the only building in their vicinity. There were no beds available so they sat up all night on chairs!

During their entire stay the weather was miserable, but that did not deter the good ladies from Philadelphia. They visited the camps, talking with the soldiers and distributing their gifts. They found the men in excellent spirits and heard very few complaints.

They came to realize the nearness of the enemy when they heard the church bells ring in Fredericksburg and when the music of a Confederate band came across the river very distinctly.

After spending their last night sleeping in a vacant but dry shed, the committee returned home, its errand of mercy fulfilled.[13]

As March gave way to April in a snowstorm, there was unusual excitment in camp. Preparations were made for the reception of a very important party of visitors. General Hooker ordered a new uniform coat from his tailor in Washington. The President was about to pay a visit to the Army of the Potomac.

Lincoln had had misgivings about Hooker from the beginning, as is shown in his famous letter to the general when he put him in command of the Army of the Potomac. He did not, he told Senator Browning, know what better to do, even though he was not satisfied with Hooker's conduct.[14] That was in January.

During the ensuing two months while Hooker was putting the army in shape, Lincoln was much occupied with other matters—he tried to smooth the ruffled feathers of General Sigel and General Rosecrans, witnessed some experiments with new military devices, gave at-

---

13 Philadelphia *Evening Bulletin*, Mar. 10, 1863.
14 Pease and Randall, eds., *Diary of O. H. Browning*, I, 619-20.

tention to measures passed by Congress, proclaimed amnesty for soldiers absent without leave, and set aside a day of "national humiliation, fasting and prayer."

On the military front, he was much concerned about the impending attack on Charleston. The taking of Charleston would have a strong psychological effect, favorable to the North and damaging to the South. He wanted the city captured.[15]

In that gloomy uncertain winter there was one encouraging development. The social life of the White House family gradually returned to normal after the months of quiet following the death of Willie Lincoln.

Receptions were held Saturdays, sometimes in the afternoon and again in the evening. Mrs. Lincoln received at the afternoon parties which were less formal and more intimate than the crowded evening levees. Mr. Lincoln was present when the pressure of his duties allowed it.

The evening levees, although pleasant, were somewhat of an ordeal for the President. On January 31, the crowd was so great that at one time there were a hundred or more carriages waiting in line outside, and the reception of February 14 was characterized by Benjamin B. French as a "crusher." He thought the crowd the largest he had ever seen at a reception.[16]

But the last formal party of the season climaxed all previous receptions. It was a brilliant occasion, with long lines of people waiting at the doors long before they were opened at eight thirty.

The crowd was estimated at ten thousand persons, ranging from "General Halleck down to the common soldier in patched great coat and muddy boots," and including many ladies of whom it was written—

> The white arms and raven hair
> The braids and bracelets
> The swanlike bosoms and the necklace—

vying with one another in the brilliance of their costumes.

---

[15] See Powell, ed., *Lincoln Day by Day*, III, 168, 169, 171, 172, 176, and Morse, ed., *Diary of Gideon Welles*, I, 236-37, 247, 249, for Lincoln's concern about Charleston during February and March.

[16] Washington *Evening Star*, Jan. 31, 1863; B. B. French to Mrs. Pamela M. French, Feb. 19, 1863, B. B. French Papers.

It took hours for all to reach the President, and even though there were soldiers present to keep order and prevent crowding, "hats, coats, dresses, crinoline and corns suffered terribly." It was midnight before the doors were finally closed.[17]

Mrs. Lincoln seemed to enjoy it all. She was friendly, affable, and poised. She greeted people cordially and made them feel welcome. " 'The Queen' of all this show, Mrs. Lincoln [wrote B. B. French of the final levee], at whose side I stood, was dressed in rich black satin and jewels of the richest kind."[18]

The President, while always cordial, was showing the strain, however. Thus a reporter at the reception on February 21 noted that he looked haggard and careworn, and on the evening of March 2 Jane Swisshelm said, when he greeted her: "May the Lord have mercy on you, poor man, for the people have none."[19]

Mrs. Swisshelm, a strong abolitionist, had been prejudiced against both the President and Mrs. Lincoln before coming to Washington, but she changed her view. She wrote:

> . . . I watched the President and Mrs. Lincoln receive. His sad, earnest, honest face was irresistible in its plea for confidence, and Mrs. Lincoln's manner was so simple and motherly, so unlike that of all Southern women I had seen, that I doubted the tales I had heard.[20]

This was a refreshing contrast to the sour and unfair remarks made by another visitor shortly afterward who, commenting on the city being full of sick and wounded soldiers, on the seizure of vehicles for use as ambulances, on great war meetings being held, ended her observations caustically ". . . and the lady of the President has had the taste to hold balls and levees in the midst of reverses most appalling."[21]

---

[17] Washington *Evening Star*, Mar. 3, 1863; Washington *Daily Morning Chronicle*, Mar. 3, 1863; N.Y. *Herald*, Mar. 3, 1863; French, ed., *Diary of B. B. French*, p. 119 (Mar. 3, 1863).

[18] N.Y. *Herald*, Feb. 22, 1863; French, ed., *Diary of B. B. French*, p. 120 (Mar. 3, 1863).

[19] Jane Grey Swisshelm, *Half a Century* (Chicago, 1880), p. 236.

[20] Swisshelm, *Half a Century*, p. 236.

[21] "Richmond and Washington during the War," *Cornhill Magazine*, VII (Jan.-June, 1863), 97.

Mrs. Lincoln had callers more frequently now, including Mrs. Gustavus Fox, whom she greatly enjoyed, and General and Mrs. Heintzelman. Dinner guests included General Butler and two longtime friends, Dr. Anson G. Henry and James C. Conkling.[22]

An event which attracted much attention was the private reception to the new bride and groom, "General" and Mrs. Tom Thumb, whose well-publicized marriage had taken place in New York just three days before their appearance at the White House.

Most members of the Cabinet came to the party, as did General Butler, Cassius M. Clay, and Henry Wilson. So fascinated with the midget couple were the guests that Mr. Lincoln remarked that the "General" had thrown him completely in the shade.[23]

Twice during January the President went to the Senate chamber to hear the elocutionist, James E. Murdoch. On the tenth, he went, apparently alone, and in spite of bad weather, and on the nineteenth both he and Mrs. Lincoln were present. That same afternoon, Murdoch had been at the White House where, for the first time, he read Janvier's poem "The Sleeping Sentinel."

When Murdoch repeated the poem that evening in the Senate chamber there was great applause, and the *Evening Star* reported: "Among the pieces read by Mr. Murdoch, was one entitled the 'Sleeping Sentinel,' which was particularly interesting from the fact that the President, who had pardoned the 'sleeping sentinel,'—upon which act the production was founded—was present."[24]

---

[22] Powell, ed., *Lincoln Day by Day*, III, 162, 168, 169, 170; Lincoln, *Works*, VIII, 511; Mrs. [Mary Todd] Lincoln, Letters, 1863, Ill. State Hist. Library.

[23] Washington *Evening Star*, Feb. 14, 1863; Washington *Daily Morning Chronicle*, Feb. 14, 1863; N.Y. *Herald*, Feb. 11, 14, 1863.

[24] Washington *Evening Star*, Jan. 12, 20, 1863, Feb. 9, 1864; Washington *Sunday Morning Chronicle*, Jan. 11, 1863; Washington *Daily Morning Chronicle*, Jan. 20, 1863; James E. Murdoch, *Patriotism in Poetry and Prose: Being Selected Passages from Lectures and Patriotic Readings* (Phila., 1865), p. 102; *Lincoln Lore*, No. 544 (Sept. 11, 1939). The program also included selections from Shakespeare, Longfellow, Browning, Thomas B. Read, Tennyson, and Dickens. Washington *Evening Star*, Jan. 19, 1863. Senator Browning who was present on both occasions thought that Murdoch read well, but *agonized* too much on some selections. Pease and Randall, eds., *Diary of O. H. Browning*, I, 612, 616-17.

Murdoch made a considerable contribution to the war effort at some sacrifice. Not a robust man, and subject to a recurring illness which forced him to suspend his activities at times, he nevertheless gave generously of his talents, reading and lecturing in hospitals and camps as well as to civilian audiences. The proceeds of

Twice, also, Lincoln went to the theatre to see *Henry IV* and *Hamlet*. Later, he was to attend Shakespearean plays more often, always with great enjoyment.

There was, so far as the record indicates, no music at the White House that winter. The Marine Band was not in its accustomed place for the receptions or for other occasions. Another season would pass before the well-known musicians under Scala would be present to make their contribution at White House functions.

But the President did hear music on two quite different occasions. Once, in February, he occupied a private box at Grover's Theatre to see and hear Barney Williams, the famous minstrel and comedian. The main feature was the "Lakes of Killarney," advertised as "The most magnificent spectacle ever produced in this city, with all the original music."[25] This, we may be sure, brought Lincoln real relaxation, for he was very fond of light comedy.

The second occasion was more formal. A Great War Meeting to demonstrate support for the government was planned for March 31 in the hall of the House of Representatives.

The meeting was scheduled to begin at five o'clock. Government offices had closed early so that workers could attend. At four o'clock the gallery began filling up, and at 4:30 the doors to the floor were opened and the crowd streamed in. Extra chairs were placed in the aisles, and police and committee members were on hand to keep order. An overflow meeting was arranged in the Senate chamber. In spite of bad weather, the gathering was immense.

---

his lectures were used for the benefit of sick and wounded soldiers. Murdoch, *Patriotism in Poetry and Prose, Preface*, p. 80.

Sandburg states that on one occasion Lincoln requested that Murdoch read T. B. Read's poem "The Oath," calling it "The Swear." Sandburg, *Abraham Lincoln*, II, 315. Murdoch mentions the poem but not the incident. *Patriotism in Poetry and Prose*, pp. 114-17. According to the Washington *Evening Star*, Jan. 9, 1863, Murdoch's readings for the evening of January 10 were to include "The Oath." There is no indication that Lincoln requested it on that occasion. It may have been when Murdoch was at the White House.

Lincoln heard Murdoch read again on later occasions.

25 N.Y. *Herald*, Feb. 26, 1863; Washington *Evening Star*, Feb. 23, 24, 1863. In his early days Williams had been famous for his minstrel activities. Then he did impersonations, and by the 1860's was playing Irish comedian parts. Carl Wittke, *Tambo and Bones: A History of the American Minstrel Stage* (Durham, N.C., 1930), pp. 34, 48, 222. Cf. also Lincoln, *Works*, VI, 120.

Well after five o'clock the meeting was called to order, and as was usual in those days, the program was a long one. There were resolutions and speeches in abundance.

In the reporters' gallery above the Speaker's desk the Marine Band was stationed, and on the floor directly below and facing the Speaker's desk were six large stuffed chairs.

In the midst of a stirring speech by Mr. Green Adams there was an interruption. The doors opened and in walked several Cabinet members, the President, and Tad. The Marine Band struck up "Hail, Columbia," the audience rose and cheered, hurrahed, and waved handkerchiefs, and almost drowned out the music.

To the six chairs the latecomers went, sat down, and the meeting continued. There were speeches by Judge Cartter, Horace Maynard, and Andrew Johnson. Johnson spoke for an hour and a half, but could have said it all in a half an hour, according to one listener.

And the music—it was, reports said, quite splendid. The President, sitting in the front row directly below the musicians, listened with pleasure. When a quartet sang "The Flag of Our Union" he bowed to the singers in thanks.

At the overflow meeting in the Senate chamber the band of "Scott's 900" played the "Star-Spangled Banner" and "Yankee Doodle" and a quartet sang "Hail to Our Beautiful Land."

After a time, little Tad was tired and bored. He got down from his big chair, went from one Cabinet member to another, whispered to each—perhaps asking when it would be over so that they could go home. He returned to his chair, got up on his father's lap, got down again, put on the President's tall hat, which came down almost to his shoulders. Finally he climbed into his father's lap again and nestled down on Abraham's bosom. The President stroked the boy's head and rested his chin gently upon it. It was, as one onlooker observed, "a pleasant sight."

The great meeting was a success. "There never was," reported the New York *Times*, "a meeting in Washington at all to be compared with this, in numbers, respectability and enthusiasm." But the President was tired, so tired that a sympathetic member of the vast audience was moved to write: "Father Abe looks so careworn that one could but pity him."[26]

In the late afternoon four days afterward the presidential party boarded the *Carrie Martin* headed for the army. But the steamer did not get far that night for the snowstorm that had set in made navigation hazardous. Consequently the little boat anchored in a cove for the night.

There, in the snug cabin, the President sat far into the wee hours chatting with his good friends, Dr. Henry and Noah Brooks. He began to relax. He was enjoying himself. His mood became cheerful, except when his thoughts reverted to the impending attack on Charleston.[27]

During the next morning the party reached Aquia Creek—a busy but disorderly and unimpressive place, with many ships anchored about and with the landing piled high with supplies of all kinds.

As the President and his friends transferred to the special train waiting to take them to Falmouth (it was still snowing), they were cheered by some nearby soldiers. The train was hardly "special," but it would do. It consisted of a locomotive and a freight car fitted with benches for the passengers. Even the bunting and festoons with which it was decorated could scarcely make it comfortable and warm.

From Falmouth the party, escorted by General But-

[26] Washington *Evening Star*, Apr. 1, 1863; Washington *Daily Morning Chronicle*, Mar. 31, Apr. 1, 1863; Baltimore *Sun*, Apr. 1, 1863; N.Y. *Herald*, Apr. 1, 1863; Arthur J. Larson, *Crusader and Feminist: Letters of Jane Grey Swisshelm, 1858-1865* (St. Paul, 1934), pp. 203-10; N.Y. *Times*, Apr. 1, 1863; Robert L. Kincaid, "Julia Susan Wheelock: The Florence Nightingale of Michigan during the Civil War [with excerpts from the Wheelock diary]," *Lincoln Herald*, XLVI (Oct., 1944), 44-45.

[27] Noah Brooks, "Personal Reminiscences of Lincoln," *Scribner's Monthly*, XV (Mar., 1878), 673; Noah Brooks, *Washington in Lincoln's Time* (N.Y., 1895), p. 46. Brooks concluded: "It was evident that his mind was entirely prepared for the repulse, the news of which soon after reached us." Gideon Welles came to the same conclusion two days earlier. Both Brooks and Welles mention Lincoln's eagerness to obtain Confederate newspapers from which he hoped to learn more about the expedition. Definite news of the failure reached Washington soon after the President returned from the army. Morse, ed., *Diary of Gideon Welles*, I, 259, 263, 264, 265, 266, 267-68, 273.

terfield, traveled the final distance to Hooker's headquarters in two ambulances, arriving there about noon.

Immediately the visitors were taken to their quarters—three hospital tents fitted with cots, chairs, tables, and stoves. There, with the weather outside mostly cold, raw, and unpleasant, the Commander-in-Chief, his wife and son and friends, were to live for the next several days, just as the soldiers lived in the multitude of tents around them. They were, like the Army of the Potomac, "tenting on the old camp ground."[28]

Everything had been put in readiness. For a week before, the men had been making preparations. The camps were clean and in order, and the reviewing fields had been levelled off. An air of expectation prevailed everywhere.

If only the weather had been more cooperative! The week before had been pleasant and springlike. Fires were let out and overcoats shed. The roads started to dry out and became almost passable.

The grass had begun to show green, wild flowers peeked out cautiously, the redbud, so glorious in spring, began to appear, and even the frogs in the low areas started their nightly concerts. And then came the abrupt change.

> Saturday [reported a correspondent] we looked for him, and were disappointed. Saturday night, in the driving storm that swept down tents like cob-webs, we were glad that he had not come; but on Sunday morning, with the snow piled in huge drifts about the camps, and the wind whistling fiercely over the hills, a dispatch came saying that the President was on his way. . . .[29]

But regardless of the weather, the President, once established, entered into a round of activities which lasted from morning until night. There were conferences and consultations, receptions and visitations, festive occasions and periods of sober reflexion. And especially, there were the reviews—grand, moving, awe-inspiring spectacles.

First, on April 6, came the review of the cavalry, re-

---

[28] Brooks, *Washington in Lincoln's Time*, pp. 46-47; N.Y. *Times*, Apr. 10, 1863.
[29] N.Y. *Herald*, Apr. 10, 1863.

cently reorganized in the hope that it might be more effective against the Confederates. On a broad, barren plain, formerly a tobacco field, the cavalry was drawn up, some twelve thousand or more strong, the biggest army of men and horses ever seen together, according to General Hooker.

As the President appeared with Hooker, followed by a host of officers, a twenty-one-gun salute was fired. Splashing through the mud and snow, the President, in his tall hat, riding like a veteran, passed down the line of troops, then returned and stood by Mrs. Lincoln's carriage for the review.

> It was a grand sight to look upon this immense mass of cavalry in motion with banners waving, music crashing, and horses prancing, as the vast columns came on and on, winding like a huge serpent over the hills and dales, stretching far away out of sight.[30]

That night the presidential party had dinner in General Hooker's tent.

Two days later the big review took place, with some sixty thousand men in line. Again the weather was chilly and raw. While the troops waited for the President, the wind stung the soldiers' fingers and blew off the caps of some. Horses kicked and switched at imaginary flies in their impatience.

Finally the President appeared, bugles called, a band struck up "Hail to the Chief!" and the review was on. For over three hours the troop movement continued. Noah Brooks commented:

> It was a splendid sight to witness these 60,000 men all in martial array, with colors flying, drums beating and bayonets gleaming in the struggling sunlight, as they wound over hills and rolling grounds, coming from miles away. . . .[31]

The President was delighted with the fine appearance of the men and was especially impressed with the artillery. He asked General Hooker if the fancy uniforms

---

[30] Brooks, *Washington in Lincoln's Time*, pp. 47-48; Brooks in Sacramento *Daily Union*, May 8, 1863; N.Y. *Herald*, Apr. 9, 1863.

[31] Sacramento *Daily Union*, May 8, 1863.

of the Zouaves did not make good targets, and was informed that they had the effect of encouraging pride and neatness in the wearers.

The review was an exhausting performance, however, and many spectators (artists, knights of the quill, and ladies in curls and crinoline) left before it was over. Even the President was weary that night.[32]

More reviews followed on the next two days. And always there was the music, the music of which the President was especially fond; the flourish of the bugles which brought the men to attention, the strains of "Hail to the Chief!" as the President appeared, the crashing of bands as the cavalry moved into line, and the playing of the regimental bands as each unit of infantry passed in review.

The music of the Fifth and Eleventh Corps was notable, according to Noah Brooks.

> In the First [Fifth] and Eleventh Corps drums and trumpets or fifes are the only martial music, and it is preferred by the men for marching as being firmer and more accurate. In some of these Drum corps I counted 80 snare drums and 30 trumpets; and in others there were 75 or 80 drums and half that number of fifes and piccolos. The reader who has not heard such a band can scarcely imagine the glorious and inspiring effect of the roll and beat of so large a number of drums, intermingled with the martial blare of the trumpet and the shriek of the ear piercing fife. . . .[33]

The President loved it all and was especially warm in his praise of the music of the Eleventh Corps under General Howard.[34]

There was music at headquarters, too. On the first evening in camp three bands played for the President, and one of them, the Thirty-Third Massachusetts Band, was on special assignment at headquarters for the period of the President's visit. It had been privileged to come by

[32] N.Y. *Herald*, Apr. 10, 11, 1863; *Harper's Weekly*, May 2, 1863; Brooks, *Washington in Lincoln's Time*, pp. 49-50.
[33] Sacramento *Daily Union*, May 8, 1863.
[34] N.Y. *Herald*, Apr. 10, 11, 1863; N.Y. *Times*, Apr. 10, 12, 1863; *Harper's Weekly*, May 2, 1863; Brooks, *Washington in Lincoln's Time*, pp. 48, 51.

special train and occupied a tent near that of the President.[35]

Tenting was a different and rather trying experience for Mrs. Lincoln, for in addition to the inconveniences of such living, there was the unpleasant weather which certainly meant discomfort for her.

Yet Mary Lincoln bore up well, and it did the soldiers good to see her there. Lady visitors always aroused interest, and this was especially true of the President's wife, for many had never seen a President's wife! They cheered Mary Lincoln as well as the President.[36]

Mrs. Lincoln went to at least two of the reviews and sat in her carriage through long hours watching them. She went riding in the camp areas and was interested in all that she saw.

Only one disturbing incident occurred, and it proved to be minor and Mr. Lincoln brought her out of it. When the President visited General Sickles' headquarters there was a reception for him. As a wager and with the approval of General Sickles, that vivacious and charming lady, the Princess Salm-Salm, greeted the President with a big kiss! Everyone was delighted; the President was somewhat surprised.

When Mrs. Lincoln heard of the incident, she gave him a lively quarter hour. She did not approve of other women kissing her husband. Her annoyance at General Sickles melted only after they had left camp. On the way back to Washington the General accompanied the party but was snubbed by Mrs. Lincoln.

Finally, at dinner, the President remarked to Sickles:

"I never knew until last night that you were a very pious man."

General Sickles was taken aback, and replied that the President must be mistaken.

"Not at all," said Lincoln. "Mother says you are the

---

[35] Washington *Evening Star* Apr. 6, 1863; N.Y. *Herald*, Apr. 10, 1863; N.Y. *Times*, Apr. 10, 1863; Underwood, *Thirty-Third Massachusetts Infantry*, pp. 19-20. To their disgust, the members of the Massachusetts Band had to hike the seven miles back to their camp in the snow and mud, and it was reported that their steps could be traced by the instruments abandoned in the snow!

[36] Brooks, *Washington in Lincoln's Time*, p. 284; Edwin W. Stone, *Rhode Island in the Rebellion* (Providence, 1864), pp. 223-24.

greatest Psalmist in the army. She says you are more than a Psalmist, you are a Salm-Salmist."

This broke Mrs. Lincoln's resentment and she laughed with every one else, and General Sickles was forgiven.[37]

Tad, too, enjoyed the experience of "tenting on the old camp ground"—at least for a while. He went to the reviews, riding a pony and wearing his red Zouave uniform and gray cloak, and was watched over by an orderly. He followed his father wherever he went. He wanted to see the "greybacks," and Noah Brooks took him down to the river where they looked across at the battered town of Fredericksburg.

But soon the boy wanted to go home. He pestered his father until finally the President offered him a dollar at the end of the stay if he would cease his complaining. He tried to keep the bargain, but could not, but his father gave him the dollar anyway.[38]

As the days passed the President's spirit revived and his good humor became more apparent. Noah Brooks recounts one instance of the presidential wit which was appreciated by all those who heard it.

An ambulance was transporting the party to General Reynold's headquarters and the going was very rough. The driver was having a hard time with the mules. He swore at them constantly and profusely. Finally Mr. Lincoln spoke to him, saying:

"Excuse me, my friend, are you an Episcopalian?"

The man, greatly startled, looked around and replied: "No, Mr. President; I am a Methodist."

"Well," said Lincoln, "I thought you must be an Episcopalian, because you swear just like Governor Seward, who is a churchwarden."[39]

In the evenings when the officers gathered after dinner and talked and told stories, the President contributed his share and seemed to relax.

---

[37] Julia Lorrilard Butterfield, *A Biographical Memorial of General Daniel Butterfield* (N.Y., 1904), pp. 159-62; Brooks, *Washington in Lincoln's Time*, pp. 68-70; W. A. Swanberg, *Sickles the Incredible* (N.Y., 1956), pp. 174-76.

[38] Brooks, *Scribner's Monthly*, XV, 673; Brooks, *Washington in Lincoln's Time*, pp. 48, 283; George L. Kilmer, unidentified clipping, Lincoln National Life Foundation.

[39] Brooks, *Washington in Lincoln's Time*, pp. 50-51.

Thus when the visitors returned to Washington, the President appeared refreshed, invigorated and encouraged. But he was still concerned about General Hooker's overconfidence, saying, "It is about the worst thing I have seen since I have been down here."[40]

And when it was remarked that the rest had been good for him, he shook his head and replied: "I don't know about the 'rest,' as you call it. I suppose it is good for the body. But the tired part of me is inside and out of reach."[41]

Even so, "tenting on the old camp ground" had been a worthwhile experience.

Scarcely a month later the President returned to the camp for a brief visit. This time there were no reviews or festivities; there was no gaiety and no music. For this was just after Chancellorsville. He was greatly shaken. What would the country say? What would the soldiers think?

Some like Vallandigham and Seymour thought that they spoke for the country; others looked upon the draft riots as a rebuke to the administration and the President.

Defiant citizens of New Orleans sang the "Bonnie Blue Flag" day and night and nurtured their children on it in kindergartens; Southern sympathizers in Baltimore cheered Jeff Davis in the streets and sang Confederate songs; in the capital city "secession females" rode down Pennsylvania Avenue singing Southern songs and cheering Jeff Davis, a crowd of rowdies outraged loyal citizens by their loud singing of the "Bonnie Blue Flag" at eleven o'clock at night, and that indomitable Southerner, Belle Boyd, sang "Take me back to my own sunny South" from her prison window while an admiring crowd listened from across the street; at an anti-administration meeting in New York violent anti-Negro songs were circulated; reports from the army indicated that the most popular songs among the men were "Give Us Back Our Old Commander," and "When This Cruel War Is Over."[42]

[40] Brooks, *Scribner's Monthly*, XV, 674.
[41] Brooks, *Scribner's Monthly*, XV, 673.
[42] N.Y. *Tribune*, Mar. 11, Apr. 2, 8, 9, May 18, 23, 1863; Baltimore *Sun*, Apr.

But for a Vallandigham and a Seymour there were George William Curtis and John A. Andrew, and others; down in Louisiana, Union troops marching out of Baton Rouge sang "Old John Brown," a party of officers stopping at a fine plantation made use of the owner's elegant French piano while singing "John Brown" and "Year of Jubilo," and the residents of New Orleans were treated to the "Red, White and Blue" and the "Star-Spangled Banner" at a testimonial to Admiral Farragut.

The Confederate singers in Baltimore were arrested, but more important, a Fourth of July program, widely supported, included the "Star-Spangled Banner" and "Hail, Columbia," and at a flag presentation ceremony for a colored regiment, with thousands present, the "John Brown Song" was sung so impressively that "It would have humanized and melted even the New York mob, and arrested them in their nefarious deeds, could they have heard it, as it mounted to heaven just as the crimson twilight was fading away."[43]

In Washington the persistence of "Southern airs" was perhaps more annoying than serious. The "secession females" were arrested and Belle Boyd was eventually sent South for a second time.

Meanwhile, in an army hospital not far away, the lady nurses, taking time out briefly from their ministrations, sang most sweetly and well for the convalescent soldiers, much to their comfort; the Marine Band gave its concerts regularly; and on the streets bands played for the troops that marched constantly to and fro.[44]

A loyal Unionist who knew the ghastly consequences of battle and who saw the troops in the streets frequently was moved, one day, to say:

Just before sundown this evening a very large cavalry

1, 1863; N.Y. *Herald*, Mar. 13, 1863; Washington *Sunday Morning Chronicle*, Apr. 5, 1863; Belle Boyd, *Belle Boyd in Camp and Prison: Written by Herself* (N.Y., 1867), p. 238; *New Hampshire Sentinel* (Keene), Jan. 22, Aug. 13, 1863.

[43] N.Y. *Tribune*, Mar. 31, May 19, 23, Aug. 17, 1863; Baltimore *Sun*, Apr. 1, July 6, 1863.

[44] Roy P. Basler, ed., *Walt Whitman's Memoranda during the War [&] Death of Abraham Lincoln* (Bloomington, 1962), pp. 21-22; Washington *Evening Star*, June 8, Oct. 5, 1863; Washington *Daily Morning Chronicle*, July 3, 6, 1863; Lincoln, *Life with the Thirty-Fourth Massachusetts Infantry*, pp. 98-99.

force went by—a fine sight. The men evidently had seen service. First came a mounted band of sixteen bugles, drums and
cymbals, playing wild martial tunes—made my heart jump.[45]

After all, there was plenty of Union music in the city.
At the front the pessimism of "When This Cruel War
Is Over" was but temporary. The old inspiring songs
were played and sung: the "Star-Spangled Banner,"
"Hail, Columbia," the "Red, White and Blue," and "Yan-
kee Doodle." "John Brown's Body" was a favorite, and
the most popular of all was "Rally 'Round the Flag."
It was sung in Maryland, in Tennessee, in Mississippi.
It swept from camp to camp—

> Yes, we'll rally 'round the flag, boys,
> Rally once again—
> Shouting the Battle-Cry of Freedom.[46]

And the draft—if it provoked riots in New York and
other cities, it was also accepted elsewhere with patriotic
feeling and with music. In one district in Philadelphia after the drawing of names the entire assembly sang the
"Star-Spangled Banner"; in Dover, New Hampshire, the
conscripts cheered the enrolling officer, formed a parade
headed by the mayor, and went off to the music of a band;
in Laconia, New Hampshire, the draftees paraded
through the streets to the music of a fife and drum corps
and ended up by lighting a bonfire.[47]

Among those whose names were drawn in New Hampshire that summer was a young man in the town of Merrimack. At the scheduled time he, along with a score of
others, reported to the enrolling officer in Concord. But
as it turned out, he was not accepted. Beside his name
on the record was the notation: "Exempted, feebleness
of constitution."

The young man went home to his family. He was
destined to serve his country's cause, not as a soldier, but

---

[45] Basler, ed., *Walt Whitman's Memoranda*, p. 19.

[46] N.Y. *Tribune*, May 29, July 15, 1863; *Musical Rev. and World*, XIV (Sept. 26,
1863), 234; *New Hampshire Sentinel* (Keene), July 16, Oct. 15, 1863.

[47] N.Y. *Tribune*, July 28, Aug. 26, 1863; *New Hampshire Sentinel* (Keene),
Oct. 15, 1863.

in another way. On the draft record his occupation was listed as "musician," and it was as a musician that he made his contribution.

Not only did he go about the cities and towns of New England singing for the folks at home, he was the composer of one of the great and enduring songs of the war, a song that gave comfort, hope, and courage, a song that was sung in the South as well as in the North, a song which for fifty years afterward brought tears and fond memories to veterans as they gathered at reunions and encampments. For the song was "Tenting on the Old Camp Ground," and the young man was Walter Kittredge.

As with thousands of other young men that summer of 1863, Kittredge's draft call set him to thinking. He thought of his family and the New Hampshire hills; and he thought of the army far away at the front, made up of young men just like himself. He thought of the hardships, the suffering, and the pain that they endured; he thought of the long nights with their inevitable longing for home and for peace once more; and there came to him the words and music of the song.

Once Kittredge had put the song on paper he took it to a Boston publisher. It was rejected. He then showed it to his friend Asa Hutchinson. The Hutchinsons sang it at one of their concerts, and it was an instantaneous success. Published by Oliver Ditson Company at the urging of Hutchinson, the song was soon heard everywhere. Within two months 10,000 copies were sold, and by the end of the war sales reached 100,000.[48]

---

[48] Records of the Provost Marshal General's Office, Vol. 19, Draft Book, 2nd District, New Hampshire, 73 (Photostat), National Archives; George Calvin Carter, *Walter Kittredge: Minstrel of the Merrimack* (Manchester, 1953), *passim*; Gordon Hall Gerould, " 'Tenting on the Old Camp Ground,' and Its Composer," *New England Magazine*, XX (Aug., 1899), 723-31 (New Series) ; J. M. French, "Tenting on the Old Camp Ground," *The Granite Monthly*, LXI (Jan.-Dec., 1929), 123-27.

Kittredge recovered from the rheumatic fever that had been the cause of his rejection in the draft and led a long, busy, active life. He composed songs, compiled songbooks, and went about giving entertainments of readings and music. He received thousands of letters prompted by "Tenting Tonight" and his royalties on the piece continued for many years. In 1896 the royalties were larger than in any previous year! He sang "Tenting Tonight" with John Hutchinson every day for a week at a big antislavery meeting in Philadelphia in 1866, and at a Grand Army of the Republic meeting in Washington in 1892. He died on July 8, 1905, and was buried in the cemetery adjoining the Congregational Church in Merrimack. Appropriately enough, the music at the funeral service included "Tenting on the Old Camp Ground."

It seems very probable that President Lincoln, who heard so much of the music of the war, both at home and when visiting the army, must at one time or another have heard "Tenting Tonight."

It was the kind of a song that the President would have appreciated, for he knew full well the real meaning of all that the piece so effectively expressed.

For not only had he witnessed the great reviews and consulted with the officers, he had walked alone through the camps and had talked and laughed and sympathized with the men in their tents, and had learned what life was like for them. And he had spent hours in the hospital tents with the sick and wounded, and his visits there did the men a world of good even though his tender sympathy and earnest concern brought tears to the eyes of many.

In the White House there was the counterpart. Behind the front of official business there were always the human problems—the pleas of loved ones for the release of a boy from prison, the requests to visit a hospital, the solicitation for the exemption of a boy whose aged mother needed him at home, a request to go to the front to find a missing brother, and those appeals for pardons—could the President ever forget that William Scott, the "sleeping sentinel," whom he pardoned early in the war, had later died a hero's death on the battlefield?

Moreover, the President who experienced all these things knew also the heartache of personal loss in the death of Ellsworth and Baker and Mrs. Lincoln's half brothers. It is pleasant to imagine him after a day filled with such problems sitting by a window in the White House as dusk was falling finding relief for his tired body and comfort for his weary spirit as Carl Schurz played softly on the nearby piano—old favorites which they both loved, and then the song that touched the heart of the nation in 1863 and for years after—

> We're tenting to-night on the old camp ground,
>   Give us a song to cheer
> Our weary hearts, a song of home,
>   And friends we love so dear.

Many are the hearts that are weary tonight,
Wishing for the war to cease;
Many are the hearts that are looking for the right,
To see the dawn of peace.
Tenting to-night, tenting to-night,
Tenting on the old camp ground.[49]

---

[49] William H. Townsend of Lexington, Kentucky, recalls having seen a letter in which Carl Schurz described such an occasion. John Lair, *Songs Lincoln Loved* (New York and Boston, 1954), p. viii.

CHAPTER XIII

AFTER GETTYSBURG—A SEA OF ANGUISH

THOSE FIRST FEW DAYS OF JULY, 1863, WERE DAYS OF anxiety, apprehension, and concern for the people of the North. Then came the news of Gettysburg and Vicksburg, such news as Unionists had long awaited, news that brought a revival of spirit and provoked spontaneous outbursts of celebration everywhere. Bells were rung, parades were organized, cannons were fired, fireworks were displayed, all to the inevitable accompaniment of the music of the Union.

In New York on the Fourth, the chimes on Trinity Church were heard at six o'clock in the morning and again at noon with a program that included "Hail, Columbia," "Yankee Doodle," "Old Dog Tray," "Columbia, the Gem of the Ocean," "Last Rose of Summer," the "Star-Spangled Banner," and "Home, Sweet Home." In the afternoon Dodworth's Band gave a concert in Central Park which attracted an estimated 30,000 people who heard "Viva l'Amérique," "The Flag of the Free," "Volunteers Welcome Home March," and a "Bunch of Melodies."[1]

Even the dissident Democrats observed the day. At the Academy of Music speeches were given by such notables as Seymour, Pendleton and O'Gorman, and a band contributed the "Marseillaise," "Hail, Columbia," and the "Star-Spangled Banner." Following the last number, the guarantees of the Constitution were read, with comments, to the enthusiastic approval of the audience.[2]

At a Tammany celebration an Old Folks Quartette sang the "Red, White and Blue," and a soloist offered

---

[1] N.Y. *Times*, July 4, 1863 ; N.Y. *Herald*, July 6, 1863.

[2] N.Y. *Herald*, July 6, 1863.

"Mother I Am Come Home to Die," and "The Minstrel Boy to the War Is Gone."[3]

In Philadelphia there were parades, a flag presentation at the camp for colored soldiers, a program of music and speeches at the Union League headquarters, and at the Chestnut Street Theatre the orchestra played the "Star-Spangled Banner," "Yankee Doodle," and "Hail, Columbia," with the audience joining when the "Star-Spangled Banner" was repeated.[4]

Activities in Washington resembled an "old-fashioned Fourth of July." The day began with "the explosion of powder in all directions," and at ten o'clock a huge parade, headed by the Marine Band and veterans of the War of 1812, proceeded from the City Hall to the White House grounds. There an elaborate program was carried out, consisting of musical selections, prayers, the reading of the Declaration of Independence, and an oration by Hiram Walbridge.

All morning rumors of the victory at Gettysburg filtered through the crowd, and great was the excitement when the oration of the day was interrupted so that Mayor Wallach could officially announce the outcome of the battle. As the band struck up the "Star-Spangled Banner" there were cheers and cheers and "gunpowder explosions louder than ever." The day ended with a "magnificent display" of fireworks on the White House grounds.[5]

Meanwhile, at Gettysburg, as the Union troops rested after the battle, bands marched through the streets playing national airs and General Meade was serenaded at his headquarters.[6]

Mrs. Meade, then in Philadelphia, was also favored

---

[3] N.Y. *Herald,* July 6, 1863.

[4] Philadelphia *Evening Bulletin,* July 6, 1863.

[5] Washington *Evening Star,* July 3, 6, 1863; Washington *Daily Morning Chronicle,* July 3, 6, 1863; Washington *Sunday Morning Chronicle,* July 5, 1863; Sacramento *Daily Union,* July 28, 1863; N.Y. *Herald,* July 6, 1863. The exercises were arranged by William O. Stoddard who consulted with Mrs. Lincoln concerning the program. Stoddard, *Inside the White House,* pp. 206-9; Stoddard, *Lincoln's Third Secretary,* pp. 180-81. The President took no part in the proceedings. He was too busy.

[6] N.Y. *Tribune,* July 7, 1863. The *Tribune* the same day carried a story that General Schimmelfennig, cut off from his men and knocked down by some Rebels out for plunder, then hid in a cellar for two days, coming out when he heard a band playing "Yankee Doodle." Coffin, *The Boys of '61,* p. 299.

with a serenade. About eleven o'clock in the evening an immense crowd gathered at her residence. Birgfeld's Band played several selections—the "Star-Spangled Banner," "Hail, Columbia," and "Yankee Doodle." The mayor made a brief speech, there was much cheering and applause, the band played the "Battle Hymn of the Republic," and the crowd dispersed.[7]

As one reporter expressed it in commenting on the day's events, ". . . people were famishing for a success at the hands of the Army of the Potomac, and having got it, they applaud to the skies."[8]

But if there was a doubt in the minds of some on Independence Day, there was none on July 7 when the news of Vicksburg was confirmed. Again there were great outbursts of patriotic fervor. An observer wrote: "We have had the dark hour. The dawn has broken. . . . Bells are ringing wildly. . . . Citizens grin at one another with fairly idiotic delight."[9]

In New York flags were flown and a salute of one hundred guns was fired; in Boston the bells were rung and in Newburyport bells and a salute honored the occasion; in Albany there were salutes, fireworks, and music; Lancaster and Reading were in a state of unrestrained relief and excitement; in Wilmington, Delaware, boys fired pistols into empty barrels and an enthusiastic citizen climbed to the ridgepole of his house and rang his dinner bell vigorously.[10]

In Philadelphia there was a great meeting in Independence Square. The Union League paraded to the square led by Birgfeld's Band. A prominent minister offered an appropriate prayer, several addresses were given, and

---

[7] Philadelphia *Inquirer*, July 6, 9, 1863; N.Y. *Evening Post*, July 6, 1863. This is one of the few instances when the press referred to the "Battle Hymn of the Republic." Usually the "John Brown Song" was mentioned. General Meade was pleased that Mrs. Meade was complimented by the people of Philadelphia. However, he was a little embarrassed when at Frederick he was serenaded and presented with a bouquet by a delegation of ladies. He apologized to the ladies for being so busy. To Mrs. Meade he wrote: "The people of this place have made a great fuss with me." George Meade, *The Life and Letters of George Gordon Meade* (N.Y., 1913), II, 132-33; N.Y. *Tribune*, July 10, 1863.

[8] Philadelphia *Evening Bulletin*, July 9, 1863.

[9] William Thompson Lusk, in Commager, ed., *The Blue and the Gray*, II, 642-43.

[10] Philadelphia *Evening Bulletin*, July 8, 1863; N.Y. *Tribune*, July 8, 1863; Lusk, in Commager, ed., *The Blue and the Gray*, II, 642-43.

when the band played a hymn from the steeple of Independence Hall, the multitude was thrilled. When the ceremonies ended, the procession marched back to League headquarters to the tune of "John Brown's Body." In the evening buildings were illuminated, and fireworks were set off in the streets. "It was," said one newspaper, "the 4th of July over again, enlarged and improved."[11]

That same evening strains of music were heard outside the White House as a large crowd gathered to serenade the President. Music by the "powerful and almost matchless band" of the Thirty-Fourth Massachusetts Regiment and cheers from the crowd brought the President to the door. In his impromptu response, Lincoln alluded to the birthday of the nation when ". . . for the first time in the history of the world a nation by its representatives, assembled and declared as a self-evident truth that 'all men are created equal.'" He made reference to the great battle just ended in Pennsylvania at which ". . . those who opposed the declaration . . . 'turned tail' and run." As was his wont he praised the men in the army and closed by saying, "Having said this much, I will now take the music."[12] The crowd cheered, the band struck up "Hail, Columbia" and the serenaders went on to honor Secretary Stanton and Secretary Seward. But though in his remarks to the serenaders the President had referred to the outcome of the battle as a "glorious theme" worthy of a speech, he was distressed, greatly distressed, because General Meade did not follow through and try to destroy Lee's army.[13]

---

[11] Philadelphia *Inquirer*, July 8, 1863; Philadelphia *Evening Bulletin*, July 7, 8, 10, 1863.

[12] Washington *Evening Star*, July 8, 1863; Washington *National Intelligencer*, July 9, 1863; Washington *Daily Morning Chronicle*, July 8, 1863; N.Y. *Herald*, July 8, 1863; Lincoln, *Thirty-Fourth Massachusetts Infantry*, p. 112. According to Noah Brooks, Lincoln "took the music" later when Charles Sumner conveyed to him the disapproval of some "nice Boston folks" for his use of the expression "'turned tail' and run." They considered it quite undignified. Noah Brooks, *Abraham Lincoln* (N.Y., 1888), p. 449; Brooks, *Washington in Lincoln's Time*, p. 254.
One man in Richmond expressed his views as follows: "It appears that President Lincoln has made a speech in Washington in exultation over the fall of Vicksburg, and the defeat of an army contending against the principle that all men were created equal. He means the negro—we mean that white men were created equal—that we are equal to Northern white people, and have a right, which we do not deny to them, of living under a government of our own choice." J. B. Jones, *A Rebel War Clerk's Diary* (N.Y., 1935), I, 378.

[13] The instances which reveal Lincoln's disappointment are numerous. The evening before the serenade he wrote to General Halleck that he was "a good deal

Forty-eight hours earlier, after a busy day, the President went across the river to visit the troops stationed there. It was toward evening. As he approached the headquarters of the First Brigade, Colonel Thomas R. Tannatt, then in command of the unit, invited him to watch the evening review.

As was the custom, the several bands were playing for the review, and it being Sunday, they chose religious selections. The President asked if the band nearby could play "Lead, Kindly Light." The musicians gladly obliged, and as the music poured forth, the President, his face showing the terrific strain that he had undergone in recent days, repeated the words, as if to himself—

> Lead, kindly light, amid th' encircling gloom,
> Lead Thou me on.
> The night is dark, and I am far from home;
> Lead Thou me on.
> Keep Thou my feet; I do not ask to see
> The distant scene;
> One step enough for me.

The President was deeply affected. His face was wet with tears. The hymn was full of meaning. It fitted his mood, and was utterly appropriate for the dark uncertain days through which the nation was passing.[14]

Even while the President was repeating the words of the hymn that Sunday evening, many people were on their way to Gettysburg to minister to the wounded and suffering. Among the volunteers was a young Quaker lady,

---

dissatisfied"; the very morning of the seventh of July he spoke "with a countenance indicating sadness and despondency," although he was greatly cheered when the news of Vicksburg arrived; by the twelfth he was convinced that Meade would be too late, and on the fourteenth he was so upset that he adjourned the Cabinet meeting abruptly and poured out his distress to Secretary Welles as they walked to the War Office. Later that day Welles found Lincoln lying on a sofa in Stanton's office "completely absorbed, overwhelmed with the news."

That same day he wrote the letter to General Meade which was never sent. It reveals his great disappointment—"Your golden opportunity is gone [he wrote], and I am distressed immeasurably because of it." It also shows that Lincoln foresaw more long months of effort, sacrifice, and suffering. "As it is, the war will be prolonged indefinitely." Lincoln, *Works*, VI, 318, 328; Morse, ed., *Diary of Gideon Welles*, I, 363, 370-71; Bates, *Lincoln in the Telegraph Office*, p. 157. Cf. also Dennett, *Lincoln . . . in the Diaries . . . of John Hay*, pp. 66, 67, 70-71.

[14] Browne, *Every-Day Life of Lincoln*, II, 499-500. This incident had not previously appeared in print. Browne was especially concerned that it be included in the revised (1913) edition of *The Every-Day Life of Abraham Lincoln*. F. F. Browne Papers, The Newberry Library, Chicago.

Cornelia Hancock. Her first glimpse of the aftermath of the battle came soon after she arrived. She wrote:

> Every barn, church, and building of any size in Gettysburg had been converted into a temporary hospital. We went the same evening to one of the churches, where I saw for the first time what war meant. Hundreds of desperately wounded men were stretched out on boards laid across the high-backed pews as closely as they could be packed together. The boards were covered with straw. Thus elevated, these poor sufferers' faces, white and drawn with pain, were almost on a level with my own. I seemed to stand breast-high in a sea of anguish.[15]

That was but the beginning. The next evening she wrote: "There are no words in the English language to express the suffering I have witnessed today." A month later she said: "It does not appear to me as if one death is anything to me now." Still later this gentle Quaker girl expostulated: "I think war is a hellish way of settling a dispute." Yet she stayed as did others, for nearly two months, working to a state of near exhaustion in the great effort to alleviate pain and suffering, and when she left, she said, ". . . as soon as there is another battle, I shall go again."[16]

The spontaneous impulse to do something for the victims of battle which caught up Cornelia Hancock and hundreds of others was organized with remarkable speed, especially in the cities nearest to Gettysburg. The Sanitary Commission, Christian Commission, Ladies' Relief Associations, the Adams Express Company and other groups immediately went into action. As the doctors, nurses, and other helpers converged on Gettysburg, supplies began to pour in.

In Philadelphia, church services were suspended that first Sunday in July, and the women requisitioned sewing machines, collected clothing and linen, food and delicacies. Supplies and money came from New Jersey, New Hamp-

---

[15] Henrietta Stratton Jaquette, *South After Gettysburg: Letters of Cornelia Hancock 1863-1868* (N.Y., 1956), p. 6. Another young lady, Sallie Robbins Broadhead, of Gettysburg, observed that same morning: "What a beautiful morning! It seems as though nature was smiling on thousands suffering. One might think, if he saw only the sky, and earth, and trees, that everyone must be happy; but just look around and behold the misery made in so short time by man." Earl Schenck Miers and Richard A. Brown, eds., *Gettysburg* (New Brunswick, 1948), p. 269.

[16] Jaquette, *South After Gettysburg*, pp. 10, 19, 24, 27.

shire, and Massachusetts, to be forwarded to Gettysburg. In two days $14,000 was received from Boston, and in a short time this was increased to over $50,000. Wounded men arrived in great numbers and were cared for in hospitals filled to overflowing, or, when possible, treated and sent home.[17]

Both citizens and organizations in Baltimore did yeoman service in relief. On the evening of July 4 the first load of supplies left the city for Gettysburg, twenty tons of ice, sixty boxes of lemons, and a quantity of linen, sent by the Adams Express Company. The following day this patriotic firm had its supervisors at Gettysburg to take charge of the distribution of supplies, had begun to organize a hospital and ambulance corps, had sent off its first contingent of nurses, and had dispatched five more wagons loaded with supplies. Its relief work continued daily as did that of the Sanitary and Christian Commissions and of individual citizens. Within two weeks over $34,000 had been contributed in money and two cars, one of them a refrigerator car, were being dispatched daily by railroad.

In addition, the people of Baltimore made heroic efforts to care for the wounded arriving from Gettysburg. They came by the trainload—on July 6 a six-car trainload reached the city, on July 10, 2,000 arrived, on July 12, a seven-car trainload, on July 20, 800 more came. All were cared for.[18]

The work of the Sanitary Commission was indicated in the reports of its secretary, Frederick L. Olmsted. Within three days more than one hundred wagons had been dispatched to Gettysburg and five railroad cars were on the way. Other cars were leaving Boston, Philadelphia, and New York daily. A special relief station was established at Gettysburg where the personal needs of one

---

[17] Philadelphia *Evening Bulletin*, July 7, 9, 11, 1863; Washington *National Intelligencer*, July 11, Aug. 10, 1863; Batimore *Sun*, Aug. 6, 1863; Mrs. Edmund A. Souder, *Leaves from the Battle-field of Gettysburg* (Phila., 1864), p. 6.

[18] Baltimore *American*, July 6, 7, 10, 1863; Baltimore *Sun*, July 6, 7, 10, 11, 13, 20, 21, 24, 1863. Two of the city's leading musical organizations, the National Union Musical Association and the German Singing Association, gave concerts, the proceeds of which were contributed for relief. Baltimore *American*, July 10, 15, 18, 21, 1863.

thousand men not hospitalized were cared for each day. In the ten days after the battle there were transported to Gettysburg 39,844 pieces of clothing, 11,700 pieces of bed linen, 11,000 towels and napkins, 4,000 pairs of shoes, 8,500 dozen eggs, 3,800 pounds of concentrated beef soup, 12,500 pounds of condensed milk, 116 boxes of lemons, and sixty tons of perishables in refrigerator cars.[19]

Thus, with this great humanitarian effort, conditions at Gettysburg improved, and the town slowly got back to normal. Wounded men recovered and were sent home, others were transferred to hospitals elsewhere, many were to sleep forever there on the battlefield.

The President, meanwhile, issued a proclamation calling upon the people to set aside August 6 as a day of national thanksgiving, praise, and prayer. The proclamation was almost like a prayer in itself. "It has pleased Almighty God to hearken to the supplications and prayers of an afflicted people . . ." it began.

It reminded the nation of the cost of the victory. ". . . these victories have been accorded not without sacrifices of life, limb, health and liberty. . . . Domestic affliction in every part of the country follows in the train of these fearful bereavements."

It invited the people to go to church, there to

> . . . render the homage due to the Divine Majesty, for the wonderful things he has done in the Nation's behalf, and invoke the influence of His Holy Spirit to subdue the anger, which has produced, and so long sustained a needless and cruel rebellion, to change the hearts of the insurgents, to guide the counsels of the Government with wisdom adequate to so great a national emergency, and to visit with tender care and consolation . . . all those who, through the vicissitudes of marches, voyages, battles and seiges, have been brought to suffer in mind, body or estate, and finally to lead the whole nation, through the paths of repentance and submission to the Divine Will, back to the perfect enjoyment of Union and fraternal peace.[20]

---

[19] Baltimore *Sun*, July 24, 1863 ; Philadelphia *Evening Bulletin*, Aug. 1, 1863.

[20] Lincoln, *Works*, VI, 332-33. Ten days later Jefferson Davis also issued a proclamation setting aside a day of "fasting, humiliation, and prayer." Moore, *Rebellion Record*, VII, Doc. 370-71. On August 7, the N.Y. *Herald* printed the two proclamations side by side, with editorial comment which contained a typical

The proclamation was in harmony with the feelings of many people after the first days of rejoicing and celebration. It fitted the mood of Cornelia Hancock; it fitted the mood of an Ohio doctor who, upon hearing the news of the battle, walked twelve miles to the nearest railroad station in order to get to Gettysburg as quickly as possible; it fitted the mood of Mrs. Edmund Souder, of Philadelphia, who gave up her vacation at the cool seashore to help; it fitted the mood of Mrs. Souder's companions who waited eight hours in the broiling sun without complaint at Hanover Junction for a train to Gettysburg; and it struck a responsive note in the hearts of hundreds of others who hastened to the scene of the battle.[21]

It likewise expressed the sentiment of thousands who attended church services regularly during that hot summer—the solemn services on July 4 which were in contrast to the joyous celebrations, the impressive ceremony in Independence Square on July 7, the Sunday meetings at which members of the Christian Commission urged support of the humanitarian work going on at Gettysburg, the daily services at Camp Curtin, the special service of prayer and thanksgiving in Faneuil Hall in Boston.[22]

And from these services there echoed across the land one hymn, sung above all others—

> Praise God from Whom all blessings flow,
> Praise Him all creatures here below,
> Praise Him above, ye heav'nly host;
> Praise Father, Son, and Holy Ghost.[23]

barb, aimed at Davis' proclamation, characterizing it "the dismal wail of Jeff." Actually it was dignified and appropriate.

Mrs. Lincoln, who suffered from the intense Washington heat and whose head injury, received when she was thrown from her carriage early in July, was slow in healing, left the city for a trip to New England. She spent the first two weeks of August in New Hampshire, and on the sixth she and her two sons were in a party of 130 that took the popular carriage road drive to Mount Washington. She was the first First Lady to tour New England extensively. James Duane Squires, "Mrs. Abraham Lincoln's Visit to Mount Washington in 1863," *Appalachia* (Dec., 1961), pp. 452-57.

[21] Jaquette, *South After Gettysburg*, chap. I; Souder, *Battle-field of Gettysburg*, pp. 11-15, 54.

[22] Philadelphia *Evening Bulletin*, July 6, 8, 13, 20, 1863; N.Y. *Times*, July 10, 1863.

[23] At the band concert in Central Park on July 4, a most startling effect was produced when, in the last number, "Bunch of Melodies," the band went from a lively waltz into "Old Hundred"; at the meeting in Independence Square on July 7, when the band played "Old Hundred" from the steeple of Independence Hall, the effect was very impressive; the climax of the meeting in Faneuil Hall in Boston came in the singing of "Old Hundred"; an observer at a Sunday service in

At Gettysburg there was much that was in keeping with the mood and sentiment of the President's Proclamation. Nurses were surprised at the courage and fortitude of the wounded. Whether Union or Confederate, the men did not complain, they bore no enmity toward each other, and so often, when refreshment or assistance was offered, the response was, "Help the others, they need it more than I."[24]

As they went from tent to tent and from cot to cot, providing hot chocolate, tea, milk, punch, fruit, and a word of cheer, those who ministered were frequently asked to recite or sing a favorite hymn—for the boy from Maine, "There Is Rest for the Weary," and for the boy from Virginia, "Jesus, Lover of My Soul," "There Is a Fountain Filled with Blood," and "Rock of Ages"; for the soldier from Massachusetts, "There Is a Happy Land," and for the soldier from Texas, "Am I a Soldier of the Cross?"

Each evening when darkness came and the busy world was hushed there could be heard the notes and music of other hymns, "Soldiers of Christ, Arise," "All Hail the Power of Jesus' Name," and at the end, the Doxology— "Praise God, from Whom all blessings flow."

As time went on the churches were emptied of their wounded, services were resumed, and the townspeople and soldiers sang together—

> Rock of ages, cleft for me,
> Let me hide myself in thee.

Toward the end of July a soldier on the quiet streets remarked that it was just like "an old-fashioned Sunday."[25]

---

camp near Baltimore commented that the singing of "Old Hundred" "never sounded more natural." N.Y. *Herald*, July 6, 1863; Philadelphia *Evening Bulletin*, July 8, 1863; N.Y. *Times*, July 10, 1863; N.Y. *Tribune*, July 30, 1863.

In April, 1862, a commentator expressed the hope that "Old Hundred," which he said had become the "Te Deum" of America, would be heard more often. If he were in the army, he would want to enter battle to the tune of "Hail, Columbia" and "Yankee Doodle," and close with "Old Hundred." *Dwight's Journal of Music*, XXI (Apr. 19, 1862), 22-23. His hope was realized, as "Old Hundred" was probably played and sung, with various sets of words, more often than any other hymn, as for instance, in the summer of 1863 after Gettysburg.

[24] Jaquette, *South After Gettysburg*, p. 12; Souder, *Battle-field of Gettysburg*, pp. 24-36.

[25] Frank Moore, *The Civil War in Song and Story* (N.Y., 1889), pp. 490-93;

To be sure, the men in camp and on the field sang, even hymns, for the sheer emotional relief that was thus provided. Down in Tennessee earlier that same year a Sunday's singing included "Dixie," "Gay and Happy," "I'm a Pilgrim," and "There Is a Happy Land," and at the end of the war a group in the same regiment mixed "John Brown" and "Dixie" quite irreverently with orthodox hymns. Said one participant, "It seems to relieve the spirits. . . ."[26]

To be sure, also, not all men sought solace in religion and its music, for some fortified themselves with the bottle and found relief in rollicking songs and songs of nostalgic sentiment.[27]

But for many it was equally true that the singing of hymns renewed their hope, revived their spirits, and restored their faith. At Yorktown, in April, 1862, when the men had joined in singing "Old Hundred" one Sunday evening, a soldier was moved to thus describe the incident:

> There was a silence for a moment, and then there was wafted across the air the music of that glorious anthem, "Old Hundred," in which it seemed a thousand voices were participating. . . . Never before have we heard anything so magnificently grand as that same "Old Hundred," sung by the soldiers of the Union army on the plains of Yorktown. The air was made vocal with music, and the woods around reverberated with the mighty strain. Beneath the canopy of heaven the soldier gazed upward into the starlight [sic] sky and sang unto God, "from whom all blessings flow," an anthem that stirred the heart of man with the best and holiest emotions.[28]

The boys in gray who shared in the hymns at Gettysburg to their comfort relied upon these same hymns on other occasions, just as did the boys in blue, for both read

---

Souder. *Battle-field of Gettysburg*, pp. 17, 18, 37, 48, 61; Philadelphia *Evening Bulletin*, July 23, Aug. 5, 1863; Baltimore *Sun*, July 23, 24, 30, 1863.

[26] Jenkin Lloyd Jones, *An Artilleryman's Diary* (Madison, Wis., 1914), pp. 31, 320.

[27] Paul M. Angle and Earl Schenck Miers, eds., *Tragic Years: 1861-1865* (N.Y., 1960), I, 429; N.Y. *Tribune*, July 30, 1863. At Vicksburg during a band concert celebrating the surrender of the city the soldiers got quite hilarious and the bandleader became so drunk that he had to give up. Jones, *Artilleryman's Diary*, p. 79. Cf. "Evil and Goodness," chap. X, in Bell Irvin Wiley, *The Life of Billy Yank* (Indianapolis, 1951).

[28] Moore, *Rebellion Record*, V, 10.

the same Bible, both prayed to the same God, and both sang the same hymns.

Thus on a dark and dreary night a group of Confederates gathered for a prayer meeting and sang "When I can read my title clear," or again, a chaplain, standing on a stool in the mud in a camp in Florida, opened a service with "How Firm a Foundation."[29]

Sometimes the men on both sides sang together, as when a Confederate private was taken to the river for baptism. The Union troops across the stream looked on with interest, and when the Confederates began to sing "There is a fountain," they joined in. The convert was then immersed "to the satisfaction of all."[30] On another occasion a Confederate chaplain remarked: "To me it is a happy thought that in the two confronting camps, often at the same hour, there rose with voice and heart the common strain—'All Hail the Power of Jesus' Name.' "[31]

As with all types of music, the hymns of the people admitted of no real boundaries. Rather did they constitute a common bond of sympathy and understanding and a reminder that all men were as one before the Judgment seat.

For the ordeal of war with its imminence of death did something to the souls of men. It increased their concern about the unknown future and tested their convictions regarding the purposes and compassion of their Maker. Nothing brought this concern and these convictions into focus as did the hymns which were sung and heard. As a Northern soldier remarked after attending a service in a church in Alabama:

> A good choir with the deep-toned organ opened the service with fitting music. . . . The solemn notes of the organ had awakened feelings that are too apt to lie dormant in the soldier's breast, those that raise the mind above the din of common life, and look to a future of immortality, purity, which all hope to obtain ere long.[32]

---

[29] J. Wm. Jones, *Christ in Camp; or Religion in Lee's Army* (Richmond, 1888), pp. 309, 621.

[30] Bell Irvin Wiley and Hirst D. Milhollen, *They Who Fought Here* (N.Y., 1959), pp. 145-46.

[31] Jones, *Christ in Camp*, p. 14.

[32] Jones, *Artilleryman's Diary*, p. 174.

And so it was with Abraham Lincoln. He whom Herndon and other early contemporaries knew (or thought they knew) as a confirmed skeptic, became a man of pronounced religious feeling, convinced that the war was part of God's great purpose, and from which would come some greater good.

This growing belief was revealed in his "Meditation on the Divine Will," written in the fall of 1862:

> The will of God prevails. In great contests each party claims to act in accordance with the will of God. Both *may* be, and one *must* be wrong. God can not be *for*, and *against* the same thing at the same time. In the present civil war it is quite possible that God's purpose is something different from the purpose of either party—and yet the human instrumentalities, working just as they do, are of the best adaptation to effect His purpose. I am almost ready to say this is probably true—that God wills this contest, and wills that it shall not end yet. . . .[33]

And as time went on his increased conviction was again expressed in his letter to Mrs. Gurney:

> The purposes of the Almighty are perfect, and must prevail, though we erring mortals may fail to accurately perceive them in advance. We hoped for a happy termination of this terrible war long before this; but God knows best, and has ruled otherwise. We shall yet acknowledge His wisdom and our own error therein. Meanwhile we must work earnestly in the best light He gives us, trusting that so working still conduces to the great ends He ordains. Surely He intends some great good to follow this mighty convulsion, which no mortal could make, and no mortal could stay.[34]

Further, Lincoln's close identity with the New York Avenue Presbyterian Church and its minister seemed to parallel his religious development. From the first he and his family became associated with this church, just a few blocks from the White House. There they attended the Sunday after they began their residence in the White House, there they took a pew, and there they worshipped.

---

[33] Lincoln, *Works*, V, 403-4.
[34] Lincoln, *Works*, VII, 535.

The New York Avenue Presbyterian Church was then a new edifice, having been constructed in 1860 and dedicated on October 14 of that year. Its congregation, formed by the merger of the Second Presbyterian and F Street churches, was under the leadership of Dr. Phineas D. Gurley.

Dr. Gurley, strong, able, genuine, was a competent and successful leader of his flock. He was also quite musical, as was his mother before him. In college he had played the flute and had sung in the college choir. He gave constant encouragement to the choir in the New York Avenue Church, and its musicians were said to have been about the best in the city.[35]

Dr. Gurley became not merely the "preacher to the President." He was closely associated with the Lincoln family and was often at the White House. With him the President had many discussions on secular as well as religious subjects. Lincoln is said to have remarked, "I like Gurley. He don't preach politics. I get enough of that through the week, and when I go to church I like to hear the gospel." When Willie Lincoln died, Dr. Gurley conducted the funeral service and consoled the family. He was probably the closest and perhaps only real spiritual advisor that Mr. Lincoln ever had.

From this rather stern but devoted Presbyterian pastor Lincoln heard the Word of God. He listened attentively, and during the long prayer he stood, as had been the custom in the Presbyterian Church back in Springfield, Illinois. Visitors at the church were struck by the revelation in his appearance of the tremendous burdens he bore. Noah Brooks, after attending a service late in 1862, remarked of the President:

---

[35] The relationship of the Lincolns with the New York Avenue Presbyterian Church is discussed in Frank E. Edgington, *A History of the New York Avenue Presbyterian Church* (Washington, 1962). Many prominent persons were worshippers there or at the two churches which merged into it. They included John Quincy Adams, Andrew Jackson, John Marshall, Franklin Pierce, James K. Polk, and John C. Calhoun. The present edifice contains a very beautiful Lincoln Chapel and the original Lincoln pew.

I am indebted to Mr. Edgington for generously sharing with me his rich background of knowledge of the church and of Lincoln's association with it. I am also indebted to Miss Constance Adams, of Washington, D.C., and Mrs. E. R. Millar, of Alexander, Arkansas, granddaughters of Dr. Gurley, for information graciously supplied.

His hair is grizzled, his gait more stooping, his countenance sallow, and there is a sunken, deathly look about the large cavernous eyes, which is saddening to those who see there the marks of care and anxiety, such as no President of the United States has ever before known.[36]

The music at the New York Avenue Church must have been comforting to the President for it included many hymns that were familiar to him as they were to people generally, both in the North and in the South—"Rock of Ages," "Father, Whate'er of Earthly Bliss," "When All Thy Mercies, O My God," "Alas, and Did My Saviour Bleed," and "There Is a Fountain." It is not unreasonable to assume that from these old hymns, as well as from the preaching and counseling of Dr. Gurley, Lincoln drew some of his inner strength.

And had he known, he would have appreciated the singing of "There Is a Fountain" for the Virginia boy at Gettysburg, for he had been familiar with the hymn since his frontier days in Indiana; he would have understood the feelings of the boy from Texas who asked for "Am I a Soldier of the Cross?" for it was said to have been a favorite with him; he would have been at one with the congregation in the church in Gettysburg as it sang "Rock of Ages," for he knew it well, and he had once repeated it for a dying woman back in Illinois.

He surely knew the grandeur and full meaning of the Doxology, for it had a prominent place in Presbyterian worship.[37] He had heard it sung by soldiers as yet un-

---

[36] Sacramento *Daily Union,* Dec. 30, 1862; Brooks, *Washington in Lincoln's Time,* p. 2.

[37] Presbyterian hymnbooks included many sets of words under the heading "Doxologies." *Psalms and Hymns Adapted to Public Worship, and Approved by the General Assembly of the Presbyterian Church in the United States of America* (Phila., 1830) contained ten Doxologies; one edition of *Psalms and Hymns Adapted to Social, Private, and Public Worship in the Presbyterian Church in the United States of America* (Phila., 1843) contained twenty-two Doxologies and another edition contained twenty-four. Metcalf and Nutter Collections, Boston University School of Theology Library. These early volumes contained words only. Tunes were "lined out" by the precentor.

The records are not entirely clear as to exactly which hymnbook was used in the New York Avenue Church, but very likely it was *Psalms and Hymns.* Perhaps *Devotional Hymns,* first published in 1842, was also used. When the church building was razed in 1950, preparatory to the building of the present edifice, the box deposited in the old cornerstone, October 6, 1859, was opened and everything listed in its contents was there except the copy of the hymnbook! But at any rate, the hymnbook or books in use during the Civil War period were standard Presbyterian

tried, and he had heard it sung by Negro refugees at the contraband camp.[38]

As it was sung at Gettysburg and elsewhere that summer of 1863, it became, one might say, a response to the call to "thanksgiving, praise and prayer" in the President's Proclamation—

> Praise God from Whom all blessings flow,
> Praise Him all creatures here below.[39]

Four months later the President himself went to Gettysburg to dedicate as a permanent resting place a portion of that field which in July had been "a sea of anguish." The Marine Band played the second musical selection on the program that November day. It was "Old Hundred."

publications which contained all of the old hymns that were familiar to Lincoln from his earlier days as well as some he came to know later.

The first pipe organ was installed in the church in 1874. It was used for nearly three score and ten years, and when a new organ was installed in 1942, some of the case work from the original instrument was built into it. Cf. Edgington, *History of the New York Avenue Presbyterian Church, passim.*

[38] Augustus Woodbury, *A Narrative of the Campaign of the First Rhode Island Regiment, in the Spring and Summer of 1861* (Providence, 1862), pp. 38-39; N.Y. *Herald*, Oct. 19, 1861; Washington *Evening Star*, Oct. 19, 1861; Washington, *They Knew Lincoln*, pp. 86-87.

[39] On August 6, the day set aside by the President's Proclamation, stores and business establishments were generally closed. Church services were held, but in many places attendance was not large due to the excessive heat. In Baltimore many sought relief by going to the shore or out on the water. Roads and railroads leading out of the city were crowded. Baltimore *Sun*, Aug. 8, 1863. In Lutherville the National Union Musical Association gave a big concert for the benefit of the wounded. Baltimore *American*, Aug. 3, 6, 1863. In Philadelphia the Union League Headquarters was illuminated, and a band concert was given. Philadelphia *Evening Bulletin*, Aug. 7, 1863. In Washington the day was quiet. The President attended the service at the New York Avenue Church and then went out to the Soldiers' Home. N.Y. *Herald*, Aug. 7, 1863; Dennett, ed., *Lincoln . . . in the Diaries . . . of John Hay*, p. 74.

CHAPTER XIV

THE MUSIC AT GETTYSBURG

WHEN PRESIDENT LINCOLN STEPPED FROM THAT GAILY decorated special train at Gettysburg on the evening of November 18, 1863, for his brief but highly significant visit, the town was in readiness for him and for the ceremony in which he was to take part the next day. Since the first of the month the townspeople had been busy with preparations. Bright new flags flying in the breeze on the village "Diamond," at the cemetery, and on Round Top, and flags and bunting in profusion on public buildings and private houses gave the town a true holiday appearance.[1] Then, too, for several days visitors had been arriving in ever-increasing numbers. Distinguished guests and ordinary citizens, they came from far and near, by train, carriage, and by wagon.

Ward Hill Lamon and Benjamin B. French made a special trip from Washington to confer with David Wills on final plans for the dedication. Edward Everett arrived early and spent considerable time familiarizing himself with the battlefield and the countryside. Many of the other early comers could be seen wandering over the battlefield hunting for souvenirs or searching for the graves of loved ones.[2]

As the crowd grew larger and larger, excitement heightened, and the town, its normal population of 2,400 having increased to upwards of 15,000, took on an air of celebration.[3] This holiday atmosphere which had been

[1] N.Y. *Herald*, Nov. 20, 1863; Philadelphia *Evening Bulletin*, Nov. 20, 1863; Philadelphia *Press*, Nov. 21, 1863; Washington *National Intelligencer*, Nov. 21, 1863; Washington *Evening Star*, Nov. 20, 1863.

[2] French, ed., *Diary of B. B. French*, pp. 122-23; N.Y. *Herald*, Nov. 20, 1863; Philadelphia *Inquirer*, Nov. 21, 1863.

[3] N.Y. *World*, Nov. 21, 1863; Philadelphia *Inquirer*, Nov. 20, 21, 1863.

building up during the early days of the month reached a climax the evening of the President's arrival. The next morning, however, it was gone. A different mood had taken hold of the multitude, a mood that was more solemn, sober, and serious. The changing atmosphere and contrasting moods of that Wednesday and Thursday of November, 1863, reveal the spirit and feeling of a people at war, and in no way are the spirit and feeling better expressed than in the music at Gettysburg.

"Music," said *The Adams Sentinel* (of Gettysburg) the day before the President arrived, "is the most delightful rational entertainment that the human mind can possibly enjoy." Maybe so. But the music at Gettysburg just after this item appeared was much more than "delightful rational entertainment"; it was the revelation of the soul of a people who knew the exaltation of victory, the bitterness of defeat, and the sorrow of irreparable loss.[4]

Although there was one band in town when the President's train reached the little railroad station at dusk (about 6:30 some reporters said), and although there were two bands on the train itself, there was, strangely enough, no music to greet the President on his arrival. Perhaps it was too near the supper hour, and people, including musicians, were too hungry!

Had there been any music during the long trip from Washington to Gettysburg? There were musicians aplenty—the United States Marine Band made the entire trip and the Second United States Artillery Band had boarded the train at Baltimore.

None of the party that day seems to have made any reference to music during the trip. John Hay did not mention it, saying only, "We had a pleasant sort of trip." Those who wrote in later years, MacVeagh, Nicolay, Cochrane, were much occupied with recounting other matters —MacVeagh how he "instinctively felt [as the President arose to speak at the cemetery] that the occasion was taking on a new grandeur, as of a great moment in history"; Nicolay on the writing of the "few appropriate

---

[4] *The Adams Sentinel* (Gettysburg), Nov. 17, 1863; Baltimore *American*, Nov. 20, 1863.

remarks"; while Cochrane wanted the world to know
that he had handed Lincoln a copy of the New York
Herald so that the President could "see what they say
about us."[5]

And, of course, as time went on, the important fact
turned out to be whether or not during the trip Lincoln
borrowed a pencil from Andrew Carnegie and wrote out
the "remarks" on a scrap of paper! Actually, the speech
was already partially written, and was finished at Gettysburg.

But even so, a trainload of people, a journey of several
hours, two bands of musicians, and no music? It wasn't
likely! At Baltimore, where the cars were uncoupled at
the Baltimore and Ohio station and dragged, one by one,
up to the Northern Central station, the Marine Band
piled out of the train and entertained both travelers and
spectators with some of its music. This music and the
cordial attitude of the Baltimoreans (in contrast to the
attitude displayed in February and April, 1861) made
the transfer less tedious than it otherwise might have
been.[6]

Then, as the train gathered speed on its journey to
Hanover Junction and thence to Gettysburg, with the
President and his party lunching in the baggage car converted into a diner, the members of the Marine Band
again took up their instruments and "the route out into
Pennsylvania was made to resound with martial airs."[7]
And although it is not so stated, it is not unreasonable to
think that the Second United States Artillery Band also
joined in with selections of its own. Thus, the musicians
contributed to the occasion en route even though they did

---

[5] Dennett, ed., *Lincoln . . . in the Diaries . . . of John Hay*, p. 119 ; Wayne Mac-
Veagh, "Lincoln at Gettysburg," *The Century Magazine*, LXXIX (Nov., 1909),
20-23 ; John G. Nicolay, "Lincoln's Gettysburg Address," *The Century Magazine*,
XLVII (Feb., 1894), 596-608 ; Henry C. Cochrane, "With Lincoln to Gettysburg
1863," *Abraham Lincoln Memorial Meetings held by the Pennsylvania Commandery
of Military Order of the Loyal Legion of U.S. in the years 1907-1908-1909-1911.*
(Address, Feb. 13, 1907.)

[6] Edward Hungerford, *The Story of the Baltimore and Ohio Railroad, 1827-1927*
(New York-London, 1828), II, 36-37 ; Baltimore *Gazette*, Nov. 19, 1863 ; Washington *National Republican*, Nov. 19, 1863 (item from the Baltimore *Sun*) ; Philadelphia *Press*, Nov. 21, 1863.

[7] N.Y. *Times*, Feb. 12, 1909.

not formally announce the arrival of the President's party with music!

A large crowd was on hand at the little railroad station to greet the President, but there was no formality except for a brief welcome by David Wills and other dignitaries. The travelers scattered "like a drop of quicksilver spilt," John Hay noted, and the President was escorted directly to the now famous Wills' house on the "Diamond."

The excitement created by the arrival of the presidential train subsided somewhat and the crowd thinned out—but not for long. People began to appear again from all directions, and soon the square was filled. The mood of the crowd as it gathered in the village that evening was not serious. Quite the contrary—a spirit of joyous exuberance and gaiety was everywhere in evidence. The visitors were in a holiday mood; this was a time of celebration!

Just a few hours earlier, a military review had taken place, in anticipation, one might say, of the special events to come. And now into the crowded square and to the Wills' house paraded a group of serenaders headed by the band of the Fifth New York Artillery Regiment, the same unit which had marched so well in review that afternoon.

Patriotic music and cheers filled the air as the eager crowd waited. There was a stir of restlessness, for the President did not appear immediately. It seemed a rather long interval before the door finally opened and Mr. Lincoln stepped out.

When the applause subsided, the President spoke briefly, his words being "chiefly an apology for not making any speech," as one reporter put it. He said:

> I appear before you, fellow-citizens, merely to thank you for this compliment. The inference is a very fair one that you would hear me for a little while at least, were I to commence to make a speech. I do not appear before you for the purpose of doing so, and for several substantial reasons. The most substantial of these is that I have no speech to make. [Laughter.] In my position it is somewhat important that I should not say any foolish things.

A VOICE—If you can help it.

MR. LINCOLN—It very often happens that the only way to help it is to say nothing at all. [Laughter.] Believing that is my present condition this evening, I must beg of you to excuse me from addressing you further.

Then, amid cheers and applause, the President retired. He had been in Gettysburg perhaps a little over an hour when, hearing the call of the people outside, he had appeared before them in response to the music of serenaders and a band.

Lincoln's brief remarks did not please the crowd, for the people wanted a speech—a rousing speech—and did not get one. But although disappointed, the crowd was not unfriendly, even though when the President had said, "In my position it is somewhat important that I should not say any foolish things," a voice had called out, "If you can help it," and even though John W. Forney saw fit later to berate his audience for not cheering the President.

There was considerable levity in the crowd as the President spoke, and the "If you can help it" may have been good-natured banter. The Philadelphia *Inquirer* commented that his remarks produced "great merriment!" Other accounts mention the applause ("prolonged," said some) when he retired, and contrary to Forney's observation, one newspaper mentioned that the President was cheered lustily.[8]

Perhaps of even greater significance was the fact that the President did not share the mood of the crowd. He was concerned with the importance of the events of the morrow, he wanted to give more thought to his part in the ceremony, and he wanted nothing to mar the occasion. It has been said that the cruel story circulated after

[8] There was marked variation in newspaper accounts of the serenades. Some papers, including the N.Y. *Herald*, Nov. 20, 1863, printed the version as given here; other accounts did not contain the "If you can help it." Washington *National Intelligencer*, Nov. 21, 1863; Philadelphia *Daily News*, Nov. 20, 1863. Very brief accounts were given in the Philadelphia *Inquirer*, Nov. 21, 1863, and in the Washington *Daily Morning Chronicle*, Nov. 21, 1863. The longer accounts mention the enthusiasm with which the President was greeted and the applause when he retired. The good humor of the crowd was noted in the Philadelphia *Inquirer*, *supra*, and in the Baltimore *American*, Nov. 20, 1863. No indication has been found that the audience was unfriendly, except from the remarks of Forney.

his visit to Antietam (a story arising from a musical incident) was in his thoughts at Gettysburg, and it may well be that he also remembered the criticism that resulted after the serenade of July 7 on the occasion of the celebration for the victories of Gettysburg and Vicksburg when he had used the expression that the enemy " 'turned tail' and run."

The President was not unaccustomed to serenades, although he was never wholly at ease when one occurred; nevertheless, back in the White House he was usually able to satisfy serenaders when he had no speech to make, and on some occasions, his words were especially well chosen. It is regrettable that, even though he shared not the spirit of the occasion, he could not have found a happier choice of words as he responded to his first serenade in Gettysburg.[9]

However, the disappointed serenaders soon recovered their enthusiasm, and went to serenade others. Secretary Seward, staying next door, obliged them with a patriotic speech; the noise and excitement increased as several groups of singers milled about, often singing lustily in competition with each other. The other bands joined in and lent their best efforts to the occasion.

Nine o'clock came. The President, who had gone to his room soon after the serenade to work on his speech, conferred with Mr. Wills and went to work again—words on paper—"a few appropriate remarks." Outside the din continued. There were shouting and laughter and music in all directions as the serenaders filled the air with notes of familiar songs. Sharing the holiday spirit, although somewhat bored by it all, were the President's two secretaries. Strangely enough, they were not with the President that evening, but were rather celebrating and trying to amuse themselves. John Hay, with Wayne Mac-Veagh and Secretary Stanton's son, after a visit to the local college, and a supper of oysters, found themselves

---

[9] His response on July 7, 1863, apart from the " 'turned tail' and run" expression, was felicitous and appropriate; his second brief repsonse at Frederick, Maryland, on October 6, 1862, as he was on his way back to Washington from his visit to the army at Antietam, might easily have been adapted to the situation at Gettysburg.

with John W. Forney, in the latter's room, where they
"drank a little whiskey with him."

They then went out and wandered around listening to
the serenades and serenaders. Having enough of that,
they returned to Forney's room, together with John Nicolay and several other friends. Here, after more whiskey, they had their own music—Nicolay sang his little
song "Three Thieves," and they all sang "John Brown."
That not being sufficient, they acquired a band in the
streets, and arranged a simulated serenade so that
Forney, now very talkative, could make a speech.

The music sounded, Forney appeared, chastised the
crowd for not cheering the President earlier, and then
rambled on for a time. MacVeagh and Judge Shannon
also spoke, after which they all went upstairs again.
Then, according to Hay, "We sang more John Brown and
went home." Not very edifying, but still a part of the
music at Gettysburg![10]

Two hours passed—it was eleven o'clock. The President, still at work, went next door to confer with Secretary Seward. The crowd outside had not diminished
greatly, and the excitement continued at a high level.
Down at the railroad station another train arrived, full
of important dignitaries, and with more music. This
train was the "Governors' special," to which cars from
Baltimore had been joined at Hanover Junction for the
last part of the trip.

The travelers on the "Governors' Special"—some four
hundred of them according to one report—were weary
and hungry. Their train had left Harrisburg at 1:30 P.M.
and was supposed to have connected with the President's
train at Hanover Junction. But delays occurred and hence
the train arrived several hours late.[11]

Expecting to stop at York for dinner, the travelers had
only a lunch before leaving Harrisburg. But by the time
the train arrived at Goldsboro many were already hun-

[10] Dennett, ed., *Lincoln . . . in the Diaries . . . of John Hay*, pp. 119-21.

[11] Philadelphia *Evening Bulletin*, Nov. 19, 1863; Philadelphia *Press*, Nov. 21,
1863. The governors were thus not present for the early evening serenades. They
were also too late to dine with the President at the Wills' house.

gry.[12] As soon as the train stopped there was a rush of generals, governors, and others for the small restaurant in town, and its entire stock—everything from petrified gingerbread to green apples—was immediately bought up.

Amid a "shifting Kaleidoscope of Governors, ginger bread and generals" some fared better than others, but none too well. Governor Seymour dined on persimmons, Governor Brough had crackers and cheese, while ex-Secretary Cameron feasted on a green apple. Ex-Governor Dennison won the approval of the fair sex, for, having secured an armful of stale ginger cakes, he gallantly carried them to the ladies' car!

There was still hope that dinner, or at least some food, might be obtained at York, but there was none. The train made only a short stop at the town, so short in fact, that several brave souls who had gotten off to search for food were left at the station! Their predicament provided some amusement for the hungry people aboard "all the way to Gettysburg."

The one redeeming feature of this rather hectic journey was the music of the band. Governor Curtin had invited a well-known German band from Philadelphia to participate in the ceremony at Gettysburg, and by its excellent music along the way, it contributed much to relieve the monotony of the trip. Fortunately, the members of the band were among the lucky ones who had obtained refreshments at Goldsboro, and as if in gratitude, the musicians then and there "proceeded to discourse music of the most entertaining description."

The playing of the band brought townsmen to the scene, and when (just before the train was to depart) the musicians struck up national anthems "in spirited style," the citizens gave three cheers for the governor of the state. Apparently the much-appreciated music of the band, from Harrisburg to Gettysburg, did not overtax the musicians, for their music the next day was of high quality and was praised whenever mentioned.

---

[12] Goldsboro, although but a small village, was the most important station between Harrisburg and York. It was about halfway on the approximately thirty-mile run.

In marked contrast to the strenuous journey and inadequate arrangements of the "Governors' special" was the pleasant and well-planned (though also long) trip of the city officials of Baltimore.[13] Their special car, together with the car of the state officials of Maryland, left Baltimore at three o'clock for Hanover Junction and Gettysburg. The Baltimore contingent numbered about fifty persons, and so carefully were plans made for the party that nobody lacked for food or lodging.

The Baltimore car, decorated the full length of the ceiling with an American flag, was a sleeper from the Baltimore and Ohio Railroad. It contained a buffet which was stocked with food and refreshments for the entire journey. Using the well-appointed car for sleeping quarters and for meals, the Baltimoreans did not have to depend upon chance accommodations en route or while in Gettysburg.

With the Baltimore officials went a group of well-trained singers, the National Union Musical Association of Baltimore. Like the Philadelphia band on the "Governors' special," the Musical Association was to participate in the exercises the next day, and also, like the band, it provided entertaining and inspiring music on the trip to Gettysburg. At every station stop the singers sang national airs—"We Are Coming, Father Abraham," and the "Battle-Cry of Freedom"—and to vary the program from time to time they sang humorous songs. One such song of about fifty verses, each a sort of repetition of the preceding one, which "was sung with fine effect" began:

> We were there all the while
> At the siege of Carlisle—

The entertainment provided by the Musical Association and the good cheer dispensed at the buffet by one Captain James were ample compensation for the slowness of the journey. When the Baltimore car was attached

---

[13] Baltimore *American*, Nov. 20, 23, 1863; Baltimore *Gazette*, Nov. 18, 19, 21, 1863; Baltimore *Sun*, Nov. 19, 1863.

to the "Governors' special" at Hanover Junction for the final part of the trip to their common destination, and the two groups mingled, many of the less fortunate travelers on the "special" enjoyed the hospitality and refreshments of their Baltimore friends. They were also "regaled with several songs by the Baltimore Glee Club . . . who, by their performance, greatly relieved the otherwise tedious journey." Perhaps the band joined in also.

Once off the train at Gettysburg, many of the latest arrivals dispersed to whatever lodgings were available. But not the singers of the Musical Association. In spite of the late hour, they wanted to pay their respects to the President. Marching to the square, they joined the crowd outside the Harper residence and began to sing. Amid the applause of the crowd, they filled the night air with "inspiring and appropriate" selections, including "Our Army Is Marching On" and, again, "We Are Coming, Father Abraham."

Mr. Harper came to the door and introduced the President who, having just finished his conference with Secretary Seward, was about to return to his own room. Mr. Lincoln bowed, but declined to speak. He bid the gathering "Good night," and then walked at a brisk pace to the Wills' house. The crowd seemed satisfied and gave a tremendous cheer.[14]

It was well after midnight when the weary President climbed into bed. Twice he had been serenaded by singers, some of whom had kept the air filled with music during much of the evening, and some of whom, even now, were not ready to end their singing, cheering, and shouting. Benjamin B. French, who stopped at Mr. Harper's that night, recorded that before he dropped off to sleep between one and two o'clock, he heard a full chorus sing admirably the whole of a "well-known production." Appropriately

---

[14] Washington *Daily Morning Chronicle*, Nov. 21, 1863; Philadelphia *Press*, Nov. 21, 1863; Baltimore *Gazette*, Nov. 21, 1863; Baltimore *Sun*, Nov. 21, 1863; Baltimore *American*, Nov. 20, 1863, quotes the President as saying, as he left the Harper residence, "I can't speak tonight, gentlemen. I will see you all tomorrow." According to another source, Lincoln, seeing the street and sidewalk full of people, said to the guard, "You clear a way and I will hang onto your coat." Orton H. Carmichael, *Lincoln's Gettysburg Address* (New York-Cincinnati, 1917), p. 50.

enough, that "well-known production" was "We Are Coming, Father Abraham, Three Hundred Thousand More!"[15]

At length, however, the music ceased, and the square became empty. The tired singers sought their lodgings for the night, and a restless sort of stillness spread over the town as they stowed themselves away in temporary quarters—the lucky ones in comfortable beds, the less fortunate in church pews, on parlor floors, or in the halls of the local college.[16]

People were astir early in Gettysburg the next morning. The weather, fortunately, was fair and moderate. "Day dawned on Thursday with an unclouded sky, giving assurances of lovely weather," reported a local newspaper.[17] At seven o'clock the clear notes of a bugle sounded from Cemetery Hill, as if calling the citizens to the day's activities, and cannon boomed out a thirty-four-gun salute to the President. By nine o'clock the village square was jammed with people, and in the side streets traffic tangles of carriages and wagons added to the confusion.

Marshals and their aides, easily identified by their yellow scarfs, tricolored rosettes, black and white shoulder knots, and buff-colored gauntlets, were hurrying to and fro, making a determined effort to get the military and civilian units and dignitaries into line for the procession.

When the President appeared at ten o'clock, and mounted the "beast" that had been provided for him, he was immediately surrounded by the crowd. As the people pressed close, he shook hands with many, and one can imagine Chief Marshal Lamon bustling up to end the visiting and get the President into line so that the already delayed procession could get started on its way.

Finally all was in readiness—a minute gun boomed in the distance, the bands struck up "in fine confusion," and the parade began its march up Baltimore Street toward the cemetery. "The procession filing around the roads,

---

[15] French, ed., *Diary of B. B. French*, pp. 123-24.
[16] Philadelphia *Evening Bulletin*, Nov. 20, 21, 1863; Philadelphia *Inquirer*, Nov. 20, 21, 1863.
[17] *The Compiler* (Gettysburg), Nov. 23, 1863.

the bands playing down the valley, were glorious in sight and sound," wrote one observer, and another commented on the colorful uniforms, the regalia of the fraternal societies, the wounded veterans of the Army of the Potomac carrying a flag inscribed to their fallen comrades, and the bright uniforms of the musicians.[18]

All four bands were in line: the United States Marine Band, the Second United States Artillery Regiment Band, the Band of the Fifth New York Artillery, and Birgfeld's Band of Philadelphia. Curiously enough, while it can be easily determined where in the procession the Odd Fellows marched and where the officers of the Adams Express Company were, it cannot be readily ascertained, except by deduction, exactly where the bands were located! But, then, it didn't really matter, as they were well spaced and answered each other effectively as the parade moved forward.[19]

There was a marked contrast between the mood and atmosphere that morning and the mood and atmosphere of the evening before. The gaiety and holiday spirit were gone and the people were now more serious and restrained; the atmosphere of celebration had disappeared and over the town and the people had spread a mantle of solemnity. The night before, people had been celebrating the victory of the bloody battle fought on this very soil four months earlier; the next morning they were remembering the awful cost of that victory and were about to honor the dead.

The music that filled the town the night before but reflected that mood of victory and spirit of celebration—"We Are Coming, Father Abraham," "John Brown's Body," the "Star-Spangled Banner";[20] the music that

[18] Boston *Journal*, Nov. 23, 1863; Philadelphia *Press*, Nov. 21, 1863; N.Y. *Herald*, Nov. 20, 1863.

[19] The official Order of Procession did not indicate the location of any of the bands in the parade. Newspaper accounts did not agree on the location of the bands, and did not name all four bands. Cf. Baltimore *Gazette*, Nov. 21, 1863; Cincinnati *Commercial*, Nov. 20, 1863; Philadelphia *Evening Bulletin*, Nov. 20, 1863; Philadelphia *Inquirer*, Nov. 20, 1863.

[20] One newspaper contained a report deprecating the noisy celebration on the evening of November 18. The report said that the crowd had nothing else to do except make a noise or hear a speech, that many had come to have a good time, and it didn't matter much whether the occasion was a wedding or a funeral. There was, the report continued, no malicious intent in the parading, shouting, singing

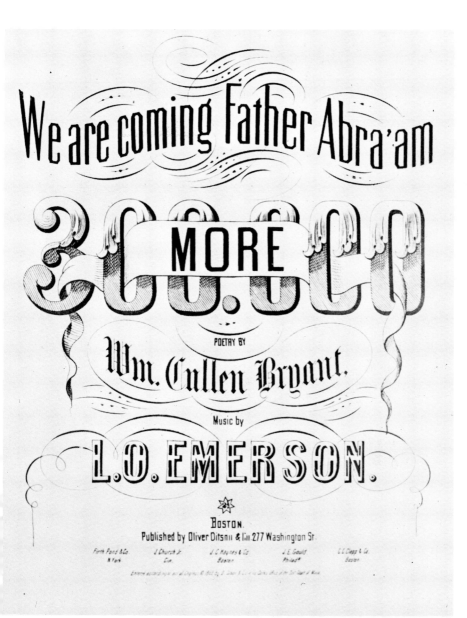

"WE ARE COMING FATHER ABRA'AM"

The words of this popular song were actually written by a New York financier, James S. Gibbons. Although Gibbons' poem was put to music by a number of composers, none of the sheet-music editions gives credit to the real author! Lincoln was familiar with the piece and heard it on numerous occasions.

PLATE XVIII

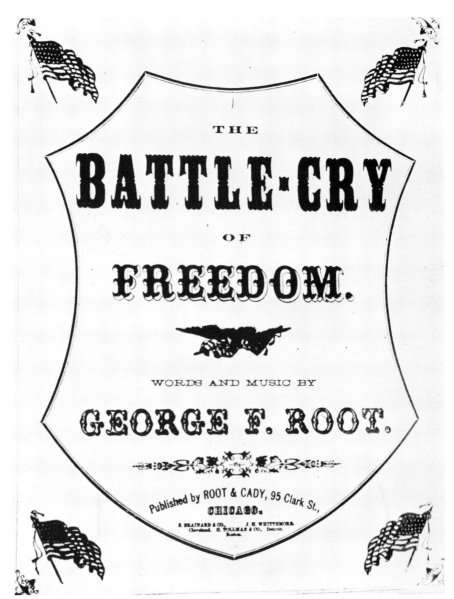

"THE BATTLE-CRY OF FREEDOM"

Composed in response to the President's call for more troops in the summer of 1862. Lincoln heard the song's stirring notes many times.

PLATE XIX

GREAT WAR MEETING IN WASHINGTON, D.C.

It was meetings such as this one that brought a response to the President's call for "three hundred thousand more." This meeting, which Lincoln attended, began about five o'clock and lasted well into the evening, ending with a display of fireworks.

(*Harper's Weekly*, August 23, 1862)

PLATE XX

FREEDOM TO THE SLAVES
Proclaimed January 1st 1863, by ABRAHAM LINCOLN, President of the United States.
"Proclaim liberty throughout All the land unto All the inhabitants thereof." ___ LEV XXV. 10

"FREEDOM TO THE SLAVES"
A reproduction of a Currier & Ives print dealing with slavery and emancipation
PLATE XXI

COURTESY DEPARTMENT OF LINCOLNIANA, LINCOLN MEMORIAL UNIVERSITY, HARROGATE, TENN.

"THE PRESIDENT'S EMANCIPATION MARCH"

The composer, George E. Fawcett, sent a copy of this piece to the President, who acknowledged it with thanks. The composition is said to have attained wide popularity.

COURTESY DEPARTMENT OF LINCOLNIANA, LINCOLN MEMORIAL UNIVERSITY, HARROGATE, TENN.

"THE JOHN BROWN SONG"

An early edition with "New and Revised Words." There are six verses referring to John Brown of Osawatomie and Harpers Ferry.

PLATE XXII

WARD HILL LAMON

Lincoln's close friend and constant companion. Lamon loved to sing and frequently did for Lincoln both in Illinois and in Washington.

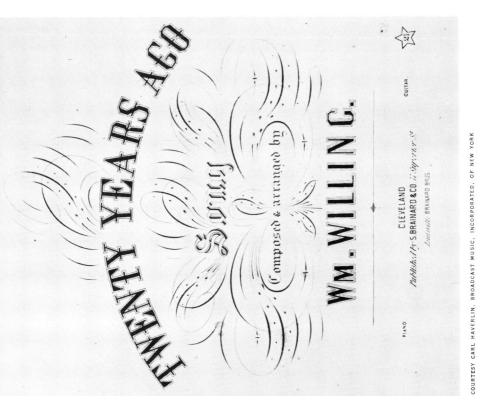

"TWENTY YEARS AGO"

The "little sad song" that Ward Lamon sang for Lincoln during the Antietam visit was one of Lincoln's favorites.

LINCOLN WITH ALLAN PINKERTON AND GENERAL JOHN A. McCLERNAND

One of several photographs taken during the President's visit to Antietam in October, 1862.

"COMMODORE" NUTT

One day in October, 1862, a meeting of the Cabinet was interrupted while P. T. Barnum's protégé, George Washington Morrison ("Commodore") Nutt sang "Columbia, the Gem of the Ocean" for the President and the members of the Cabinet.

PLATE XXIV

WALTER KITTREDGE'S SONG
Popular among soldiers in the North and South, it is still a favorite today

"TENTING ON THE OLD CAMP GROUND"
Walter Kittredge received many requests for autographed copies of "Tenting Tonight." The original of this copy is in the collection of Broadcast Music, Incorporated, of New York.

"WHEN THIS CRUEL DRAFT IS OVER"

Opposition to the draft expressed in song

"WHEN THIS CRUEL WAR IS OVER"

This song struck a responsive chord in the hearts of many during the dark days of the war.

PLATE XXVI

THE GRAND REVIEW

When Lincoln went down to visit the Army of the Potomac in April, 1863, he witnessed small reviews and then a grand review. At the Grand Review General Hooker wore a brand-new uniform coat and rode a horse that he had just received as a gift from admirers in New York. The President was clad in his usual black coat and tall

NEW YORK AVENUE PRESBYTERIAN CHURCH, WASHINGTON, D.C.

Here Lincoln worshipped, sought solace, found strength, and gave thanks. At that time the church edifice was new, having been dedicated October 14, 1860. The church served the congregation until 1950 when it was demolished and replaced by the present structure, dedicated December 21, 1951. The present church contains many reminders of the Lincolns—the Lincoln pew from the earlier church, the Lincoln Chapel, and the Lincoln Parlor wherein is placed the manuscript of Lincoln's draft of a bill, July 14, 1862, for compensated emancipation.

PLATE XXVIII

REV. PHINEAS D. GURLEY, D.D.
Minister of the New York Avenue Presbyterian Church, pastor and friend of the Lincoln family in Washington.
PLATE XXIX

ADAPTED TO

SOCIAL, PRIVATE, AND PUBLIC WORSHIP

IN THE

PRESBYTERIAN CHURCH

IN THE

UNITED STATES OF AMERICA.

APPROVED AND AUTHORIZED BY THE GENERAL ASSEMBLY.

To which are added, The Form of Government of the Presbyterian Church in the United States of America, The Directory for Worship, and the Shorter Catechism.

PHILADELPHIA:

PRESBYTERIAN BOARD OF PUBLICATION.

TITLE PAGE OF AN 1843 EDITION OF A WIDELY USED PRESBYTERIAN HYMNAL

One such as this was used in the New York Avenue church, and Abraham Lincoln was undoubtedly acquainted with it. It contains the familiar hymns (words only) referred to in the text.

FOR THE

ARMY AND NAVY,

PUBLISHED BY THE

AMERICAN TRACT SOCIETY,

150 NASSAU-STREET, NEW YORK.

FRONT COVER OF A HYMNBOOK DISTRIBUTED TO SOLDIERS AND SAILORS

Probably published in 1863. The book is small, measuring only 2¾x4¼ inches, and is less than a quarter of an inch thick.

PLATE XXX

"NATIONAL CONSECRATION CHANT OR HYMN"

Sung by the National Union Musical Association of Baltimore just before President
Lincoln made his dedicatory address at Gettysburg on November 19, 1863.

THE FINAL MUSICAL NUMBER ON THE PROGRAM AT THE CEMETERY
AT GETTYSBURG

Sung by volunteer singers from the churches of Gettysburg

PLATE XXXI

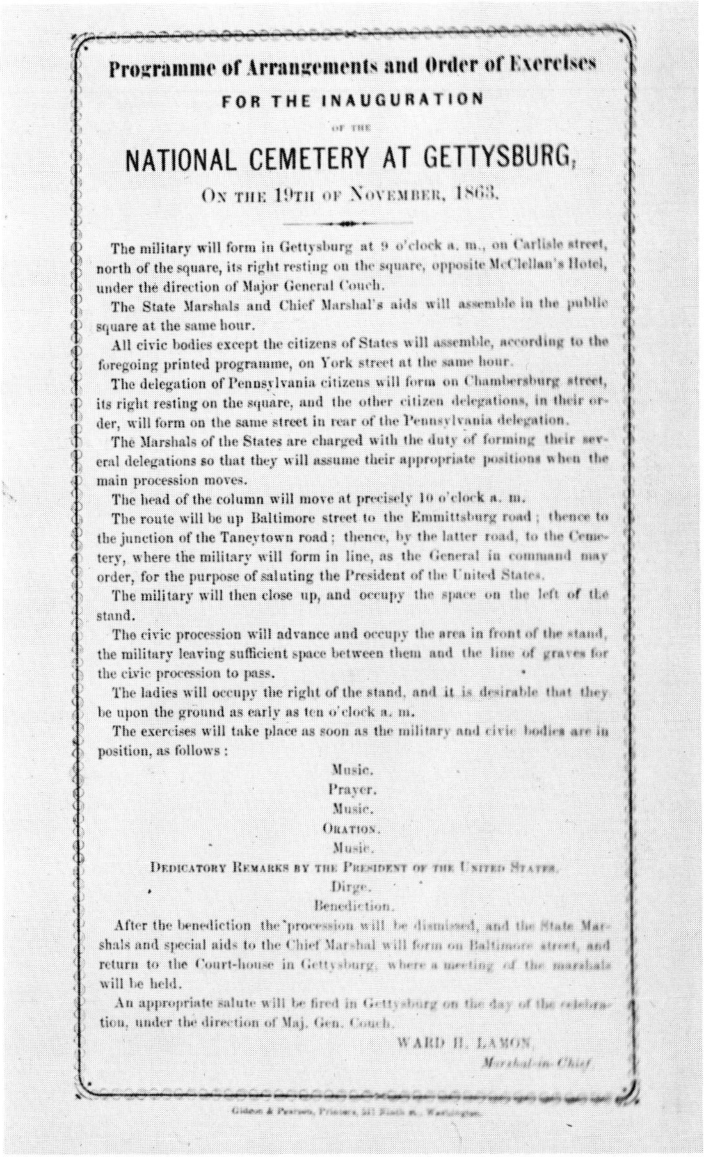

Programme of Arrangements and Order of Exercises

FOR THE INAUGURATION

OF THE

NATIONAL CEMETERY AT GETTYSBURG,

ON THE 19TH OF NOVEMBER, 1863.

The military will form in Gettysburg at 9 o'clock a. m., on Carlisle street, north of the square, its right resting on the square, opposite McClellan's Hotel, under the direction of Major General Couch.

The State Marshals and Chief Marshal's aids will assemble in the public square at the same hour.

All civic bodies except the citizens of States will assemble, according to the foregoing printed programme, on York street at the same hour.

The delegation of Pennsylvania citizens will form on Chambersburg street, its right resting on the square, and the other citizen delegations, in their order, will form on the same street in rear of the Pennsylvania delegation.

The Marshals of the States are charged with the duty of forming their several delegations so that they will assume their appropriate positions when the main procession moves.

The head of the column will move at precisely 10 o'clock a. m.

The route will be up Baltimore street to the Emmittsburg road; thence to the junction of the Taneytown road; thence, by the latter road, to the Cemetery, where the military will form in line, as the General in command may order, for the purpose of saluting the President of the United States.

The military will then close up, and occupy the space on the left of the stand.

The civic procession will advance and occupy the area in front of the stand, the military leaving sufficient space between them and the line of graves for the civic procession to pass.

The ladies will occupy the right of the stand, and it is desirable that they be upon the ground as early as ten o'clock a. m.

The exercises will take place as soon as the military and civic bodies are in position, as follows:

Music.

Prayer.

Music.

ORATION.

Music.

DEDICATORY REMARKS BY THE PRESIDENT OF THE UNITED STATES.

Dirge.

Benediction.

After the benediction the procession will be dismissed, and the State Marshals and special aids to the Chief Marshal will form on Baltimore street, and return to the Court-house in Gettysburg, where a meeting of the marshals will be held.

An appropriate salute will be fired in Gettysburg on the day of the celebration, under the direction of Maj. Gen. Couch.

WARD H. LAMON,

Marshal-in-Chief.

Gideon & Pearson, Printers, 511 Ninth st., Washington.

OFFICIAL PROGRAM, NATIONAL CEMETERY AT GETTYSBURG, NOVEMBER 19, 1863

The official program gives no information at all concerning the bands that played, the musical group that sang, or the names of the musical selections of the day.

PLATE XXXII

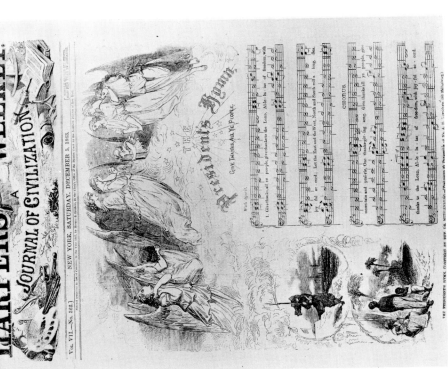

COVER PAGE OF SHEET-MUSIC EDITION OF "THE PRESIDENT'S HYMN"

With music by J. W. Turner, a Boston composer who wrote more than a dozen war songs.

"THE PRESIDENT'S HYMN"

"Give Thanks, All Ye People," written by Dr. William A. Muhlenberg, a prominent Episcopal minister of New York City, was inspired by President Lincoln's Proclamation for a National Thanksgiving. It soon came to be known as "The President's Hymn," and was sung in many churches on Thanksgiving

echoed over the hills and valleys the next morning was
of a different sort, quite in keeping with the solemnity of
the occasion. Who even today is not moved to solemn
thoughts and cherished memories when a bugle calls, and
who today is not filled with sober realization of the fearful sacrifice that war demands when he hears the cannon boom?

It was fitting, then, that the day began with the call of
the bugle, it was fitting that the cannon boomed as the
vast assemblage moved toward the spot of dedication, and
it was fitting, also, that the bands played solemn notes of
march and dirge as they came to that hallowed ground.

It was near twelve o'clock, noon. The dignitaries and
guests were at their places on the platform, the military
units were in position at the left of the stand, and the
several musical organizations (six in all) stood directly
in front. Benjamin B. French, in the temporary absence
of Chief Marshal Lamon, stepped forward and gave a
signal. It was the signal for the opening number of the
program, a dirge entitled "Homage d'un Heros."

This piece was composed especially for the occasion
by Adolph Birgfeld, business manager and director of
German opera at the Academy of Music in Philadelphia.
Birgfeld (whose name was spelled incorrectly in the official report and was spelled in various ways in other
sources) trained his own German band and directed it
at public functions and also at the opera when extra musicians were needed there. He and his band, invited by
Governor Curtin to attend the ceremony, had come will-
ingly and had insisted on paying their own expenses.

As noted earlier, Birgfeld's Band had enlivened the trip
of the "Governors' special" to Gettysburg. It was the
only Pennsylvania band at the ceremony, and was given
the "place of honor" on the program by its assignment
to play this opening number. Its playing was highly
praised; the Chicago *Tribune* called the dirge "magnifi-

---

and horn-blowing, but it was in bad taste and out of place. Interestingly enough,
this was the N.Y. *World!* N.Y. *World,* Nov. 21, 1863.

cent," "a piece eloquently suited to the occasion . . . performed with pre-eminent skill. . . ."[21]

Then followed the lengthy prayer of the Chaplain of the House of Representatives, Reverend T. H. Stockton, after which the United States Marine Band played that grand old hymn, known and sung by all, at home and in the army camp, "Old Hundred."[22]

Two hours later. As a fitting companion piece in verse and song to the highlight of the occasion, the oration of Mr. Everett, there was another musical selection, listed in the official report as a "Hymn composed by B. B. French, Esq."

It is well known that French wrote his "Ode" on sudden inspiration when, at Gettysburg with Lamon a few days before the ceremony arranging details for the program, he learned that no prominent poet had been persuaded to write a piece for the occasion. French's verses were printed in newspaper accounts of the ceremony, in official reports, and found their way into the literature of Gettysburg generally. Somehow, in a manner not now known, the hymn came into the hands of Wilson G. Horner, the young and popular leader of the National Union Musical Association of Baltimore.

Horner, too, was equal to the occasion. Between the time that French completed his verses (November 13) and the day of the ceremony (November 19), Horner composed appropriate music, set the words to the music, and apparently introduced the piece to his singers.

Consequently, when Mr. Everett finished speaking, it was the Musical Association of Baltimore, led by Horner using a small American flag as a baton, that sang the "Consecration Hymn" to the music composed by its own versatile director.[23]

These Baltimoreans were a loyal and hardy lot of singers. They had organized their Musical Association early

---

[21] Chicago *Tribune*, Nov. 21, 1863.

[22] Curiously enough, the selection was referred to by some as "The grand old hymn of Luther!" Washington *National Intelligencer*, Nov. 21, 1863; Baltimore *American*, Nov. 20, 1863.

[23] Washington *Daily Morning Chronicle*, Nov. 21, 1863, observed that when some "idiot" proposed three cheers for Mr. Everett, no one responded. The audience had more sense.

in the war (with emphasis on the *National Union* in their name) and had given many hours in singing for soldiers at camps and hospitals. They had sung their way to Gettysburg on the train the day before, had serenaded the President only a little before midnight, had slept on the parlor floor at the MacCreary residence, had marched to the cemetery, stood two hours in the November air (a thing in itself which would be catastrophic for many singers), and in spite of all this, they sang the hymn "in fine style," "with excellent effect," and "in a manner that elicited the admiration of all!" A Baltimore reporter summed it up as follows:

> The Glee Club of Baltimore conspicuously participated in the ceremonies of the dedication, their musical talent and patriotism contributing not a little to give *eclat* to the occasion.[24]

There was still another musical number on the program. After the President had spoken, a volunteer choir from the churches of Gettysburg, accompanied by Birgfeld's Band, sang another dirge, which was expressly composed for the occasion by James G. Percival and Alfred Delaney:

> O! it is great for our Country to
>   die, whose ranks are contending,
> Bright is the wreath of our fame; glory
>   awaits us for aye;
> Glory, that never is dim, shining on with
>   a light never ending,
> Glory that never shall fade, never O!
>   never away!

A Philadelphia paper termed the piece "a beautiful dirge," and a local paper had high praise for the choristers. Their singing, the local paper reported, was "an exquisite performance, and has rarely been excelled on such an occasion."

John Hay was not so impressed, however, for this was

---

[24] Baltimore *American*, Nov. 23, 1863. The organization was inaccurately referred to as the "Baltimore Glee Club." Its correct name was the National Union Musical Association of Baltimore. *Ibid.*, Nov. 21, 1863.

probably the selection to which he referred (rather flippantly) in his diary when he wrote that "the music wailed and we went home." After a brief benediction and another cannon salute, the ceremonies were over.[25]

It was rather late in the afternoon when the presidential party finished its tardy lunch at the Wills' house, but the activities were not yet over, and neither was the music. For nearly an hour the President was the "victim of a 'hands shaking' that must have taxed his good nature to the utmost," and then he took that famous walk with John Burns to the Presbyterian Church for the five o'clock meeting.

Meanwhile, the several bands alternating with each other on the "Diamond" outside, "kept the air resonant with melody till sunset," and, in addition, the Marine Band escorted Mr. Lincoln and Mr. Burns to the church.[26]

Down at the railroad station there was more music. A huge crowd had gathered there; some of the people in the vast crowd had been there several hours. All were waiting for trains to take them home. They would have to wait a while longer, as no trains were scheduled to leave until after the departure of the President's train.

Although tired, they were patient and orderly, and their weariness was at least partly relieved by music. The tireless Baltimore singers were there and sang, not once, but many times, "a constant succession of patriotic and popular songs!"[27]

When the President made his hasty exit from the church and proceeded to the crowded station to board his train at 6:30 (or thereabouts), his twenty-four-hour visit

---

[25] Philadelphia *Evening Bulletin*, Nov. 20, 1863; *The Adams Sentinel* (Gettysburg), Dec. 8, 1863; Dennett, ed., *Lincoln . . . in the Diaries . . . of John Hay*, p. 121. Seventy years later, the last survivor of the Gettysburg choir, Mrs. M. O. Smith, of Hanover, aged ninety-two, was a guest of honor at the Anniversary celebration at Gettysburg. *Gettysburg Times*, Nov. 19, 1958. A contemporary of Mrs. Smith, George D. Gitt, recalled at that time that as Mr. Lincoln was leaving the platform after the exercises, he leaned over and shook hands with the singers, including Mrs. Smith. George D. Gitt, "I Saw and Heard Lincoln at Gettysburg," *Liberty*, X (Nov. 25, 1933), 36-38; Wirt Barritz, "November 19, 1863," *St. Nicholas Magazine*, LXI (Nov., 1933), 13-15, 29.

[26] Washington *Evening Star*, Nov. 20, 1863; Washington *Daily Morning Chronicle*, Nov. 21, 1863; Boston *Journal*, Nov. 23, 1863.

[27] Washington *Daily Morning Chronicle*, Nov. 21, 1863.

was ended.[28] Presumably that same train chugging from Gettysburg with the President's party aboard and with the Chief Executive stretched out ill in a drawing-room, carried also the Marine Band and the Second Regiment Band. But it was more than likely that the instruments were silent on the homeward journey, for the musicians, too, had had two very strenuous days.

Washington was still and silent when the train arrived just before one o'clock the next morning.

In Gettysburg the town was fast reapproaching normal, for people seemed in as much of a hurry to leave as they had been to get there a day earlier. The streets, which twenty-four hours before had been alive with people, now had a sort of empty look, and instead of music and songs which had filled the air, there was a growing silence.

Up at the cemetery, where slept the honored dead, all was silent, too. The people had gone, and with them had gone the music; a verse from B. B. French's "Ode" provided a benediction which would echo through the years to come:

> Here let them rest,
> And summer's heat, and winter's cold,
> Shall glow and freeze above this mould,
> A thousand years shall pass away,
> A nation still shall mourn this clay,
> Which now is blest.

---

[28] One reporter embellished his account of the services at the church by stating that after the President had listened a few minutes to the main speaker, he was so discouraged by the notes of the speech that he bent his head on the back of the pew in front of him and went quietly to sleep! N.Y. *World*, Nov. 21, 1863.

CHAPTER XV

"GIVE THANKS, ALL YE PEOPLE"

ON THURSDAY AFTER HIS RETURN FROM GETTYSBURG, THE President was in bed, ill with a mild case of varioloid which kept him confined for three weeks. But his spirits were good, and for him and the people of the North the skies brightened as the year 1863 came to an end. That Thursday—the last Thursday in November—became a day of special significance and a turning point in the morale of the Union.

In the weeks following the July victories at Gettysburg and Vicksburg there was a letdown. Meade could not be induced to move against Lee, and after the defeat at Chickamauga, the President's attempts to get action in Tennessee were in vain. He prodded and urged. To General Rosecrans he wrote: "You and Burnside now have him [the enemy] by the throat, and he must break your hold, or perish."[1] Even the change in command produced no immediate results.

On the home front there were irritations and frustrations, such as the interference with the draft by judges who issued writs of *habeas corpus,* Blair's speech at Rockville, Maryland, and the continual wrangling between the Radicals and Conservatives in Missouri.

When he left for Gettysburg on November 18, Lincoln was depressed and distressed. Tad was not feeling well, and Mrs. Lincoln was upset. He returned from Gettysburg, ill himself, and convinced that his speech there had been a "flat failure."[2]

But the next day he received a felicitous note from

---

[1] Lincoln, *Works,* VI, 510.
[2] Milton H. Shutes, *Lincoln and the Doctors* (N.Y., 1933), pp. 85-86; Lamon, *Recollections,* p. 171.

Edward Everett congratulating him on his speech at
Gettysburg, and the following day, his illness having been
diagnosed as a mild case of smallpox, he was in good
enough spirits to remark: "Now I have something that
I can give to everybody."³

He was heartened by the news from Tennessee, and on
Wednesday, November 25, upon hearing details of Or-
chard Knob and Lookout Mountain, he telegraphed his
thanks to General Grant. And then on Thursday came
further good news from Chattanooga. It was entirely
fortuitous but eminently appropriate that that day had,
by his own proclamation, already been designated as a
day of National Thanksgiving!

For many years that remarkable woman, Sarah Josepha
Hale, editor of *Godey's Lady's Book* and campaigner for
good causes, had been urging the establishment of such
a day. In her first book, *Northwood*, written in 1827, she
devoted an entire chapter to the description of a New
England Thanksgiving; in the 1840's she began a sys-
tematic effort to have the last Thursday in November
recognized throughout the nation as Thanksgiving Day.
She editorialized in *Godey's*, she wrote letters to Presidents, governors, and countless other prominent persons
urging the establishment of Thanksgiving on that day.⁴

To Mrs. Hale, the great significant fact of the American experience had been the union of all the states. A
National Thanksgiving Day, with its historical and sentimental connotations, would, she thought, serve to focus
attention upon and strengthen the Union and perhaps
also check the disruptive influences aroused by the growing controversy over slavery. In February, 1860, she
wrote:

> We believe our Thanksgiving Day, if fixed and perpetuated,
> will be a great and sanctifying promoter of this national
> spirit. . . . Let Thanksgiving, our American Holiday, give us

³ Shutes, *Lincoln and the Doctors*, p. 86. Another version of Lincoln's quip was:
"Now let the office-seekers come, for I have something I can give to all of them."
Ruth P. Randall, *Mary Lincoln*, p. 329.

⁴ Ruth E. Finley, *The Lady of Godey's: Sarah Josepha Hale* (Philadelphia and
London, 1931), chaps. XI, XII.

American books—song, story, and sermon—written expressly to awaken in American hearts the love of home and country, of thankfulness to God, and peace between brethren.[5]

Her campaign had had some measure of success. By 1859 thirty states and three territories celebrated on the last Thursday in November, and the day was observed by Americans in foreign capitals and on American naval vessels at sea. A year later it was celebrated in Japan, and at the Thanksgiving Dinner in Berlin the menu contained all the traditional dishes except pumpkin pie! When the war came, Mrs. Hale urged the setting aside of the day as an armistice, adding, "The way is already prepared. . . . Shall the 28th of November [the last Thursday] be this year an American Thanksgiving Day?"[6]

On September 28, 1863, Mrs. Hale made a direct appeal to President Lincoln, urging him to issue a proclamation declaring the last Thursday in November a "Day of National Thanksgiving."[7] She also addressed a letter of similar vein to Secretary of State Seward. Seward replied on September 29: "I have received your interesting letter . . . and have commended the same to the consideration of the President."[8]

To Seward was given the assignment of drafting the proclamation. This he did, and on Saturday of that week, October 3, he read the document to Secretary Welles who recorded in his *Diary*: "I complimented the paper as very well done, and him for his talent in the preparation of such papers, which pleased him. . . ."[9] That same

[5] "The New National Holiday," *Godey's Lady's Book*, Feb., 1860, R. T. Lincoln Coll., 26702-3.

[6] "Thanksgiving—the New National Holiday," *Godey's Lady's Book*, Nov., 1860; "Thanksgiving Day: The Last Thursday in November," *Godey's Lady's Book*, Nov., 1861, R. T. Lincoln Coll., 26703-4.

[7] Sarah Josepha Hale to Abraham Lincoln, Sept. 28, 1863, R. T. Lincoln Coll., 26699.

[8] Finley, *The Lady of Godey's*, p. 200.

[9] Morse, ed., *Diary of Gideon Welles*, I, 449-50. Welles had some reservations about the "Nationalizing process." Thanksgiving had always been a matter for the states, and there might still be occasions when state observance would be more appropriate. It would hardly do, he thought, to make the "National Day" mandatory.

In 1860, Thanksgiving was duly observed in Lincoln's own state on November 29. Henry Villard, then in Springfield, noted: "A lot of country people came in on Thanksgiving Day. One garrulous old lady said she well remembered Abe when still a boy in his old home in Kentucky. She expressed great astonishment at his elevation to the highest office in the land. 'Why,' she said, 'he was the gawkiest,

day the proclamation, signed by the President, was given
to the public. It began:

> The year that is drawing to its close, has been filled with
> the blessings of fruitful fields and healthful skies. To these
> bounties, which are so constantly enjoyed that we are prone
> to forget the source from which they come, others have been
> added, which are of so extraordinary a nature, that they can-
> not fail to penetrate and soften even the heart which is ha-
> bitually insensible to the ever watchful providence of Almighty
> God.

Then, after recounting the accomplishments and progress of the past year, all in the midst of a civil war of
"unequalled magnitude and severity," it continued:

> No human counsel hath devised nor hath any mortal hand
> worked out these great things. They are the gracious gifts
> of the Most High God, who, while dealing with us in anger for
> our sins, hath nevertheless remembered mercy.

It called upon the people to give thanks, to remember
those who had suffered by war, and to

> fervently implore the interposition of the Almighty Hand to
> heal the wounds of the nation and to restore it as soon as
> may be consistent with the Divine purposes to the full en-
> joyment of peace, harmony, tranquility and Union.[10]

The proclamation met with instant approval. Newspapers printed it, discussed it at length, and urged its
observance. Governors, as in the past, issued proclamations, and even some mayors did the same.[11]

---

dullest looking boy you ever saw,' but she added: 'There was one thing remarkable
about him—He could always remember things better than any other boy in the
neighborhood.' " Henry Villard, *Lincoln on the Eve of '61* (N.Y., 1941), pp. 30-31.
   The New York *Tribune*, Dec. 1, 1860, carried a dispatch stating: "Quite a number of country people were in town, and paid their respects to the President-elect.
Mr. Lincoln, like the rest of Anglo-American mankind, feasted on a roast turkey,
and having special cause to thank his Maker, attended Divine Service."
   In 1861, Lincoln ordered government departments closed on November 28, because Washington and Georgetown observed Thanksgiving. Lincoln, *Works*, V, 32.
The Lincolns had as dinner guests General Banks, Colonel John Cochrane, ex-
Governor Newell of New Jersey, and Mr. and Mrs. Joshua Speed. N.Y. *Times*,
Nov. 29, 1861; N.Y. *Herald*, Nov. 29, 1861.
   On Thanksgiving Day, 1862, Lincoln was extremely busy, and Mrs. Lincoln re-
turned from a trip to New York. Powell, ed., *Lincoln Day by Day*, III, 152.
   [10] Lincoln, *Works*, VI, 496-97, and note.
   [11] Boston *Journal*, Oct. 5, 1863; Philadelphia *Evening Bulletin*, Oct. 5, 31, 1863;
Washington *National Intelligencer*, Nov. 24, 1863; N.Y. *Tribune*, Nov. 21, 23, 26,
1863. *The Compiler* (Gettysburg), Oct. 12, 1863, commented briefly that the Pres-

The Boston *Daily Journal,* rejoicing that Thanksgiving Day would now have a double sanction, national as well as state, observed:

> Such an extension of a time-honored local custom may be regarded as typical of the spread of New England principles, until they are avowed and applied by the Chief Magistrate of the Republic.[12]

In far-off Oregon, the leading journal spoke with a nostalgic New England flavor:

> We are summoned by National and State Proclamations, to devote this day to services, expressive of our profound gratitude to the ALMIGHTY RULER for the great benefits which He has granted to us. . . . While the sons and daughters of New England live, and wherever they wander, the anniversary festival of thanksgiving and praise, will never fail to remind them most effectively of the precious privileges and honest pleasures enjoyed by them when among "the old folks at home."[13]

Thus was the precedent set. Thanksgiving Day became one of our most significant national holidays.[14]

Among those inspired by the President's proclamation was Dr. William A. Muhlenberg, of New York City. An Episcopal minister, writer of hymns and of books on religious subjects, founder of a boys' school and college and a home for the less fortunate, Dr. Muhlenberg was best known for his interest in St. Luke's Hospital which he established and administered.

Soon after the Thanksgiving proclamation was issued, this busy man, whose life was devoted to helping others,

---

ident had issued a proclamation setting aside the last Thursday of November as a day of Thanksgiving and Prayer. On Nov. 16, 1863, it carried a much longer account of Governor Seymour's proclamation and quoted three paragraphs from it. This was but natural, for *The Compiler* neither favored the administration nor was in favor with it. Its editor had more than once been arrested by Federal authorities.

[12] Boston *Journal*, Nov. 25, 1863.

[13] *Morning Oregonian* (Portland), Nov. 26, 1863.

[14] The editors of *Lincoln Lore*, Louis A. Warren and R. Gerald McMurtry, have written extensively on Thanksgiving. See *Lincoln Lore*, Nos. 33, 294, 397, 449, 503, 555, 763, 972, 1024, 1180, 1233; Louis A. Warren, *A Lincoln Memorial to Thanksgiving: Address Delivered at the Dedication of the Abraham Lincoln Statue, Hingham, Massachusetts, on September 23, 1939* (n.d.) (pamphlet); Louis A. Warren, *Little Known Facts About Thanksgiving and Lincoln's Proclamation* (1939) (pamphlet). Cf. also J. G. Randall, "Lincoln and Thanksgiving," *Lincoln Herald*, XLIX (Oct., 1947), 10-13.

sat down and wrote and put to music a "metrical version" of it which he entitled "Give Thanks, All Ye People." On November 2, 1863, the hymn was published by S. T. Gordon, and a second edition followed a week later.[15] The new hymn came to the attention of Dr. Henry W. Bellows, head of the United States Sanitary Commission. Dr. Bellows thought that it should have a different title and should be published and sung in the churches on Thanksgiving Day.

Accordingly, he wrote to Secretary Seward suggesting that the President's consent be obtained to calling the song "The President's Hymn." Seward acted promptly and telegraphed Lincoln's response: "Let it be so-called."

Shortly, new editions of the hymn appeared under the new title, "The President's Hymn," and Dr. Bellows wrote to a number of newspapers inviting their attention to it. His letter to the press tells the story:

NEW YORK, Tuesday, Nov. 17, 1863
To the Editor of the New-York Times:
Inclosed you will find a hymn; written by our beloved and revered fellow-citizen, Dr. Muhlenberg, founder of St. Luke's Hospital, and writer of the immortal hymn, "I would not live alway." Will you not give it a place in your columns, and use your editorial influence to induce our people throughout the loyal States to sing it in the churches on the approaching Thanksgiving as "The President's Hymn"?

It has a right to that designation. It is, as a comparison of the two will prove, a metrical version of the President's Proclamation, which this year, for the first time, made our "Harvest Home" a National Festival; a significant and blessed augury of that "more perfect Union," in which, with God's blessing, the war shall leave us as a people.

Solicitous to have the highest authority given to the use of this National Hymn, I obtained the reluctant consent of its writer (author also of the music to which it is set) to ask our Chief Magistrate's permission to style it "The President's Hymn." The Secretary of State, through whom the application was made, telegraphed me a few hours afterwards the President's leave—in the decisive style which has now become so familiar to our people—"Let it be so-called." May we not

---

[15] Stewart W. McClelland *et al.*, *Lincoln's Thanksgiving Proclamation Named the Last Thursday in November as a Day of National Thanksgiving and Praise* (Harrogate, Tenn., 1945) (pamphlet).

hope that millions of our people will, on Nov. 26, be found uniting in this National Psalm of Thanksgiving, and that "The President's Hymn" will be the household and the Temple song of that solemn and joyful day? It will help to join our hearts as citizens thus to blend our voices as worshippers; and the blessings of Union, Liberty and Peace will sooner descend on a people that can thus unite in its praise and hosannas.

Respectfully yours,
HENRY W. BELLOWS[16]

President Lincoln had not only designated and caused to be observed the first National Thanksgiving, but was instrumental in the naming of a hymn for the occasion.

Glorious Victory!
General Grant's Great Success
Bragg Routed and Driven From
Every Point.
Successful Battle on Tuesday.

Thus did the New York *Times* announce the war news on Thanksgiving Day.[17] It was so everywhere. The war news captured the headlines, and the details filled many columns. But at the same time the newspapers gave some attention to the significance of the day, often with the added meaning now associated with it by the news of victory.

The *Tribune,* contrasting the discouraging situation at the end of 1862 with the present outlook, especially since the news from Chattanooga, editorialized:

This has been a year of signal mercies; solemnly as it draws to a close the President summons the Nation to acknowledge them as the gift of God. Mercies signal and abundant; an almost uninterrupted tide of military successes and of national progress. For the first time . . . the Rebellion *visibly* totters to its fall. . . .[18]

---

[16] N.Y. *Times,* Nov. 22, 1863; Philadelphia *Inquirer,* Nov. 19, 1863; *Morning Oregonian* (Portland), Dec. 31, 1863; Mary A. Hedrick, *Incidents of the Civil War During the Four Years of Its Progress* (Lowell, Mass., 1888), p. 159. Other musical compositions written in honor of the day included: "Oh, Praise the God of Mercies," by E. Turney and W. H. Walter; a "National Thanksgiving Ode," by C. C. Haven (to be sung to the tune "Old Hundred") ; and a "Thanksgiving Hymn," by R. F. Fuller.

[17] N.Y. *Times,* Nov. 26, 1863.

[18] N.Y. *Tribune,* Nov. 26, 1863.

The Adams Sentinel, of Gettysburg, was much more lyrical. It said:

> As the National jubilee, less than five months ago, was cele-
> brated in immortal deeds upon the heights of Gettysburg,
> by the brave army under Meade, so now has the National
> Thanksgiving been made forever memorable upon the heights
> of Chattanooga by the army of General Grant. As though
> by some Divine dispensation, each of these national occasions
> has been signalized by a magnificent triumph to the Union
> arms; so that henceforth the observation of both anniversaries
> will become a patriotic and a Christian duty. These days will
> teach us rightly to estimate the value of our Federal Union,
> and gratefully to remember the men who have given up their
> lives that it might not "perish from the earth."[19]

The following day the New York *Times* reported: "It is doubtful whether any day of Thanksgiving has been so generally and so *purposely* observed as yesterday," and the *Evening Bulletin* of Philadelphia commented: "Thanksgiving was celebrated in this city, yesterday, more heartily than any festival of a similar character for years." The *Bulletin* went on to say: "The glorious war news of the day gave an additional zest to the occasion, and Grant's victory was the theme of hilarious conversation everywhere."[20]

Business establishments and offices were closed, public buildings and governmental departments were shut down, amusement houses were full, and special parties were held.

In New York the entertainment program included Verdi's *Macbeth,* a concert by the "Excelsior Old Folks" (in costume), and a performance by Christy's Minstrels; in Brooklyn the "powerful" play *The Drunkard* was billed for the day.[21]

In Baltimore many went on excursions to the country, and the Odd Fellows held a levee; in Washington there was a benefit ball at the Navy Yard and a big party at the Armory Hospital. Canterbury Hall and Ford's Thea-

---

[19] *The Adams Sentinel* (Gettysburg), Dec. 1, 1863.
[20] N.Y. *Times,* Nov. 27, 1863; Philadelphia *Evening Bulletin,* Nov. 27, 1863.
[21] N.Y. *Times,* Nov. 25, 1863; N.Y. *Tribune,* Nov. 26, 1863.

tre offered extra afternoon performances, and a circus troupe in Philadelphia, by way of observing the day adequately, advertised three showings of its program.[22]

Nor were the more serious aspects of the day of Thanksgiving neglected. Religious services, concerts, special programs of entertainment and bounteous dinners were provided at the army hospitals, largely through the efforts of relief associations.

At the "Home for Friendless Children" in New York the usual Thanksgiving dinner was served and a special chapel service was held in the afternoon. Many visitors were present. The New England Soldiers' Relief Association invited all soldiers temporarily in the city to a Thanksgiving dinner at its quarters. The expenses of the dinner were met by a patriotic merchant. Four hundred convalescent soldiers at the Central Park Hospital were provided a fine dinner and a musical program by the Rose Hill Ladies' Relief Association.[23]

Even Sing Sing Prison observed the day in "an interesting and appropriate manner." At the morning chapel service a chaplain read *three* proclamations—that of the President, the Governor, and George Washington's of seventy-four years before! The music by a "choir of prisoners" was reported as excellent and included a hymn composed by one of the "residential convicts." After the service the men had yard liberty as well as a sports program, and the day ended with a grand Thanksgiving dinner.[24]

Dr. Bellows' suggestion that "The President's Hymn" be sung was followed in many instances. At the annual meeting of the Rose Hill Ladies' Relief Association, at which Dr. Muhlenberg was present, the piece was on the program. It was sung at the "Home for Friendless Children." It was sung at the Central Methodist Church and the North Presbyterian Church in New York, at the

[22] Baltimore *Sun*, Nov. 26, 28, 1863; Washington *Evening Star*, Nov. 21, 1863; Washington *National Intelligencer*, Nov. 26, 1863; Philadelphia *Press*, Nov. 23, 1863.

[23] N.Y. *Tribune*, Nov. 26, 27, 1863; N.Y. *Times*, Nov. 26, Dec. 5, 1863; Baltimore *Sun*, Nov. 25, 26, 28, 1863; Philadelphia *Evening Bulletin*, Nov. 27, 1863.

[24] *Morning Oregonian* (Portland), Jan. 13, 1864.

Church of the Intercessor in Philadelphia, and at churches in Washington.[25] Another prominent feature of the services that day was the collection of funds for charitable and relief organizations, particularly the Christian Commission. The appeal of the Commission was effective. "A million of men in hospital and camp and on shipboard wait in perishing need," it read. The response was generous. In the Philadelphia area over $27,000 was contributed. At a special evening service in the Church of the Epiphany the edifice was filled and hundreds could not gain admission. The collection amounted to nearly $15,000. In a Methodist church in Harrisburg $1,000 was contributed for the Commission.[26]

In the frontier city of Portland, Oregon, three churches and one synagogue raised $735.95, and other contributions brought the city's total to $940.75. One of the largest contributions, $223.50, that of the Presbyterian church, was attributed to its excellent music. The choir leader had selected new music just received from the East and had trained his singers carefully. Thus, concluded a news report: ". . . it is hardly to be wondered at that the melodious blending of patriotism and devotion should inspire the congregation to the highest degree of liberality, and make their donation one of the largest."[27]

The excited and enthusiastic minister of a small church in Ohio almost lost the opportunity to preach his Thanksgiving sermon. The service had begun. "The President's Hymn" had been sung and a collection of sixty dollars had been taken for the Sanitary Commission. The minister had started his sermon but was interrupted by the sexton who walked up to the pulpit and handed him the latest newspaper.

---

[25] N.Y. *Tribune*, Nov. 24, 25, 27, 1863; N.Y. *Times*, Nov. 25, 27, 1863; Philadelphia *Evening Bulletin*, Nov. 27, 1863; Sacramento *Daily Union*, Dec. 24, 1863.

At the Church of All Souls of which he was the pastor Dr. Bellows had printed copies of the hymn placed in the pews the Sunday before Thanksgiving. He made a long announcement explaining how the hymn was written and how it came to be called "The President's Hymn." He urged parishioners to take the hymn home and learn it for the coming service. "Notices read in Church this morning." Henry W. Bellows Papers (Folder 1863 Misc.), Massachusetts Historical Society.

[26] N.Y. *Tribune*, Nov. 25, 1863; Philadelphia *Evening Bulletin*, Nov. 27, Dec. 7, 1863.

[27] *Morning Oregonian* (Portland), Nov. 25, 28, 30, 1863.

The preacher paused, looked at the paper, and shouted, "Glorious news." He forthwith read the headlines that told of the victory at Chattanooga, called for three cheers for the Stars and Stripes, and led the congregation in the singing of the Doxology.

Then, saying to his flock, "Now, I have too much good sense to think that you would rather hear me preach than hear the news," he proceeded to read, subject to interruption by cheers from his listeners, all the dispatches and the editorial.

The service ended with the usual benediction but not before the congregation voted to return that evening, hear the sermon, and take up another collection for the Sanitary Commission![28]

Thus, as the country faced yet another winter of conflict, the feeling prevailed that there was much for which thanks should be given. The President and Tad recovered from their illnesses, and Mrs. Lincoln was feeling better. General Grant's accomplishments were appreciated; the President expressed his "profoundest gratitude"; and Congress ordered a medal struck in Grant's honor.[29]

Lincoln's Annual Message met with unusual approbation. A dispatch from Washington to the New York *Tribune* reported:

> It is safe to say that no President's Message since George Washington retired into private life has given such general satisfaction as that sent to Congress today by Abraham Lincoln. The President, who is in much improved health today, is greatly gratified at the reception given to his Message and the congratulations which pour in upon him from all sides.[30]

---

[28] Philadelphia *Evening Bulletin,* Dec. 1, 1863; *Morning Oregonian* (Portland), Jan. 6, 1864.

[29] Lincoln, *Works,* VII, 53, 79.

[30] N.Y. *Tribune,* Dec. 10, 1863. John Hay was greatly impressed with the many favorable reactions. He wrote: "Whatever may be the results or the verdict of history the immediate effect of this paper is something wonderful. I never have seen such an effect produced by a public document. Men acted as if the millennium had come." Senator Chandler was "delighted" and Charles Sumner beamed; Congressman Boutwell considered it "an able and shrewd paper," and Owen Lovejoy thought it "wonderful." Even Horace Greeley approved, pronouncing it "devilish good." Dennett, ed., *Lincoln . . . in the Diaries . . . of John Hay,* pp. 131-32. It was Lincoln's explanation of his Amnesty Proclamation with its implications for reconstruction that drew men's attention. About one third of the Message was devoted to this subject. Two of Lincoln's assertions are worth noting: "I shall not attempt to retract or modify the emancipation proclamation; nor shall I return to slavery any person who is free. . . ." "Saying that reconstruction will be accepted if presented in a specified way, it is not said it will never be accepted in

The Adams Sentinel approved wholeheartedly, saying,

> If we had ever despaired of success, we could no longer despair, now that we have read this calm and earnest message, which, itself so quiet and firm, must kindle a new enthusiasm for the cause. It is principle, right, liberty, that is the soul of the President's message.[31]

For personal reasons many were, of course, grateful to the President. An old Illinois associate, Usher F. Linder, was made glad when Lincoln released his son, a prisoner of war, and sent him home.[32] Private Miles O'Reilly, whose visit to the White House on Thanksgiving Day, must have cheered the President, expressed his thanks in poetry. Sometime earlier, after a short stay in custody for injudicious remarks concerning the military, the humorist wrote:

> Long life to you, Misther Lincoln;
> May you die both late and aisy;
> An' whin you lie wid the top of aich toe
> Turned up to the roots of a daisy,
> May this be your epitaph, nately writ;
> "Though thraitors abused him vilely,
> He was honest an' kindly, he loved a good joke,
> An' he pardoned Miles O'Reilly."[33]

More significantly, there was a growing sentiment that the country had something else for which it should be thankful. Although the malcontents continued to complain, the critics to ridicule, and the humorless to groan, an increasing number of discerning men became con-

---

any other way." Lincoln, *Works*, VII, 51, 52. The first statement reassured the friends of freedom; the second allowed Lincoln room to maneuver and adjust to changing conditions in the future.

Confederate politicians were greatly upset. A resolution was introduced into the Confederate Congress calling Lincoln an "imbecile and unprincipled usurper who now sits enthroned upon the ruins of constitutional liberty in Washington. . . ." Congressman Miles objected to the resolution, saying, "The true and only treatment which that miserable and contemptible despot [Lincoln] should receive . . . was silent and unmitigated contempt. This resolution would appear to dignify a paper emanating from that wretched and detestable abortion, whose contemptible emptiness and folly would only receive the ridicule of the civilized world." It should be tabled. It was! N.Y. *Tribune*, Dec. 28, 1863.

[31] *The Adams Sentinel* (Gettysburg), Dec. 15, 1863.

[32] Lincoln, *Works*, VII, 94-95.

[33] *New Hampshire Sentinel* (Keene), Oct. 29, 1863; N.Y. *Herald*, Oct. 3, 20, 23, Nov. 28, 1863.

vinced that, above all else, the nation should be thankful
for Abraham Lincoln himself!

Here and there in the countless sermons preached that
fourth Thursday in November and in speeches and editorials, this conviction was expressed. Rev. Dr. Newman,
preaching in the Fourth Street Methodist Episcopal
Church in New York, said:

> Let us rejoice that as time wears on, and the war continues,
> the wisdom, patriotism, and policy of the Administration is
> better appreciated by the loyal States, and a heartier support
> is now given to our noble President than ever before. . . .
> Under his humane and wise administration, Slavery is doomed.
> . . . and Liberty is the proffered inheritance of every citizen.
> Let the name of Abraham Lincoln go down to posterity with
> that of the illustrious Washington, embalmed in the fragrance
> of human affections, and garlanded with the flowers of a na-
> tion's gratitude.[34]

At the First Baptist Church in Brooklyn, the minister,
Dr. Sarles, expressed his view: "I think that we have
great reason to thank God for a faithful, honest President. . . . He has placed over us a faithful man, and we
ought to be devoutly thankful for so great a blessing."[35]

Reporting on the sermon of Rev. William H. Furness
at the Unitarian Church in Philadelphia, the *Evening
Bulletin* commented: "Among other admirable passages,
his sermon contained an eloquent tribute to President Lincoln, as one of the gifts for which we have to be thankful."[36]

And Henry Ward Beecher, man of strong opinion that
he was, declared:

> We owe a debt of deep gratitude to God for the Chief Mag-
> istrate of our land. He is wisely and surely pioneering the
> way to the liberty of this nation. One man there was whom
> God's hand had ordained to break our foreign bondage. If
> it were possible to honor more than him another whom God
> has ordained to break the bondage of a worse oppression in
> our land, then the second should be greater than the first:
> but joined together one and inseparable, we shall hereafter

---

[34] N.Y. *Tribune*, Nov. 27, 1863.
[35] N.Y. *Times*, Nov. 29, 1863.
[36] Philadelphia *Evening Bulletin*, Nov. 27, 1863.

hear on jubilees the shouts "Washington and Lincoln!—the Fathers!"[37]

At Gettysburg, the editorial writer, preparing his script for the local paper, wrote: "If Mr. Lincoln, at the beginning of the war, seemed to be one of those fortunate men who had greatness thrust upon them, he has since shown the higher power to achieve greatness by unsurpassed fidelity to a national trust and comprehension of a world's revolution."[38]

Across the ocean in London, noted the same issue of the Gettysburg paper that contained this editorial praise, the *Spectator* said:

> Mr. Lincoln has been tested as few Governors have ever been tested, and though he may not always have risen fully to the level of a great emergency, he has seldom failed to display a noble impartiality, a great firmness of purpose, and a

---

[37] N.Y. *Times*, Nov. 27, 1863; N.Y. *Tribune*, Nov. 27, 1863. Of the eighteen sermons reported on in the *Times* on November 27, Beecher's was the only one that gave unqualified thanks for Abraham Lincoln. The *Tribune* contained Dr. Newman's tribute as well as Beecher's in its coverage of eighteen sermons. A few days later when Beecher again paid tribute to Lincoln in a speech to the American Anti-Slavery Society, his remarks brought great applause. N.Y. *Tribune*, Dec. 4, 8, 1863.

Beecher was far from being a consistent admirer or supporter of Lincoln and the administration. In fact, he was more often a harsh critic. While editor of *The Independent*, Beecher berated the President unmercifully. After Second Bull Run he wrote: "At present, the North is beaten. . . . It is a supreme and extraordinary want of executive administrative talent at the head of the Government that is bringing us to humiliation. . . . Let it be known that the Nation wasted away by an incurable consumption of Central Imbecility." Lincoln, after reading some criticisms of this sort, threw the papers on the floor, saying indignantly, "Is thy servant a *dog* that he should do this thing?" Carpenter, *Six Months at the White House*, p. 230. Cf. Rice, ed., *Reminiscences of Abraham Lincoln*, pp. 248-49, and Paxton Hibben, *Henry Ward Beecher: An American Portrait* (N.Y., 1942), *passim*.

Dr. Bellows who had done so much to further the cause of a National Thanksgiving, was severely criticized for his sermon on Thanksgiving Day. The sermon was thought by some to be tinged with "Copperheadism" and "defeatism." Bellows' loyalty was even questioned. He received a number of critical letters and his loyalty was the subject of discussion in the sacred precincts of the Union League Club!

Bellows was embarrassed and upset. To the Vice-President of the Union League Club he wrote: ". . . I am deeply mortified to find it possible that any sane & serious person should think it possible for me to be tainted with [disloyalty]." Henry W. Bellows to Jonathan Sturges, Dec. 11, 1863, Bellows Papers.

The fact of the matter was that Bellows had been so busy that he had not had time to prepare a Thanksgiving sermon. Instead, he used one that he had written before the battle of Gettysburg in which he discussed the war philosophically and in which he tried to explain "both sides." When the criticism arose he realized that it had been a mistake to deliver such a sermon, at least on Thanksgiving Day. James Freeman Clarke advised him to forget it, saying, "You will be sure, in a month or two, to obliterate the memory of this discourse, by some noble and splendid thing." James Freeman Clarke to Henry W. Bellows, Dec. 18, 1863, Bellows Papers. Cf. Other letters in Bellows Papers; N. Y. *Times*, Nov. 27, 1863; Nevins and Halsey, eds., *Diary of George Templeton Strong*, III, 375, 377.

[38] *The Adams Sentinel* (Gettysburg), Dec. 15, 1863.

sagacious, if not somewhat utilitarian, judgment. . . . We believe a juster man never held the reins of government.[39]

In Boston, James Russell Lowell prepared a long article in defense of the administration. He gave his opinion: "History will rank Mr. Lincoln among the most prudent of statesmen and the most successful of rulers." And Lowell further said: "Never did a President enter upon office with less means at his command, outside his own strength of heart and steadiness of understanding, for inspiring confidence in the people, and so winning it for himself, than Mr. Lincoln."[40]

Again in London, at the Thanksgiving Dinner in St. James's Hall, Charles Francis Adams made a fine speech emphasizing what the country had to be thankful for under President Lincoln. "He has succeeded," said Adams, "because he has, from the beginning to the end, impressed upon the people the conviction of his honesty and of his fidelity to one great purpose."[41]

"Give Thanks, All Ye People"

"The President's Hymn" did not become popular as did so many songs of the war, but for many people, as they looked forward with increased confidence in the President,

---

[39] The article was entitled "A Good Word for Mr. Lincoln." It began: "It is some amends for the ridicule which has been so unsparingly heaped by certain foreign presses upon Mr. Lincoln, that the *London Spectator*, one of the most intelligent and most respectable journals in Europe, finds occasion for the following words about him. . . ."

[40] [James Russell Lowell], "The President's Policy," *North American Review*, CCII (Jan., 1864), 239, 241.

[41] Preceding the toasts and speeches the President's Proclamation was read, a prayer was offered by a runaway Negro then much in the news, and a hymn composed for the occasion was sung. N.Y. *Tribune*, Dec. 15, 1863; N.Y. *Times*, Dec. 20, 1863.
  Others who spoke appreciatively of the President at this time were Frederick Douglass and a Professor Martin, who, in a speech before the National Literary Society, said: "President Lincoln had done a few of the noblest things ever achieved by the head of a great nation." N.Y. *Tribune*, Dec. 8, 14, 1863. Gideon Welles in his careful manner commented on the last day of the year: "The President has well maintained his position, and under trying circumstances acquitted himself in a manner that will be better appreciated in the future than now." Morse, ed., *Diary of Gideon Welles*, I, 500.
  Dissidents included Wendell Phillips and the New York *Herald*. The *Tribune* in a chronological listing showed how the *Herald* had changed from a supporter to an opponent of Lincoln, its position on December 21 being: "We abandon 'Honest Old Abe' as a hopeless case. We have puffed him, we have praised him, and have helped him in every way, but can get no good out of him. To use one of his own similes, he is a crooked stick that cannot be bent, and that will have to be broken." N.Y. *Tribune*, Dec. 29, 1863.

and with a renewed spirit and with new hope, its words and sentiments had real meaning.[42]

> Give thanks, all ye people, give thanks to the Lord,
> Alleluias of freedom, with joyful accord:
> Let the East and the West, North and South roll along,
> Sea, mountains and prairie, One thanksgiving song.

- - - - - - - - - - - - - - - - - - - -

> Our guilt and transgressions remember no more;
> Peace, Lord! righteous Peace, of Thy gift we implore;
> And the Banner of Union, restored by Thy Hand,
> Be the Banner of Freedom o'er All in the land.

---

[42] In 1864, Thanksgiving was duly celebrated, and again Mrs. Hale was active in urging its observance. Sarah Josepha Hale to William H. Seward, Oct. 9, 1864, R. T. Lincoln Coll., 37081; *Lincoln Lore*, No. 1461.

Governor Bramlette of Lincoln's native state recommended that the day ". . . should be so observed by all the citizens of Kentucky, with that becoming reverence and thankfulness to Almighty God, for His manifold mercies bestowed, even while scourging us with war." Philadelphia *Evening Bulletin*, Nov. 22, 1864.

Newspapers reported the day's activities in detail, noting especially that church services were held, collections taken, and that organized efforts to provide dinners for soldiers in hospitals and in camps and for sailors at sea were highly successful. To the blockading squadron were shipped 30,000 pounds of turkey and chicken, to the armies on the Potomac and James about 220,000 pounds, plus great quantities of apples, cakes, doughnuts, cheese, cranberries and canned fruit. No wonder poultry was high—twenty-five cents a pound! In the reports of sermons preached there were thanks expressed for the results of the election, but few references to the President. Henry Ward Beecher observed: "The election had determined that Mr. Lincoln was not a tyrant but a just Christian magistrate, fearing God and loving man." At the New York Avenue Presbyterian Church in Washington "The President's Hymn" was sung. Lincoln was at the service. Philadelphia *Evening Bulletin*, Nov. 19, 22, 23, 25, 28, 1864; Washington *National Intelligencer*, Nov. 22, 24, 26, 1864; Baltimore *Sun*, Nov. 24, 26, 1864; *The Adams Sentinel* (Gettysburg), Nov. 29, 1864; N.Y. *Herald*, Nov. 24, 25, 1864; Washington *Daily Morning Chronicle*, Nov. 25, 1864.

CHAPTER XVI

WASHINGTON IS GAY

THE OPTIMISM AND GOOD SPIRIT THAT PREVAILED AS THE
year 1864 dawned were nowhere more evident than in the
social life of the wartime capital. A busy social season
was anticipated, and the New Year's Reception at the
White House set the pace.

As early as December 9, an Iowa lady, alert to such
developments, wrote:

> The White House is to be very gay this winter. That the
> President, having safely recovered from varioloid, the word
> has gone around that strangers are to be well entertained at
> the Presidential mansion this year.[1]

By the end of the month there was general agreement
that this was indeed the case. On December 19 a select
party, by invitation only, had been given at the White
House for Russian naval officers then in the city. It was
an elaborate and brilliant affair. The officers were re-
splendent in their uniforms, the diplomatic corps and
army were well represented, and the ladies, one and all,
were "magnificently dressed." Washington was impressed
—and eager for more![2]

New Year's Day was quite wintry. The night before
had been the coldest of the season. Water pipes froze
"as tight as the money market," and an icy blast which
had blanketed the Midwest with snow swept over the city.
Although the sun came out, it did not dissipate the extreme chill in the air.

---

[1] [Mrs. John A. Kasson] *Iowa Jour. of Hist.*, LII (Jan., 1954), 79.

[2] Washington *Sunday Morning Chronicle*, Dec. 20, 1863; [Mrs. John A. Kasson]
Iowa Jour. of Hist., LII (Jan., 1954), 82; John T. Stuart to his wife, Dec. 20,
1863, Stuart-Hay Papers.

Nevertheless, by ten o'clock that morning crowds gathered outside to watch the parade of dignitaries entering the White House for the annual reception. For two hours they stood waiting; then the doors were opened and they, the general public, swarmed in. So great was the crush that the doors were closed every fifteen minutes to allow those already inside to pay their respects and make their exits.

Even so, the White House was jammed. John Nicolay wrote that he had never seen such a crowd; Orville H. Browning, making his New Year's Day rounds, did not attempt to go in; many toes were trampled on and there was some damage to hats, bonnets, and dresses.[3]

Noah Brooks, in his dispatch to the Sacramento *Daily Union*, gave a vivid description of the affair:

> These gentry [diplomats, military and other dignitaries] made a brave show, as they marched up in all their gold lace and toggery, General Halleck leading the military crowd, Seward leading his pet lambs of the diplomacy, and Admiral Davis sailed in at the head of the Squadron of naval officers. The Foreign Ministers were especially gorgeously arrayed, being covered with stars, garters and medals of honor; the rush for a glimpse of these gay birds was very great, and Secretary Seward looked very like a molting barnyard fowl among peacocks, in such an illustrious company. The rush of the great multitude was as great as in former years; and the crushing and jamming of bonnets and things was fearful. One woman became separated from her family, and a tender female shriek being heard, the paterfamilias of the lost one was sure that it was the voice of his beloved which he heard; likewise his son, a youth of tender years, was led to believe that his mother was killed; whereat he bawled exceedingly, and there was a great deal of excitement at the entrance to the great drawing-room, where all of this took place, until every Jack got his Jill and all went well again.[4]

Shortly after this auspicious beginning it was announced that Mrs. Lincoln would receive her friends every Saturday from one to three o'clock in the afternoon

---

3 Washington *Evening Star*, Dec. 29, 30, 1863, Jan. 1, 1864; Washington *Daily Morning Chronicle*, Jan. 2, 1864; N.Y. *Herald*, Jan. 3, 1864; John G. Nicolay to Therena Bates, Jan. 2, 1864, Nicolay Papers; Pease and Randall, eds., *Diary of O. H. Browning*, I, 653.

4 Sacramento *Daily Union*, Feb. 4, 1864.

and that evening levees would be held on Tuesdays. These gatherings were invariably reported as "largely attended," "very largely attended," or "brilliantly attended."

If the weather was bad, fewer people came out; if it was pleasant, there was certain to be a crowd. Thus the evening reception on January 12 brought out a relatively small number of people while on the afternoon of January 23, with the weather springlike, an "immense throng" appeared and the party "exceeded all previous ones in brilliancy."[5]

After a month the social routine of the White House was well established and so was that of the rest of the city. "Washington is gay," reported one correspondent on the twelfth. "Mrs. Lincoln's reception on Saturday last, inaugurated the season. The President's first levee was given this evening. Tomorrow night the great hotel hops commence, beginning at Willard's. On Thursday night Secretary Seward will have a splendid reception. On Friday, Speaker Colfax's receptions will commence. Through all the Winter there will be elegant parties. . . ."[6]

Speaker Colfax's receptions and those at the White House were the most popular. Again Noah Brooks provided the best description of the White House functions:

> Most visitors go in party dress on Tuesday evening—the women wearing laces, feathers, silks and satins rare, leaving their bonnets in an anteroom; the gentlemen appear in light kids and cravats. . . . Mixed in are the less airy people dressed in quieter style. At Saturday receptions ladies wear walking dress; not half so fine a show as by gaslight, when glittering crowds pour through the drawing-rooms into the great East Room, where they circulate in a revolving march to the music of the Marine Band.[7]

And of the President and Mrs. Lincoln, he added:

---

[5] Washington *Evening Star*, Jan. 7, 9, 13, 16, 23, 27, 29, 1864; Washington *Sunday Morning Chronicle*, Jan. 24, 31, 1864; N.Y. *Herald*, Jan. 10, 13, 17, 1864.

[6] N.Y. *Times*, Jan. 13, 1864. There was even a "Law of Receptions": Cabinet members—about semi-monthly (by invitation); the Speaker of the House—every Friday evening (no cards necessary); the President—every other Tuesday evening (no cards); Mrs. Lincoln—a matinee on Saturdays, one to three in the afternoon (no cards); families of cabinet ministers and of the Speaker—at home to receive callers on Wednesdays. N.Y. *Times*, Jan. 20, 1864.

[7] Sacramento *Daily Union*, Feb. 27, 1864.

Uncle Abraham stands by the door which opens into the Blue Room, flanked by Marshal Lamon and his private secretary, who introduce the new arrivals. . . . The President shakes hands, says "How-do," and the visitor is passed on to where Mrs. Lincoln stands, flanked by another private secretary and B. B. French, the Commissioner of Public Buildings, who introduce the party; then all press on to the next room, where they admire each other's good clothes, criticize Mrs. Lincoln's new gown, gossip a little, flirt a little, yawn, go home, and say "What a bore!" Such is our Republican Court, and the most bored man in it is Old Abe, who hates white kid gloves and a crowd.[8]

The schedule was carried out to the last reception of the season, that of April 19. Crowds continued to come;[9] toes were trampled on and hats and dresses disarranged; the last reception was so packed that women actually shrieked with pain.[10]

The high point was reached on March 8 when General Grant appeared. Many had never seen him before. The President greeted him cordially and turned him over to Secretary Seward, who, in turn, presented him to Mrs. Lincoln. Then Seward led him to the East Room. The multitude, orderly, and somewhat in awe, cheered. The General mounted a sofa and proceeded to shake hands all around, perspiring profusely all the while. After an hour of this he accompanied Mrs. Lincoln in the evening promenade. Soon after, he left for his hotel and the party ended.[11]

---

[8] Sacramento *Daily Union*, Feb. 27, 1864. Commissioner French found the receptions strenuous. He wrote: ". . . the American Empress demands my personal presence for 2 hours every Saturday, and 3 every alternate Tuesday—and *no vittles & drink given!*—kids $2.25 per pair! Isn't it awful?" B. B. French to H. F. French, Jan. 31, 1864, B. B. French Papers.

[9] On March 22 a driving storm which left nine inches of snow on the ground kept many away. A Massachusetts boy in camp near Annapolis called it "a genuine New England Snow Storm cold as the very devil." On April 10, B. B. French wrote: "I was at the reception yesterday, as usual. It has either rained or snowed, or done something it ought not to, out of doors, at *every* reception for the past 2 months. Yesterday the rain descended in torrents, still *they came*, & would come if a Sodomitic Shower were in full progress." B. B. French to Pamela French, April 10, 1864, B. B. French Papers.

[10] Washington *Evening Star*, Apr. 20, 1864.

[11] Washington *Evening Star*, Mar. 9, 1864; N.Y. *Herald*, Mar. 12, 1864; Sacramento *Daily Union*, Apr. 9, 1864; *Memoranda*, Mar. 8, 1864, Nicolay Papers; Horace Porter, *Campaigning with Grant* (N.Y., 1897), pp. 19-21.

Grant had no liking for social functions, and avoided them when possible. He failed to appear at Grover's Theatre on the evening of March 10, and Mr. Grover came out and apologized for the General's absence. Washington *Evening Star*, Mar. 11, 1864. He also missed the dinner planned for him at the White House on March 12, which led the President to remark that it was like the play *Hamlet*

One welcome feature of White House functions this winter was a return to the custom of having the Marine Band present. When, on December 18, 1863, Secretary Welles wrote to Colonel Harris of the Marine Corps,

> There will be a "Reception" at the Executive mansion tomorrow, the 19th inst., from 1 to 3 p.m.
>
> You will direct the Marine Band to assemble there at 12:30 P.M.,

and when he issued a second order to Colonel Harris on December 29,

> You will issue the necessary directions for the Marine Band to be in attendance at the Reception on New Year's Day, at eleven o'clock A.M., precisely, . . .

this welcome custom was officially revived.[12]

Not since February, 1862, just before Willie died, had such an order been issued. For nearly two years there had been no music in the White House. Now there was music again.[13] Henceforth, every party was brightened by the playing of the band. Its music, duly praised by the press, contributed much to the now gay atmosphere at White House functions.

The President, of course, was very fond of band music, but it is doubtful if he knew what was being played—or even that the band was "discoursing some of its finest music"—as he stood before the long lines of visitors saying "How do," in his genial Western manner.[14]

---

with Hamlet left out. Serenaders in the streets tried to seek the General out, but to no avail. They concluded that he had no music in his soul as no tune would bring him out. Washington *Evening Star*, Mar. 14, 1864 ; N.Y. *Herald*, Mar. 18, 1864.

[12] Gideon Welles to Colonel J. L. Harris, Dec. 18, 29, 1863, Officers of the Marine Corps No. 7, Letter Book.

[13] Welles' orders were sent to Colonel Harris regularly before each party.

[14] In later years many people "remembered" incidents that had occurred at presidential receptions. Some may have actually happened. Many have the "flavor of the times" ; others may be doubted. Veterans remembered the cordiality of the President as he shook hands with them ; one soldier was annoyed because Mrs. Lincoln put her handkerchief over her white kid glove before offering her hand (his hands were clean) ; from an unidentified source came the recollection that at one reception the Marine Band played the favorite selection of the President, the "Soldiers' Chorus" from *Faust*. A Mrs. J. E. Comfort recalled that her remark to the President that she had been enjoying the beautiful roses in the conservatory brought from him the response that once he had come to a spot where hundreds of roses were in bloom—their perfume was overpowering and almost

Mrs. Lincoln particularly enjoyed the receptions. She had put aside her mourning clothes and now dressed in the latest fashion. She was cordial, gracious and hospitable. Social affairs were good for her.[15] But the constant pressure of two mass receptions a week evidently wore on the President. In January his health seemed good. Noah Brooks, commenting after the New Year's Day reception, said:

> The President looks better since he has had the varioloid.
> I don't mean to insinuate that the disease has added any new charms to his features; but his complexion is clearer, his eyes less lack-luster and he has a hue of health to which he has long been a stranger.[16]

As time went on other observers reported that although he was in excellent spirits he did look "somewhat worn." At the reception on March 22 he sat down. This was most unusual. On April 12 the reception was postponed because he was indisposed.

Perhaps, however, the full calendar of entertainment outside the White House helped to offset the strain of routine business and routine social functions. This entertainment was varied and much of it was musical. It included Shakespearean plays, popular comedy and trag-

---

made him faint; and another time as he rode through a dense woods at evening scores of nightingales were singing—no bird's music was sweeter than the nightingale's, but in this instance the music became like a severe pain. "So you see," he concluded, "there can be too much even of flowers and music." W. E. Barker, Sioux City (Iowa) *Journal*, Feb. 7, 1915; Col. W. D. Dickey, Brooklyn *Daily Eagle*, Feb. 10, 1918; clipping, *Christian Register*, n.d.; clipping, n.d., Lincoln National Life Foundation.

[15] Two minor incidents illustrate the social difficulties of the First Lady. In January Fernando Wood gave a big reception. On the table, prominently displayed, was a bouquet with a card affixed which read: "With the compliments of Mrs. Lincoln." Word got around that Mrs. Lincoln had supplied *all* the flowers *and* the Marine Band for the party of this "notorious apostle of peace." The fact was that Mrs. Wood had asked for flowers and Mrs. Lincoln replied that there were none beyond those needed for the White House. As a matter of courtesy, she had sent with her reply a small bouquet. From this the story was manufactured and spread. Cf. N.Y. *Times*, Jan. 28, Feb. 4, 1864; Cincinnati *Gazette*, Feb. 4, 1864; *Leslie's Illus. News*, Feb. 20, 1864; *Harper's Weekly*, Feb. 27, 1864; Mrs. Lincoln to General Sickles, Feb. 6, 1864, Mary [Todd] Lincoln Letters, 1864.

A "Ladies Anti-Extravagance Movement" was organized in Washington and other cities to encourage women to avoid ostentatious luxury and wear simple and somber clothing. A committee approached Mrs. Lincoln to ask her support. She refused. The movement did not get very far; there was no response in social circles, and to some the whole idea was a humbug and a fraud and was likely proposed by some old maid who had nothing to wear anyway! Cf. N.Y. *Times*, May 17, 24, 1864; N.Y. *Herald*, May 17, 27, 1864; *Leslie's Illus. News*, May 28, 1864.

[16] Sacramento *Daily Union*, Feb. 4, 1864.

edy, musical drama and a musical "extravaganza," two concerts, and several operas.[17]

There is no doubt but that Lincoln's greatest pleasure in entertainment during these winter and spring months came from the plays of Shakespeare. Five times he saw Edwin Booth and once Edwin Forrest. Not only did he see *Richard III* (twice),[18] *Julius Caesar*, the *Merchant of Venice, Hamlet* and *King Lear*, but he discussed Shakespeare with actor Hackett and recited passages to Carpenter, the artist.[19]

On the evening of January 25, the Lincolns had a box at Grover's Theatre for the first appearance in Washington of Felicita Vestvali in *Gamea, or the Jewish Mother.*

The play centered upon the tortures undergone by a Jewish mother whose child was, against her wishes, brought up a Roman Catholic. Vestvali, "one of the greatest lyric tragic artistes," had played the part of Gamea many times with brilliant success. Her impersonation of the mother was, according to the *Chronicle,* "a marvel"; her portrayal of the mother's emotions was so real as to electrify the audience and cause it to burst into spontaneous applause.

The incidental music, "replete with gems," included both solos and chorus selections—"The Mystic Chant," "The Mother's Prayer," "The Cradle Song," "Silvia Is Mine Again," and a "Gondolier's Barcarole."

---

[17] The three lectures that he attended during these months (by Anna Dickinson, George Thompson, and Rev. J. R. Warner) might also be considered as entertainment. Miss Dickinson, of course, had some sharp comments to make, but ended by complimenting the President. He sat in the front row. Now and then he had a half solemn and half grinning expression as if something reminded him of a story. Cincinnati *Gazette*, Jan. 18, 1864; [Mrs. John A. Kasson] *Iowa Jour. of Hist.*, LII (Jan., 1954), 83. At the lecture by George Thompson a band enlivened the occasion. Washington *Evening Star*, Apr. 7, 1864. Mr. Warner's lecture on Gettysburg was listened to "with rapt attention," and the day afterward the President expressed his pleasure to the speaker when he called at the White House. Washington *Evening Star*, May 19, 1864; Washington *Daily Morning Chronicle*, May 19, 20, 1864.

[18] The second presentation was a "grand gala night" in honor of General Grant. The theatre was decorated for the event and Grover had secured Charles Koppitz from Philadelphia to conduct the orchestra. The theatre was crowded and Koppitz prepared some "choice apropos music." When Grant failed to appear, Mr. Grover went before the audience and apologized. It was later announced that any who were disappointed could get their money back. Washington *Evening Star*, Mar. 10, 11, 1864.

[19] Powell, ed.. *Lincoln Day by Day*, III, 246; Carpenter, *Six Months at the White House*, pp. 49, 58.

With Koppitz' orchestra providing the instrumental accompaniment, Vestvali's singing was as well done as her acting. The play, the music, and the acting were all rated as excellent.[20]

The President evidently shared this sentiment, for he and his family, together with Charles Sumner, were present for another performance of *Gamea* three evenings later! Not only that, but the very next evening he again saw the "Magnificent Vestvali," this time in the musical drama, *The Brigand,* complete with "all the original music, and a full chorus."

Vestvali's acting and singing captivated the entire audience. Her musical selections, which included a drinking song, "Hurrah!," "The Brigand's Prayer," "Gentle Zitella," and "The Brigand's Dying Song," created quite a furore.

In less than a week Mr. and Mrs. Lincoln were back at Grover's Theatre to witness another triumph by Vestvali in *The Duke's Motto.* The play, full of exciting incidents, had had a long run in New York, and was equally popular in Washington.

Vestvali's impersonation of the Hunchback brought down the house. Her songs included "The Dashing Cavalier," "La Manola," and "Sweet Blanche, with Mingled Hopes and Tears."

To have attended four performances by the same actress in less than two weeks was something of a record for a busy wartime executive. The *Daily Chronicle* could not have been far wrong when it commented that the "Magnificent Vestvali" seemed to have charmed the President as she had "the balance of mankind."[21]

On Monday, February 8, Mr. and Mrs. Lincoln saw another popular current production. This time it was *The*

---

[20] Washington *Evening Star,* Jan. 26, 27, 1864; Washington *National Intelligencer,* Jan. 25, 26, 1864; Washington *Daily Morning Chronicle,* Jan. 25, 26, 1864. Cf. Odell, *Annals of the New York Stage,* VII, 559, 618, VIII, 244. Cf. also, *Leslie's Illus. News,* June 13, 1863.

[21] Washington *Daily Morning Chronicle,* Jan. 29, 30, Feb. 4, 1864; Washington *Evening Star,* Jan. 29, 30, Feb. 4, 1864; Washington *National Intelligencer,* Jan. 29, 30, Feb. 3, 4, 5, 1864. During this ten-day period (Jan. 25-Feb. 3) there were two receptions at the White House and the President attended the second anniversary meeting of the Christian Commission. The Saturday previous (Jan. 23) he also went to the theatre!

Sea of Ice, with Laura Keene in the leading role. *The Sea of Ice* was a five-act spectacular drama, full of comedy, pathos, and tragedy. Opening with a "whistling song and chorus," it unfolded the story of a party cast adrift on the ice by mutineers, with all perishing except an infant girl. She, by a miracle, survived, was brought up by Indians, educated in Paris, and finally determined to find and destroy the murderer who cast her and her parents adrift years before. The play ended with an "awful retributive denouement."

So popular was the play that it attracted a crowded house for four nights. Miss Keene won high praise for her acting.[22]

It was perhaps about this time that the President and Tad went to an "extravaganza," which, although of questionable taste and dubious merit, gave both one of their biggest thrills.[23] It was billed as

The grand fairy spectacle of the
Seven Sisters
And the birth of Cupid in
The Bower of Ferns.[24]

The Seven Sisters was a sort of *revue* made up of scenes or tableaux based on the earthly adventures of the seven daughters of Pluto, in which local events, persons, and incidents were introduced in a humorous and satirical fashion.

The production was lavishly praised—it was "a magnificent, dazzling, gorgeous, fairy, spectacular extravaganza." It offered "superb costuming, brilliant scenery, beautiful effects, astonishing transformations, elegant tableaux, fairy dances, grand marches. . . ." In addition an extra large "corps de ballet" was featured.[25]

---

[22] Washington *Evening Star,* Feb. 8, 9, 1864; Washington *National Intelligencer,* Feb. 8, 10, 1864; Washington *Sunday Morning Chronicle,* Feb. 14, 1864. The play was first produced by Laura Keene in the depression year, 1857, and was so successful that she revived it yearly. Odell, *Annals of the New York Stage,* VII, 33.

[23] The production ran for two weeks in March, 1864, and for two weeks in November. Mr. Lincoln and Tad may have attended in November, but they more likely went in March. There seems to be no way of fixing the exact date.

[24] Washington *National Intelligencer,* Mar. 14, 1864.

[25] Washington *Sunday Morning Chronicle,* Mar. 13, 1864; Washington *National Intelligencer,* Mar. 14, 1864. *The Seven Sisters* was first produced by Laura Keene

Because there was criticism by the press, certain objectionable passages were eliminated. Said one newspaper:

> The tedious, drawling, painful, trashy interpolations—especially of "Lady Pluto's" offensive *wit* and pot-house politics —into the dialogue of this piece, deserve indignant and emphatic reprehension. Some of it was outrageous, and most of it was in wretched taste.[26]

After the expurgation, the play was described as "now a pure, racy, enjoyable thing."[27]

But purge or no purge the production was popular and played to crowded houses each night. The last tableau made a spectacular finish. It was, according to the *Intelligencer*, "the theme of wonder and comment in our community. Each night new beauties appear. . . . The eye is dazzled and the sense puzzled to see so many gorgeous and pleasing effects . . . finally blending into one grand picture of unsurpassed loveliness and brilliancy. . . ."[28]

It was this final tableau which brought particular pleasure to the President and Tad, for it was on this occasion that Tad joined the singers on the stage as the entire cast sang the "Battle-Cry of Freedom." There was a thrill of excitement as the audience recognized the President's son, and as the music of the song filled the

in November, 1860. It had the longest run of any production up to that time, 253 performances. Early in 1861 tableaux were introduced in keeping with the secession crisis: Columbia at the tomb of Washington, the States, the Ebony Wedge, a slave auction, Calhoun's Dream, Washington at Valley Forge, Liberty and Diogenes, Union and Liberty Forever, an Apotheosis of Washington and the Union. Uncle Sam appeared "with an eagle under his arm." Odell, *Annals of the New York Stage*, VII, 310-12.

More changes were introduced later. If the President and Tad saw the "extravaganza" in November, they had an added treat, for at that time an important personage had joined the cast—Miss Lotta, from California (Charlotte Crabtree). In her part in *The Seven Sisters*, she was described as "The Sauciest, Most Piquant, and Vivacious Star of the present period," and "the brightest and most Dashing Comic Actress of the Age." Washington *National Intelligencer*, Nov. 14, 15, 16, 18, 1864.

Although the production was a great success, it cost Miss Keene heavily in prestige as a dramatist and artist. Odell, *Annals of the New York Stage*, VII, 384.

[26] Washington *National Intelligencer*, Mar. 16, 1864. The *Sunday Morning Chronicle*, on the other hand, thought it not immoral or indecent, but wholesome satire, respectable fun and genuine wit. It criticized the production for disparaging remarks at certain statesmen and because it was derogatory toward Negroes. Washington *Sunday Morning Chronicle*, Mar. 20, 1864.

[27] Washington *National Intelligencer*, Mar. 28, 1864.

[28] Washington *National Intelligencer*, Mar. 22, 1864. John Nicolay called it "a sensational extravaganza, good for nothing, except for one very gorgeous scene at the close." John G. Nicolay to Therena Bates, Mar. 21, 1864, Nicolay Papers.

hall, there was an expression of surprise and pleasure on the face of Abraham Lincoln.[29]

Sunday, June 19, 1864, was a solemn day in Washington. There was an atmosphere of sadness in many churches that morning; in the afternoon a somber crowd of twenty-five thousand persons lined the streets to witness the funeral procession of eighteen young women who were killed in a horrible explosion at the Arsenal two days before.

After a short service at the Arsenal, the procession, headed by a band playing mournful dirges, wended its way to the Congressional Cemetery. Along the route a choir sang "Sister, thou wast mild and lovely," in memory of one of the victims. In one of the carriages as mourners for the dead rode Edwin M. Stanton and Abraham Lincoln.[30]

That evening the President attended a sacred concert at Ford's Theatre. Madame Cecilia Kretschmar, assisted by Theodore Habelmann and Joseph Hermanns, provided the program. Kretschmar was well known for the many concerts she had given to raise funds for sick and wounded soldiers. Habelmann and Hermanns were prominent members of a German opera troupe.

In their best professional manner the artists gave a most creditable performance. The audience was enthusiastic. So was the President. He expressed himself as "highly entertained" by the singing of these popular artists.[31]

Earlier in the season the President, Mrs. Lincoln, and Secretary Seward had attended a concert of quite a different type. On the evening of March 24, they were in

---

[29] Bullard, *Tad and His Father*, pp. 51-65. Cf. chapter IX, *supra*. This tableau was added sometime after the summer of 1862.

[30] Washington *Evening Star*, June 17, 20, 1864; Washington *National Intelligencer*, June 18, 20, 1864; Washington *Sunday Morning Chronicle*, June 19, 1864; Washington *Daily Morning Chronicle*, June 20, 1864; Sacramento *Daily Union*, July 12, 1864; B. B. French to H. F. F., June 19, 1864, B. B. French Papers. Explosions like this were all too common during the war. In this case, a monument of simple beauty was erected to the victims in the Congressional Cemetery. Washington *Evening Star*, Nov. 26, 1864; *Leslie's Illus. News*, Nov. 16, 1867.

[31] Washington *Evening Star*, June 18, 1864; Washington *Sunday Morning Chronicle*, Jan. 25, 1863, June 26, 1864; William Roscoe Thayer, *The Life and Letters of John Hay* (Boston and New York, 1915), I, 147.

the front row of the elite audience at Willard's Hall to hear the program offered by Louis M. Gottschalk, "the unrivaled."

Gottschalk was assisted by Charlotte Varian, "the superb soprano," Carlo Patti, violinist and brother of the famous Patti sisters, and Theodore Habelmann, the well-known operatic tenor. The program was typically "Gottschalk." It was varied, and, of course, included a number of Gottschalk's own works:

Part I

1. Violin Solo—"Élégie" _____Ernst
   Signor Carlo Patti
2. Aria from the "Barber of Seville" _____Rossini
   Theodore Habelmann
3. Transcription of the "Miserere"
   from "Trovatore" _____Gottschalk
   Louis M. Gottschalk
4. "Slumber On, Baby Dear"
   (A Mother's Cradle Song) _____Gottschalk
   Charlotte Varian
   (accompanied by Gottschalk)
5. a. "La Savane" (Ballad Creole)
   b. "Forest Glade" (Polka Brilliante) ____Gottschalk
   Louis M. Gottschalk

Part II

6. a. Andante from the Sonata
   "Pathétique" _____Beethoven
   b. "Ojos Criollos" (Danse)
   for four hands _____Gottschalk
   Louis M. Gottschalk and S. Behrens
7. Scene and Aria from "La Traviata" _____Verdi
   Charlotte Varian
8. Violin Solo "Carnival de Venice" _____Paganini
   Signor Carlo Patti
9. Song "My Father's Home" _____Gumbert
   Theodore Habelmann
10. Fantasia on themes from the
   "Daughter of the Regiment,"
   composed and performed by
   Louis M. Gottschalk

According to reports, the audience was highly pleased; it was delighted with the contributions of the singers and the violinist, and was "charmed and thrilled" by Gottschalk's playing. "He never was more brilliant," said the *Chronicle*.

What the President's reaction to the program was is not known. Very likely he enjoyed to the utmost Gottschalk's encore—his medley of patriotic airs, "L'Union." He and the rest of the audience would probably have been surprised had they known that Gottschalk thought that he had played badly, and was furious with himself because of it![32]

In April and June, thanks to the efforts of Leonard Grover, a German opera company came to Washington for a series of performances. Interest was at a high pitch in social circles, and society turned out in large numbers to support this new cultural triumph. Society at this time included not only Cabinet officers, judges, diplomats, and their wives, but also Mr. and Mrs. Lincoln.

Opera was not entirely new to Washington or to the Lincolns. Lincoln saw his first opera, *Un Ballo in Maschera*, on February 20, 1861, during his stop in New York when he was on his way to his inauguration. In January, 1862, Mrs. Lincoln and Robert saw the *Barber of Seville*, and the President accompanied Mrs. Lincoln to a performance of scenes from *Il Trovatore*. In May of that year the President appeared at Ford's Theatre where Clara Louise Kellogg was playing in the *Daughter of the Regiment*.[33]

By 1863 there were signs that Washington was to have a genuine "opera season." A well-known Italian company came to the city for a week's stay. Not since before the war had a first-class opera troupe been willing to risk the expense of an extended visit there. This time public support was generous and the singers played to crowded houses each evening. Music, it was said, was being re-

[32] Washington *Daily Morning Chronicle*, Mar. 24, 25, 1864; Washington *Evening Star*, Mar. 24, 1864; Washington *National Intelligencer*, Mar. 24, 1864; Gottschalk, *Notes of a Pianist*, p. 246.

[33] Washington *Evening Star*, Jan. 23, 24, May 28, 1862.

vived and the city was becoming a real center of culture. The "revival" was allegedly due to the influx of Northerners. In former times, society sought entertainment in listening to violent speeches and in hissing and cheering brawling congressmen from the House galleries. Politics was the "ruling passion" and music fled. "Music," said the *Chronicle*, "the sensitive child of Peace, and language of noble aspiration, trembled at the treachery and fled from the ruffianism of Washington."

Now things were changed. The Yankees were in control and even in wartime they brought with them the arts of peace. Finding in music "one of the most pleasant and useful auxiliaries to social pastime and enjoyment" (as presidential secretary Nicolay put it), people were now crowding the concert and opera halls instead of packing the House galleries!

Nicolay, himself, went almost every night. The President and Mrs. Lincoln attended twice with Senator Sumner as their guest.[34] The New York *Herald*, quick to note the presidential move, suggested that the Lincolns come to Manhattan to hear more opera. Mrs. Lincoln could shop and the President could have his fill of opera, and the change would do them both a world of good![35]

Thus when the German opera troupe arrived in April, 1864, Washington was quite "opera-minded," and the pleasure anticipated by music lovers was enhanced by the fact that the season was to be one of mostly *German* opera, not Italian! For German opera was becoming more and more popular. It was considered much more substantial and worthwhile; the artists were said to be better singers, better actors, and not given to temperamental instabilities that were characteristic of Italian artists.

Reflecting this viewpoint, reports from Philadelphia praised the German company highly and announced it as a "positive delight" to have had a season of fourteen performances with no Verdi, no anvil chorus, no gypsy

---

[34] Washington *Sunday Morning Chronicle*, Apr. 26, 1863; John G. Nicolay to Therena Bates, Apr. 19, 26, 1863, Nicolay Papers; Lincoln, *Works*, VI, 185; Philadelphia *Sunday Dispatch*, Apr. 26, 1863.

[35] N.Y. *Herald*, Apr. 23, 1863.

hags, seductions, stabbings or burnings—not a murder in the whole season! Instead, there had been love, romance, innocent intrigue, and humor.[36]

When the German troupe had completed its June series in Washington, one critic—after praising the singers and orchestra—concluded flatly that German opera was far superior to Italian, and warned the Italian stars:

> Once fairly in competition with this German troupe and the Italians will find that their pretty tricks, their lovely wrangles, their tender "sudden indispositions," that affectation and imperiousness which have nauseated us with some of their prima donnas and tenors—these capers of overspoiled warblers, the Italians will find so put to the blush by the manly, working, healthy mode of the Germans, that we shall soon cease to be annoyed by what of this has so much and so long offended.[37]

Three times in April and once during the June series, the President attended the opera. Each time he saw the best, for the operas were excellently performed, the acting was superior and the music of top quality.

On the evening of April 2 *Faust* was played. Although the weather was miserable, with rain pouring down, the house was full. It was "Extra Grand Toilet Night," consequently many attended in full dress. Secretary Seward and his family occupied the box opposite the President's.[38]

The performance was lavishly praised by the critic for the *Intelligencer*:

> The troupe now at Grover's give us the opera. We have it complete from the orchestra to the chorus. We have the action, the passion, the sparkle of the drama . . . subordinated to the story on the stage. Such an entertainment is not a merely disjointed carnival of sweets, where *bon bons* are pelted at our heads in mobbish confusion—but it is the legitimate rendition of the opera.[39]

---

[36] *Dwight's Journal of Music*, XXII (Feb. 7, 1863), 356-57, (Feb. 14, 1863), 363, from the Philadelphia *Evening Bulletin*, Jan. 12, Feb. 8, 1863. The fact that *Dwight's Journal* chose to print these comments was in itself of some significance.

[37] Washington *National Intelligencer*, June 11, 1864.

[38] A complete orchestra of thirty pieces and a chorus of thirty-four were imported from New York. In addition, there was a full brass band for appropriate scenes, as in *Faust*. Washington *Sunday Morning Chronicle*, Mar. 27, 1864; Washington *Evening Star*, Apr. 2, 4, 1864.

[39] Washington *National Intelligencer*, Apr. 4, 1864.

As for the leading singers, the reporter summed up their achievements in words of unqualified praise:

> In the whole range of operatic triumph there is no history which stands out more proudly than does that which Frederici, Hermanns, and Himmer have made for Faust. We do not believe that three stars of equal magnitude have ever adorned the American stage—that is, appearing together and in the same opera.[40]

Two evenings after *Faust* the Lincolns were present for *Der Freischütz*, and again the critic was generous. He wrote:

> We write this fresh from Der Freischütz . . . we thrill with the inspiration of a night whose best hours have been passed with the masters of a great art. Let not him or her who paid for a ticket to hear Der Freischütz (or Faust) imagine that the price was counted out! Genius is above rubies. You cannot *buy* the inspiration which flows from a Weber or a Guunot [*sic*].[41]

On Tuesday, April 5, the weather was so stormy that the usual reception at the White House was postponed, but the Lincolns went to the performance of *Martha*, nevertheless! Of the evening's production the *Star* reported:

> It was, to say the least of it, a more decided artistic triumph than was ever achieved in this country by any other opera company. Every solo, duet, trio, quarto, quintette and chorus in the piece was rapturously applauded, and half a dozen of them were necessarily repeated before the audience would permit the piece to proceed.[42]

The more discerning comment in the *Intelligencer* was: "*Martha* we could never reconcile ourselves to as an opera—these artists however, made it not only endurable, but a feast."[43]

---

[40] Washington *National Intelligencer*, June 10, 1864. *Faust*, first heard in New York in November, 1863, easily became the most popular of all operas. For ten years Clara Louise Kellogg was considered the greatest "Marguerite." In March, 1864, when she was ill, Marie Frederici took the part. She was capable and popular. Odell. *Annals of the New York Stage*, VII, 581, 582, 583.

[41] Washington *National Intelligencer*, Apr. 7, 1864.

[42] Washington *Evening Star*, Apr. 6, 1864.

[43] Washington *National Intelligencer*, June 3, 1864.

One evening in June during the second visit of the German company the President went alone to the opera. He heard *Fidelio*. It was well done, principally because of the accomplished acting and singing of the popular Madame Johannsen.[44]

The opera season was over. Lincoln had seen and heard four performances which were hailed as outstanding successes in a season of success. Did he enjoy his operatic experiences? We do not exactly know. He could, while at the opera, relax and muse or think if he did not care to listen and follow; he was free from interruption and from requests for favors; he could there avoid politicians and generals, and he could by being there please Mrs. Lincoln.

But whereas he often, with great enjoyment and from a fund of quite intimate knowledge, discussed Shakespeare's plays and recited long passages from them, he was never known to discuss operatic plots or characters, to hum an operatic tune or expound on the merits of Italian versus German opera! The most that can be said is that the "Soldiers' Chorus" from *Faust* was one of his favorite pieces.

On the second day of July the Lincolns moved out to the Anderson Cottage at the Soldiers' Home for the summer. The gay social season, with its receptions, concerts, plays, and operas, was over. Very likely, the President was glad. There was plenty to take up his time and energy. And as it turned out, there were excitement and music that summer of 1864.

---

[44] Washington *National Intelligencer*, Apr. 7, June 8, 1864. In December, and again in March, 1865, the Lincolns attended more opera. The President saw *Faust* twice, Mrs. Lincoln saw *Martha* twice, and they went together in March to hear *The Magic Flute* and *La Dame Blanche*. Mrs. Lincoln also had plans for attending more opera later that month, but her trips to City Point interfered. Washington *Evening Star*, Dec. 6, 8, 1864, Mar. 16, 22, 1865; Washington *Daily Morning Chronicle*, Mar. 8, 1865; Pierce, ed., *Memoir and Letters of Charles Sumner*, IV, 232-34; Carl Sandburg and Paul M. Angle, *Mary Lincoln, Wife and Widow* (N.Y., 1932), pp. 222, 224; Ruth P. Randall, *Mary Lincoln*, p. 348; N.Y. *Times*, Jan. 20, 1930.

CHAPTER XVII

THE SINGING CHAPLAIN AND
THE SINGING PILGRIM

BY 1864 CIVILIAN RELIEF WORK, BOTH ON THE HOME FRONT and battlefront, was operating extensively and effectively. The Sanitary Commission, headed by Henry W. Bellows, Unitarian minister, and the Christian Commission, under the leadership of George H. Stuart, Philadelphia merchant, collected, packaged, and forwarded to the armies incredible quantities and varieties of food, clothing, hospital supplies, delicacies, writing materials, and a host of other supplies, all of which contributed immeasurably to the welfare, health, and morale of the men who were engaged in the bloody business of war.

Equally important were the ministry and services of the volunteer unpaid workers of the commissions. They nursed the sick, cared for the wounded, consoled the downhearted, and aided the distressed. When help was most needed, they were there to give it. A committee from Peoria, Illinois, provided meal tickets for soldiers en route, while a committee from Baltimore acquired a steam engine to pump water to lay the dust at the hospital camp at City Point. The Cincinnati committee provided reams of writing paper (35,000 sheets a day at one time) for General Thomas' soldiers, and the same group sent twenty cows to Nashville to provide milk for 2,400 sick and wounded men; the subsistence committee at Pittsburgh gave day and night meal service to soldiers passing through the city, and a call at Saratoga for ice produced $3,200 and saw the ice on its way in twenty-four hours; diet kitchens made possible proper food for men too ill to take regular hospital rations, and two members of the

Christian Commission traveled the long journey to California to raise money for the work.[1]

The Sanitary Commission, in addition to its work on the battlefield and in camps, established homes in a number of cities to care for returning soldiers. In Washington it had several houses and lodges, including one at the wharf, a central one on North Capitol Street, and a special lodge for persons who had come to the city in search of missing relatives. By fall of 1863 the home on North Capitol Street had provided 86,986 nights' lodgings and 331,315 meals; it helped the men obtain their back pay and pensions, got in touch with their relatives, procured railroad tickets for them, and provided them with clothing. The home's bedrooms and bathrooms were clean and its reading rooms were cheerful. The commission cleaned up Camp Convalescent and made it livable—it had been called "Camp Misery" because conditions there were so bad.[2] When it was over there were many testimonials to the value of this work. Blunt-spoken General Sherman, who was sometimes annoyed by the energetic zeal of the volunteer workers, paid tribute to the Christian Commission (which might be applied to the Sanitary Commission also). Writing to George H. Stuart in January, 1866, he said,

> That the agents for the application of this charity did manifest a zeal and energy worthy of the object, I myself am a willing witness; and I would be understood as heartily endorsing, without reserve, their efforts, when applied to the great hospitals and rendezvous in the rear of our great armies. . . .
>
> Now that the great end is attained, and in our quiet rooms and offices we can look back on the past with composure, I am not only willing, but pleased with the opportunity, to express my belief that your charity was noble in its conception, and applied with as much zeal, kindness, and discretion as the times permitted.[3]

---

[1] Lemuel Moss, *Annals of the United States Christian Commission* (Phila., 1868), pp. 323, 331, 343-44, 346, 352-54, 527, 663 ff.

[2] *The United States Sanitary Commission: A Sketch of Its Purposes and Its Work* (Boston, 1863), Part III.

[3] Moss, *Annals of the Christian Commission*, pp. 238-39.

This vast work required money. To the constant appeals of the two commissions, the people responded generously. The Christian Commission relied mainly on contributions of individuals at church services and patriotic meetings. The popular response was impressive. General Sherman commented, "That the people of the United States should have voluntarily contributed six millions of dollars for the moral welfare of the soldiers employed, in addition to other and vast charitable contributions, is one of the wonders of the world."[4]

Probably the most effective means employed to raise money was through fairs conducted by the Sanitary Commission. Beginning at Chicago in October of 1863, fairs were organized in cities large and small, and millions of dollars were thus attained. The fairs were successful, not only financially, but socially, and, of equal importance, as unifiers and stimulators of moral support for the Union cause.

The President recognized the importance of the work of the commissions and gave them more than passing support. He met with members of the commissions and contributed to their work.[5] He received many invitations to attend fairs, contributed autographs, letters, and important documents to be sold there, received gifts from them, and was present on four occasions at fairs and twice at anniversary meetings of the Christian Commission.[6]

[4] Moss, *Annals of the Christian Commission*, p. 238.

[5] Carpenter, *Six Months at the White House*, pp. 161-62; Moss, *Annals of the Christian Commission*, p. 299; Sidney Kramer, "Lincoln at the Fair," *Abraham Lincoln Quarterly*, III (Sept., 1945), 340-58.

[6] Documents that Lincoln contributed included the Proclamation of the Act to Suppress Insurrection, July 25, 1862, to the Philadelphia fair, the Preliminary Emancipation Proclamation, Sept. 22, 1862, to the Army Relief Bazaar at Albany, the original draft of the Emancipation Proclamation to the fair at Chicago, copies of the Gettysburg Address to the fairs at New York and Baltimore, and a copy of the Proclamation of Amnesty and Reconstruction, Dec. 8, 1863, to the fair at Cincinnati. Lincoln, *Works*, V, 341, n., 433, n.; VI, 30, n., 539-40; VII, 21, n., 22, 53, n.

It is of interest that Lincoln received a gold watch from the Chicago fair as a prize to the donor whose contribution brought the highest sum, the Emancipation Proclamation having been sold for three thousand dollars. By contrast, a mammoth ox (named General Grant) which, having been given to him by a patriotic Bostonian, Lincoln forthwith contributed to the Sailors' Relief Fair in Boston, sold for $3,200! For this he received no prize! Lincoln, *Works*, VII, 75; VIII, 96, and n.

Among the gifts received by Lincoln was a song of seven verses, "National Union Hymn. Written by an old citizen of Ohio. Tune 'Old Hundred' For the Western Sanitary Fair." The hymn was sung at the Cincinnati fair and the

The fair held at the Patent Office in Washington during February and March, 1864, for the benefit of the Christian Commission and the families of soldiers in the District, was not an extensive enterprise. And yet Lincoln thought it of sufficient importance to attend both the opening and closing ceremonies. Thus it was that on the evening of February 22 he appeared at the Patent Office and was ecorted to the platform as the Second District Regiment Band played "Hail to the Chief!"

The exercises included a prayer, a long address by L. E. Chittenden of the Treasury Department, and a patriotic poem by Benjamin B. French. Inevitably, there were calls for the President to say something. Lincoln was taken unawares. He had not expected to make a speech and apologized.[7]

The audience accepted his apology good-naturedly, with laughter and applause, but not so Mrs. Lincoln, who was sitting in the front row directly before him. At the end of the evening, as the Presidential party waited for a carriage, Mrs. Lincoln remarked:

> That was the worst speech I ever listened to in my life. How any man could get up and deliver such remarks to an audience is more than I can understand. I wanted the earth to sink and let me through.[8]

However, Lincoln redeemed himself at the closing ceremonies of the fair on March 18. The hall was jammed with people; young ladies screamed and older ladies had their corns trod upon. The Knights Templar, in full regalia, opened a passage so that the President, Mrs. Lincoln, and other dignitaries could reach the platform. A band played "Hail to the Chief!"[9]

After General Sickles and General Oglesby made patriotic addresses, it was the President's turn. He paid

---

author sent the copy to the President. G. Richards to Abraham Lincoln, January 14, 1864, R. T. Lincoln Coll., 29475, 29482-3.

[7] Washington *Evening Star*, Feb. 23, 1864; Washington *Daily Morning Chronicle*, Feb. 23, 1864; N.Y. *Herald*, Feb. 24, 1864; Lincoln, *Works*, VII, 197-98.

[8] As remembered by Richard Oglesby who was with the presidential party. Sandburg and Angle, *Mary Lincoln, Wife and Widow*, p. 112.

[9] Washington *Evening Star*, Mar. 18, 19, 1864; Washington *Daily Morning Chronicle*, Mar. 19, 1864; N.Y. *Herald*, Mar. 19, 1864; N.Y. *Times*, Mar. 19, 1864.

tribute to the soldiers, expressed appreciation of the fairs, and complimented the ladies:

> In this extraordinary war extraordinary developments have manifested themselves, such as have not been seen in former wars; and amongst these manifestations nothing has been more remarkable than these fairs for the relief of suffering soldiers and their families. And the chief agents in these fairs are the women of America.
>
> I am not accustomed to the use of language of eulogy; I have never studied the art of paying compliments to women; but I must say that if all that has been said by orators and poets since the creation of the world in praise of woman were applied to the women of America, it would not do them justice for their conduct during this war. I will close by saying God bless the women of America![10]

By the middle of April the Lincoln's had received invitations to several fairs—Boston, Lancaster, and the biggest of all, in New York. But the President accepted the invitation to be present at the opening of the fair in Baltimore on April 18.

That the date was of more than passing significance was noted in Baltimore. It was ". . . a day ever memorable for the first assault and maltreatment of the soldiers of the sister State of Pennsylvania . . . and the prelude to the atrocities committed in our streets against the patriotic sons of Massachusetts on the nineteenth."[11] As it turned out, Mr. Lincoln was also aware of the day and referred to it in his brief speech that evening. Perhaps that was why he decided to be present.

When Lincoln arrived in Baltimore shortly after six o'clock, a large crowd was on hand to greet him. A holiday had been declared for the city, the weather was fine, and a long parade had brought out thousands during the afternoon. The President's appearance added to the excitment.[12]

At six thirty the doors of the fair building were opened for the first time and crowds poured in. Although some

---

[10] Lincoln, *Works*, VII, 254.

[11] Baltimore *American*, Apr. 13, 1864; Baltimore *Sun*, Apr. 14, 1864.

[12] Baltimore *American*, Apr. 19, 1864.

minor finishing touches were still to be made, the main hall presented a beautiful spectacle. Overhead the arches were decorated and illumined with a thousand sparkling gaslights. In the center of the hall there was a floral temple thirty feet high made of many varieties of flowers and shrubs. Around the hall were exhibits and stands prepared by organizations that had contributed to the occasion.

Among the major attractions were the art gallery, the fish pond, and a children's table featuring "Flora Mc-Flimsey" with her entire wardrobe, and the New England Kitchen.

The idea of a New England Kitchen for serving meals, first tried at the Brooklyn fair, had met with such success that the Baltimoreans constructed one also. It was arranged in old-fashioned style with a fireplace and a spinning wheel. Thus, said the *Sun*, ". . . the days of childhood are brought back again with their pleasing recollections, when peace prevailed throughout the land, nor brother raised his hand against brother. To thousands who will visit the fair, the New England kitchen will be as familiar as their home, but to the younger generation it will be an object of curiosity."[13]

Newspapers gave generous attention to the unique contribution to the fair in which the President himself had a part—the volume prepared by Colonel Alexander Bliss, *Autograph Leaves of Our Country's Authors*. They noted that John P. Kennedy had prepared the introduction for the work, and that the first two contributions were the "Star-Spangled Banner" and the President's speech at Gettysburg. Copies were on sale and the originals were to be sold "either by raffle or otherwise."[14]

Music for the fair was under the direction of Professor James M. Deems, well-known and highly respected teacher

---

[13] Baltimore *American*, Apr. 18, 19, 1864; Baltimore *Sun*, Apr. 19, 20, 21, 1864. The kitchen proved so popular that in a few days it had to be enlarged. Baltimore *Sun*, Apr. 23, 1864.

[14] Baltimore *American*, Apr. 18, 1864; Baltimore *Sun*, Apr. 19, 1864. Cf. F. Lauriston Bullard, *"A Few Appropriate Remarks": Lincoln's Gettysburg Address* (Harrogate, 1944), chap. III; *The Unique and Final Holograph Manuscript of Lincoln's Gettysburg Address* (Catalogue), Parke-Bernet Galleries, Inc. (N.Y., 1949); David C. Mearns and Lloyd A. Dunlap, *Long Remembered: The Gettysburg Address in Facsimile* (Washington, 1963).

and composer of Baltimore. A stand had been built for the musicians near the entrance to the main hall. At eight o'clock, as President Lincoln, Governor Bradford, General Wallace, and others entered and approached the speakers' platform, the crowd cheered, waved handkerchiefs, and the band struck up the familiar "Hail to the Chief!"

The program was not unduly long. It began with a prayer, a hymn, and opening remarks by Governor Bradford. The band then played "Hail, Columbia," after which the President gave his short speech. A Chinese quilt was presented to Mrs. Bradford by Senator Wilson of Massachusetts; General Wallace made an address followed by a final musical selection.

The music was of particular significance. The singers were the National Union Musical Association, the same group that had sung Benjamin B. French's hymn at Gettysburg the previous November; the hymn following the prayer was Oliver Wendell Holmes' "Army Hymn," a copy of which he had submitted for the *Autograph Leaves*.

When General Wallace had finished his address, a young man stepped up beside the President to sing. He was Wilson G. Horner, prominent in musical circles and active in patriotic affairs in Baltimore. Horner had led the National Union Musical Association in the singing of French's hymn at Gettysburg, and earlier in this same month of April had sung at the White House for the President. The song that had so pleased the President on that occasion, Horner now sang again, with the Musical Association joining in the chorus. It made a climactic ending for the exercises:

> We are coming, Father Abraham,
> Five hundred thousand more,
> From Mississippi's winding stream
> And from New England's shore—[15]

When Horner finished there was a rush as people

---

[15] Baltimore *Gazette*, Apr. 19, 1864; Baltimore *Sun*, Apr. 19, 1864; Baltimore *American*, Apr. 19, 1864; Washington *Evening Star*, Apr. 4, 1864.

pressed forward to shake hands with the President. Finally the crowd moved away enough so that he could go about and observe the exhibits. Several bouquets and a beautiful afghan were presented to him. It was nearly eleven o'clock when he was escorted from the hall to the home of William J. Albert.[16] The evening was not over, however, for at the Albert home a levee was held at which many distinguished guests were present to greet the Chief Executive. It had been a strenuous day. As he left Baltimore the next morning to return to Washington, the President expressed his pleasure in his visit. Baltimore had indeed changed since February, 1861![17]

Two months later the President journeyed to Philadelphia to attend the fair there. This visit was more strenuous—and less pleasant—than his Baltimore trip. The fair was much larger and more elaborate, and those in charge were very anxious to have Lincoln attend. Unable to be there for the opening June 7, he sent Methodist Bishop Simpson to represent him, and rather reluctantly agreed to make the trip himself June 16-17.[18]

Arriving in Philadelphia just before noon, the President was welcomed by a huge crowd. With difficulty, his carriage, preceded by the Jefferson Cornet Band, made its way to the Continental Hotel. At a fire station the fire bells were rung. At a recruiting station a band struck up the "Star-Spangled Banner."

At four o'clock the mayor and welcoming committee appeared to escort the President to the fair. So great were the crowds that it took an hour to reach the fairgrounds. Once inside, the crowd was so dense that at one time the President had to be "rescued" and led to a

---

[16] The President stayed with Mr. Albert that night. The invitation sent to him is in the Nicolay Papers (Correspondence, No. 3).

[17] Baltimore *American*, Apr. 19, 20, 1864; Baltimore *Sun*, Apr. 20, 1864. Mrs. Lincoln made a one-day visit to the fair on the following day. She was cordially received, accepted a present for her thoughtfulness in sending flowers for the fair, and ate at the New England Kitchen. Baltimore *American*, Apr. 21, 1864; Baltimore *Sun*, Apr. 21, 1864; Washington *Daily Morning Chronicle*, Apr. 23, 1864; Sally C. Baynes *et al* to Mrs. [Mary Todd] Lincoln, Apr. 19, 1864, R. T. Lincoln Coll., 32500-1.

[18] *Harper's Weekly*, June 11, 18, 1864; *Leslie's Illus. News*, June 25, 1864; *Our Daily Fare*, June 8, 21, 1864; Charles J. Stillé, *Memorial of the Great Central Fair for the U.S. Sanitary Commission Held at Philadelphia, June, 1864* (Phila., 1864), *passim*; Frank H. Taylor, *Philadelphia in the Civil War* (Phila., 1913), pp. 263-65; John Welsh to Abraham Lincoln, May 23, 1864, R. T. Lincoln Coll., 33266-7.

private room. He had little time to visit the exhibits or hear the music of the bands.

The banquet at seven o'clock was long, formal, and tedious. Toasts were given, speeches made, and the President was presented with a medal and a staff. Edward Everett made a graceful and complimentary speech expressing the hope that the country would not swap horses in the middle of the stream. Lincoln's speech, which began, "War, at the best, is terrible, and this war of ours, in its magnitude and its duration, is one of the most terrible," was short, well delivered, and well received.

Near midnight, after visits to the Union League Club, and the National Union Club, the President finally returned to his hotel, but not to immediate rest, for a huge crowd awaited him there. Fireworks were shot off, a band played "Auld Lang Syne," "Rally 'Round the Flag," "Yankee Doodle," and the "Star-Spangled Banner." The crowd started singing and kept it up. It called for the President. He finally appeared and spoke briefly.[19]

It had been a very strenuous day. Later, when invited to the fair to be held in Chicago, Lincoln humorously recalled, ". . . for all the time I was in Philadelphia I was crowded, and jostled, and pulled about, and cheered, and serenaded, until I was more used up than I ever remember to have been in my life. I don't believe I could stand another big fair."[20]

Unlike the Sanitary Commission, the Christian Commission did not sponsor fairs. Rather, it depended upon church and patriotic services, and especially the yearly anniversary meetings to raise money and generate enthusiasm for its work.

The anniversary meetings became occasions for great outpourings of people. The two that Lincoln attended were particularly memorable for it was there that the inspired music of a singing chaplain and a singing pil-

[19] Philadelphia *Inquirer*, June 16, 17, 18, 1864; Philadelphia *Evening Bulletin*, June 16, 17, 21, 1864; N.Y. *Times*, June 17, 1864; N.Y. *Herald*, June 17, 1864; Washington *Daily Morning Chronicle*, June 18, 1864; *Our Daily Fare*, June 17, 18, 1864; *Lincoln Lore*, No. 1315 (June 21, 1954).

[20] Mary A. Livermore, *My Story of the War. . . .* (Hartford, 1894), pp. 579-80.

grim gave him the greatest musical thrills of his presidential years.

The First Anniversary Meeting in Washington was held in the hall of the House of Representatives on the evening of February 22, 1863. The weather was miserable. For twenty-four hours a violent storm had raged. It had snowed and rained and the streets were full of slush and mud. Nevertheless, a large crowd gathered. Secretary Chase presided and for nearly four hours the audience listened to reports, plans, and addresses. A successful precedent was set for future years.

Although he was invited to attend and preside at the meeting, the President did not go. He brought the matter up at a cabinet meeting, but only Chase seemed to favor his accepting the invitation. Evidently Lincoln considered that it was not sufficiently important for him to make the effort to go. His letter extending his best wishes but declining the invitation was read at the meeting.[21]

A year later it was different. The President went and was glad that he did go. Again a huge audience assembled in the hall of the House of Representatives. Vice-President Hamlin opened the meeting with an "eloquent and effective" speech. George H. Stuart, hardworking chairman of the Commission, then gave a detailed report on the Commission's work.

The list of speakers was long—it included Speaker Colfax, Senator Sherman, General Martindale, and several ministers active in the cause. A band in the gallery played at intervals.

During Mr. Stuart's report the President and Mrs. Lincoln arrived. The entire audience rose, cheered, applauded, and waved handkerchiefs. Mr. Stuart finished

---

[21] Washington *Evening Star,* Feb. 23, 1863 ; Philadelphia *Evening Bulletin,* Feb. 23, 1863 ; N.Y. *Times,* Feb. 27, 1863 ; Morse, ed., *Diary of Gideon Welles,* I, 238 ; Moss, *Annals of the Christian Commission,* p. 132 ; U.S. Christian Commission to Abraham Lincoln, Feb. 12, 1863, R. T. Lincoln Coll., 21693-4 ; Abraham Lincoln to Rev. Alexander Reed, Feb. 22, 1863, R. T. Lincoln Coll., 21896-7 ; Lincoln, *Works,* VI, 110-11, 114-15. Perhaps the President was too exhausted to attend. At the reception on February 21, he was reported as looking "haggard and careworn." *Leslie's Illus. News,* Feb. 28, 1863. That same day, however, James C. Conkling was invited to an informal dinner at the White House on Sunday evening. Mrs. [Mary Todd] Lincoln, Letters, 1863, Ill. State Hist. Library.

his report and the band played the "Star-Spangled Banner."[22]

Soon after came the climax of the meeting. Charles C. McCabe, known as the "singing chaplain," recently released from Libby Prison, rose and began to speak.

The chaplain was an effective speaker as well as a good singer, and the audience, including the President, listened intently to his thrilling tale of his capture at Winchester, Virginia, in June, 1863, and of his imprisonment at Libby.[23]

He recounted his efforts to bolster the spirits of the other prisoners—how he started the "University of Libby," organizing classes in French, Spanish, Greek, Latin, rhetoric and grammar, mathematics, and other subjects, and especially how he got them to sing.

A singing society was organized and concerts were given with programs that included French, Irish, Hungarian, Scotch, and German songs, sometimes ending with "Home, Sweet Home." So good was the music that even the natives of Richmond gathered outside to listen; they did not object to "We Are Coming, Father Abraham" and "Rally 'Round the Flag," but somehow, they did not care for "Yankee Doodle!"[24] On the other hand, the commandant of the prison thought the singing somewhat of a nuisance, saying, ". . . you Yankees seem disposed to sing anywhere, and we have to endure it even here."[25]

Finally McCabe gave a graphic description of what happened in Libby during the early days of July, 1863. The prisoners were moody and anxious. They knew a big battle was about to occur on Northern soil. They waited. Rumors filtered in that the Army of the Potomac

[22] Washington *Evening Star*, Feb. 3, 1864; Washington *National Intelligencer*, Feb. 4, 1864; Philadelphia *Evening Bulletin*, Feb. 3, 1864; N.Y. *Tribune*, Feb. 3, 1864; N.Y. *Times*, Feb. 3, 1864; *United States Christian Commission, for the Army and Navy: For the Year 1863* (Phila., 1864).

[23] Washington *Evening Star*, Feb. 3, 1864; Washington *Daily Morning Chronicle*, Feb. 3, 1864; Philadelphia *Evening Bulletin*, Feb. 3, 1864; Baltimore *Sun*, Feb. 4, 1864.

[24] Frank Milton Bristol, *The Life of Chaplain McCabe, Bishop of the Methodist Episcopal Church* (New York, Chicago, Toronto, 1908), *passim*.

[25] Bristol, *Life of Chaplain McCabe*, p. 96.

had again been defeated. The prison was filled with gloom.

A friendly Negro soon gave them the real news— Gettysburg! Spirits lifted and Chaplain McCabe once again led the ragged and dirty prisoners in song. They sang all the patriotic songs; they sang "Praise God from Whom All Blessings Flow," and made the prison ring with a new song that the singing chaplain had taught them. At this point McCabe and Colonel William H. Powell, a comrade who had nursed him through a severe fever at Libby, began to sing that same song—

> Mine eyes have seen the glory of the
> coming of the Lord—

The audience rose. When the singers came to the chorus, everyone joined in—

> Glory, glory, hallelujah!
> His truth is marching on.

McCabe and Powell sang all the verses with the audience joining in each time. But before the last notes had died away, a voice was heard, "Sing it again!" It was the voice of the President!

And so amid great enthusiasm they sang it again. Lincoln's face was wet with tears.

Many in the excited audience paused to shake hands with the President as they left the meeting. It had been an occasion long to be remembered, made so by the singing chaplain.[26]

Shortly thereafter, Chaplain McCabe attended a Saturday reception at the White House. The President recognized him and complimented him highly, saying, "Take it all in all, the song and the singing, that was the best I ever heard."[27]

---

[26] Washington *Evening Star*, Feb. 3, 1864; Washington *Daily Morning Chronicle*, Feb. 3, 1864; Philadelphia *Evening Bulletin*, Feb. 3, 1864; Baltimore *Sun*, Feb. 4, 1864; Bristol, *Life of Chaplain McCabe*, chap. XXI.

[27] Bristol, *Life of Chaplain McCabe*, p. 203. In his Journal, McCabe also wrote: "My vanity was considerably delighted. Sure, and how could I help it?" Subsequently, by his singing, McCabe played a major part in making the "Battle Hymn" familiar to people throughout the North.

So well known was the work of the Christian Commission by 1865, and so popular had its anniversary meetings become, that on January 29 of that year, the day set for the Third Anniversary gathering, the crowd at the hall of the House of Representatives was tremendous.[28] Every seat was taken, many were standing, and hundreds were unable to get in at all.

As in previous years the meeting was long, beginning at seven o'clock and lasting until eleven thirty. After a Scripture reading, a prayer, and introductory remarks by Secretary Seward who presided, the meeting proceeded to get down to business.

Mr. Stuart gave his usual detailed report on the work of the Commission, following which there were no fewer than eight addresses. The remarks of newspaper correspondent A. D. Richardson, recently back from a lengthy stay in Confederate prisons, aroused particular interest.

The music for the occasion was more elaborate than in previous years, notably in the presence and contributions of the Washington Handel and Haydn Society. Opening the program with Bellini's stirring "Mighty Jehovah," these trained musicians during the evening led the audience in "America," sang the popular "Far away the campfires burn" in fine style, offered the "Hallelujah Chorus," and at the conclusion joined with the audience in the long-metered Doxology.[29]

But these selections were not the ones which pleased the President the most. (He had arrived during the Scripture reading and thus missed "Mighty Jehovah.")[30]

---

[28] The business meetings of the Commission were held in the E Street Baptist Church on January 26-27. On the morning of the twenty-seventh the delegates (to the number of one hundred or more) called on the President. Mr. Stuart introduced the group and Mr. Lincoln responded with a "neat and characteristic speech." Bishop Janes offered a prayer and the President shook each delegate by the hand. Washington *National Intelligencer,* Jan. 27, 1865; Baltimore *Sun,* Jan. 27, 28, 1865; N.Y. *Herald,* Jan. 27, 28, 1865; N.Y. *Times,* Jan. 28, 1865; Lincoln, *Works,* VIII, 241-42; Moss, *Annals of the Christian Commission,* pp. 213-16; J. G. Holland, *The Life of Abraham Lincoln* (Springfield, 1866), pp. 439-40.

[29] Washington *National Intelligencer,* Jan. 28, 30, 1865; Baltimore *Sun,* Jan. 30, 31, 1865; Philadelphia *Evening Bulletin,* Jan. 30, 1865; Moss, *Annals of the Christian Commission,* pp. 216-17.

[30] The President received a personal invitation from Mr. Stuart and a printed invitation. In his letter Mr. Stuart wrote: "Your presence with us, last year, added greatly to the interest of our meeting, and to its influence for good throughout the

Chaplain McCabe, whose singing the year before had so thrilled Lincoln, was again present. After describing his fund-raising efforts in Lincoln's home territory in central Illinois in the summer of 1864, he sang once more the "Battle Hymn of the Republic." Once more the audience, including the President, rose spontaneously and once more everyone joined in the chorus—

> Glory, glory, hallelujah!
> His truth is marching on.[31]

A little earlier in the program another singer took the center of the stage. He was Philip Phillips, a born musician, whose whole life had been bound up in music. As a boy Phillips had learned to play the melodeon and had attended a singing school. Before he was twenty he had a singing school of his own. Later he became associated with a musical publishing house, compiled songbooks, and went about the countryside selling music and melodeons and organizing singing societies.

With the coming of the war Phillips spent much time singing in camps and hospitals and to soldiers everywhere he met them. Because of his constant traveling and singing he was known as the "singing pilgrim."[32]

Phillips' song for the Anniversary Meeting, entitled "Your Mission," was quite different from the "Battle Hymn." Its several verses were poignant with sentiment and personal meaning for a people who had been through nearly four years of war. It began:

> If you can not on the ocean
>   Sail among the swiftest fleet,
> Rocking on the highest billows,
>   Laughing at the storms you meet;
> You can stand among the sailors,
>   Anchor'd yet within the bay,
> You can lend a hand to help them,
>   As they launch their boats away.

---

country. It was an occasion never to be forgotten by those who were there." George H. Stuart to Abraham Lincoln, Jan. 24, 1865, R. T. Lincoln Coll., 40249-50, 40261.

[31] Washington *National Intelligencer*, Jan. 30, 1865; Philadelphia *Evening Bulletin*, Jan. 30, 1865; Moss, *Annals of the Christian Commission*, p. 217.

[32] Alexander Clark, *Philip Phillips: The Story of His Life* (N.Y., 1883), *passim*.

As Phillips sang, Lincoln was deeply moved and tears ran down his face. Taking his program he wrote a message on the back of it and sent it up to Secretary Seward. It read:

Near the close let us have "Your Mission" repeated by Mr. Philips. Dont say I called for it

LINCOLN

To the satisfaction of all, Phillips complied with the request and repeated the song.[33] Observers recalled that the verse which affected the President the most was:

If you can not in the conflict
　　Prove yourself a soldier true,
If, where fire and smoke are thickest,
　　There's no work for you to do;
When the battlefield is silent,
　　You can go with careful tread,
You can bear away the wounded,
　　You can cover up the dead.

For a second time music at an Anniversary Meeting of the Christian Commission had given the President strong and thrilling emotional satisfaction.[34] Indeed, no music of the entire war affected him more deeply than the two songs sung by the singing chaplain and the singing pilgrim on these noteworthy occasions.

Some three months later Chaplain McCabe was in Chicago. The city was draped in mourning and the people were quiet and sober, waiting for the arrival of the funeral train. On the evening of April 30, a memorial service was held in the city. Speaker Colfax gave the ad-

---

[33] Washington *National Intelligencer*, Jan. 30, 1865; *The Christian Advocate*, July 4, 1895; Moss, *Annals of the Christian Commission*, pp. 216-17; Lincoln, *Works*, VIII, 245-46. The day after the meeting, Phillips wrote to Lincoln asking for a copy of his message requesting that "Your Mission" be repeated. Lincoln evidently complied for, years later, Phillips wrote that he had the "written request" in his possession and regarded it "as a rare relic." Philip Phillips, *Round the World with Descriptive Songs and Gem Solos* (N.Y., 1887), p. 37.

[34] "There were stirring songs of patriotism that night, whose choruses were like the clash of symbals [*sic*]; but that which he wished to hear again was the simple and touching ballad, 'Your Mission'. . . . At one verse of the ballad sung with exquisitely simple pathos . . . his face worked with deep emotion. This was the verse. . . ." So wrote one of the officials who was on the platform that evening. Rev. C. M. Butler, *Funeral Address on the Death of Abraham Lincoln, Delivered in the Church of the Covenant, April 19, 1865* (Phila., 1865), pp. 16-17.

dress and upon request McCabe sang the "Battle Hymn of the Republic."

> Mine eyes have seen the glory of the
> coming of the Lord—

On May 2, McCabe went down to Springfield along with hundreds of others. At a service the following evening he was again asked to sing the "Battle Hymn."

> I have seen him in the watchfires
> Of a hundred circling camps—

After the meeting a quiet group of people gathered at the home of Governor Oglesby and again McCabe was asked to sing.

> As he died to make men holy,
> Let us die to make men free—

Although he had wondered about singing the "Battle Hymn" on such occasions, in the end it did not seem inappropriate to do so. "They wanted it sung because Mr. Lincoln loved it so," he wrote.[35]

On the evening of February 11, 1866, members and friends of the Christian Commission gathered for the Fourth and Final Anniversary Meeting of the organization. Again the hall of the House of Representatives, now draped in memory of Abraham Lincoln, was crowded to capacity and thousands were unable to gain admittance.

As on former occasions, the meeting was lengthy. There were prayers, reports, remarks, addresses. Philip Phillips, the singing pilgrim, led the great assembly in the first hymn.

> Jesus shall reign where e'er the sun
> Does his successive journeys run.

---

[35] Bristol, *Life of Chaplain McCabe*, pp. 211-14. For forty years after the war, McCabe led a busy and active life and in 1896 was elected a bishop in the Methodist Episcopal Church. At his funeral service in Evanston, Illinois, Dec. 24, 1906, a baritone soloist sang the "Battle Hymn of the Republic" in tribute to the singing chaplain. Bristol, *Life of Chaplain McCabe*, pp. 415-16.

Later the audience joined in singing "America," and, at the close, the Doxology. Phillips sang "We Are Rising as a People" and "Home of the Soul."

The climax of the evening took everybody back to the meeting of the year before. Phillips was scheduled to sing, but before he commenced, the presiding official, Speaker Colfax, announced dramatically:

> Before singing the beautiful and impressive hymn, "Your Mission," next in order on the programme, let me read a brief note from the paper I hold in my hand. On the 29th of January, 1865, at the last anniversary meeting of this Commission, when hostile armies were contending together in deadly strife, this poem was sung as a part of the exercises of the evening. Abraham Lincoln, with his tall form, his care-furrowed face, and his nobly throbbing heart, was here, and, after listening in tears, he sent up, written upon the back of this programme (holding up the precious sheet), in that plain, familiar handwriting, by that hand that now lies cold in the grave, this request:—
>
> *Near the close, let us have "Your Mission" repeated by Mr. Philips. Dont say I called for it*
>
> LINCOLN[36]

Phillips then sang, once again, "Your Mission." The song ended:

> Do not, then, stand idly waiting,
>   For some greater work to do;
> Fortune is a lazy goddess,
>   She will never come to you.
> Go and toil in any vineyard,
>   Do not fear to do or dare,
> If you want a field of labor,
>   You can find it anywhere.

For years the memory of Lincoln's request that "Your Mission" be repeated, and the response of Philip Phillips, the singing pilgrim, remained in the minds of many who

---

[36] Washington *Evening Star*, Feb. 12, 1866; Philadelphia *Evening Bulletin*, Feb. 12, 1866; Moss, *Annals of the Christian Commission*, pp. 233-34; 256-57. The following day, Feb. 12, 1866, in the same place the Congress heard George Bancroft's eulogy on Lincoln. The program opened with the Marine Band playing the "Miserere" from *Il Trovatore*. Washington *Evening Star*, Feb. 12, 1866; M. A. De Wolfe Howe, *The Life and Letters of George Bancroft* (N.Y., 1908), II, 158.

had been at those thrilling Anniversary Meetings of the
Christian Commission in 1865 and 1866.[37]

---

[37] Seventeen years later, in recalling the incident, George H. Stuart said: "I have eyes that could weep with President Lincoln, when Mr. Phillips sang his touching songs in Washington." Philip Phillips, *Song Pilgrimage Round the World* (New York and London, 1882), p. 31. In 1887 Phillips referred to the occasion in his *Round the World*, p. 37; it was described in detail in Phillips' obituary in *The Christian Advocate*, July 4, 1895, and in the Philadelphia *Times*, Sept. 18, 1898. It is mentioned in Esther Singleton, *The Story of the White House* (N.Y., 1907), II, 93, and in Emanuel Hertz, *Abraham Lincoln: A New Portrait* (N.Y., 1931), I, 356-57.

A publication called *Heart Throbs* (n.p., n.d.) called it Lincoln's favorite song "which he encored no less than eighteen times when sung at a Sunday School convention in Washington." (This has not been substantiated.) Sandburg, *Abraham Lincoln*, IV, 116, describes it incorrectly, placing the event in the White House.

In 1915, Henry W. Knight, who had been in the Seventh Maine Regiment, stated that he had been present when Lincoln sent his message to Seward the evening of Jan. 29, 1865. Unidentified clipping, Lincoln National Life Foundation.

Phillips' singing is also mentioned in Elizabeth K. Vincent, *In the Days of Lincoln* (Gardena, Calif., 1924), p. 13.

In May, 1921, a request in the "Queries and Answers" column of the New York *Times Book Review and Magazine* for information on "Your Mission" resulted in twenty-one replies. The two replies printed in detail have the essential facts correct. N.Y. *Times Book Review and Magazine*, June 12, 26, 1921.

CHAPTER XVIII

SUMMER MUSIC

THE EARLY SUMMER OF 1864 WAS A TIME OF FRUSTRATION, disappointment, and dissension. Grant's failure before Richmond and his entrenchment at Petersburg meant more long months of struggle. Demands for a negotiated peace continued to find supporters while, on the other hand, dissenters within Republican ranks, even after the collapse of the Frémont movement, still hoped for the replacement of Lincoln by a more "vigorous" candidate in the coming election.

Lincoln, however, maintained his confidence in Grant and in the ultimate outcome; his two quick visits to see the commander (June 20-23 at City Point and July 31 at Fort Monroe) and Grant's trip to the capital in August strengthened the understanding between the two men working in harmonious relationship. His accord with Grant was forcefully expressed in his telegram to the general on August 17:

> I have seen your despatch expressing your unwillingness to break your hold where you are. Neither am I willing. Hold on with a bull-dog gripe, and chew & choke, as much as possible.[1]

As for the ultimate result, Lincoln's problem was to condition the public not to expect a quick victory and at the same time prevent undue pessimism. He said to Noah Brooks in June:

> I wish, when you write or speak to people, you would do all you can to correct the impression that the war in Virginia will end right off and victoriously. To me the most trying

---

[1] Lincoln, *Works*, VII, 499.

thing of all this war is that the people are too sanguine; they expect too much at once. . . . I shall be satisfied if we are over with the fighting in Virginia within a year.[2]

Again in August, in an interview with Benjamin B. French, the President expressed the same thought. French reported:

I had a long, and very pleasant talk with the president day before yesterday while his barber was shaving him. He said we must be patient, all would come out right—that he did not expect Sherman to take Atlanta in a day nor that Grant could walk right into Richmond, but that we should have them both in time. So I was encouraged. . . .[3]

The peace advocates within his own party gave the President much trouble. Greeley's badgering, the Niagara fiasco, and the futile Jaquess-Gilmore trip to Richmond failed to silence their agitation. Coupled with this was the growing feeling among prominent Republicans that the President could not be reelected in November.

By late August, even Lincoln began to show great concern. On the twenty-third of that month he had members of the Cabinet sign, unseen, the now famous memorandum:

This morning, as for some days past, it seems exceedingly probable that this Administration will not be re-elected. Then it will be my duty to so co-operate with the President elect, as to save the Union between the election and the inauguration; as he will have secured his election on such grounds that he can not possibly save it afterwards.[4]

In ten days all was changed. Sherman had entered Atlanta and Farragut had won decisively at Mobile. The President ordered one-hundred-gun salutes fired in celebration, and at Trinity Church, in Philadelphia, the special Thanksgiving service on September 11 was begun with the singing of "The President's Hymn."[5]

---

[2] Brooks, *Washington in Lincoln's Time*, p. 149.

[3] Benjamin B. French to H. F. French, Aug. 9, 1864, B. B. French Papers.

[4] Lincoln, *Works*, VII, 514, and n., 514-15; Dennett, ed., *Lincoln . . . in the Diaries . . . of John Hay*, pp. 237-38. Cf. also, Lincoln, *Works*, VII, 517, and n., 517-18.

[5] Philadelphia *Evening Bulletin*, Sept. 10, 1864.

The social season that spring had ended in June. Both
Mr. and Mrs. Lincoln attended the opera during its final
performances, and on Sunday, June 19, the President and
Secretary Hay went to the concert at Ford's Theatre.
The entire program, which Lincoln pronounced "highly
entertaining," was, indeed, a fitting climax for the season's social activities. Every selection of the popular
artists, Kretschmar, Habelmann, and Hermanns, was received with appreciative applause by the audience which
filled the house to capacity. The *Chronicle* gave unqualified praise, saying, "Words cannot express the fine singing done by these artists." Secretary Hay commented
humorously:

> I went last night to a Sacred Concert of profane music at
> Ford's. Young Kret[s]chmar and old Kret[s]chpar were
> running it. Hs. [Hermanns] and H. [Habelmann] both sang:
> and they kin if anybody kin. The Tycoon and I occupied a
> private box, and both of us carried on a hefty flirtation with
> the M. girls in the flies.[6]

Later in the month Lincoln and Tad and the two secretaries spent a pleasant evening at Grover's Theatre.
Kate Vance, the beautiful, versatile equestrienne was
playing in *Rockwood: or Dick Turpin the Highwayman.*
Kate took the part of Dick Turpin. Her steed "Don Juan"
(an "educated charger") made for much excitement during the performance. "The feats of this magnificent animal last night," said the *Star*, "were truly astonishing,
bounding over the mountain paths, leaping gaping
abysses, jumping hedges and fences, &c." The presidential party must have enjoyed the play, for they stayed
to the end.[7]

Well before this there were harbingers of the summer
to come. On May 7, a warm sunny day, a great crowd
gathered on the south lawn of the White House for the
first summer concert by the Marine Band. When Lincoln
appeared, there were calls for a speech. He declined, sug-

[6] Washington *Evening Star*, June 18, 19, 1864; Washington *Daily Morning
Chronicle*, June 20, 1864; Washington *Sunday Morning Chronicle*, June 26, 1864;
Thayer, *Life and Letters of John Hay*, I, 147.

[7] Washington *Evening Star*, June 30, 1864; Washington *National Intelligencer*,
June 29, 30, 1864.

gesting that three cheers be given for General Grant and his men then engaged in the great struggle in the Wilderness. The cheers were given with a will and the President sat back to enjoy the music.[8]

Two evenings later an excited multitude, filled with rumors of a great victory in Virginia, streamed onto the White House grounds, led by the band of the Twenty-Seventh Ohio Regiment. As the tall form of the President appeared, the crowd quieted down and waited expectantly. Lincoln thanked them all for coming, expressed his gratification for Grant's success thus far, but reminded his audience that there was a great deal more to be done. The crowd responded with a cheer and soon went on its way.[9]

An unusual kind of parade converged on the White House on the morning of May 30. The Sunday School Union of the city, made up of pupils in the churches, to the number of over five thousand, began to gather in Lafayette Square at nine o'clock. Forming in orderly lines, the boys and girls moved toward the White House with banners flying and bands playing "Hail, Columbia" and other "inspiring strains."

Lincoln appeared in a window and bowed, but made no speech. Each unit paid its respects as it passed the President and many cheered as they went by. Services were held in the churches after the parade. For the children it was exciting; for the President the interruption must have been a pleasure.[10]

June 9 was an important day for Lincoln. On that day he received official notice of his renomination, met delegates from the National Union League (to whom he made his remark, ". . . it was not best to swap horses when crossing streams"), was congratulated by Philadelphia

[8] Washington *Daily Morning Chronicle*, May 7, 1864; Washington *Sunday Morning Chronicle*, May 8, 1864; Lincoln, *Works*, VII, 332.

[9] Washington *Evening Star*, May 10, 1864; Sacramento *Daily Union*, June 2, 6, 1864; Lincoln, *Works*, VII, 334. Lincoln was, in fact, uneasy and anxious concerning the battle in Virginia. He was unable to sleep on the night of May 6. On the day of the serenade he was further distressed by bad news from General Banks' expedition on the Red River. Morse, ed., *Diary of Gideon Welles*, II, 25-26.

[10] Washington *Evening Star*, May 30, 31, 1864; Washington *Daily Morning Chronicle*, May 30, June 1, 1864.

delegates to the convention in Baltimore, and in the evening was serenaded by a huge crowd headed by the Ohio delegation and Captain A. Menter's celebrated American Cornet Band.[11]

After the band played "Hail to the Chief!" and the "Soldiers' Chorus," the President came out. Somewhat uneasy, he confessed that serenades bothered him, saying, ". . . the hardest of all speeches I have to answer is a serenade. I never know what to say on these occasions." Recovering quickly he humorously expressed his satisfaction with what had just taken place in Baltimore, and ended, as he often did, by calling for three cheers for General Grant and his men.

The cheers were given heartily together with extras for Lincoln and Johnson. The band contributed selections from *The Bohemian Girl* and *Maritana,* and ended with an "American Overture." The music "unsurpassed in execution and unequalled in sweetness" was a fitting conclusion to a busy and exciting day.[12]

Lincoln's four-day trip to City Point started on June 20. After a rough voyage from which he quickly recovered, he conferred with Grant and Butler, reviewed troops, inspected the lines, and saw the spires of Petersburg. As he went through the lines he heard once more the music that he enjoyed so much, for the bands were ready and played as he passed by. At nightfall as he sat with a group of officers in front of Grant's tent, Lincoln relaxed and told stories. Very likely, too, he heard music in the distance, inasmuch as it was the custom of the bands to play each evening.

The boys in blue nearby and the boys in gray over yonder swapped coffee and newspapers for newspapers and tobacco during daytime lulls; in the evening they both

[11] Washington *Evening Star,* June 10, 1864 ; Lincoln, *Works,* VII, 380-84.

[12] Washington *Daily Morning Chronicle,* June 10, 1864; N.Y. *Herald,* June 10, 1864; N.Y. *Times,* June 10, 1864; Lincoln, *Works,* VII, 384. For a week Lincoln had been greeting delegations to the Baltimore Convention. According to the New York *Herald,* he entertained the delegates with stories. "His anecdotal powers were in complete order," said the *Herald* on June 4, "and he furnished to his numerous visitors enough funny stories during the day to make the Convention merry for a week." By June 9, however, there was such a swarm of delegates at the White House that he had no time for "anecdotizing." N.Y. *Herald,* June 10, 1864.

listened to the music of the bands, for the appeal of music transcended the battle lines between them. Even "My country, 'tis of Thee" and "Mine eyes have seen the glory" were not objectionable to the Confederates.

Whether he heard the evening music or not, Mr. Lincoln returned to Washington refreshed, revived, and with a sunburn. He was in good spirits.[13]

When on the second of July the President's family moved to the Soldiers' Home for the summer, life was a lot less strenuous. There were few formal engagements and social affairs; Congress was about to adjourn and there would be less pressure on the President from that quarter.

Even the Fourth of July was relatively quiet in Washington. The President was busy signing bills at the Capitol. There were no big parades or celebrations. Bells were rung, outings were held, bands played here and there, and Negro Sunday School children held a picnic on the grounds between the White House and the War Department. In the evening there were fireworks. Out at the Soldiers' Home, Tad arranged and set off his own pyrotechnic display.[14]

The big musical feature of the summer months was the weekly concerts by the Marine Band at the Capitol and on the White House grounds. The President's interest in the music of the band was apparent in his attendance at the first concert (May 7) and at others during the summer.

Although the concerts were for pure pleasure they became the center of two minor, but to music lovers, serious controversies, one of which involved the President himself.

During the summer of 1861 Mr. and Mrs. Lincoln and the boys often sat out on the south portico during the

---

[13] Washington *National Intelligencer*, June 27, 1864; N.Y. *Herald*, June 25, 1864; Porter, *Campaigning with Grant*, pp. 216-24; Dennett, ed., *Lincoln . . . in the Diaries . . . of John Hay*, pp. 195-96; Morse, ed., *Diary of Gideon Welles*, II, 58. On Sunday evenings the men sang hymns: ". . . 'Old Hundredth' and "Pleyel's Hymn' would come rolling in over the works, from a thousand throats, to mingle harmoniously with thoughts of peace." Small, ed., *Road to Richmond*, p. 153.

[14] Washington *Daily Morning Chronicle*, July 6, 1864; Cincinnati *Gazette*, July 6, 1864; Sacramento *Daily Union*, July 27, 1864; Dennett, ed., *Lincoln . . . in the Diaries . . . of John Hay*, p. 207.

concerts, and Mrs. Lincoln had been responsible for the erection of the tent to protect the musicians from sun and sudden showers. From May until November hundreds of visitors had gathered there weekly to hear the music.

With the advent of warm weather in 1862 the public anticipated that the concerts would begin as in former years. Notices to that effect appeared in the press. But Mrs. Lincoln, still suffering grievously from the death of Willie only a few months earlier, was adamantly opposed to music on the White House grounds that summer.

This aroused public criticism and protest and it was then rumored that the concerts would begin after the family had moved to the summer White House. This suggestion was in turn rejected and after two weeks of uncertainty it was announced: "There positively will be no music in the President's grounds this summer."[15]

A disappointed citizen with more understanding than most critics made a compromise suggestion in a letter to the *Star.* Signing himself "Pure Delight," he wrote:

> Coinciding, as I do, in the eminent propriety of dispensing with all assemblages of a gay or hilarious character about the President's house, on account of the recent bereavement therein, permit me to suggest to the Commissioner of Public Grounds, the Secretary of the Navy, or whoever has authority in the matter, the consideration of having the Marine Band give their Wednesday or Saturday performance in some other locality in the western portion of the city. It is a great treat to small and large children, and is greatly enjoyed. I would suggest Lafayette Square, the Circle, or some of the angles; but please let us have the music occasionally in that quarter.[16]

Even this compromise suggestion brought no results. To the great disappointment of the concertgoers there was no music on the White House lawn that summer. A year later the question arose again—should there be concerts at the White House? That the public wanted them was certain. Secretary of the Navy Welles brought the matter to the attention of the President and advised that the concerts be resumed.

---

[15] Washington *Sunday Morning Chronicle,* May 25, June 8, 1862 ; Washington *Evening Star,* June 6, 1862 ; Washington *National Intelligencer,* June 7, 1862.
[16] Washington *Evening Star,* June 18, 1862.

Mr. Lincoln demurred, fearing Mrs. Lincoln would object. Welles then suggested that they be given in Lafayette Square. The President hesitated and finally passed the problem right back to Welles, telling him to do what he thought best.

Welles acted promptly. That same day (June 8) he sent a message to Colonel Harris of the Marine Corps:

> You will direct the Marine Band to renew their performances at the Capitol on Wednesdays, and at Lafayette Square (instead of the President's, as formerly) on Saturdays from 5:30 to 7:30 P.M.[17]

With evident satisfaction Welles noted in his *Diary* the following Saturday: "We had music from the Marine Band to-day in Lafayette Square. The people are greatly pleased."[18]

The concerts continued until October 5 that year, and as if by way of compensation the band of the Seventeenth Infantry also gave concerts in Lafayette Square on several Tuesday and Friday afternoons throughout the summer![19] By 1864 Mrs. Lincoln apparently no longer objected to having the concerts in the traditional place. The Marine Band was back.

The second controversy was of quite a different nature. It centered on the question—what type of music should be played at band concerts during wartime? Should programs be made up largely of operatic airs and dance tunes or should they contain mostly patriotic and martial music?

Throughout the war the question was debated. Newspapers discussed it and even the President's official family became involved. In the end the advocates of patriotic and martial music made a little progress. Programs which in 1862 were made up almost exclusively of operatic and dance numbers were, by 1864, somewhat better balanced.[20]

---

[17] Welles to Harris, June 8, 1863, Officers of the Marine Corps. No. 7, Letter Book.
[18] Morse, ed., *Diary of Gideon Welles*, I, 327.
[19] Washington *Evening Star*, July 9, 14, 17, 21, Sept. 29, 1863.
[20] Programs given in Central Park, New York, were essentially similar to those

Although the tendency of bandleaders to favor operatic selections was noted in 1861,[21] it was not until 1862 that criticism became sharp and persistent. While disappointment over the ban on concerts at the White House was still rife, Bandleader Scala's first program at the Capitol (June 7, 1862) drew adverse comment for it included no "national airs." Apart from the first number, "Lincoln's Union March" (Scala's own composition), the entire program was made up of operatic selections plus the popular "Mont Blanc Polka."[22]

The second program (June 11) was likewise preponderantly operatic, although it opened with "Hail, Columbia," and ended with "popular airs."[23]

When the third program, again heavily operatic, was performed, a reporter from the *Sunday Chronicle* was aroused, even though Scala had deferred to public opinion by ending the concert with a "Polka, with popular selections, including national airs." While granting that the program had included more popular airs than the first concert, and thus showed improvement, the irate reporter maintained that this was not enough, for, he said, ". . . although Snobs cry, 'brayvo!' after a long imported rigmarole, the People prefer the good old-fashioned airs, marches, and dancing tunes."[24]

Persisting in his crusade for more patriotic music, the

given in Washington, but Dodworth did include more popular and patriotic selections each time. Cf. N.Y. *Evening Post*, Aug. 7, 1861; N.Y. *Herald*, Sept. 21, 1861, July 6, 1863, July 3, 1864.

[21] N.Y. *Times*, May 17, 1861.

[22] Washington *Evening Star*, June 7, 1862. Said the N.Y. *Times* that same day: "It is remarked that the national airs were not prominently included in the list of pieces performed."

[23] Washington *Evening Star*, June 11, 1862. The entire program as announced:
    "Hail, Columbia"
    Quickstep from "Parisina"
    Mazurka
    Terzetto from "Belisario"
    Waltz "Georgette"
    Grand Medley
    Polka from "I Poliuto"
    Popular Airs

[24] Washington *Evening Star*, June 14, 1862; Washington *Sunday Morning Chronicle*, June 15, 1862. The program, as announced in the *Star*:
    Grand March from "The Prophet"
    Quickstep from "Parisina"
    Mazurka Galop
    Duet from "I Puritani"
    Waltz
    Finale of the second act from "I Poliuto"
    Polka, "with popular selections, including national airs."

critic reported in July that his broad hint that the Marine Band (supported by the United States Treasury) cease its "discordant attempts to perform operatic airs," and play more "good old-fashioned national tunes" had aroused wide-spread popular approval; he further admonished and advised Bandleader Scala:

> Crashing through the crotchets, dashing past the bars—tooting out the quavers higher than the stars—maccaroni airs, we heard, through the month of June—now, Scala, let us hear, every Yankee tune.[25]

That the crusade was not overly successful, however, is revealed in the critic's brief comment on September 21 that during the summer ". . . few have gone to hear the Marine Band toot their foreign overtures."[26]

In the summer of 1863 the controversy involved, of all people, Secretary Welles! Welles had already braved the wrath of Mrs. Lincoln by ordering the Marine Band to give its regular Saturday concerts in Lafayette Square just across from the White House. Early in July he instructed the band to play more martial and national music. When on July 11, the band complied, presidential secretary Nicolay was upset and forthwith went to Welles to protest.

Nicolay was fond of music. In his Springfield days he sang and played his flute on many occasions. In Washington, in spite of his busy schedule, he frequently managed to be present at dances, concerts, and the opera. He obviously liked "quality" music and he thought that band concerts should be a means of refining and cultivating the public taste for good music.

Upon presenting his views to Welles, Nicolay found the Secretary of the Navy adamant. Welles admitted that he was no musical expert but insisted that the concerts should serve a patriotic purpose in wartime. In his *Diary* Welles, commenting on the interview, wrote:

> . . . his [Nicolay's] refined music entertained the few effem-

---

25 Washington *Sunday Morning Chronicle*, July 6, 1862.

26 Washington *Sunday Morning Chronicle*, Sept. 21, 1862.

inate and the refined; it was insipid to most of our fighting men, inspired no hearty zeal or rugged purpose. In days of peace we could lull into sentimentality, but should shake it off in these days. Martial music and not operatic airs are best adapted to all.[27]

There the matter rested as far as Welles was concerned. The concerts in 1864 began auspiciously. A hot spell during the first week of May was followed by rain and cooler weather which made everything green and fresh-looking. The reporter for the *Chronicle* waxed philosophical. Writing after the Wednesday concert at the Capitol, he saw it as a symbol of assurance that the country would not be destroyed and of hope that freedom would prevail. It was, he said, ". . . as if God had given the lovely evening to prove that the morning of the day of victory would soon be here."[28]

Complaints about the musical selections still were heard but as the summer weeks passed the concerts seemed to meet with greater approval. Although the programs were still generously operatic, they invariably included a "Medley" of patriotic pieces and frequently additional "national airs" such as the "Star-Spangled Banner" and "Yankee Doodle."

The reporter for the *Chronicle*, highly critical two years before, now became a staunch supporter of both the programs and Bandleader Scala. Thus he characterized the program of June 4 as Scala's "choice morceaux." Scala's rule, he said, was to vary the programs to suit all tastes, to choose both old and new compositions. Furthermore, Scala was now training the band in several new pieces to be used later in the season. This was gratifying and the public was quite generally satisfied.[29]

---

[27] Morse, ed., *Diary of Gideon Welles*, I, 368; Nicolay, *Lincoln's Secretary*, pp. 25-26, 100, 331. In his letters to his fiancée Nicolay frequently mentioned going to dances, concerts, and the opera.

[28] Washington *Daily Morning Chronicle*, May 12, 1864.

[29] Washington *Daily Morning Chronicle*, June 4, 1864; Washington *Sunday Morning Chronicle*, June 5, 1864. The program of "choice morceaux":
Grand March from "The Prophet"
Medley Quickstep of American Airs
Overture from "La Dame Blanche"
Finale of the second act from "I Poliuto"
American Quadrille
Waltz "Il Bacio"

A week later he reiterated that the new pieces being prepared would be pleasing to the public and that the concerts were now becoming very popular. The program of July 30 was made up of "gems," and that of August 6 was ". . . all that the most fastidious lover of harmony could desire," "a rich selection." The last program in August was rated as excellent.[30]

Obviously, the programs were now more in accord with public taste, and equally obvious were the improved performances of the band. In 1862 the *Chronicle* had some harsh words to say about the musicians:

> Bandmaster Scala has evidently good musical taste, but he should discharge some of his old tooters, who are often half asleep, and enlist some smart performers on the cornet-a-piston and valve-trumpet, to give his music a snap.[31]

By 1864 the attitude of the *Chronicle* was quite changed. It was pleased with the musicians as well as with the music. Thus, the program of July 30 was "rendered with skill and beauty," "executed as only the Marine Band can perform," and a month later the music was reported as getting better each time.[32]

Citizens as well as the press took a proprietary interest in the concert proceedings. When, in July, the flagpole at the music stand was left bare for some weeks, this was cause for adverse comment. The *Chronicle* remarked that the omission from the program of musical "gems" on July 30 of both the "Star-Spangled Banner" and "Rally 'Round the Flag" was quite in keeping with the bare flagpole. An interested citizen in a letter to the same journal, after asking why there was a music stand and a handsome flagpole but no flag flying, stated that surely there was no more appropriate occasion for flying the flag

---

"Mrs. Sprague's Polka"
Schottische
"Brilliant Galop"
"When in the Silent Night"
"Star-Spangled Banner"
"Yankee Doodle"

[30] Washington *Sunday Morning Chronicle*, June 12, July 31, Aug. 7, 28, 1864.
[31] Washington *Sunday Morning Chronicle*, June 15, 1862.
[32] Washington *Sunday Morning Chronicle*, July 31, Aug. 28, 1864.

than when the Marine Band played national airs on the grounds of the Executive Mansion. It should be displayed, he added, and then the "Star-Spangled Banner" and "Rally 'Round the Flag" would have real meaning.[33]

Commissioner French was apparently stirred to action by the comments for, on the following Saturday, the flag was flying—no longer would the band play around a bare flagpole! In addition French had a flagpole erected at the Capitol for displaying the flag there when the band gave its Wednesday concerts.[34]

As was natural with humankind the vast crowds that attended the concerts included all sorts of people, some of whom were music lovers, and some of whom were not. But all had a good time.

One observer with a good sense of humor characterized the crowd as including solons and snobs, wives of proconsuls, sons of praetors, and daughters of aediles; then there were military beaux and dashing belles, ". . . some of them aristocratic pearls of great price, and some other pearls of beauty and of price, but of more Cleopatrean configuration"; likewise there were incorrigible young men who smoked, and ". . . *dear* little bare-legged children who clap their hands for a good brisk tune, but who turn away from the mournful selections from dull operas." To complete the picture there were naughty boys who called the red-uniformed musicians "lobsters."[35]

Occasionally there were amusing distractions at the concerts. On June 4, 1864, a group of Indians from Kansas, outfitted in full regalia, feathers, paint, and weapons, appeared. The Indians had been to the opera (*Der Freischütz*) the night before where they had had a jolly time. They had laughed loudly during tense and somber scenes, and once when an actor put a goblet to his lips as if to drink, one brave called out, "Firewater!" They quieted

[33] Washington *Sunday Morning Chronicle*, July 31, 1864; Washington *Daily Morning Chronicle*, July 30, 1864.

[34] Washington *Sunday Morning Chronicle*, Aug. 7, 28, 1864; Washington *Daily Morning Chronicle*, Aug. 27, 1864.

[35] Washington *Sunday Morning Chronicle*, June 22, 1862; Washington *Daily Morning Chronicle*, June 15, 1862.

down when a hundred opera glasses were aimed in their direction, but stayed through the entire performance.

Now, standing on the portico of the White House, excited by the presence of such a large crowd, the Chief of the warriors began to make a speech. He said, according to an Indian trader who interpreted for him, that he had come a long distance to see the Great Father with whom he had important business to transact; he was pleased to see such a large crowd of good-looking white people; he intended to educate his sons in the ways and habits of the whites.

After finishing his speech and receiving congratulations from the amused onlookers, the Chief stepped down and shook hands all around, at the same time accepting contributions from all who offered them. A bystander remarked that already he was acquiring some civilized habits.[36]

Whenever he could Lincoln went out to the portico to hear the weekly concerts. It is quite unlikely that he was at all concerned about the type of music that was played. He just wanted to listen. Whatever the program, he would have agreed with the remarks of a reporter that Scala's music ". . . makes the . . . beautiful grove reverberate with the delicious concord of sweet and soul-stirring melody every Saturday afternoon. . . ." The program on the day that this complimentary remark was made included:

> A Grand March
> Quickstep—"Queen of Roses"
> Overture from "Zanetta" ("Never Play with Fire")
> Bolero from "The Sicilian Vespers"
> Quadrille—Strauss
> Polka
> Medley of Patriotic Airs—The "Battle-Cry of
> Freedom," &c.[37]

Toward the end of the program the President appeared

---

[36] Philadelphia *Evening Bulletin*, June 6, 1864; Washington *Sunday Morning Chronicle*, June 5, 1864.

[37] Washington *Daily Morning Chronicle*, June 11, 1864; Washington *Sunday Morning Chronicle*, June 12, 1864.

on the portico. Thus on that day he was at least able to hear the final "Medley of Patriotic Airs" which included the "Battle-Cry of Freedom."

On July 30 Lincoln probably missed the concert entirely as he started that afternoon for Fort Monroe. Of the musical "gems" played that afternoon, which included a march from *Masaniello*, the "Nightingale Waltz," and a "sweetly plaintive cavatina" from *Belisario*, he would have particularly enjoyed one number, the "Soldiers' Chorus" from *Faust*.[38]

Nor did the President mind the great crowds that thronged the grounds—if only they would let him alone. So often when he appeared there were clapping, cheering, and calls for a speech. Thus on one such occasion he finally got up and went inside, saying to the artist Carpenter as he stretched out on the sofa, "I wish they would let me sit out there quietly, and enjoy the music."[39]

Although the band concerts continued into the fall, events in September turned people's attention to new developments. Sherman's entrance into Atlanta, with bands playing "Hail, Columbia," "Red, White and Blue," and other rousing pieces, thrilled the North.[40]

Sep Winner's "Our Nation Calls for Peace Again" met with little response. Rather, Henry Clay Work's stirring "Marching Through Georgia" reflected the spirit of the hour. Even while preparations were under way in Atlanta for the great march, bands played in the square and a series of seventeen concerts and entertainments took place to the delight of soldiers and some of the citizens.[41] But soon the guns would boom once again.

In Chicago bands treated the Democrats gathered in convention to national airs, with "Dixie" added for good

---

[38] Washington *Sunday Morning Chronicle*, July 31, 1864.

[39] Carpenter, *Six Months at the White House*, p. 143.

[40] Underwood, *Thirty-Third Massachusetts Infantry*, p. 233.

[41] Underwood, *Thirty-Third Massachusetts Infantry*, pp. 236-38; Adolf A. Hoehling, *Last Train from Atlanta* (N.Y., 1958), pp. 460, 514-15. It is of interest that in Atlanta operatic music was not especially featured, nor was martial music, although, of course, there was some of both. At the concert on Sept. 24, 1864, the program included "Then You'll Remember Me," "Ever of Thee," "Mary of Argyle," and "Come Where My Love Lies Dreaming"—the kinds of songs that Lincoln particularly enjoyed.

measure and "Hail to the Chief!" for McClellan.[42] Lincoln and Johnson supporters in Washington, after raising a forty by twenty-six-foot banner, paraded to the White House to serenade the President.[43] Toward the end of the month the Washington *Chronicle* published the words of a new song:

Union, Abe and Andy!

Look out! Look out! that meddling shout,
From Maine to Rio Grande,
Drives treason back, and clears the track,
For Union, Abe and Andy.[44]

The gentle music of the summer quickly faded into the background, and no wonder—a spectacular military march and an exciting election campaign were under way.

---

[42] N.Y. *Tribune*, Sept. 1, 1864; Washington *National Intelligencer*, Sept. 2, 1864.

[43] Washington *Evening Star*, Sept. 14, 1864; N.Y. *Tribune*, Sept. 14, 1864; Lincoln, *Works*, VIII, 4.

[44] Washington *Daily Morning Chronicle*, Sept. 24, 1864.

CHAPTER XIX

A STORY OF A SONG

ON SEPTEMBER 12, 1864, THE NEW YORK TRIBUNE CARRIED a notice of a contest for campaign songs for the coming presidential election. Prizes of ten dollars were to be given for each of five songs, four of which were to be humorous ". . . with sharp hits at McClellan, Jeff Davis and traitors."[1]

Events were to demonstrate that there was little need for a contest to stimulate songwriters, for during the two months preceding the election there was a great abundance of campaign music. Indeed, the air became almost saturated with it day and night.

With the coming of the Democratic Convention in Chicago, campaign music began in earnest. "Chicago was wild . . . with brass bands and cheering Democrats," reported Noah Brooks, and the delegates at the Wigwam were entertained by first-rate bands playing the "Star-Spangled Banner," "Yankee Doodle," and other popular airs, to which they generously added "Dixie" and, hopefully, for McClellan, "Hail to the Chief!"[2]

A correspondent (Republican) at the convention, tired out after a day of Democratic revelry, speechmaking, and brass bands, reported to his paper:

> My last recollections, as I sank to rest, were that Lincoln had deliberately set fire to the Capital, and was at that moment on the ground playing on the violin, while Seward was going through the figures of a fascinating reel. . . .[3]

---

[1] N.Y. *Tribune*, Sept. 12, 1864.

[2] Brooks. *Washington in Lincoln's Time*, p. 186; N.Y. *Tribune*, Sept. 1, 1864; Washington *National Intelligencer*, Sept. 2, 1864. In the streets there were soldiers by the scores singing, "Give us back our old Commander." This brought enthusiastic applause everywhere. Chicago *Times*, Aug. 30, 1864.

[3] Washington *Daily Morning Chronicle*, Sept. 5, 1864.

At a Democratic meeting in New York a soloist was joined by the audience in chorus as he sang ". . . a song, low dogged and pro-slavery. . . ." to the "John Brown" tune:

> Tell Ole Abe to let the nigger be;
> We don't want the darkies free—
> Glory, glory, Hallelujah!

while out at Harpers Ferry on a moonlit night a band led a whole brigade in the real "Old John Brown."[4]

President Lincoln was also much absorbed in politics. As Republicans and Democrats gathered in countless political meetings to express their sentiments in speech and song, Lincoln conferred with numerous and sundry important politicians. Twice during the month he was serenaded by admirers; while he was being serenaded by Treasury clerks on the evening of September 10, supporters in Philadelphia were treated to "The Union Now and Forever" and "We Are Coming, Father Abraham"; two evenings later a Union rally in New York closed with "Red, White and Blue" and the next afternoon Lincoln made a few remarks to a huge crowd of Lincoln-Johnson enthusiasts who had marched to the White House, led by a fine band.[5] General Sheridan's victory over General Early prompted Lincoln to send congratulations to Sheridan and that same evening an audience in Brooklyn heard the song, "Good News from Sheridan Again."[6]

Frémont's withdrawal from the campaign and Blair's resignation from the Cabinet simplified matters for the Republican leaders even as the rank and file in New York were being stimulated by "Rally for the Union," "Flag of the Free," "Friends of the Country" and "The Slave

---

[4] N.Y. *Tribune*, Sept. 2, 5, 1864.

[5] Washington *Sunday Morning Chronicle*, Sept. 11, 1864; Philadelphia *Evening Bulletin*, Sept. 12, 1864; N.Y. *Tribune*, Sept. 13, 1864; Washington *Evening Star*, Sept. 14, 1864; Lincoln, *Works*, VIII, 4.

[6] Lincoln, *Works*, VIII, 13; N.Y. *Tribune*, Sept. 21, 1864. One verse of the Sheridan song went as follows:
> Good news from Sheridan again,
> He's up and took the Early train,
> The Union boys are sure in battle;
> They've paid the rent for stealing cattle.

Ship." Up in Westchester, parading Democrats were
". . . tunefully threatening to hang Abe Lincoln to a sour
apple tree." Lincoln conferred with Govenor Curtin in
an effort to improve their mutual relations and Washington Republicans sang "Rally 'Round the Flag."[7]

By the end of the month issues were being clarified—
at least to some. In Philadelphia Republicans added to
their "Rally 'Round the Flag" repertoire that lively song
of symbolic significance, "Kingdom Coming." Democrats in the same city carried banners showing President
Lincoln on his knees before an "outlandish negro" with
guns and bayonets. A Democratic congressman warned in
a speech:

> If this Administration is permitted to go on, when the sol-
> diers come home they will steal, murder, rob, and rape your
> mothers, wives and daughters, and you will be powerless.
> There will be no law to protect you.
>
> This Administration must be put down and whipped out.[8]

At a huge McClellan meeting in New York a versatile
participant who was both singer and orator sang to
Father Abraham:

> We are coming, Father Abraham,
>   Two millions strong I'm sure,
> To drive you from the White House;
>   Abe, your acts we can't endure.
> You suppressed the habus [sic] corpus, Abe;
>   You imprisoned without cause,
> And trampled on our sacred rights
>   The constitution and laws.
>
> - - - - - - - - - - - - - -
>
> We are coming, Father Abraham,
>   In all our strength and pride,
> To hurl you from the place you hold,
>   As not worthy to preside.
> You have long play'd the usurper,
>   But you'll find it will not do;
> For we'll make McClellan President,
>   In spite of your whole crew.[9]

---

[7] N.Y. *Tribune*, Sept. 22, 23, 1864; Powell, ed., *Lincoln Day by Day*, p. 286;
Washington *Daily Morning Chronicle*, Sept. 29, 1864.

[8] Philadelphia *Evening Bulletin*, Oct. 1, Sept. 19, 30, 1864.

[9] N.Y. *Herald*, Sept. 18, 1864.

The speaker then went on to make ". . . some eloquent observations on the disastrous condition of the country." The campaign was under way.

October, 1864, might well have been called "Rally 'Round the Flag" month—at least as far as Republicans were concerned. From the first day of the month until the last, "Rally 'Round the Flag" was heard constantly at rallies and parades. In addition, "John Brown," "Yankee Doodle," and "Columbia, the Gem of the Ocean" were not neglected, and songs of more recent origin were sung enthusiastically—"Babylon Is Fallen," "It's All Up in Dixie," together with "There's a Good Time Coming."

Democrats went into action in support of McClellan. They laid claim to the "Star-Spangled Banner" by reason of the fact that vice-presidential candidate Pendleton's wife was the daughter of Francis Scott Key, and hence legatee of his estate. Their new music emphasized McClellan—"McClellan and the Union," "Hurrah for McClellan," "McClellan Mazurka," "McClellan and Pendleton Polka," and they were especially fond of "McClellan Is the Man"—

O General McClellan, he is the man;
He licked the Rebels at Antietam.[10]

A "novel feature" was introduced at a Republican rally in Philadelphia when a girls' glee club appeared and sang the "Star-Spangled Banner" and "Rally 'Round the Flag." Not to be outdone, the Democrats presented a chorus of thirty-four young ladies in red-white-and-blue costumes who sang "The Cry of Liberty" so effectively that it had to be repeated.[11]

Naturally President Lincoln continued to be intensely absorbed in the political drama. The October elections found him at the telegraph office constantly. While he eagerly waited there for the returns from the "October

---

[10] Chicago *Times*, Sept. 9, 1864; Detroit *Free Press*, Oct. 8, 24, 1864; Washington *National Intelligencer*, Sept. 22, 1864; Nevins and Halsey, eds., *Diary of George Templeton Strong*, III, 475.

[11] Philadelphia *Evening Bulletin*, Oct. 7, 1864; Philadelphia *Daily Age*, Oct. 20, 1864.

states" his supporters and opponents sang it out across the land.

Republicans gathered in Philadelphia began with "Babylon Is Fallen" and "John Brown"; when the news indicated victory they paraded with bands leading them in "John Brown" and "Rally 'Round the Flag." Glum Democrats on the sidelines hurled epithets—"nigger worshippers" and "abolitionists"—in their direction. In noisy Chicago "John Brown" filled the air, and in New York a glee club sang "Rally, Freemen, Rally" and "It's All Up in Dixie."[12]

Democrats held a huge meeting and parade in Pittsfield, Illinois, with speeches, serenades, and three bands playing, and in Detroit the rallying songs included "The Right Man in the Right Place."[13]

As they endeavored to capitalize on the "Give Us Back Our Old Commander" theme, the Democrats might have noticed certain portentous signs. There was, for instance, the stiffening resistance of the Union lines when a band played "Yankee Doodle" and "Kingdom Coming" during a fierce assault at Resaca, Georgia. There was the seeming widespread popularity of humorous pro-Lincoln songs and the soldiers' vote.

A Voice from the Army

(To be sung to the tune of "Just Before the Battle, Mother")

Just before election, brothers,
We are thinking most of you,
While on picket, or in trenches,
"With the enemy in view."

(Chorus)

Hark! it is the bugle sounding,
Grant still finds us work to do,
But, oh! we'll not *forget those traitors*,
When this bloody war is thro'.

---

[12] Philadelphia *Evening Bulletin,* Oct. 12, 1864; Sacramento *Daily Union,* Nov. 5, 1864; N.Y. *Tribune,* Oct. 14, 1864.

[13] Chicago *Times,* Oct. 12, 1864; Detroit *Free Press,* Oct. 12, 1864.

An Election Song
(To the tune of "Yankee Doodle")

Yankee Doodle, keep it up—
Yankee Doodle Dandy,
This is the way we soldiers vote,
For Honest Abe and Andy.[14]

President Lincoln and Republicans in general had reason to be happy over the election returns. Again large crowds paraded to the White House from downtown Washington to serenade the Chief Executive. The demonstration on October 21 was a mammoth affair. So long was the parade that it was estimated that it took forty minutes for the marchers with their torches, lanterns, banners, and transparencies to pass a given spot. Lights in the houses along the route, fireworks, and booming cannon added to the excitement. Slogans on the banners left no doubt as to the sentiments of their bearers:

> Bully for Phil. Sheridan. We have broken through Stonewall, passed through Longstreet, caught the Early bird, and given him his Phil.

> We have lost our legs and arms but not our patriotism. (Transparency carried along with five ambulances and forty-five soldiers, each of whom had lost a leg or an arm.)

> We are coming, Father Abraham, 2,000,000 voters more.

---

[14] N.Y. *Tribune*, Oct. 24, 1864; Washington *Daily Morning Chronicle*, Oct. 15, 1864; N.Y. *Herald*, Oct. 19, 1864. Philadelphia *Evening Bulletin* ran an editorial entitled "Our Old Commander" in which it said:
> There was a pretty little song, got up by some one of the many lyrists of the so-called Democratic party, the burden of which was
>
> "Give back our old commander."
>
> It was supposed to be sung by the united voice . . . of the Army of the Potomac, who, by a rather uncomplimentary fiction, were supposed to be unable to fight the rebels without "Little Mac" at their head.
> - - - - - - - - - - - - - -
> It is thus rendered plain [by their votes in the October elections] that the soldiers do not want "their old commander" to be President. If they are all afforded facilities for voting at the election in November, they will show that at least nine-tenths of them want to have for President their old commander-in-chief, Abraham Lincoln. The charm of McClellan's name is wholly gone, with the soldiers as well as with the civilians of the land. Philadelphia *Evening Bulletin*, Oct. 18, 1864.

We furnish Copper, but no Copperheads.
(Banner carried by a Michigan group.) [15]

The President's appearance at the serenades brought the usual cheering and music. His remarks, brief and pertinent, were answered by more prolonged cheering, after which the crowds moved on for further celebration elsewhere.[16]

The Democratic press took rather a dim view of these tributes to Lincoln, particularly the serenade of October 19, arranged by loyal Marylanders to celebrate their new constitution which ended slavery in that state.

The Detroit *Free Press* asserted that the constitution was a "bogus instrument" inasmuch as half the people of the state were disenfranchised and a majority was really against it. The *Daily Age* of Philadelphia also stated that the constitution was put across by fraud and that "honest Old Abe" knew it was.

Both papers were skeptical of the crowd, the *Free Press* maintaining that it was but a "hired band of serenaders," and the *Age* insisting that it was made up of office holders, contractors, and New England camp followers. The *Age* added that never had there been such a shameful spectacle on the White House grounds since they were converted into a "commons" for Negro picnics.[17]

The New York *Daily News* ran an editorial entitled "Mr. Lincoln and His Serenaders" which began: "Some of the toadies so plentiful in Washington have recently

---

[15] Washington *Evening Star*, Oct. 20, 22, 1864; Washington *Daily Morning Chronicle*, Oct. 20, 22, 1864; Cincinnati *Gazette*, Oct. 20, 1864. When the marchers passed McClellan banners there were groans and the bands stopped playing. A McClellan banner was destroyed by fire—accidentally or on purpose, with Democrats claiming that it was the latter. The banner was later replaced and there were cheers from bystanders when a speaker said, "We will give back your old commander." Washington *Evening Star*, Oct. 22, 25, 29, 1864.

[16] Lincoln, *Works*, VIII, 52-53, 57-58.

[17] Detroit *Free Press*, Oct. 25, 1864; Philadelphia *Daily Age*, Oct. 21, 1864. The reference to Negro picnics stemmed from the fact that twice during the summer Negro groups had used the White House grounds. On July 4 Negro Sunday School children held an assembly there and on August 4 a huge crowd held a celebration in observance of the ending of "Black Laws" in the District. These were the first instances of Negro groups thus having use of the White House grounds. Cf. Lincoln, *Works*, VII, 419; Washington *National Intelligencer*, Aug. 4, 6, 1864. "With negro picnics in the White House grounds, and negro cronies [Frederick Douglass] in the White House itself, displaying their teeth at the Presidential wit, white people will have to wait a long time for their turn." Philadelphia *Daily Age*, Sept. 27, 1864.

paid Mr. Lincoln the honor of a serenade. . . ." The editorial went on to say:

> Mr. Lincoln treated his fawning serenaders to what his peculiar phraseology would call "a little speech". . . . The tyrant reminded his base sycophants that he addressed them as sons of that Poland of America—the deeply wronged State of Maryland. Mr. Lincoln declared that he accepted their spaniel-like licking of his hand as a commendation of their "new constitution". . . .[18]

As the month came to a close there was no letup in political activity. The President discussed and conferred, and both parties kept on rallying.

On banners and transparencies the Democrats expressed their sentiments about President Lincoln:

In Chicago
"Lincoln demands blood, the people demand peace."

In Boston
"Abolish Old Abe and Restore the Union."

In Philadelphia
"Abe Lincoln, First in War and First in the
Pockets of his Countrymen."

In Detroit
"Blessed are the Peacemakers, God and McClellan
are the only hope of our severed Union."[19]

The Negro question, too, loomed large as an issue. In Chicago a Republican rally was labelled an "abolition meeting" given over to "abolition harangues" with the Hutchinsons singing "what was called a song of freedom which consisted of two line verses with hallelujah refrain."[20] At a Democratic meeting in Philadelphia the proceedings were interrupted by a youngster calling out, "Three cheers for the White Men of the Twelfth Ward !" A transparency in the parade at Pittsfield, Illinois, bore the slogan: "McClellan for president, and white men for husbands," while a banner carried aloft at Philadelphia

---

[18] N.Y. *Daily News*, Oct. 24, 1864.
[19] Chicago *Times*, Nov. 7, 1864 ; Boston *Courier*, Nov. 8, 1864 ; Philadelphia *Daily Age*, Oct. 31, 1864 ; Detroit *Free Press*, Nov. 5, 1864.
[20] Chicago *Times*, Oct. 28, 1864.

proclaimed: "No Tyranny; No Niggers; White Men are as Good as Niggers when they Behave Themselves."[21]

The Democratic musical arsenal was augmented by new words to be sung to that most valuable musical asset, thus far monopolized by Republicans—"Rally 'Round the Flag." The new words, in six verses and chorus, gave the new theme:

> Yes, we'll rally to the ballot-box, rally once again,
> Shouting the battle cry of freedom;
> Rally from the hillside, rally from the plain,
> Shouting the battle cry of freedom.

Chorus:
> The Union forever, hurrah, boys, hurrah,
> Here's an end to oppression, an end to the war,
> And we'll rally round the ballot-box, rally once again,
> Shouting the battle cry of freedom.

> We are marching to the polls, boys, for 'Little
>   Mack' to vote,
> Shouting the battle cry of freedom,
> To restore our severed Union; we will our lives devote:
> Shouting the battle cry of freedom.[22]

But slogans did not win votes and an occasional good song was not enough, as the election results showed on the night of November 8. While the opposition had music in quantity, it did not have the songs that could compare with those of the Lincolnites—in emotional punch, patriotic fervor, or crusading conviction. Nor did the occasional use of "Dixie" and other Southerners' songs help the Democratic cause.[23]

---

[21] Philadelphia *Daily Age*, Oct. 20, 31, 1864; Chicago *Times*, Oct. 12, 1864.

[22] Detroit *Free Press*, Oct. 31, 1864.

[23] To cite but three examples, the opposition had nothing that could compare with "We Are Coming, Father Abraham," "The Battle-Cry of Freedom," and the "John Brown Song." In the far Northwest a newspaper raised the question, "Does the Democratic party ever sing patriotic songs?" At a Union meeting one would hear hundreds of voices swelling the chorus of "Rally 'Round the Flag." Further, Union soldiers went into battle "fired with patriotic impulses." But the Copperheads march to the same tunes as do the rebels, "Dixie" and the "Bonnie Blue Flag." *Morning Oregonian* (Portland), Nov. 5, 1864.

The Old Guard felt otherwise. It said: "Song rarely flourishes well in an atmosphere of lies and fraud. The genuine enthusiasm which is essential to good song writing, cannot be found among a party who know themselves to be in the wrong; hence, all the Republican songs of this campaign are dull and pointless, com-

On that election evening Lincoln splashed through the mud and rain on his way to the telegraph office to get the returns. In New York spokesmen at Tammany Hall were giving a final warning to a noisy audience against the "anti-Catholic bigotry" and "nigger-loving" of the Republicans. As the returns came in confident Republicans in the same city sang "Old Hundred" and "John Brown." Outside the War Office where Lincoln waited, jubilant crowds, unmindful of the weather, paraded and sang.

> Yes, we'll rally 'round the flag, boys;
> Rally once again—
> Shouting the Battle-Cry of Freedom![24]

Earlier that same day Lincoln discussed politics with Secretary Hay. In the course of the conversation he remarked:

> It is a little singular that I, who am not a vindictive man, should have always been before the people for election in canvasses marked for their bitterness: always but once; when I came to Congress it was a quiet time. But always besides that the contests in which I have been prominent have been marked with great rancor.[25]

Certainly Lincoln's remark applied to the campaign just ended, for there was much more to it than has been thus far described. Lincoln was subject to bitter, unfair, and unscrupulous attacks that were filled with rancor. His person and his manner were held up in ridicule and contempt; his motives were sinister, his integrity nonexis-

---

pared with the pathos and humor of the Democratic songs." It then gave us an example of Democratic music:

> "The Democratic Creed"
> (Air: "A man's a man for a' that.")
> Regardless of the hireling's cry,
> Of Copperhead and all that,
> We still despotic power defy,
> And dare to speak, for all that.
> For all that, and all that,
> The traitor band, and all that,
> We still believe the South have rights
> As well as North, for all that.

The Old Guard, II, 261 (Nov., 1864).

[24] *The Bangkok Recorder*, Jan. 16, 1865 (from a report of a correspondent of the London *Daily News* in New York) ; Washington *Evening Star*, Nov. 9, 1864.

[25] Dennett, ed., *Lincoln . . . in the Diaries . . . of John Hay*, p. 233.

tent and his acts heartless or ruthless, or both. He was worse than Nero or any other "base tyrant" that had ever lived.

Journalists and politicians who urged that the campaign be conducted on the decent ground of policy and principle were ignored by partisans of vehement ill-will who, themselves, lacked both decency and principle.[26]

The lowest of all the low attacks on the President had its origin nearly two years earlier, after Lincoln had visited the Army of the Potomac following the battle of Antietam. It centered on a song—"a little sad song"— and it became known as the "Antietam Incident."[27]

The sights and scenes at Antietam, the destruction, the loss of life and the suffering moved the President deeply. Worried and distressed, Lincoln was not revived in spirit as he usually was when he visited the army. During a rough ride in an ambulance from one camp to another, nowhere near the battlefield, Lincoln asked Ward Lamon to sing "the little sad song" that Lincoln loved. Lamon complied, but the singing of "Twenty Years Ago" made the President even more melancholy.

To offset this melancholy and to cheer the weary President, Lamon then, as he had often done before, sang snatches of two or three little comic songs of which "Piccayune Butler" was one. That was all there was to it. The Antietam Incident was forgotten—but not for long.

The trip to Antietam (October 1-4, 1862) was covered extensively by the press. In some cases opposition newspapers gave more details than friendly journals, but there was no mention of the President having requested a song

---

[26] The Washington *National Intelligencer*, Sept. 3, 1864, endorsed the sentiment expressed by the New York *Commercial Advertiser*: "Why cannot this campaign be fought out upon principle, and why should the personal character of candidates be assailed, and the country made to ring with charges wantonly made and entirely unsusceptible of proof?"

Vice-Presidential candidate Pendleton, in a speech in Cincinnati, urged: "Let us indulge in no personal animosities or personal abuse. . . . Let us appeal to reason and judgment, and experience—let us appeal to the minds and hearts and consciences of our fellow-citizens." Philadelphia *Daily Age*, Sept. 15, 1864.

In contrast, four days later a speaker in Philadelphia exclaimed: "Last New Year the emancipation was celebrated at Washington, by the contrabands calling upon Lincoln, and those who witnessed the scene say Lincoln stood slobbering over the negro like an imbecile, as he is." Philadelphia *Daily Age*, Sept. 19, 1864.

[27] Chapter XI, *supra*.

at any time. Nor was there any reference to singing for more than two months.[28]

Before the year ended, however, distorted stories of the Antietam Incident had begun to circulate. On Sunday, December 21, there appeared the following:

A Story of a Song

President Lincoln loves a good story. In fact, President Lincoln tells good stories—and tells a great many of them too. So long as they *are* good he is not so very particular as to when and where he tells such stories or has them told. He introduces them everywhere and on every occasion—sometimes to illustrate a principle and sometimes to provoke a laugh. The same thing may be said of President Lincoln's relish for a good comic song. Perhaps he don't sing himself in a manner calculated to render Brignoli envious, or fill Susini with doubts (to use the green-room diction) as to his next year's "little sal;" but he enjoys a keen appetite for a jolly song well delivered by another, and he has a gratefully abiding remembrance of the man who can thus impart entertainment.

While riding, for instance, over the field after the sanguinary battle of Antietam, the President said nothing while General McClellan was pointing out the place our brave volunteers fell by scores and gallantly laid down their lives in defence of the Union. He remained profoundly silent while McClellan, with trembling lip, eulogised the valor of a division which had left eight hundred dead in one small spot, their rudely-made graves marking their last resting place. Perhaps the President was thinking of the moaning widows and fatherless children, crying for bread, those eight hundred had left behind them! But at that moment his eye caught a glimpse of a familiar uniform.

"Isn't that Major So-and-so?" said he.

"It is," was the response.

"Send for him! Send for him at once!" he quickly answered.

The major was summoned, and came.

"General," said the President, "the major sings one of the best songs you ever heard. I tell you it's a jolly good one! Come, Major, let us have it right on the spot!"

And the song was given—all who *could* leave, however, without discourtesy to the chief magistrate of the United States, withdrawing from the sod that covered the bones, on that battle-field, of their once gallant comrades.

Could we furnish a better proof of President Lincoln's appreciation of a good song or a good singer? As to his good taste, we are not discussing it at this moment. Neither are

---

[28] Cf. N.Y. *World*, Chicago *Times*, *The Crisis* (Columbus), Boston *Courier*, and Harrisburg *Weekly Patriot and Union* for these months.

we prepared to speak of the time and the place as *apropos* to
the "jolly good song" in question. Those are all matters we
leave to the reader and his or her judgment. We simply desire to show what a passion the President has for a comic
story and a mirthful song; and (as the instance we have
given comes to us, as genuine, from high authority,) we think
we have pretty clearly established our position.

The next day, December 22, a prominent New York
Republican, disturbed about the story, penned a letter
to Assistant Secretary of the Navy Gustavus V. Fox,
which read:

My dear Sir
    The enclosed I cut from the Sunday Times of yesterday
such stories are doing *us* much harm   if not true please say
so   I would send it to the President myself but my motive
might be mistaken
- -
                        Yours very truly
                        GEO W BLUNT[29]

Fox replied on December 30: "The slip of paper from
the Sunday Times, about Pres Lincoln calling for a song,
whilst riding over the field with Gen'l McClellan is too
absurd to contradict. No one here ever heard of it."[30]
The story had not yet reached Washington, but it would
eventually.

On the day after Blunt wrote to the Assistant Secretary
of the Navy the New York correspondent of the London
Standard composed his dispatch. In it was another version of the Antietam Incident (see Chapter XI):

By the bye, it is a fact that President Lincoln, when he visited
the battle-field of Antietam, before the corpses had been
buried, called upon an officer, who had been reported to him
as a good song singer, to "step out and sing me a song," and
then in an open plain, in hearing of the dying, and in sight of
the sightless dead, the officer sung [*sic*] for the President of
the United States "Jim along, Josey."

---

[29] George W. Blunt to Gustavus V. Fox, Dec. 22, 1862, Gustavus Vasa Fox Papers,
New-York Historical Society. A clipping containing "A Story of a Song" was
pasted on the reverse side of the letter. It was evidently clipped from *The Sunday
Times and Noah's Weekly Messenger*, Dec. 21, 1862.

[30] Gustavus V. Fox to George W. Blunt, Dec. 30, 1862, Fox Papers, Letter Press
Copy.

... there is not a man, woman, or child in this country that is not of the decided opinion that if the meanest soldier in the army could be placed in the position of Lincoln and in the President's chair, that the country would be benefited, and possibly saved from the awful anarchy to which we are drifting as rapid as electricity. Still call out the singing officer, and let him sing, "Jim along, Josey," among the corpses and the dying. What a splendid, but much abused, ruler old Nero was. His tyranny never slaughtered as many bodies as Lincoln's incompetency, and though he fiddled while Rome was burning, he never called out one of his officers to sing "Jim along, Josey."

Printed in the *Standard* on January 6, 1863, this version returned to the United States to be picked up and spread by anti-administration journals.[31]

As the sniping continued, Lincoln's propensity for jokes and story-telling was linked with the Antietam Incident and was distorted in the same way. Thus *The Old Guard*, a magazine "devoted to the principles of 1776 and 1787" (and consequently violently opposed to the Lincoln administration) opened its attack by saying: "We have great confidence in Mr. Lincoln as a good storyteller, an excellent joker, and a first class buffoon; but no confidence in him whatever, as a military strategist."[32]

The Metropolitan Record, a Catholic family paper, soon joined in. It was one of the first journals to repeat the London *Standard* story. In March it referred to Lincoln as "Our jocular and anecdotal Chief Magistrate. . . ." On May 2 it printed the following:

We know—the world knows—how the Chief Magistrate contrives to keep up his spirits in the midst of difficulties . . . and we recollect a story that was told of his having called upon one of the officers during a visit to the bloody field of Antietam to sing for him "Jim along Josey," or some other spirit-stirring negro melody. We are not certain whether the officer

---

31 London *Evening Standard*, Jan. 6, 1863. Before the end of the month the story appeared with the added comment that it was "Piccayune Butler" rather than "Jim Along, Josey" that was sung. Mrs. Charles P. Daly, wife of an eminent New York judge, believed the story, stating in her diary on January 23, in her gossipy fashion, "The incident was told me by someone in Lincoln's company on the occasion." Harold Earl Hammond, ed., *Diary of a Union Lady 1861-1865* (N.Y., 1962), p. 218.
32 *The Old Guard*, II [1] (Feb., 1863), 47. The magazine was published in New York by C. Chauncey Burr & Co., and later by Van Evrie, Horton & Co.

did this, but if he did not, it was not the fault of our lively and loquacious Executive.

In olden times it was customary for the monarch to wile away his tedious hours by the droll antics and the witticisms of a court fool. The ever-flowing humor and inexhaustible fund of jokes possessed by the sixteenth magistrate of the United States renders what was an indispensible adjunct to the court of olden times entirely unnecessary at the White House, for the principal occupant of the Presidential mansion is a sort of dual character, and so saves the Nation the expense of supporting a jester.[33]

An editorial in the *Record* in June, entitled "Which is the Most Humiliating—Peace or War?" blamed the administration for the country's plight and said of the President: "Look and estimate if you can the character of the man who can tell his ribald jests while the country is bleeding at every pore."[34]

During the summer and fall of 1863 *The Old Guard* continued the attack. In August it published a poem, "Old Abe's Foot Down," in which these lines appeared:

> But crack your low jokes, Massa Lincoln—
> Only white men to ruin are hurled—
> So put your foot down, Massa Lincoln,
> And trample them out of the world.

This was followed by the observation: "Louis XIV was a great libertine; but, notwithstanding the notorious obscenity of Lincoln's jokes, we do not believe he is that. . . ." The journal then suggested: ". . . Lincoln

[33] *The Metropolitan Record* (N.Y.), Mar. 28, May 2, 1863, republished in *The Washington Despotism Dissected* (N.Y., 1864), pp. 17, 73. An oblique reference to the Antietam Incident can be seen in a song then current in Connecticut. "White Soldier's Song," both anti-Negro and anti-Lincoln, contained this verse: (Tune "John Brown")

> Tell Abe Lincoln on Antietam's bloody dell,
> Tell Abe Lincoln where a thousand heroes fell,
> Tell Abe Lincoln and his gang to go to h . . . ,
> And we'll go marching *home*.

The N.Y. *Tribune*, Mar. 18, 1863, labelled the song "the genuine Copperhead hiss!" The song appears in J. F. Feeks, *Democratic Presidential Campaign Songster No. 1. McClellan and Pendleton.* (N.Y., [1864]), pp. 26-27, with some variations in wording. After the verse here quoted there is, in the *Songster*, a notation: "The . . . verse is based upon the incident of Lincoln's calling for a 'comic song' while passing over the field of Antietam with McClellan after the battle, and being shown where so many brave men had fallen." It is also included in *Copperhead Minstrel: A Choice Collection of Democratic Poems and Songs. . . .* (N.Y., 1864), pp. 55-56.

[34] *The Metropolitan Record* (N.Y.), June 13, 1863, in *The Washington Despotism Dissected*, pp. 113-14.

should have a medal representing himself as standing between a dungeon and a grave yard, holding a white man's skull on the point of a sword with a negro baby resting in his bosom."

For all of this, *The Old Guard* advocated: "Hit him in the head with such hard, honest words as shall stop his vulgar joking and laughing, and bring him to a realizing sense of the agonies of a perishing nation."[35]

Lincoln's visit to Gettysburg in November, 1863, afforded an opportunity for further exploitation of the Antietam Incident. The *Daily Age* of Philadelphia, referring to the ceremony as a "wake," asked, "Will the President unite, on this occasion, in a solemn litany for fatherless children and widows, and all who are desolate and oppressed, or will he in jocund vein ask Marshal Lamon for a song, as he did at Antietam?"

After giving its version of the events of the evening of November 18—they were of "a lively character" and Mr. Lincoln made a joke or two—the *Age* concluded:

> It is thus that the President of the United States and his confidential advisers disport themselves in the presence of the historic field where two hundred thousand of their countrymen, four months ago, met in deadly conflict. It is thus that they render homage to the heroic dead. With the groans of the wounded still resounding in the air—the corpses of the slain still unburied—the bereaved still clad in the emblems of mourning, and their tears still flowing—these men meet to laugh and joke and electioneer.[36]

In view of its consistent antipathy, it is not surprising that the *Illinois State Register* used the occasion to editorialize:

Old Abe at Gettysburg

Nothing could have been more inappropriate than to have invited that prince of jokers, Old Abe, to be present at the consecration of the Gettysburg Cemetery. But having been invited, it was hoped . . . that he would at least refrain from his clownish jokes while standing over the new made graves

[35] *The Old Guard*, I (Aug., 1863), 210; (Sept., 1863), 238; (Oct., Nov., Dec., 1863), 270.

[36] Philadelphia *Daily Age*, Nov. 18, 20, 1863. The paper did give grudging approval of Lincoln's speech in its issue of Nov. 21, 1863.

of thousands who had been slain in the recent battle. . . .

. . . we have seen it stated that while riding on the battle
field of Antietam, in the presence of thousands of fresh
made graves, and where the ground had not yet drank [*sic*]
up the blood of the slain, Abraham Lincoln, the president of
the United States, called on one of the party to sing a negro
song, to enliven the scene! . . . "Nero fiddled while Rome
was burning," and Abraham Lincoln perpetrates his miserable jokes while standing upon the graves of his countrymen, . . .[37]

As it became clear during the early months of 1864
that Lincoln would run for reelection, the Chicago *Times*
did its best to discredit him. He was, said the *Times*, not
only a "smutty joker" and a clown; what was worse, he
was a humbug and a hypocrite.

Old Abe is going in for re-election on a most remarkable
and funny record. He wants to be re-elected joker. He points
to his expiring term with pride and pleasure, as a great joke.
The record is a sorry joke to the country. . . . Is it possible
that the great American nation are to be wheedled into the
support of a candidate . . . whose chief claim to support . . .
is that he is a clown?[38]

In April the *Times* printed a lengthy letter in which
Washington and Lincoln were contrasted: Washington
had formed the Union and Lincoln had broken it; Washington never went back on a promise but Lincoln seldom
kept one; Washington always respected the civil power;
Lincoln trampled civil authority under the "iron heel of
despotism"; Washington was known for his dignity and
good conduct, Lincoln was distinguished for his smutty
jokes. "Washington," said the letter, "prayed for assistance from On High when going into battle, and devoutly thanked God for victories gained; Lincoln, it is
said, asked a companion to sing 'Jump Jim Crow' upon
the bloody field of Antietam."[39]

With the renomination of Lincoln an accomplished fact

---

[37] *Illinois State Register* (Springfield), Nov. 24, 1863.

[38] Chicago *Times*, Feb. 25, Mar. 2, 1864.

[39] Chicago *Times*, Apr. 5, 1864. That this account was sent in by a correspondent
reveals that the Antietam Incident (in the "Jump Jim Crow" version) was becoming more than just newspaper talk.

the opposition press naturally bestirred itself even more vigorously. From June until November the attack went on steadily, with "Lincoln the joker" and "Piccayune Butler" frequently the target. It sometimes seemed as if Lincoln could scarcely make a move or utter a word without their being dragged into the picture.

The nominating convention was a farce, said the *Essex Statesman,* and as for the President, "There is no personal attractive quality in Mr. Lincoln . . . he is ugly in person and has an ungainly way of telling a smutty story at an exceedingly inappropriate moment."[40]

Lincoln's remark about not swapping horses when crossing streams brought the comment from a Boston paper: "Thus, at the seat of government, we have jests and their concomitants, almost in the hearing of the groans of thousands upon thousands of dying soldiers. . . ."[41]

The Chicago *Times,* in a long editorial entitled "Lincoln's Love for the Soldiers" called the President cruel, heartless and thoughtless, for when convention delegates called at the White House,

> He entertained them with amusing anecdotes, and it is estimated that within sight of the windows where the company was congregated, three soldiers died during each one of Mr. Lincoln's laughable recitals. In happy harmony with this was the request for "Picayune Butler," when he was surveying the wounded and corpses on the field of Antietam.[42]

Lincoln's attempt to apply his Amnesty Plan in Florida was a joke, said the *Freeman's Journal,* almost as good a joke as his riding among the fresh graves and the burial parties at Antietam, slapping Marshal Lamon on the knee, and asking him to sing "Jump Jim Crow"; his trip to the Sanitary Fair in Philadelphia provoked the

---

[40] *Essex Statesman* (Salem, Mass.), June 11, 1864.

[41] Boston *Courier,* June 10, 1864.

[42] Chicago *Times,* Sept. 21, 1864. The London *Herald* correspondent in New York reported that the Baltimore Convention had done its work—it had nominated an ex-rail splitter and an ex-tailor, a joker and a Merry-Andrew. The latter won against his competitors in Tennessee because he could tell the nastiest stories. London *Herald,* June 24, 1864. The correspondent was the same person who had sent the "Antietam Incident" to the *Evening Standard,* Jan. 6, 1863.

Chicago *Times* to observe: "While the nation is steeped to its very lips in blood, its Chief Magistrate is retailing old jokes in the Presidential Mansion, or else is on electioneering tours among the people"; his wish to have ex-governor Tod of Ohio in the Cabinet prompted the comment that if the greatest joker in the Northwest was qualified to be President, then the best story-teller in Ohio was qualified to head the Treasury.[43]

General Early's raid led the Philadelphia *Age* to charge that "the Great Imposter and Imbecile" engaged in "puerile twaddle about abolition" when the rebels were at the very gates. "But," it added, "what else could be expected from one who called for a vulgar negro song to drown out the shrieks and groans of his dying countrymen at Antietam?"[44]

On the other hand, when Lincoln went out to Fort Stevens to see what was taking place he again showed his true character, said the Chicago *Times*, when he remarked after seeing a bullet bounce from a wall and strike a soldier's leg, "That was a good carom!"[45] The *Times* also thought the call for 500,000 men a capital joke. "It is almost as good a 'joke' as his calling on Marshal Lamon to sing 'Picayune Butler' amid the sepulchres of Gettysburg."[46]

Lincoln's solicitude for the sick and wounded also brought ridicule. The *Age*, after recounting Napoleon's custom of having an officer distribute money to the wounded men after a battle, remarked, "Imagine Mr. Lincoln sending Mr. Seward round the military hospitals . . . after having ordered a negro song to be sung as he rode over the field where they lay!"[47]

The nomination of McClellan gave the opposition a candidate to support. Now the contrast could be made

---

[43] *New-York Freeman's Journal and Catholic Register*, June 11, 1864; Chicago *Times*, June 18, 20, 1864; Boston *Courier*, July 8, 1864. To a caller who had waited two hours to see him, Lincoln is reported to have said: "Dave Tod, sir, tells the best story of any man in Ohio!" Chicago *Times*, July 13, 1864.

[44] Philadelphia *Daily Age*, July 11, 1864.

[45] Chicago *Times*, July 23, 1864. When the *Times* repeated the story on Sept. 7, it had a cannonball tear a soldier's limb off.

[46] Chicago *Times*, Aug. 4, 1864.

[47] Philadelphia *Daily Age*, Sept. 13, 1864.

between the two candidates, and it was. Twice McClellan had saved the capital only to be dismissed after the crisis had passed. During the battle ". . . Old Abe sat trembling and frightened, and ready for flight from the Capital, but as the news of the result . . . came from the victor, McCLELLAN, he at once revived. . . ." He was so excited and relieved that ". . . amid heaps of the dead and dying on the battlefield, he called for negro songs, shocking and disgusting all within his hearing."[48]

McClellan, large-souled and fearless, noble and humanitarian, was noted for his concern for his men, for their health, welfare, and safety, whereas Lincoln, ". . . riding over the blood-stained field of Antietam, called for a negro song, to drown the sighs of the living and the groans of the dying."

> Remember that field of Antietam [said a speaker at a Democratic rally]. Remember that when the wreck of war was lying around, and the bodies of the heroes of the Union were lying stiff and stark on the ground, that there was one man, who should be the father of his people, who, at that moment, could not be satisfied with anything less than a comic song. [Hisses.] You do well to hiss it—for from the heart of every Christian man, all over the earth, there came a cry of disgust at that disgraceful petition. [Enthusiasm.] There was another man there, who was used to war, and knew its horrors, who, when he heard that ribald jest, turned his horse's bridle and rode away. His name was George B. McClellan. [Deafening cheers.]

"Which will you choose," asked the *Age,* "the Hero who won Antietam or the Jester who called for a vulgar negro song . . . ?" How could Christian men vote for the "smutty joker" who was guilty of such conduct on the field of battle?[49]

---

[48] Detroit *Free Press,* Sept. 23, 1864.

[49] Philadelphia *Daily Age,* Sept. 21, 28, Oct. 4, 22, 31, Nov. 4, 1864. An embellishment of the Antietam Incident, to the obvious detriment of the President, appeared in the *Journal of Commerce* in October. After describing the scene at which Lincoln called for "Paradise Butler" [*sic*], the party moved to a hospital area near South Mountain. It came upon four men carrying a dead soldier, followed by two Sisters of Charity. McClellan ordered a halt while the little procession passed. He then went up to the stretcher-bearers, ". . . uncovered the face of his dead comrade, asked his name and where he fell, and then lifting his hat, stood with uncovered head while they passed on to the burial place. Then the President and the General . . . having done fitting honor to the soldier of the people, went on their way." The story was entitled "Two Characters Drawn—Look on This Picture."

Supplementing the several versions of the Antietam Incident borrowed freely from one another by opposition journals and orators were poems and campaign songs of equal caliber. One of the most gruesome poems was entitled "Lincoln at Antietam":

> Dead upon dead were huddled thick,
> The very air with death was sick;
> The wounded waited, with ebbing life,
> Their turn for the surgeon's tired knife.
>> But carelessly rode Old Abe along,
>> And called in that scene for a negro song.
>
> Youth and manhood lay weltering there,
> With the sweat of agony matting the hair;
> And the bravest in battle heard with awe
> The crushing sound of the busy saw.
>> But carelessly rode Old Abe along,
>> And called in such scene for a negro song.
>
> Mothers, daughters, sisters, wives,
> Knit by love to those precious lives,
> How must your hearts for news athirst
> Have throbbed and sunk and bled, or burst,
>> While carelessly rode Old Abe along,
>> And called 'mid those graves for a negro song.[50]

In contrast, the campaign song, "The Cry of Liberty," was almost genteel:

> Too long a worthless despot sits,
>> Dispensing jokes for laws;
> And shoddy lords and shoddy thieves,
>> Disgrace our Country's cause:
> And deeds of savage cruelty,
>> Dishonor our fair name:
> While Abolition fiends have filled
>> Our land with guilt and shame.
>
> Our courts of justice have been closed,
>> By the sound of Seward's bells;
> Our bravest and our best were dragged
>> Like thieves to felon cells;
> While provost marshals grimly sit,
>> And mock our country's wrongs;

Philadelphia *Daily Age*, Oct. 12, 1864; *Essex Statesman* (Salem, Mass.), Oct. 12, 1864.
[50] Detroit *Free Press*, Oct. 24, 1864; *The Old Guard*, II, (Nov., 1864), 262.

And *Honest* Abraham laughs and jokes,
And sings his ribald songs.[51]

Democratic campaign songsters contained many of the anti-Lincoln songs sung in parades and at rallies. Words were adapted to Northern tunes and parodies on Northern verse were popular. Thus the "Battle-Cry of Freedom!" became "Shouting Our Battle-Cry—'McClellan'!" and Father Abraham was assured in various versions of "We Are Coming, Father Abraham" that his days in the White House were numbered.

Songsters contributed, also, to the caliber of the campaign for in some of them were printed low and vicious verses on Lincoln as a joker and on the Antietam Incident. The *Copperhead Minstrel* included three such songs. In the very first song in the book were the lines:

What if blood in rivers run,
Souls with horror freeze all—
Uncle Abe must crack his jokes,
Pop goes the weasel.[52]

The *Democratic Presidential Campaign Songster* contained "The Cry Is Mac, My Darling," "White Soldier's Song," and "Shouting Our Battle-Cry—'McClellan'!" The final verse of the latter read:

And we want no smutty jokes, but we
want a man of deeds,
To lead us with the firm hand of reason;
So we'll dress Old Abraham up in a Cabinet
widow's weeds,
And mark him "The last joke" of the season.[53]

In *Campaign Document, No. 19,* which featured "The

---

[51] Philadelphia *Daily Age*, Sept. 12, 1864. Later in the month the paper alleged that a rumor was abroad that "Old Abe," "the celebrated clown," would appear at Concert Hall with his trained dog to tell some jokes ". . . and sing the famous negro melody so admirably performed under his direction at Antietam." Philadelphia *Daily Age*, Sept. 30, 1864.

For further examples of anti-administration poems and songs, see *The Crisis* (*Columbus*), June 29, July 27, 1864; *Essex Statesman* (Salem, Mass.), June 22, 1864; N.Y. *World*, Oct. 8, 10, 14, 1864; Philadelphia *Daily Age*, Oct. 24, 1864; *The Old Guard*, II (Nov., 1864), 261-62.

[52] *Copperhead Minstrel*, pp. 3-5.

[53] Feeks, *Democratic Presidential Campaign Songster No. 1*, pp. 5-6.

Cry Is Mac, My Darling," there was "A Song for the Boys," to be sung to the tune of "Yankee Doodle." Two of the nine verses alluded to the President:

> Old Uncle Abe is a used up babe,
>   With all his jokes and toddy;
> The Copperheads have seen the threads
>   That were not in the shoddy.
> - - - - - - - - - - - - - - -
> Our "Little Mac" is just the man
>   To restore the nation's glories;
> He never will on the battle-field
>   Indulge in smutty stories.[54]

In terms of persistent, powerful and scurrilous abuse, neither the songsters, nor the songs, nor the contributions of opposition journals in general, could compare with the editorials printed in the New York *World*. The *World's* malicious work was compounded in that other papers quoted it liberally, seeming to accept it as the ultimate source of authority and truth. Its editorial "Lincoln and Johnson" on June 9 beginning "The age of statesmen is gone; the age of rail-splitters and tailors, of buffoons, boors and fanatics has succeeded . . ." set the tone.

Editorials on June 20, "On Calling Things by Their Names," on June 27, "Is Mr. Lincoln a Buffoon?" and on October 1 on "The Ambitious Buffoon," all built up to a venomous conclusion featuring the Antietam Incident.[55]

The editorial on September 9, while not as graphic or detailed as others on the Antietam Incident, turned out to have special significance. A copy, together with a verse of a campaign song which was printed in the same col-

---

[54] *Campaign Document, No. 19. Campaign Songs.* (N.Y., [1864]), p. 11. Two songsters which contained no calumnious references were: William D. Potts, *Campaign Songs for Christian Patriots and True Democrats, Accompanied with Notes* (N.Y., 1864), and Sidney Herbert, . . . *McClellan Campaign Melodist: A Collection of Patriotic Campaign Songs in Favor of the Constitution and the Union, the Election of General McClellan, the Restoration of Federal Authority, and the Speedy Extermination of Treason* (Boston, 1864).

[55] The New York *Herald* time and again berated the opposition press, especially the *World*, for the indecency of the campaign being conducted. On Oct. 2, in an editorial, "The Degradation of the Party Press," it took the *Tribune* to task for its attacks on McClellan and then went on: "But the Bohemians of the *World*, in their shocking depravity, seem to be incurable. Regardless alike of truth, decorum and the policy, as politicians, of a decent respect for the confidences of the family sanctum, their conduct is scandalous and disgraceful to all concerned." N.Y. *Herald*, Oct. 2, 1864. Cf. other editorials in the *Herald* for Sept. 27, Oct. 5, 9, 11, 1864.

umn, was sent to Ward Lamon by a prominent Republican who wanted to know if there was any truth in it.

Lamon drafted a sharp reply which he showed to the President. Lincoln thought it too strong. He then carefully wrote out a complete account of what had actually happened. But the account was not sent. Lincoln advised Lamon, "Keep this paper, and we will see about it."[56]

Early in the campaign the *Intelligencer* pointed out that vilification and bitterness ". . . augur only a poverty of intellectual resources in combination with a superabundance of malignity."[57] As it turned out, the campaign made very clear the truth of the *Intelligencer's* observation. Lincoln, with his understanding of politics, concluded that it was best not to recognize the "superabundance of malignity" that was aimed at him. As for the Antietam Incident, he expressed himself to Lamon in homely but effective frontier terms:

> . . . there has already been too much said about this falsehood. Let the thing alone. If I have not established character enough to give the lie to this charge, I can only say that I am mistaken in my own estimate of myself. In politics, every man must skin his own skunk. These fellows are welcome to the hide of this one. Its body has already given forth its unsavory odor.[58]

---

[56] A. J. Perkins to Marshal Lamon, Sept. 10, 1864; Lincoln's own account of the Antietam Incident, Lamon Papers; Lamon, *Recollections of Abraham Lincoln*, pp. 141-48. This volume contains a facsimile of the President's account, following page 144.

Although Lamon says (p. 146) that the statement was never given to the press, he did send a statement to the inquirer, A. J. Perkins, some two and a half weeks after Lincoln said, "Keep this paper. . . ." This statement varies slightly from the President's account, but was obviously based upon it. Lamon could not refrain from mentioning the controversy that had been stirred up. At the end of his letter to Perkins, he wrote: ". . . certainly no objections were made by General McClellan or anyone else at the time, to anything said or done by myself or any of the party—It has only occurred to them since to endeavor to torture something, however small, out of an act that was innocently perpetrated by myself without any promptings from my well abused friend President Lincoln." Ward H. Lamon to A. J. Perkins, Sept. 30, 1864, Lamon Papers.

In his letter of acknowledgment Perkins said that he would use Lamon's statement "if not forbidden by you." A. J. Perkins to W. H. Lamon, Oct. 5, 1864, Lamon Papers. Whether he did or did not use it is thus far not known.

In the Herndon Papers there is a four-page manuscript entitled "History of the Antietam Episode as written by Marshal Lamon for his second volume of the Life of Lincoln," sent to Jesse W. Weik by Gilbert A. Tracy. Tracy transcribed it from an account which he says was written by Lamon ("the only copy in existence"), and given to him by Mrs. Teillard. It varies somewhat from the account in Lamon's *Recollections* (edited by Dorothy Lamon) and from the account Lamon sent to A. J. Perkins. Gilbert A. Tracy to Jesse W. Weik, Jan. 12, 15, Dec. 20, 1914, Herndon-Weik Collection, Library of Congress. (Microfilm.)

[57] Washington *National Intelligencer*, Sept. 3, 1864.

[58] Lamon, *Recollections of Abraham Lincoln*, p. 142.

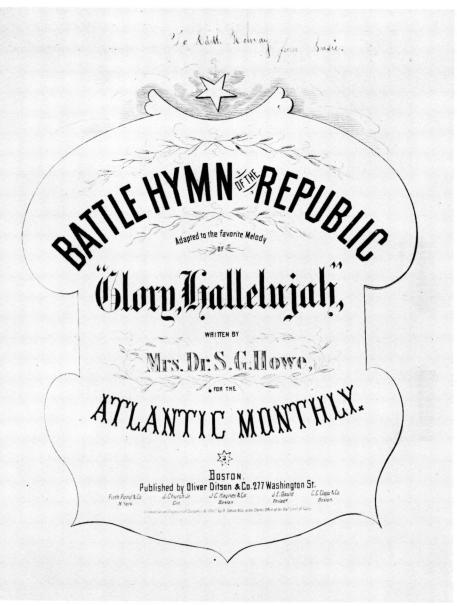

"BATTLE HYMN OF THE REPUBLIC"

Julia Ward Howe composed the words of this famous song on November 21, 1861, after witnessing a review of troops at Bailey's Cross Roads. When Lincoln heard the song at the Second Anniversary Meeting of the Christian Commission, he called out, "Sing it again!"

PLATE XXXIV

A Story of a Song.

President Lincoln loves a good story. In fact, President Lincoln tells good stories—and tells a great many of them too. So long as they *are* good he is not so very particular as to when and where he tells such stories or has them told. He introduces them everywhere and on every occasion—sometimes to illustrate a principle and sometimes to provoke a laugh. The same thing may be said of President Lincoln's relish for a good comic song. Perhaps he don't sing himself in a manner calculated to render Brignoli envious, or fill Susini with doubts (to use the green-room diction) as to his next year's "little sal;" but he enjoys a keen appetite for a jolly song well delivered by another, and he has a gratefully abiding remembrance of the man who can thus impart entertainment.

While riding, for instance, over the field after the sanguinary battle of Antietam, the President said nothing while General McClellan was pointing out the place where our brave volunteers fell by scores and gallantly laid down their lives in defence of the Union. He remained profoundly silent while McClellan, with trembling lip, eulogised the valor of a division which had left eight hundred dead in one small spot, their rudely-made graves marking their last resting place. Perhaps the President was thinking of the moaning widows and fatherless children, crying for bread, those eight hundred had left behind them! But at that moment his eye caught a glimpse of a familiar uniform.

"Isn't that Major So-and-so?" said he.

"It is," was the response.

"Send for him! Send for him at once!" he quickly answered.

The major was summoned, and came.

"General," said the President, "the major sings one of the best songs you ever heard. I tell you it's a jolly good one! Come, Major, let us have it right on the spot!"

And the song was given—all who *could* leave, however, without discourtesy to the chief magistrate of the United States, withdrawing from the sod that covered the bones, on that battle-field, of their once gallant comrades.

Could we furnish a better proof of President Lincoln's appreciation of a good song or a good singer? As to his good taste, we are not discussing it at this moment. Neither are we prepared to speak of the time and the place as *apropos* to the "jolly good song" in question. Those are all matters we leave to the reader and his or her judgment. We simply desire to show what a passion the President has for a comic story and a mirthful song; and (as the instance we have given comes to us, as genuine, from high authority,) we think we have pretty clearly established our position.

COURTESY GUSTAVUS V. FOX PAPERS
THE NEW-YORK HISTORICAL SOCIETY,
NEW YORK CITY
THE
"ANTIETAM INCIDENT"

One of the earliest versions of the "Antietam Incident." The item was sent to Gustavus Fox, Assistant Secretary of the Navy, by George W. Blunt, a prominent New York Republican, on December 22, 1862. It had appeared the previous day in the *Sunday Times and Noah's Weekly Messenger*. In his reply Fox said, "No one here ever heard of it." This was before the malicious story had spread to Washington.

PLATE XXXV

"PICCAYUNE BUTLER"

The song which became the basis of the "Antietam Incident"

PLATE XXXVI

U. S. Christian Commission,
BRANCH OFFICE,
Washington, D. C., Jan. 30, 1864.

Rev. S. I. Bowler, *Local Agent,*
300 H. Street, Washington, D.C.

DEAR SIR:

You are respectfully invited to attend the SECOND ANNIVERSARY MEETING of the U. S. CHRISTIAN COMMISSION, on TUESDAY EVENING NEXT, Feb. 2, at 7½ o'clock, in the Hall of the House of Representatives.

Vice-President HAMLIN will preside. A summary of the last Annual Report will be given by GEO. H. STUART, Esq., Chairman of the Commission.

Brief statements of the practical work of the Commission, on the field and in hospitals, will be made by REV. R. J. PARVIN and GEO. J. MINGINS, Delegates, &c., and address delivered by the Hon. Secretary, Hon. SCHUYLER COLFAX, and Brig. Gen. MARTINDALE.

No tickets will be issued, but you are cordially invited to a seat on the floor of the House, to which this Circular will admit yourself and family.

Very truly, yours, &c.,

GEO. H. STUART,
Chairman U. S. C. C.
WM. BALLANTYNE,
Chairman District Committee.

PRINTED INVITATION TO THE SECOND ANNIVERSARY MEETING
OF THE CHRISTIAN COMMISSION

Lincoln received personal as well as printed invitations to be present at the anniversary meetings, and he attended two of them.

BISHOP McCABE

Charles C. McCabe, the "Singing Chaplain," as he appeared in later years. At the Second Anniversary Meeting of the Christian Commission, February 2, 1864, his ... in Libby Prison and his singing of the "Battle

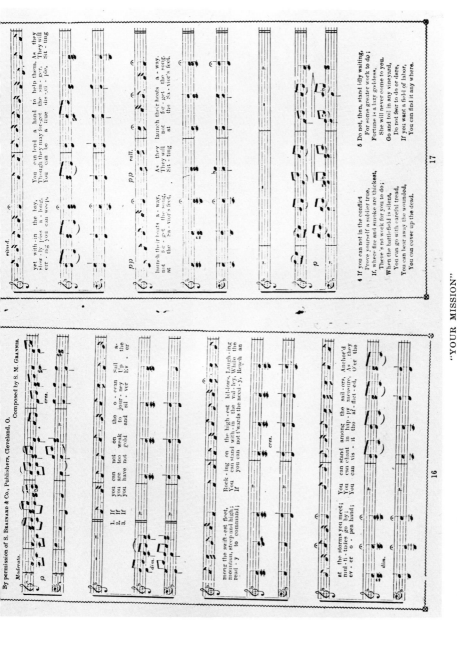

"YOUR MISSION"

Lincoln was greatly affected by Philip Phillips' singing of "Your Mission" at the Third Anniversary Meeting of the Christian Commission, January 29, 1865, and asked that the song be repeated.

PLATE XXXVIII

U. S.
Christian Commission

CENTRAL OFFICE.
11 BANK STREET.

Philadelphia, Jan 30th 1863

Hon President Lincoln
Washington D C
My Dear Sir
I learn through Mr Geo H
Steuart (President of our Christian Commission)
that you made the request to him in writing
for me to repeat my little song "Your Mission"
at our Anniversary last Sunday night

The honor created in me a strong desire to
have the request in writing as you gave it to
him. But Mr S wanted it himself. and said
I could apply to you for another and you send
it to me by mail.

This little favor in your own hand writing
I should appreciate nearly as highly as having
the honor of singing many songs together
with Two (2) hearty votes for you during the
last five years

Very truly yours
Philip Phillips
Address   Cincinnati Ohio

I will send to you my last little Singing Book
for your little Boy containing the Song "Your Mission"
40354

THE "SINGING PILGRIM," PHILIP PHILLIPS, REQUESTS A COPY OF
PRESIDENT LINCOLN'S NOTE ASKING THAT "YOUR MISSION" BE
REPEATED
The President evidently complied, for years later Phillips stated that he had the
"written request" and valued it highly.
PLATE XXXIX

Around the World

RICHLY ILLUSTRATING A TOUR THROUGHOUT TWENTY COUNTRIES WITH

Philip Phillips

"THE SINGING PILGRIM"

A Pictorial Tour OF THE GLOBE. ILLUSTRATED BY PEN AND PENCIL, INCLUDING EXPERIENCES, SIGHTS AND IMPRESSIONS OF MEN AND THINGS, THROUGHOUT Every State in the Union AND TWENTY DIFFERENT COUNTRIES, WITH AN INTRODUCTION By Rev. J. H. VINCENT, D.D., LL.D.

TRAVELS, PERSONS, INCIDENTS, SKETCHES, ANECDOTES, WORKS, ART AND NATURE.

PUBLISHED BY
THE PHILLIPS PUBLISHING CO.
BIBLE HOUSE, NEW YORK.

"THE SINGING PILGRIM"

Philip Phillips' whole life was bound up in music as a singer, player, composer, and publisher. During the Civil War his appearance in camp and hospital earned him his title. Lincoln was greatly affected by Phillips' singing at the Third Anniversary Meeting of the Christian Commission, January 29, 1865, and requested that Phillips repeat his song, "Your Mission." The title page of Phillips' book, *Round the World*, shows how the "Singing Pilgrim" appeared more than twenty years after the war.

PLATE XL

FELICITA VESTVALI

Vestvali was considered "one of the greatest lyric tragic artistes" of the times. Lincoln saw her in several of her best performances.

LOUIS M. GOTTSCHALK

Lincoln heard Gottschalk at a concert in Willard's Hall on March 24, 1864. Gottschalk, although born in the South, was always loyal to the Union.

SIGNORE SUSINI AND ISABELLE HINCKLEY

At his first opera, in New York on February 20, 1861, Lincoln heard Miss Hinckley in *Un Ballo in Maschera*. He heard Susini in *The Daughter of the Regiment* and in *Norma*.

ADELAIDE PHILLIPS

Miss Phillips was in the cast of *Un Ballo in Maschera* with Miss Hinckley when Lincoln heard the opera in New York in 1861. She was popular as a concert and opera singer for many years.

PLATE XLI

CLARA LOUISE KELLOGG
She had the leading part in *The Daughter of the Regiment* when Lincoln attended in May, 1862. Her star role was that of Marguerite in *Faust*.

THEODORE HABELMANN
Lincoln heard Habelmann in *Der Freischütz*, in *The Magic Flute*, and in *La Dame Blanche*. He also heard this competent singer in two concerts in Washington in 1864.

PASQUALE BRIGNOLI
Lincoln heard Brignoli in *Il Trovatore*, in *The Daughter of the Regiment*, and probably in *Dinorah*. Brignoli was considered a modest actor but a fine singer.

PLATE XLII

SCENES FROM "FAUST"

Performances of *Faust* in New York in 1864 inspired the artist who drew these sketches, but the same stars who played there also took the same parts in Washington when President Lincoln attended. Josef Hermanns was especially good as Mephistopheles.

(*Frank Leslie's Illustrated Newspaper*, April 16, 1864)

PLATE XLIII

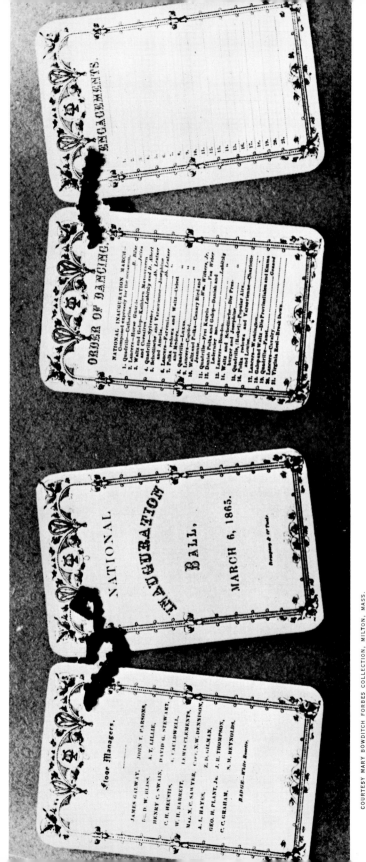

DANCE PROGRAM FOR THE INAUGURAL BALL, MARCH 6, 1865

The dance numbers were typical of the popular dance music of the time. There is little in the entire program, except possibly the "Basket" of popular airs, that would indicate there was a war!

PLATE XLIV

NATIONAL MUSIC.

VOCAL.

STAR SPANGLED BANNER.
MARSEILLES HYMN.
HAIL COLUMBIA.
YANKEE DOODLE.
AMERICA.
OUR FLAG IS THERE.
RALLY FOR THE BANNER.
BEAR ON TO VICTORY.

INSTRUMENTAL.

STAR SPANGLED BANNER	OESTEN
STAR SPANGLED BANNER	BEYER.
HAIL COLUMBIA	OESTEN
HAIL COLUMBIA	BEYER.
YANKEE DOODLE	OESTEN
YANKEE DOODLE	BEYER.
MARSEILLES HYMN	BEYER.
AMERICA	BEYER.
MUSIC OF THE UNION	GROSE.

BOSTON: OLIVER DITSON & CO., 277 WASHINGTON STREET.

J. C. HAYNES & CO.   C. H. DITSON & CO., NEW YORK.   LYON & HEALY,
LEE & WALKER,   JOHN CHURCH & CO.   CHICAGO.

Entered, according to Act of Congress, in the year 1861, by Oliver Ditson & Co., in the Clerk's Office of the District Court of Massachusetts.

BOTH THE "MARSEILLAISE" AND "YANKEE DOODLE" WERE INCLUDED IN THE NATIONAL MUSIC SERIES HERE REPRESENTED

On leaving City Point on April 8, 1865, Lincoln requested the band to play the "Marseillaise" and "Dixie." At a serenade two days later when he again asked for "Dixie," the band added "Yankee Doodle" for good measure!

PLATE XLV

By Telegraph

Navy Department
20 January 1865.

Colnel Jacob Zeilin
Commandant Marine Corps
Marine Barracks
Head Quarters

Send Marine Band to Presidents
to day at Quarter before One O'Clock

Gideon Welles
Secretary of the Navy

Recd 10.55 am

TELEGRAM ORDERING THE MARINE BAND, TO BE AT MRS. LINCOLN'S SATURDAY AFTERNOON RECEPTION, JANUARY 28, 1865

Secretary Welles sent such messages whenever the band was needed at the White House. On this day many prominent people were present. Mrs. Lincoln wore a black satin dress and a white lace shawl. Mr. Lincoln was not present.

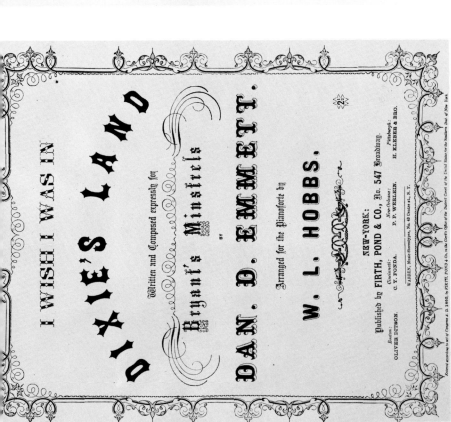

"DIXIE" WAS ONE OF LINCOLN'S FAVORITE PIECES

He first heard it at a minstrel show in Chicago in late March or early April, 1860. His last specific request for a song was when he asked the band at the serenade on April 10, 1865, to play "Dixie."

"HAIL TO THE CHIEF!"

The words, written by Sir Walter Scott, were seldom used but the tune was played constantly. Lincoln heard it at his first serenade, and many times thereafter. Played by Withers' Orchestra when he entered Ford's Theatre on the evening of April 14, 1865, it was, so far as can be determined, the last music that Lincoln heard.

PLATE XLVI

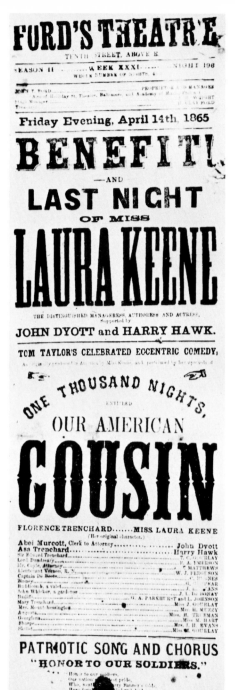

FORD'S THEATRE
TENTH STREET, ABOVE E.

SEASON II ...... WEEK XXXI ...... NIGHT 196
WHOLE NUMBER OF NIGHTS 4

JOHN T. FORD .... PROPRIETOR AND MANAGER

Friday Evening, April 14th, 1865

BENEFIT!
—AND—
LAST NIGHT
OF MISS
LAURA KEENE
THE DISTINGUISHED MANAGERESS, AUTHORESS AND ACTRESS,
Supported by
JOHN DYOTT and HARRY HAWK.

TOM TAYLOR'S CELEBRATED ECCENTRIC COMEDY,

ONE THOUSAND NIGHTS,
ENTITLED
OUR AMERICAN
COUSIN

FLORENCE TRENCHARD...... MISS LAURA KEENE
(Her original character.)

Abel Murcott, Clerk to Attorney	John Dyott
Asa Trenchard	Harry Hawk
Sir Edward Trenchard	T. C. GOURLAY
Lord Dundreary	E. A. EMERSON
Mr. Coyle, Attorney	7 MATTHEWS
Lieutenant Vernon, R. N.	W. J. FERGUSON
Captain De Boots	C. BYRNES
Binney	G. SPEAR
Buddicombe, a valet	C. BYRNE? ASS
John Whicker, a gardener	J. L. DeBONAY
Build	G. A. PARKHURST and L. JOHNSON
Mary Trenchard	Miss J. GOURLAY
Mrs. Mountchessington	Miss H. MUZZY
Augusta	Miss, H. TRUEMAN
Georgina	Miss M. HART
Sharpe	Mrs. J. H. EVANS
Skillet	Miss M. GOURLAY

PATRIOTIC SONG AND CHORUS
"HONOR TO OUR SOLDIERS."

> Honor to our soldiers,
> Our nation's greatest pride,
> Who, neath our Starry Banner's folds,
> Have fought and bled and died
> They 're the Nation's hand sawell,
> No King so great as they,
> God bless the heroes of the land,
> And cheer them on their way.'

Words by H. B. Phillips; Music Composed and Arranged by Prof. William
Withers, Jr.; Sung by Miss M. Hart, H. B. Phillips and George M. Arth.
and the Ladies and Gentlemen of the Company.

SATURDAY EVENING, APRIL 15.

BENEFIT of Miss JENNIE GOURLAY

THE OCTOROON

EDWIN ADAMS

"OUR AMERICAN COUSIN"
The playbill which was hurriedly issued for April 14, 1865, after it was
known that President Lincoln would
attend Ford's Theatre. It contained
the notice of the song, "Honor to
Our Soldiers." The song was not
sung.
PLATE XLVII

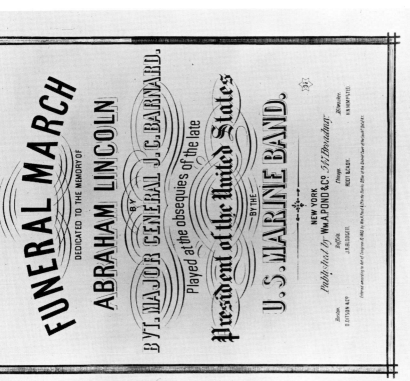

FUNERAL MARCH BY BREVET MAJOR GENERAL J. G. BARNARD

General Barnard was a musician as well as an engineer. This funeral march, which
he composed, was played as the funeral procession moved from the White House to the
Capitol on April 19, 1865. Composer's name is incorrect on the music.

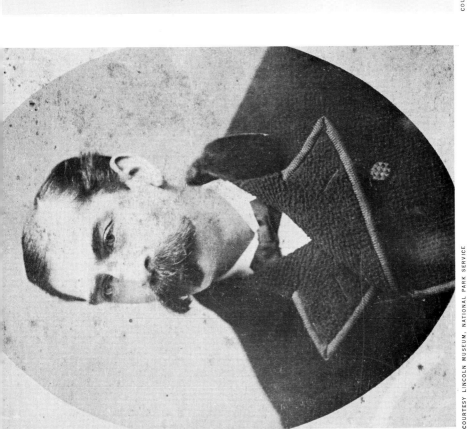

WILLIAM WITHERS

Leader of the orchestra at Ford's Theatre on the night of the assassination of President
Lincoln.

PLATE XLVIII

"FUNERAL MARCH"

One of the selections played during the funeral ceremonies at Springfield, Illinois, on May 4, 1865. The composer, E. C. Davis, was a musician of some prominence in Quincy.

"FAREWELL FATHER, FRIEND AND GUARDIAN"

This piece, for which the famous composer, George F. Root, wrote the music, became the best known of the many Lincoln funeral compositions. It was sung in Chicago and again at the final service at Oak Ridge Cemetery on May 4, 1865.

PLATE XLIX

The Antietam Incident, so far as Lincoln was concerned, was closed. The voters rendered their verdict on November 8. But the Incident was not entirely closed, for scarcely had the heat and emotion of the campaign died down when it appeared again!

Professor Goldwin Smith of Oxford University was in the United States during the exciting campaign months of 1864. Sympathetic to the Northern cause, he pointed out that there were many ties between this country and England and that, though relationships were sometimes strained, the fundamental kinship between the two peoples should keep them friendly. If the wealthy classes and the London *Times* favored the South, he said, it should be remembered that the *Telegraph* and the workers were for the North.[59]

Smith was highly critical of the damage done to good relations between the two countries by irresponsible journalists, especially American journalists from whom English writers took their cues. Writing in *The Atlantic Monthly,* he charged:

> No English speaker or journal has denounced the war or reviled the conduct of your Government more bitterly than a portion of American politicians and a section of the American press. The worst things said in England of your statesmen, of your generals, of your armies, of your contractors, of your social state and character as a people, have been but the echo of things which have been said here. If the New-York correspondents of some English journals have been virulent and calumnious, their virulence and their calumnies have been drawn, to a great extent, from the American circles in which they have lived.[60]

Two months later Smith directed some comments to those who had tried to tear Lincoln down by ridicule and by repeating the Antietam Incident. In an article in *Macmillan's* he gave his own impressions of the President whom he had interviewed soon after his reelection.

Lincoln during the interview told two or three stories

---

[59] Chicago *Times,* Sept. 21, 1864.

[60] Goldwin Smith, "England and America," *The Atlantic Monthly,* XIV (Dec., 1864), 764.

by way of illustrating a remark, but not for the sake of the stories only. To Smith, this did not indicate ". . . a particularly jocular temperament, much less an addiction to brutal levity, such as would call for a comic song among soldiers' graves, but the humour of the West, and especially of a Western man accustomed to address popular audiences, and to enforce his ideas by vivid and homely illustrations. . . ."

Lincoln's language was simple, his words full of meaning, and he used no coarse or vulgar phrases. He was a Westerner, said Smith, but he was no boor. As further evidence, Smith cited the Gettysburg Address:

> . . . looking at the substance, it may be doubted whether any king in Europe would have expressed himself more royally than the peasant's son. And, even as to the form, we cannot help remarking that simplicity of structure and pregnancy of meaning are the true characteristics of the classical style. Is it easy to believe that the man who had the native good taste to produce this address would be capable of committing gross indecencies—that he would call for comic songs to be sung over soldiers' graves?[61]

In 1866 there was published in New York a volume entitled *A Youth's History of the Great Civil War in the United States, From 1861 to 1865.* In the first paragraph the reader was informed of the purpose of the book:

> This book has been written in the cause of Truth. It has not been the object of the writer to defend any particular party or faction, but solely to vindicate democratic and republican institutions.

That the author of the volume, R. G. Horton, was associated, as proprietor and editor, with two of the most notorious anti-Republican journals of the period, the *New York Day-Book* and *The Old Guard*, gives some in-

---

[61] Goldwin Smith, "President Lincoln," *Macmillan's*, XI (Feb., 1865), 301-2. Smith concluded his article by stating that Lincoln was perhaps not a great man but he was an honest man and his reelection was good for the country and for the world. That Smith recognized the widespread use of the Antietam Incident in the campaign of 1864 is indicated by the fact that he referred to it twice in the article. In his *Reminiscences* Smith did not make specific reference to Antietam. He wrote: "The notion formed of Lincoln in England had been that of a Yankee rail-splitter with an ungainly and grotesque figure, displaying an unfeeling levity by the utterance of rather coarse jokes, from which he did not abstain even among the relics of the battle-field." Goldwin Smith, *Reminiscences* (N.Y., 1910), p. 354.

sight into the manner of the "vindication" and into the
nature of the revelation of "Truth." Abolitionism was the
cause of the country's woes and the Lincoln Republicans
had overthrown the government and established a military despotism.

Of Lincoln the author had nothing favorable to say.
Even on his way to the capital in 1861 Lincoln had shown
his true nature:

> While the country was agonized to its very heart, he amused
> the crowd which came out to greet him on his way with jokes,
> and, often, with low stories. He even made jests that were
> at once surprising and disgusting to the respectable portion of
> his own party. To a young man who, in New York city, of-
> fered to measure height with him, he replied, "No I have not
> time now to measure with you, but if you will bring on your
> sister I will kiss her." The whole style and manner of the
> man was that of a low joker, rather than that of a statesman
> and patriot.

Lincoln's lack of manners was further revealed during
an interview with a "refined and accomplished gentleman" who claimed that during a conversation, "Mr. Lincoln sat with his shoe off, holding his toes in his hand,
and bending them backwards and forwards in an awk-
ward manner."

When in Congress Lincoln had been ostracized because of his habit of telling low stories. His mind ran
in "low channels."

All of this, explained Horton, was due to Lincoln's
unfortunate background. He did not know his father, and
his mother ". . . was a person to reflect no honor upon her
child." He ran away from his "wretched home" at the
age of nine ". . . to escape the brutal treatment of the
man who had married his mother . . ." and went to work
on a flatboat on the Mississippi. It was there that he
learned to like low society, vulgar jests and stories.

With this background it was not surprising that Lincoln's administration was one of gross misrule into
which the Antietam Incident would naturally fit.

  After the battle of Antietam Mr. Lincoln had visited the

battle-field, and an incident, entirely authentic, is related, showing with what levity and indifference he viewed the scene of the dreadful carnage and slaughter.

"There," said McClellan, who was riding by his side, "we buried eight hundred gallant and noble fellows."

Mr. Lincoln, scarcely glancing at the spot, exclaimed,

"Mac, did you ever hear Major P. sing Old Dan Tucker?"

The general shook his head in evident sorrow at such desecration of the newly-made graves about him, when Mr. Lincoln, calling to Major P., who was riding a few rods in the rear, insisted that he should sing "Old Dan Tucker" for General McClellan, and it was done.

If this statement was not authenticated beyond doubt, I should hesitate to put it in here, for never before over the fresh graves on a battle-field did one whose heart ought to have wept tears of blood, indulge in such unfeeling, such unholy jests.[62]

Horton's book attained considerable popularity and Horton himself was held in some esteem. Within a year the sale of his *Youth's History* reached forty thousand copies, and when he died in 1867 a prominent Connecticut Democrat lauded him as an "Apostle of Truth," a "prophet," and "an honest, upright man, and a true friend of the people."[63]

On September 17, 1867, the fifth anniversary of the battle of Antietam, an elaborate ceremony was held at the battlefield for the laying of the cornerstone for a soldiers' monument. A crowd of about ten thousand assembled for the occasion and the dignitaries included President Johnson, members of his cabinet, foreign representatives, governors, military personnel and politicians.

The program did not go too smoothly. The weather was unfavorable—first there was a heavy shower and then it became excessively hot. There were crowding and confusion around the speakers' stand. As the meeting proceeded, some of the audience became restless. Ex-

---

[62] R. G. Horton, *A Youth's History of the Great Civil War in the United States, From 1861 to 1865* (N.Y., 1867), pp. iii, 100, 103-4, 105, 241-42.

[63] The edition of Horton's book here cited was of the "fortieth thousand." T. H. Seymour of Connecticut wrote a letter to the editor of *The Old Guard* in which he thus praised Horton. "Editor's Table," *The Old Guard*, V (Nov., 1867), 877.

Governor Bradford's oration was unduly long and to some, it took a partisan turn. There were calls for Governor Geary of Pennsylvania. The presiding officer, Governor Swann of Maryland, assured the audience that Geary would have an opportunity to speak. As it turned out, the formal program ended rather abruptly and it was only then that Geary and others had a chance to address the crowd.[64]

Unfortunately, the whole affair seemed to reflect the bitter partisan struggle then going on between Conservatives and Radicals throughout the country. The presiding officer, Governor Swann, was a Conservative, as was ex-Governor Bradford, the orator of the day. Supporters of Governor Geary and other Radicals felt that they were being snubbed and neglected; hence the demonstration during Bradford's speech.

A New York *Tribune* correspondent called the proceedings "A Farce and a Fraud"—a meeting to glorify McClellan and to aid President Johnson and Governor Swann. Again, referring to the "Antietam Farce," the *Tribune* said:

> From all accounts the affair was disgraceful in the extreme. Mr. Johnson and the members of the Cabinet with him snubbed everyone of note excepting Swann, Bradford and the other Maryland Rebels. . . . All the loyal men from here [Washington] who were present express themselves as disgusted.[65]

Further, the *Tribune* took the speakers to task for not mentioning Abraham Lincoln, and thought it significant that neither orator, poet, nor President Johnson made allusion to the immediate result of the battle, the Emancipation Proclamation.[66]

---

[64] Secretary Welles, who was present for the occasion, thought the gathering well-behaved and orderly. He blamed Governor Geary's followers for interrupting the proceedings and felt that their demonstration was "evidently preconcerted." They were ". . . rude, ill-mannered fellows who had accompanied Geary from Pennsylvania. . . ." As for Geary, he had "party designs," and ". . . made a Radical partisan's speech in a national graveyard." Morse, ed., *Diary of Gideon Welles*, III, 201-2. One of the most impartial accounts of the proceedings was that printed in the Baltimore *Gazette* Sept. 18, 19, 21, 1867. Cf. also Washington *Daily Morning Chronicle*, Sept. 18, 1867, and *Leslie's Illus. News*, Oct. 5, 1867.

[65] N.Y. *Tribune*, Sept. 18, 19, 1867.

[66] N.Y. *Tribune*, Sept. 21, 23, 1867.

Sincere and honest men were already disturbed by indecent attacks that were being made on the late President and his administration. *The Old Guard,* that same month, ran a long article comparing the career of Lincoln with that of the Roman Emperor Domitian. The Emperor's reign with its frivolous vanities and its cold and passionless cruelties had no equal except that of Abraham Lincoln. "To speak well of Abraham Lincoln," said the article, "is to praise the abominations of his life—is to speak well of despotism, of plunder, of arson, of murder!"[67]

George Templeton Strong was moved to write: "The late signs of political reaction (be the same more or less) have brought out a suspicion that the fine old rank-smelling Copperheadism of former days is not dead, but has been sleeping and begins to awake. Democratic papers now speak of Lincoln as the vilest of mankind and of Jeff Davis as the best and greatest."[68]

Coincidentally, *The Old Guard* for November carried an article "Lincoln and Davis," which bore out Strong's comment with striking accuracy. Lincoln brought more evil to mankind than any man that ever lived, and ". . . the cause represented by Abraham Lincoln is the most monstrous that ever degraded the reason or debauched the instincts of our race. . . ."

In contrast, ". . . the real . . . cause, led by Jefferson Davis, is the noblest, most beneficent, true, and glorious cause that men ever battled for on this earth, and the *means* employed were the grandest, most Christian, and chivalrous ever witnessed in the world's history." Lincoln was "the embodiment of a monstrous lunacy" while Davis was "the champion and defender of the liberty and civilization of America."[69]

The *Tribune's* sharp criticism of the Antietam ceremonies, while adding to the already poisoned atmosphere of 1867, was also a manifestation of concern over the

---

[67] *The Old Guard,* V (Sept., 1867), 650.
[68] Nevins and Halsey, eds., *Diary of George Templeton Strong,* IV (Oct. 31, 1867), 158-59.
[69] *The Old Guard,* V (Nov., 1867), 844-45.

revival of "Copperheadism." It had, however, one un-
expected and interesting result. It led to an explanation
of the origin of the Antietam Incident of 1862!

President Johnson's remarks at Antietam which were
brief and dignified did not please the *Tribune* at all. His
expressed hope that just as the soldiers buried at Antietam lay in peace after the battle, the people could live
in peace also, brought caustic comment from the *Tribune*:

> But we ask for a better example than a cemetery—a live
> policy . . . conceived in the interest of living loyalty, and not
> of dead treason.[70]

This was followed by another blast two days later:

> Mr. Johnson said the other day that he wanted us to live
> in peace as the dead soldiers are doing at Antietam. The
> "great Johnson party" has been living in peace like a dead
> man for some time past, and the great Democratic party, if
> we do our duty, will soon follow suit.[71]

Whereupon, the Boston *Post* suggested:

> Perhaps it [the *Tribune*] would have preferred that Geary,
> or some one else, had sung the song which the late lamented
> President Lincoln sang, when galloping at the head of a
> party of visitors over that field of the dead.[72]

The reference once again to the story so assiduously
circulated by the anti-Lincoln press in 1864 provoked a
refutation which provided, for the first time, some specific
factual information. In a long article in *The Independent*,
F. B. Carpenter exposed the whole matter.[73]

According to Carpenter the story of President Lincoln
calling for a comic song on the field of Antietam was invented by Joseph Scoville, the New York correspondent
of the London *Herald* and the London *Standard*.

Scoville, who claimed to have been at one time secretary
to John C. Calhoun, was a "brilliant and eccentric jour-

---

[70] N.Y. *Tribune,* Sept. 18, 1867.

[71] N.Y. *Tribune,* Sept. 20, 1867.

[72] Boston *Post,* Sept. 28, 1867.

[73] F. B. Carpenter, "Abraham Lincoln," *The Independent,* XI (Dec. 12, 1867), 1.
The article was reprinted in the Baltimore *American,* Dec. 24, 1867.

nalist." He had been associated with various ephemeral publications and had also written novels, one of which, *Vigor*, a tale of seduction in American society, was considered offensive to good taste.

During the Civil War, writing under the pen name "Manhattan," Scoville contributed regularly to the two English newspapers previously mentioned. He was strongly opposed to the Lincoln administration and his reporting, often unreliable and frequently irresponsible, brought him into question by the government more than once.

So notorious was Scoville as a sensationalist that Goldwin Smith in his article in *The Atlantic Monthly*, December, 1864, singled him out, saying:

> No slanders poured by English ignorance or malevolence on American society have been so foul as those which came from a renegade American writing in one of our Tory journals under the name of "Manhattan."[74]

As Carpenter tells it, a few weeks after Lincoln's visit to Antietam, Scoville mentioned the fact in his dispatch and "then and there invented and wrote the slander since republished many times." When questioned by a friend as to why he wrote such nonsense to the London press, Scoville replied, "Why, it was intended only as a joke. I received *ten pounds sterling for that letter*. I have to put just such stuff as that in my letters to please such fellows as they are over there."

Later, in 1864, when he was about to go before General Dix, Scoville reiterated that the story was only intended as a joke, written to please "those fellows over there."

---

[74] Goldwin Smith, *The Atlantic Monthly*, XIV (Dec., 1864), 764. There are biographical data on Scoville in Wilson and Fiske, eds., *Appleton's Cyclopaedia of American Biography*, V, 422; Allen Johnson and Dumas Malone, eds., *Dictionary of American Biography* (N.Y., 1928-44), XVI, 513; Frank Luther Mott, *A History of American Magazines 1850-1865* (Cambridge, 1938), pp. 179, 183.

In 1861 Scoville, at the request of Secretary Seward, was warned by Superintendent of Police John A. Kennedy of New York that his letters to the London *Standard* might get him into trouble. After interviewing Scoville Kennedy suggested that with some "help" in preparing leaders the administration might get more favorable articles in the two London papers. Evidently the suggestion was not acted upon. *O. R.*, Ser. II, Vol. II, pt. 2, 77-78, 498.

In his last letter to the London *Herald*, June 14, 1864 (printed June 28), Scoville related an interview with General Dix and mentioned the possibility that he might be sent to Fort Lafayette. He died suddenly on June 25, 1864.

Thus, according to Carpenter, was born the cruel story of Antietam which appeared in the London *Evening Standard*, January 6, 1863, under Scoville's pen name, "Manhattan."

But, as has already been shown earlier in this chapter, another and different version of the Antietam Incident had already appeared in print *before* Scoville wrote his dispatch.

Did Scoville write the earlier account also? It is unlikely, as the two versions are quite dissimilar in style as well as content. Furthermore, if he had written it, he probably would have said so when he was first questioned about his story as printed in the London *Standard*.

What, then, can be said of Carpenter's account in the light of the appearance of the earlier version of the story? Carpenter's writing has a ring of sincerity in it; there seems to be no doubt that he stated the facts as he understood them. But evidently he was unaware that an earlier version of the Antietam Incident had been printed before Scoville's appeared.

It is possible that Scoville saw "A Story of a Song" and from it got the idea which inspired him to write as he did for the London *Standard*, forgetting (or neglecting) to state this when he explained that he invented the story himself. It is also possible that he *did* invent his version of the Incident and knew nothing of the earlier story. In either case, Carpenter, recounting only what he was told, was writing in good faith.[75]

But if Scoville did invent his own version, the question remains, who originated the earlier version, "A Story of a Song?" The answer may never be known. In any event, both versions, as the record shows, were embellished

---

[75] When the New York *World* challenged Carpenter's story, Carpenter insisted that it was true. The purpose of his article in *The Independent*, he said, was to expose the fabrication of Scoville concerning President Lincoln at Antietam, and, he went on, ". . . it is proper that I should say that all the facts stated in that article, in reference to Mr. Scovill [*sic*], were published upon the *affidavit* of Mr. E. H. Jenny, of this city, whose acquaintance with Mr. Scovill [*sic*] extended through many years." *The Independent*, Dec. 26, 1867. N.Y. *World*, Dec. 27, 1867. Jenny was the individual who had questioned his friend, Scoville, about the article in the first place, and from whom Carpenter obtained his information. In 1867 Jenny did not deny the truth of his assertions. N.Y. *World*, Dec. 30, 1867.

freely and used abundantly during the abusive campaign
of 1864.[76]

---

[76] What actually happened at Antietam was made public in 1895 in Lamon's
Recollections of Abraham Lincoln 1847-1865, edited by Dorothy Lamon. Before the
publication of this volume one of the distorted versions appeared twice, from
the pen of a man who knew Lincoln, Donn Piatt. Piatt used the Incident in
Allen Thorndike Rice, ed., *Reminiscences of Abraham Lincoln by Distinguished
Men of His Time* (1886) and in his own *Memories of Men Who Saved the Union*
(1887).

After the publication of Lamon's *Recollections* the Antietam Incident also
appeared twice. At the turn of the century two volumes were published which,
because of the manner of their treatment of their subject, would have been quite
acceptable to the New York *World* or any other anti-administration, anti-Lincoln
newspaper in 1864, Charles L. C. Minor, *The Real Lincoln* (1901, 1904, 1928),
and George Edmonds [Mrs. Elizabeth A. Meriwether], *Facts and Falsehoods Concerning the War on the South 1861-1865* (1904). Both books, replete with untruths,
half truths, innuendos and distortions, make full use of the Incident to the
obvious detriment of Lincoln as a man and as President.

It should perhaps be added that Horton's volume of 1866 was republished in
1925 with some editorial changes and with the omission of some abusive passages.
The references to Lincoln and to the Antietam Incident were kept intact, but
the editors added after the Incident this comment: ". . . it is regrettable that
Mr. Horton does not here give his authority, 'so that no one can have a chance
to deny' the accuracy of the recital. . . ." R. G. Horton, *A Youth's History of the
Great Civil War*. Revised by Mary D. Carter and Lloyd T. Everett (Dallas [?],
1925), p. 185.

In more recent years the Incident has been mentioned in biographies of
Lincoln, studies of the Presidency, books on journalism, cartoon histories, and in
a volume on music. In all of these it is treated for what it was—an example of
irresponsible, unscrupulous and scurrilous journalism.

CHAPTER XX

THE SUN BURST FORTH

FOLLOWING THE ELECTIONS OF NOVEMBER 8, 1864, THERE
was a lessening of tension on the home front and by the
end of the year the entire war picture—for the North—
was considerably brighter. The President was busy. Mrs.
Lincoln rarely saw him before eleven o'clock in the evening but he was in good spirits and managed to snatch
some intervals of recreation.[1]

While he was at Grover's Theatre one evening enjoying
E. L. Davenport in *Hamlet,* General Sherman, preparing
to leave Atlanta, was serenaded with patriotic airs and
opera tunes—"John Brown's Body" and the "Miserere"
from *Il Trovatore* and others. As the general rode out of
the ruined city the next day the bands again struck up
"John Brown's Body." Regiment after regiment caught
up the song with such vigor that Sherman, recalling the
incident later, remarked:

> . . . never before or since have I heard the chorus of "Glory,
> glory, hallelujah!" done with more spirit, or in better harmony
> of time and place.[2]

Thanksgiving Day was widely celebrated. Through organized effort the troops in camp, hospital, and at the
front were served the traditional dinner with all the fix-
ings. As the men at Mount Pleasant Hospital gathered
for the feast provided by the Union City Committee of

---

[1] Mrs. Lincoln to Mrs. J. C. Conkling, Nov. 19, 1864, Mrs. [Mary Todd] Lincoln,
Letters, 1864 ; *Lincoln Lore,* No. 1250 (Mar. 23, 1953).

[2] N.Y. *Herald,* Nov. 17, 1864 ; Underwood *Thirty-Third Massachusetts In-
fantry,* p. 240 ; Daniel Oakey in Robert Underwood Johnson and Clarence Clough
Buel, eds., *Battles and Leaders of the Civil War* (N.Y., 1884, 1887, 1888), IV, 672 ;
Hoehling, *Last Train From Atlanta,* pp. 536-37 ; William T. Sherman, *Memoirs of
General W. T. Sherman, Written by Himself* (N.Y., 1875), II, 179.

Boston a band played "Rally 'Round the Flag," and afterward treated the inmates to a long program of music; in Milledgeville, Georgia, the band of the Thirty-Third Massachusetts Regiment gave a concert; in Danville, Virginia, Union prisoners fared but meagerly, however, and went to bed uncomfortable.[3]

The President went to the special service at the New York Avenue Presbyterian Church. Dr. Gurley preached a one-hour sermon based upon verse thirty of the sixty-ninth Psalm:

> I will praise the name of God with a song, and will magnify him with thanksgiving.

The choir sang "The President's Hymn" ("Give Thanks, All Ye People") and concluded the service with the "Hallelujah Chorus." A collection amounting to $256 was taken for the work of the Christian Commission. The President, evidently without sufficient funds at the time, asked the collectors to call at the White House later for his contribution, probably a "handsome sum."[4]

One of the pleasantest incidents of the month for Lincoln was the visit to the White House of that picturesque frontiersman, Seth Kinman. Born in Pennsylvania, onetime resident of Illinois, and at this time living in California, Kinman, six feet tall, clad in buckskins and carrying his long rifle and wearing his hunting knife, created a sensation wherever he appeared in the streets.

On his visit to the White House Kinman brought with him an elk horn chair and a violin. The chair which he had fashioned himself during the course of seven years' time he presented to Lincoln as a gift. The President

---

[3] N.Y. *Herald*, Nov. 15, 17, 20, 22, 25, 1864; Washington *Evening Star*, Nov. 25, 1864; Underwood, *Thirty-Third Massachusetts Infantry*, p. 246. "Thanksgiving Day came, and we had little to be thankful for, personally," wrote Abner R. Small. "We were alive, but that was about all. The prison authorities issued meat, such as it was, for our dinner, and a vile sort of bean soup for our supper. . . . Captain Bailey raised thirty-five dollars by the sale of a ring, and on the strength of that I borrowed a pint of rice and bought a pint of molasses, and we made a 'pudding' to celebrate with, and went to bed uncomfortable." Small, *Road to Richmond*, pp. 175-76, 230-31.

[4] Washington *Daily Morning Chronicle*, Nov. 25, 1864. The reporter thought the choir's singing of the "Hallelujah Chorus" "one of the finest pieces of church vocal music to which we have ever listened." The New York Avenue Church had the reputation of producing some of the best church music in the city.

was much intrigued. He sat in the chair, said it was the handsomest of its kind he had ever seen, and accepted it with pleasure.

All the while telling amusing stories of his frontier life the frontiersman next showed the President and the others present his long rifle which he claimed his father had used in the Black Hawk War. Lincoln remarked that he had learned to shoot with just such a long rifle.

Then Kinman took up the violin and told the story of its construction. He had once owned a favorite mule that was very fond of music. Eventually the mule died and one day as he passed the bleaching bones of his former pet he was reminded of the mule's liking for music. Thinking that there was music in those bones, he gathered them up and from them constructed the violin which he now held in his hands.

Allowing that he was not much of a musician, Kinman, nevertheless, offered to play the instrument, and being urged to do so, he played, first, "John Brown's Body" and then a minstrel "breakdown piece," "The Essence of Old Virginia." Lincoln remarked that if he knew how to play the violin he would ask the frontiersman to give it to him, but inasmuch as he was not accomplished on the instrument, he would not do so! With that the visit terminated and Kinman said his farewell and went on his way.[5]

Lincoln's next musical experience was quite a contrast —an evening at the opera to hear *Faust*. The critics gave the production high praise; it was "a feast of soul," said one enthusiastic reporter.[6]

[5] Washington *Evening Star*, Nov. 26, 1864; Washington *Sunday Morning Chronicle*, Nov. 27, 1864; Washington *Daily Morning Chronicle*, Nov. 30, 1864; N.Y. *Herald*, Nov. 26, 1864; [R. Gerald McMurtry], "Lincoln's Elk Horn Chair," *Lincoln Herald*, LVII (Spring-Summer, 1955), 23. Some days after he had received the elk horn chair from Kinman, Lincoln made a remark to William E. Chandler that is of interest. When Chandler protested against the appointment of Salmon P. Chase as Chief Justice, Lincoln said ". . . that he would rather have swallowed his buckhorn chair than to have nominated Chase." Morse, ed., *Diary of Gideon Welles*, II, 196.
"The Essence of Old Virginia" was said to have been invented by William W. Newcomb and was a favorite with Dan Bryant and other minstrel players. Cf. Odell, *Annals of the New York Stage*, VII, 90-91, 187; Wittke, *Tambo and Bones*, pp. 45, 123, 190, 225. It was the kind of a piece that Lincoln would greatly enjoy.

[6] Washington *National Intelligencer*, Dec. 5, 7, 1864; Washington *Daily Morning Chronicle*, Dec. 6, 1864; Washington *Evening Star*, Dec. 6, 1864.

The following evening a group of serenaders appeared unexpectedly. A band played several patriotic pieces and then "Hail to the Chief!" Lincoln appeared, and, quite unprepared, asked Governor-elect Fenton, of New York, to speak first and give him "a peg to hang on." When his turn came he displayed his uneasiness, saying, "I believe I shall never live to be old enough to speak without embarrassment when I have nothing to talk about." But, as on similar occasions, he said the right thing:

> I have no good news to tell you, and yet I have no bad news to tell. . . . The most interesting news we now have is from Sherman. We all know where he went in at, but I cannot tell where he will come out at.

This put the crowd in a good mood and the President himself was satisfied.[7]

Again, on the ninth of December, Lincoln attended the opera, Meyerbeer's *The Huguenots,* and ten days later he was among the guests at a gala promenade concert at Ford's Theatre. This was the big musical event of the month. Ford's was elaborately decorated and illuminated. Grafulla's famous New York Seventh Regiment Band was engaged for the occasion. In spite of the wretched weather a large crowd of distinguished people was present, prominent among whom were Secretary Seward, Speaker Colfax, Assistant Secretary Fox and numerous army officers. The program was varied and popular:

Treasury Regiment Promenade Concert
Programme
Part I

1. Grand March—"Tannhauser" _____Wagner
2. Song—"Yellow-haired Laddie and
   Cuckoo Polka" _____Grafulla
3. Overture—"William Tell" _____Rossini
4. Electric Polka _____Harry Sanderson
5. Selections—"I Due Foscari" _____Verdi
6. March _____Grafulla

---

[7] Washington *Evening Star,* Dec. 7, 1864; Washington *Daily Morning Chronicle,* Dec. 8, 1864; R. E. Fenton in Rice, ed., *Reminiscences of Abraham Lincoln,* pp. 70-71; Lincoln, *Works,* VIII, 154.

Part II

7. Overture—"Zampa" _____Herold
8. Romance—"L'Eclair, and Champagne
   Gallop" _____Halevy
9. Selections—"Robert le Diable" _____Meyerbeer
10. Waltz—"Les Enroleurs" _____Lanner
11. Gallop—"A Trip to the Front" _____Gungl
12. Medley—"Popular Airs" _____Grafulla

Dancing followed this fine concert and ". . . the dancers
had all the advantages the most ambitious could desire."
The music was excellent.[8]

Apart from the gala concert, music was not a prominent
feature of the Christmas season for Lincoln, but congratulations on his part were. Good news from Nashville on
the fifteenth prompted him to send warm words of appreciation to General Thomas. More good news was received
on Christmas Day from General Sherman:

> I beg to present you as a Christmas gift the city of Savan-
> nah with 150 heavy guns & plenty of ammunition & also
> about 25000 bales of cotton.

To Sherman the President sent hearty thanks. In that
same city on that same day the band of the Thirty-Third
Massachusetts Regiment celebrated by giving a concert.
To the delight of the colored population it played "John
Brown," "Yankee Doodle," the "Star-Spangled Banner,"
and "Dixie."[9]

With victory in the air it was no wonder that the New
Year's Reception (on January 2) brought a huge crowd
to the White House. As usual, foreign dignitaries and
prominent officials were received from twelve to one
o'clock and then for two hours President and Mrs. Lin-

[8] Washington *Daily Morning Chronicle*, Dec. 19, 20, 1864; Washington *Evening Star*, Dec. 20, 1864; N.Y. *Tribune*, Dec. 20, 1864.

[9] Lincoln, *Works*, VIII, 169, 181-82; Underwood, *Thirty-Third Massachusetts Infantry*, p. 254. Out in San Francisco, where the war was far away but feelings ran strong, some followers of the pugilistic art were, one evening that same week, celebrating a prizefight in a saloon. As they sang "Rally 'Round the Flag" a disgruntled customer entered and made "an offensive political remark." A small riot ensued, a knife was drawn and shots were fired. No one was seriously injured but the two chief culprits were arrested. *Morning Oregonian* (Portland), Dec. 23, 1864.

coln met the onslaught of "citizens-at-large." Although the *Chronicle* called it an ovation, it was more accurately described by Noah Brooks as the President's "great annual jam." Lincoln shook hands with an estimated five thousand people during the two-hour ordeal.

Even though there were police to keep order, the crush was terrible; one lady had her hat smashed and her clothes so torn that she decided not to meet the President and left disappointed. Said the New York *Herald*:

> All classes, sexes, ages and conditions came rolling up, tumbling up, scrambling up, climbing up, getting up any way they could—some in order and some in great disorder, some sober, some not so sober as might be. . . . Mrs. Lincoln retired early, but the throng continued to press forward until the gates of the White House were closed and the crowd excluded.

But nevertheless, it was a gala occasion. Lincoln was in fine spirits, Robert was home for the holidays, Mrs. Lincoln was "queen like" in her bearing and manner, and all the while the Marine Band rendered excellent music in the background. A brilliant social season was assured.[10]

The President's evening receptions were held, somewhat irregularly, on Mondays during January and February, but it was Mrs. Lincoln's Saturday afternoon levees that attracted attention. They became more popular and elaborate. Mrs. Lincoln let it be known that she wished all ladies to attend in full dress and she set the example. Her costumes, frequently described to the press, met with general approval. Thus at the levee on January 21 she wore a dress of ". . . rich and very heavy black corded silk, elaborately and tastefully trimmed. . . ."

---

[10] Washington *Daily Morning Chronicle*, Jan. 3, 1865; Sacramento *Daily Union*, Feb. 21, 1865; N.Y. *Herald*, Jan. 4, 1865; N.Y. *Times*, Jan. 4, 1865; Washington *Evening Star*, Jan. 2, 1865. Pleas for more proper dress, more polite manners and deportment, and for more adequate arrangements for wraps and outer garments appeared in the newspapers. Washington *Daily Morning Chronicle*, Jan. 4, 1865; Washington *Evening Star*, Jan. 7, 1865. Receptions thereafter were more orderly and better managed, but the wear and tear of such crowds was evident. In addition people constantly cut and clipped from the curtains, hangings, and carpets for souvenirs. Occasionally people were caught in the act and arrested, but the depredations continued. Cf. Washington *Evening Star*, Nov. 15, 29, Dec. 24, 1864; Sacramento *Daily Union*, Dec. 28, 1864. John Nicolay called the White House a "dirty old rickety concern" and a "dilapidated old shanty." John G. Nicolay to Therena Bates, Mar. 26, 1865, Nicolay Papers.

Her shawl was white point lace and her headdress black velvet and lace. On February 4 her costume consisted of ". . . a purple velvet dress, trimmed with white cord and buttons, an elegant white point lace shawl, a headdress of flowers and white lace, white kid gloves and a fan."[11]

Flowers from the White House conservatory decorated each room and their fragrance filled the air. There were azaleas, japonicas, cassia, heliotrope and many "exotics" as well. As an added attraction the Marine Band now played each Saturday as well as at the Monday evening receptions. Its "delicious" music added to the enjoyment of the levees.

The presence of prominent people at these Saturday levees indicated their increasing popularity. Vice-President Hamlin, Chief Justice Chase, Baron de Stoeckl, Senator Harlan, General and Mrs. Grant appeared at various times; even the raging sleet storm of January 21 failed to keep away such notables as Generals Burnside, Butler, and Sheridan (the latter on his first visit to the White House).[12]

Secretary Nicolay, somewhat satiated with social affairs, thought that the White House receptions were well attended and spirited as compared with others. Commissioner French was kept occupied meeting Mrs. Lincoln's demands. "I never was more busy in my life, . . ." he wrote. His duties, especially his attendance on Mrs. Lincoln, were ". . . no inconsiderable weights on a man's back." The President, in spite of his many obligations, frequently assisted Mrs. Lincoln in receiving guests. The last reception was held on March 11.[13]

But if receptions with the accompanying music of the Marine Band were important in the social season, other events were of far more significance nationally. On the first day of February hardy citizens braved the winter

---

[11] [Mrs. John Kasson] *Iowa Jour. of Hist.*, LII (Jan., 1954), 87; Washington *Sunday Morning Chronicle*, Jan. 22, Feb. 5, 1865.

[12] Washington *Evening Star*, Jan. 9, 1865; Washington *Sunday Morning Chronicle*, Jan. 22, 29, Feb. 5, 12, 19, 26, Mar. 12, 1865.

[13] John G. Nicolay to Therena Bates, Jan. 15, 1865, Nicolay Papers; B. B. French to Pamela French, Feb. 8, 1865, B. B. French Papers.

weather to serenade the President once again, this time to demonstrate their approval of the passage of the resolution sending the Thirteenth Amendment to the states for ratification.

On this occasion the President had something to say. After several patriotic airs had been played he spoke, obviously with pleasure and satisfaction. "The occasion," he said, "was one of congratulation to the country and to the whole world." He was gratified that his own state of Illinois had already ratified the amendment. The amendment was ". . . the fitting if not indispensable adjunct to the consummation of the great game we are playing." It was not only a cause for congratulation, it was a "great moral victory." The band responded with more lively airs as the serenaders departed.[14]

Later there was more good news from the South. Sherman's men occupied Columbia; Charleston and Fort Sumter were finally taken. Colored troops marched through the streets of Charleston singing "John Brown's Body," Union prisoners at Columbia heard songs they had not heard in months—"Hail, Columbia" and "Yankee Doodle"—and the President was serenaded by the band from Lincoln Hospital.[15]

At Danville, Virginia, Union prisoners who had whiled away many a lonesome hour singing "Do They Miss Me at Home?," "The Vacant Chair," and "Just Before the Battle, Mother," were cheered by the news that they were to be transferred to Libby. In anticipation they struck up "Hard Times Come Again No More" and "Home, Sweet Home!" In Washington the birthday of the first President and the recent victories were celebrated

---

[14] Washington *Daily Morning Chronicle*, Feb. 2, 1865; N.Y. *Tribune*, Feb. 3, 1865; Sacramento *Daily Union*, Mar. 1, 1865; Lincoln, *Works*, VIII, 254-55. To F. B. Carpenter he remarked a few days later that the Emancipation Act which was consummated in the Thirteenth Amendment was ". . . *the central act of my administration, and the great event of the nineteenth century.*" Carpenter, *Six Months at the White House*, p. 90.

[15] *Harper's Weekly*, Mar. 18, 1865; Charles Carlton Coffin in Rice, ed., *Reminiscences of Abraham Lincoln*, p. 174; Underwood, *Thirty-Third Massachusetts Infantry*, p. 266; Washington *Daily Morning Chronicle*, Feb. 22, 1865.

by a general illumination of public buildings and the White House.[16]

On the drizzly, wet morning of March 4 Lincoln was inaugurated for the second time amid the music of bands, the salute of cannon, and the cheers of thousands of spectators who had sloshed through the muddy streets to be on hand for the ceremony.

As the inaugural procession reached the Capitol with its bands giving forth a "continual ring of music" the presidential party appeared on the platform. Lincoln had been busy all morning as well as the previous evening signing bills, and consequently had not ridden in the parade. Then he had gone to the brief—but embarrassing—ceremony for the swearing in of Vice-President Johnson. As he reached the platform outside, the familiar notes of "Hail to the Chief!" filled the air. Cannon roared and the audience cheered.

The President read his address, which sounded more like a sermon than a state paper, and took the oath of office. There were more salutes, cheers, and music. The procession formed, this time with Lincoln and Tad and Senator Foster riding in a carriage, and headed for the White House. The sun had come out and this was considered a good omen.[17]

At the reception that evening an estimated six thousand people jammed the White House. Carriages waited one or two hours before their occupants could be admitted; ladies had their clothes torn, some shrieked in pain because of the crowding; several fainted, and one lady had to be passed over the heads of the crowd to get her out where she could be revived. When the doors closed at eleven o'clock many were still left outside.

Very likely the musicians of the Marine Band who had participated in the parade, the inaugural ceremony, and

---

[16] Henry S. Burrage, "Reminiscences of Prison Life at Danville, Virginia," in Military Order of the Loyal Legion of the United States, Maine Commandery, *War Papers* (Portland, 1908), III, 43-60; Small, ed., *Road to Richmond*, p. 177; N.Y. *Times*, Feb. 23, 1865.

[17] Washington *Evening Star*, Mar. 4, 1865; Washington *Sunday Morning Chronicle*, Mar. 5, 1865; N.Y. *Times*, Mar. 5, 1865; Brooks, *Washington in Lincoln's Time*, pp. 238-40.

had then played for the evening reception found the day nearly as strenuous as had the President himself.[18]

The next morning the President was at the Capitol again, this time for the church service. Methodist Bishop Simpson preached. The music included the familiar hymn of Isaac Watts:

> Jesus shall reign where'er the sun
> Does his successive journeys run,

and the less well-known "Come, let us join our cheerful songs" (Tune—"Coronation") :

> Come, let us join our cheerful songs
> With angels round the throne;
> Ten thousand thousand are their tongues,
> But all their joys are one.

The service ended with the Doxology.[19]

Monday, March 6, was about as strenuous a day as President Lincoln ever put in during his years in the White House. Several conferences were scheduled, two formal receptions were held, a formal communication from the Senate received, the matter of the new Secretary of the Treasury was taken up, photographer Henry F. Warren of Waltham, Massachusetts, took the President's picture, and late in the evening the President and his family attended the Inaugural Ball![20]

The committee in charge of the ball, headed by Benjamin B. French, had begun making plans weeks before and its preparations were thorough. Rather than have a hall constructed the committee had decided to hold the ball in the Patent Office Building which was well-suited for such an event.[21]

---

[18] Washington *Sunday Morning Chronicle*, Mar. 5, 1865; Washington *Evening Star*, Mar. 6, 1865; N.Y. *Times*, Mar. 6, 1865; George W. Burnell in *The Daily Northwest*, Dec. 2, 1911 (clipping). It was observed that for the first time Negroes participated in the day's activities. Negro troops, fraternal groups, and a band were in the parade, many were at the inaugural ceremony, and others, including Frederick Douglass, were at the evening reception. Washington *Evening Star*, Mar. 4, 1865; Washington *Sunday Morning Chronicle*, Mar. 5, 1865; N.Y. *Times*, Mar. 5, 6, 1865; Frederick Douglass, in Rice, ed., *Reminiscences of Abraham Lincoln*, pp. 190-93.

[19] Washington *Daily Morning Chronicle*, Mar. 6, 1865.

[20] Powell, ed., *Lincoln Day by Day*, p. 318.

[21] Using the Patent Office Building would also lessen the expense. The commit-

Three connecting halls were used—a center one fifty-eight by two hundred and seventy feet for dancing and longer ones on either side for the promenade and for the supper. In the main hall there were raised seats along the sides for those who did not care for dancing and a raised platform with sofa and chairs of blue and gold for the presidential party.

The decorations, artistically arranged, consisted of flags, banners, pennants, and corps insignia. Countless gas lights provided illumination. The marble tile floor, while not too elastic for dancing, was better than a wooden floor for there was no dust or dirt.

Three bands had been hired, Withers' Band for the dancing (price $1,000), a Hospital Band for the promenade, and the Ninth Veterans' Reserve Corps Band for the supper room. Thus there was provision for continuous music throughout the evening.

By six o'clock the caterer had his tables arranged, his kitchen set up, and vast quantities of food prepared and ready. All day long curious onlookers had watched the wagons of food drive up and unload. More intrigued passersby stopped to listen to the bands as they rehearsed. All was in readiness by nine o'clock.

Guests began to arrive soon after nine and by ten o'clock many dancers and promenaders were on the floor. One admiring observer thought it impossible to do justice in describing the costumes of the ladies, so stylish and elegant were they. He noted that light lilac or pearl silks seemed to predominate, flowers and curls were much in vogue, and that many ladies had powdered their hair with silver or golden powder.

Another critic commented that "sensible high-necked dresses" predominated with only an occasional one that was "shockingly décolletée." A few costumes, he thought, were too ornate, like that of a Spanish lady whose dress was of gold cloth with raised crimson velvet flowers and

tee allocated $5,000 for the supper and $1,300 for music. Any surplus was to be used for the families of soldiers. N.Y. *Times*, Feb. 22, 1865. The description of the ball is based upon accounts in the Washington *Evening Star*, Mar. 2, 3, 6, 7, 1865; Washington *Daily Morning Chronicle*, Mar. 3, 7, 1865; N.Y. *Times*, Mar. 7, 8, 1865.

who wore a headdress made up of a velvet band with five or six enormous diamonds. On the other hand he commended those ladies who had dispensed with hoops ". . . thereby displaying their good taste as well as their regard for the appreciation of some approximation to the female form which still inheres or lingers in the mind of man. . . ."

Still another onlooker, after describing the ladies' beautiful costumes in detail, concluded that New York led in display, but Philadelphia and Washington led in beauty. With his general summation there was hearty agreement on all sides: ". . . the *coup d'oeil* from the elevated seats lining the dancing hall at any time from ten P.M., until daylight, was brilliant in the extreme."[22]

There were twenty-one numbers on the dance program after the "Inaugural March," composed especially for the occasion. The program included quadrilles, lancers, schottisches, waltzes, and polkas. The last number was a Virginia Reel.

About ten-thirty the Withers' Band struck up "Hail to the Chief!" The President's party had arrived, President Lincoln and Speaker Colfax, Senator Sumner and Mrs. Lincoln, Commissioner French and Mr. Clephane, and others. To the strains of the familiar piece the party promenaded the full length of the hall to the raised platform.

Mrs. Lincoln wore a dress of white silk, cut low, with point lace and puffs of silk, and a necklace, bracelet, and earrings of pearl. She carried a white fan trimmed with ermine and silver spangles. On her head she wore a wreath of white jasmine and purple violets. She looked well, her toilet was faultless, and her manner easy and affable. She was fully equal to the occasion.

As the band played and the dancers whirled on the dance floor there was a continual crowding of dignitaries around the President and his party. Although there were five hundred dancing and thousands promenading, yet there was plenty of room for all. Among those who

---

[22] Washington *Daily Morning Chronicle*, Mar. 7, 1865; N.Y. *Times*, Mar. 7, 1865; Washington *Evening Star*, Mar. 7, 1865.

danced were Generals Halleck and Hooker, Admiral Farragut, Senator Wilson, and Speaker Colfax.

The supper room, with place settings for three hundred persons, presented a scene of spectacular beauty. Flanking center decorations on the main table of a model of the Capitol and two monuments representing the army and the navy were eight pyramids of nougat, orange, caramel, and other confections. Miniature flags added to the color of the decorations.

Shortly after midnight the presidential party proceeded to the supper room to partake of the bounteous supply of food prepared by the caterer. The President and Mrs. Lincoln stayed only a short time, however, and then quietly left for the White House.[23] It is doubtful that they were able to do justice to the vast numbers of edibles on the extensive menu!

But when the hungry horde of dancers descended upon the supper room the scene was different. In spite of the best efforts of the waiters, the multitude was impatient. Those who could not be seated at the table carried food to the alcoves and corners and set up more intimate small parties. Some ". . . with more audacity than good taste, could be seen snatching whole *pates,* chickens, legs of veal, halves of turkeys, ornamental pyramids, and such from the tables and bearing them aloft over the heads of the shuddering crowd (ladies especially, with greasy ruin to their dresses impending), carry them off in triumph for private delectation." One gentleman looked rather ludicrous holding a large platter of smoked tongue in both hands but finding no place to go or to sit![24]

The floor became somewhat littered and confusion was rampant,[25] but eventually all were satisfied, got their

---

[23] The President had intended to stay about a half an hour. Lincoln, *Works,* VIII, 334. Actually he was there a good two hours.

[24] Washington *Evening Star,* Mar. 7, 1865; N.Y. *Times,* Mar. 8, 1865. The *Times* reporter commented: "The American people, in general, we are ashamed to say, have not yet learned how to behave at table; and that species of etiquette, not too prevalent in private, is certainly always absent at public suppers." However, with only places at table for three hundred, it would have been some time before all four or five thousand present could have been properly served.

[25] There were confusion and excitement in the kitchen also. Cooks swore at each other and one received a dish of chicken salad in the face. The police were called in, the sender of the missile was arrested, fined one dollar by the judge, and given

money's worth, and went back to the dance floor. When the ball ended at daybreak the traffic jam of carriages and hacks was some time in unravelling. But, all in all, the party was a decided success.

One week after the inaugural festivities the President was ill. Apparently exhausted and worn out, he curtailed his schedule although he did attend the opera twice. Consequently when Grant suggested that he visit City Point, the idea appealed to him. On the twenty-third he left the city on the *River Queen* and the next day was already feeling better.[26]

---

a lecture on "the impropriety of his conduct." Washington *Evening Star*, Mar. 7, 1865.

[26] N.Y. *Herald*, Mar. 14, 1865; Washington *Daily Morning Chronicle*, Mar. 15, 1865; Washington *Evening Star*, Mar. 15, 17, 1865; Morse, ed., *Diary of Gideon Welles*, II, 237, 264; Lincoln *Works*, VIII, 367, 372, and n.

CHAPTER XXI

CITY POINT—WASHINGTON—
SPRINGFIELD

THE LONG WAR WAS ALMOST OVER. FOR THAT, LINCOLN was thankful. And yet, after his first week at City Point, he was anxious and at times depressed. On the first day of April he spent hours at the telegraph station eagerly waiting for reports from Grant, and that night he paced the deck of the *River Queen*. There would be more killing, more bloodshed.

The week just past had brought Lincoln closer to the war than he had been in all the four years of conflict. The day after his arrival at City Point he had expressed the desire to see the battlefield and had gone there by special train and on horseback. There he saw the carnage of war; he saw men wounded, dying, and dead. He returned to City Point weary, "haggard and more haggard," so exhausted that he was compelled to refuse Grant's invitation to dine with him. A soldier who saw the President at the review the following day wrote:

> This day I have seen Abraham Lincoln. . . . I can never forget the care-worn face of the noble president as he rode past, while the bands played, "Hail to the Chief."[1]

Conferences at Grant's headquarters occupied much time and twice there were meetings aboard the *River Queen* of the three men from the West, Lincoln, Grant, and Sherman. From his several trips on the river Lincoln learned much and the scenes along the waterfront filled him with interest. But when Sherman left on March

---

[1] Elwin L. Page, *Lincoln on the River Queen: An Address Delivered Before The Joint Convention of the General Court of New Hampshire and His Excellency, the Governor, and the Honorable Council, Feb. 11, 1943* (Manchester [1943]), p. 4; William H. Wharff, Eleventh Maine Infantry, unidentified clipping, Lincoln National Life Foundation.

28 and Grant departed the next morning there was nothing to do except wait. Rain and more rain made the situation more depressing.

By April 1 Mary Lincoln had apparently had enough, for she returned to Washington that day. City Point was not a pleasant place for a lady and the weather made it less so. Moreover, Mary was not well. Her worst day was Sunday, March 26, when she went to the review of General Ord's troops. The going was very rough. The ambulance jounced and bounced and splattered mud in all directions as it lumbered slowly forward. She embarrassed the driver by threatening to get out and walk if he didn't move faster. She berated Mrs. Ord who had ridden beside the President on horseback, and embarrassed everyone present by her sharp words. Mrs. Ord was entirely innocent of having committed any breach of etiquette but Mrs. Lincoln was furious at her.[2]

That evening there was a dinner party on the boat followed by dancing and a good time until midnight. Mrs. Lincoln again caused embarrassment by criticizing both General and Mrs. Ord in the presence of dinner guests. When she went so far as to urge Lincoln to remove General Ord as unfit for his position, mild-mannered General Grant rose to the general's defense.

Mrs. Lincoln likewise complained at the noise the sailors were making and demanded that they cease their festivities, but the President told the men to go ahead and enjoy themselves. He and Grant talked far into the night while the band played and the officers and their ladies danced.[3]

As Lincoln waited, that which he feared and yet ex-

---

[2] John S. Barnes, "With Lincoln from Washington to Richmond in 1865," *Appleton's Magazine*, IX (May, 1907), 522-24; Porter, *Campaigning with Grant*, pp. 412-14; Adam Badeau, *Grant in Peace: From Appomattox to Mount McGregor* (Hartford, 1887), pp. 356-59, 364; Sherman, *Memoirs*, II, 332. Cf. Randall, *Mary Lincoln*, pp. 372-74; and Philip Van Doren Stern, *An End to Valor* (Boston, 1958), pp. 87-88, 92-95. Mrs. Randall emphasizes that Mary Lincoln was a sick woman, both physically and mentally. Upon her arrival in Washington she began to think of returning to City Point. Stern points out that Mrs. Lincoln had been greatly upset the previous day when she misinterpreted a remark of Adam Badeau as indicating that Mrs. Charles Griffin had seen the President alone.

[3] Porter, *Campaigning with Grant*, pp. 415-16; Barnes, *Appleton's Magazine*, IX (May, 1907), 524; unidentified clipping, Lincoln National Life Foundation. When Grant and Sherman went aboard the *River Queen* two days later Mrs. Lincoln could not see them as she was still unwell. Sherman, *Memoirs*, II, 325.

pected, more fighting, had already begun. And with the fighting came more music. At the end of March Union forces moved to Dinwiddie Court House southwest of Petersburg. With his men making temporary camp nearby, General Sheridan established his quarters in a local tavern. It so happened that some young ladies had also recently arrived at the tavern from Charleston and Petersburg. They proved to be very friendly. One evening, after making coffee for Sheridan and his staff, they and the officers gathered around the piano and whiled away the dismal hours in song. Outside it rained in torrents.[4]

General Sheridan was a firm believer in bands and band music in battle. Rather than detach the musicians as stretcher-bearers and hospital orderlies he sent them to the firing line to encourage the men with their stirring tunes. Thus as his men moved out into a sea of mud on the last day of March the bands were ordered to play without stopping. Play, the musicians did, and amid the crack of rifles and the din of battle could be heard "Hail, Columbia," "Lanigan's Ball," "Johnny Fill Up the Bowl," "Yankee Doodle," and "Hail to the Chief!" Near Five Forks when the Union forces were hard pressed a band played "Nelly Bly" ". . . as cheerfully as if furnishing music for a country picnic." The next day General Pickett's weary and hungry men, cutting trees and digging trenches in a desperate attempt to prevent Sheridan from taking Five Forks, sang "Annie Laurie" and "Dixie" ". . . as if they were banking roses for a festival." During one attack Pickett joined his men in singing "Rally 'Round the Flag, Boys!" The next morning when Pickett thanked his men they responded with cheers and sang one of his favorite hymns:

> Guide me, oh, thou great Jehovah,
> Pilgrim through this barren land.[5]

---

[4] [F. C. Newhall] *With General Sheridan in Lee's Last Campaign* (Phila., 1866), pp. 56, 61; Stern, *End to Valor*, p. 117.

[5] Stern, *End to Valor*, p. 125; Porter, *Campaigning with Grant*, p. 431; Arthur Crew Inman, ed., *Soldier of the South: General Pickett's War Letters to His Wife* (Boston and New York, 1928), pp. 128, 130, 132.

Back at City Point Lincoln could only hear the click of the telegraph but that soon became music to his ears.

At eleven o'clock on the morning of April 2 Lincoln telegraphed to Stanton: "All going finely." Petersburg was being evacuated. As the Confederates left, some of them sang a Yankee song. By coincidence, colored troops entering that battered city the next morning sang the same song:

> Say, darkies, hab you seen de massa,
>   Wid de muffstash on his face,
> Go long de road some time dis mornin',
>   Like he gwine to leab de place?
> He seen a smoke, way up de ribber,
>   Whar de Linkum gun-boats lay;
> He took his hat, an' lef berry sudden,
>   An' I spec he's run away!
>
> De massa run? ha, ha!
>   De darkey stay? ho, ho!
> It mus' be now de kingdom comin',
>   An' de year ob Jubilo![6]

That same day and hour, Jefferson Davis entered St. Paul's Church in Richmond for Sunday worship. The service began. The choir sang

> Jesus, Lover of my soul,
> Let me to thy bosom fly,
> While the nearer waters roll,
> While the tempest still is high; . . .

A message was handed to Davis and he left the church immediately. Richmond, too, must be evacuated. That evening as the withdrawal went on apace, bands covered the retreat with a concert. Federal bands answered and ". . . the night air was filled with melodious strains, conflicting somewhat, however, in their political significance."[7]

Early the following morning Lincoln went out to

---

[6] Lincoln, *Works*, VIII, 382; Rembert W. Patrick, *The Fall of Richmond* (Baton Rouge, 1960), p. 15; *Green Mountain Freeman* (Montpelier, Vt.), Apr. 18, 1865. Patrick gives a somewhat different wording of the song.

[7] Washington *Evening Star*, Apr. 5, 1865; Patrick, *Fall of Richmond*, pp. 17-18, 36, 64.

Petersburg. He wanted to see the city and confer with
Grant. His presence there brought cheers from the sol-
diers. Bands played and troops passing through sang
"We Are Coming, Father Abraham" and "Red, White and
Blue." Pleased though he was, Lincoln was under great
strain. A reporter noted:

> Perhaps I was mistaken, but the lines upon his face seemed
> far deeper than I had ever seen them before. There was no
> sign of exultation in his demeanor. He mounted a horse,
> and under a small cavalry escort rode through the town.[8]

Meanwhile, Federal troops were moving into Richmond,
which had been officially surrendered to them by the
mayor. With flags flying they marched as bands played
"Yankee Doodle," "John Brown's Body," and "Rally
'Round the Flag." Colored troops sang "John Brown's
Body" and "Kingdom Coming" with gusto. As the Stars
and Stripes were raised on the Capitol the bands played
the "Star-Spangled Banner."[9]

The devastated city was well under control when Lincoln visited it the next day. The Negroes greeted him
with tumultuous rapture. They shouted, they danced,
they crowded around him, and those who saw him first
broke into song—

> Oh, all ye people clap your hands,
>   And with triumphant voices sing;
> No force the mighty power withstands
>   Of God, the universal King.[10]

White citizens, for the most part, remained indoors.
They were fearful, distraught, and their city was in ruins.
There was an "oppressive silence" as Lincoln went
through their part of town. One woman commented:

> Mr. Lincoln has visited our devoted city today. His recep-

---

[8] Lincoln, *Works*, VIII, 384-85; Ulysses S. Grant, *Personal Memoirs of U. S.
Grant* (N.Y., 1886), II, 458-61; Brooklyn *Daily Eagle*, Feb. 10, 1918; Charles Carlton Coffin, in Rice, ed., *Reminiscences of Abraham Lincoln*, p. 178.

[9] Coffin, *Boys of '61*, p. 507; Adam Badeau, *Military History of Ulysses S. Grant,
from April, 1861, to April, 1865* (N.Y., 1881), III, 543; N.Y. *Tribune*, Apr. 6, 1865;
Patrick, *Fall of Richmond*, pp. 66-69; Stern, *End to Valor*, pp. 186-87.

[10] David D. Porter, "President Lincoln's Entry into Richmond," *Belford's Magazine*, V (Sept., 1890), 591.

tion was anything but complimentary. Our people were in nothing rude or disrespectful; they only kept themselves away from a scene so painful.

Another Richmond lady remarked that there was no "assimilation" between invaders and invaded. When the military bands began giving concerts at the old Capitol Negroes went to them in large numbers, but no whites attended, especially ladies. The concerts were discontinued.

On the other hand, a soldier from New Hampshire saw it differently:

> But it was not the colored population alone which welcomed the Union troops and their great commander-in-chief into the city of Richmond. Thousands of white citizens were glad to be again under the protection of the flag of their fathers; and some, who had been true to it from the first, keeping it safely hidden away as a sacred emblem of their loyalty, were more happy, if possible, though less demonstrative, than the negro, as they once more were allowed the privilege of spreading its bright folds to the free air of heaven.[11]

There was no untoward incident while Lincoln was in the city, but his visit was a risky thing for him to undertake, and evidently he recognized its seriousness. The reporter who had seen him in Petersburg the day before wrote: "There was no smile upon his face. Paler than ever his countenance, deeper than ever before the lines upon his forehead."[12]

The news of the fall of Richmond touched off spontaneous celebrations everywhere. In Washington cannon salutes by the hundreds announced it. Church bells rang, fire engines paraded, government employees, off for the rest of the day, sang "John Brown" and "Year of Jubilo," schoolchildren were dismissed, and people paraded and

---

[11] Judith Brockenbrough McGuire and Phoebe Yates Pember, in Katharine M. Jones, *Heroines of Dixie* (Indianapolis, New York, 1955), pp. 395, 399; A. W. Bartlett, in Paul M. Angle and Earl Schenck Miers, eds., *Tragic Years 1860-1865*, II, 1023.

[12] Charles Carlton Coffin in Rice, ed., *Reminiscences of Abraham Lincoln*, p. 183. Actually, Generals Weitzel and Shepley had done a remarkable job in putting out fires, rounding up plunderers, restoring order, clearing away rubbish and feeding thousands of needy people. Even bitter whites were surprised at the efficiency and decency of the Union troops. Patrick, *Fall of Richmond*, pp. 71-75, 98 ff.

bands played—even "Dixie." Benjamin B. French found himself caught up in the excitement as he left his house:

> On getting into the street [he wrote] I found the population apparently half crazy. Women were on the balconies and at windows waving flags, men were shouting and shaking hands and running to and fro; speeches were being made, cannons fired, bands of music moving about playing "Yankee Doodle," and I immediately found myself marching involuntarily to the music.[13]

Far into the night the celebration continued and on the following day people busied themselves in preparing for a monster illumination. When evening came the lights went on. Bands and serenaders roamed the streets. The White House was illuminated and at the Patent Office a huge crowd gathered for music and speeches.[14]

In Philadelphia bells rang, parades were formed, crowds gathered and sang the Doxology. The day ended with ". . . the utter exhaustion of the happy people. . . ." In New York there was so much excitement little work was done. People gathered in groups singing "John Brown," the "Star-Spangled Banner," and "Rally 'Round the Flag." At the Customs House ten thousand assembled, listened to speeches, and sang the Doxology. In Boston the legislature met, adjourned and sang the Doxology. A Vermont newspaper summarized the situation accurately when it said:

> It was, from one end of the national domain to the other, a spontaneous, irrepressible jubilant outpouring of the gladness of a demonstrative people; and the third and tenth of April 1865 will stand hereafter in our calendar as days when a whole nation, by the inspiration of the mighty achievements of its heroic men, blossomed with flags, resounded with the glad chimes of happy bells, and broke into shouting and singing paeans of deliverance and victory.[15]

---

[13] French, ed., *Diary of B. B. French*, p. 130.

[14] Washington *Evening Star*, Apr. 4, 5, 1865; Brooks, *Washington in Lincoln's Time*, pp. 244-49. Wrote Secretary of the Navy Welles: ". . . the city has been in an uproar through the day. . . . Washington appeared patriotic beyond anything ever before witnessed." Morse, ed., *Diary of Gideon Welles*, II, 272-73. Because of the absence of celebrating employees Welles stayed at his desk until after three o'clock.

[15] Washington *Evening Star*, Apr. 4, 1865; Taylor, *Philadelphia in the Civil War*, p. 310; *Green Mountain Freeman* (Montpelier, Vt.), Apr. 18, 1865; Allan Nevins, ed., *Diary of the Civil War 1860-1865: George Templeton Strong* (N.Y., 1962), pp. 574-75.

Events moved rapidly the next few days. Lincoln, still anxious for Grant, reviewed more troops and visited the hospitals.[16] To the west Union forces pressed ever closer on Lee. At Amelia Springs they were so close that the Confederates could hear Sheridan's bands playing "Annie Laurie" and "Home, Sweet Home." At Farmville tired Union soldiers brightened when they saw Grant on the piazza of the local hotel. By the light of bonfires and torches they paraded through the town and off into the night hurrahing, shouting, and singing "John Brown's Body."[17]

That same evening at a patriotic meeting way up in Springfield, Massachusetts, excited citizens sang "America," "Viva L'America," and, with great enthusiasm, "John Brown's Body." When an effigy of Jefferson Davis was brought in they made the hall ring with "We'll hang Jeff Davis to a sour apple tree."[18]

Lincoln made ready to leave City Point. He seemed in better health and was brighter and more cheerful. Just before the *River Queen* set sail a band arrived for a farewell serenade. Lincoln asked for two of his favorite pieces. First he requested the band to play the "Marseillaise"—twice—in honor of the Marquis de Chambrun who had come down with Mrs. Lincoln on her second visit to City Point. He then asked for "Dixie." Somewhat startled, the musicians complied. It was about eleven o'clock when the *River Queen* left for Washington.[19]

---

[16] On one occasion when those in charge wanted to show him the equipment and arrangements of a hospital, Lincoln said: "Gentlemen, you know better than I *how to conduct* these hospitals, but I came here to take by the hand the men who have achieved our glorious victories." He then proceeded to visit the men in the wards. Jaquette, *South After Gettysburg*, p. 179.

[17] Stern, *End to Valor*, p. 218; Porter, *Campaigning with Grant*, pp. 458-59. Grant was not musical. He rarely kept in step to the music of the band. He did not care for music while eating and once hurt a bandmaster's feelings by ordering him to stop playing during dinner. He was not fond of dancing either. Porter, pp. 15, 234-35, 393-94. But doubtless he appreciated the spirit of the troops at Farmville when they sang "John Brown."

[18] Springfield (Mass.) *Daily Republican*, Apr. 8, 1865. The citizens of Springfield probably sang about Davis with less personal feeling than the men and boys who paraded the streets of Richmond a few days before singing that same "We'll Hang Jeff Davis to a Sour Apple Tree." In Richmond feeling against Davis was intensifying those first days after the city fell. Patrick, *Fall of Richmond*, p. 112.

[19] Washington *Evening Star*, Apr. 10, 1864; Elihu B. Washburne, in Rice, ed., *Reminiscences of Abraham Lincoln*, pp. 43-44: Marquis Adolphe de Chambrun, *Impressions of Lincoln and the Civil War; A Foreigner's Account* (N.Y., 1952), p. 82. Washburne found the President "in perfect health and in excellent spirits," full of anecdotes and stories. On the morning of April 8 he was "erect

April 9, 1865, was Palm Sunday. As the *River Queen* steamed up the bay Lincoln read and discussed Shakespeare, especially *Hamlet*. Out around the little village of Appomattox Court House two armies, the Blue and the Gray, waited in silence. As Grant approached the McLean house a Union band struck up a tune that must have affected the emotions of men in both armies. It was "Auld Lang Syne." After the brief formalities the bands played again—the "Marseillaise," the "Star-Spangled Banner," "The Flag of Our Union" and "Dixie."[20]

That evening around the campfires the men of both armies who had swapped souvenirs and stories during the day now shared the same food, supplied by the men in blue. Finally "taps" was sounded for the last time. A gentle rain began to fall and as darkness came one of Sheridan's bands played that most nostalgic of pieces, "Home, Sweet Home." Over at Richmond where a Yankee band was celebrating, the people of the city still could not believe that it was all over.[21]

The next morning the city of Washington was once again awakened by the booming of cannon. People poured into the streets, and learning what had taken place at Appomattox, took on the holiday spirit at once. All day long it was so; bands played, and the air was full of "Rally 'Round the Flag," the "Battle Hymn of the Republic" and "Kingdom Coming."

Three times Lincoln greeted crowds of serenaders. About breakfast time employees of the Treasury Department, after milling about singing "Old Hundred," proceeded to the White House. A band played the "Star-Spangled Banner."

Meanwhile, another and larger crowd led by Navy Yard

---

and buoyant," and looked "great and grand." Lincoln remarked to de Chambrun that he had to come to America to hear the "Marseillaise." The piece was very popular in this country and was frequently heard in Washington and elsewhere. Lincoln on more than one occasion before had requested it. "Dixie," on the other hand, while not exactly "proscribed" in Washington was rarely heard during the war, and then only when sung by "secessionist sympathizers."

[20] de Chambrun, *Impressions of Lincoln*, p. 83; Bruce Catton, *A Stillness at Appomattox* (N.Y., 1958), p. 425; Chicago *Post*, Apr. 18, 1865; Toronto *Daily Leader*, Apr. 18, 1865.

[21] Stern, *End to Valor*, p. 279; Alfred Hoyt Bill, *The Beleaguered City: Richmond, 1861-1865* (N.Y., 1946), p. 284.

employees, singing and firing several howitzers along the way, reached the White House. The crowd filled the grounds and spilled out onto the Avenue. Three or four bands played while the multitude waited for the President. Tad appeared and everyone roared as he waved a Confederate flag. When Lincoln came out people ". . . fairly yelled with delight, threw up their hats again and again, or threw up one another's hats, and screamed like mad." A band struck up "America" and everybody sang.

Once the crowd quieted down Lincoln spoke. He declined to make a formal speech until later, explaining that ". . . I shall have nothing to say then if it is all dribbled out of me now." Turning to a band nearby he asked it to play the tune which was captured on April 9 and was now our "lawful property," adding, "I have always thought 'Dixie' one of the best tunes I have ever heard." The band played "Dixie" and added "Yankee Doodle" for good measure. Lincoln led in three cheers for Grant, for the army and navy, and the crowd dispersed. To the third set of serenaders who arrived about five thirty in the afternoon he said that he would make some remarks at a meeting which was being arranged for the next evening.[22]

The evening of April 11 was moist and misty, giving a peculiar glow to the illuminated city. In the glow the Capitol dome could be seen for miles. Across the river in Arlington the Lee mansion shone with lights. On the lawn were more lights and occasionally a rocket shot skyward. Thousands of ex-slaves moved about singing "Year of Jubilo."

The crowd on the White House lawn was tremendous. The air was full of waving banners, cheers, and music. When Lincoln appeared the cheers went on for some time before he was able to speak. "There was something terrible in the enthusiasm with which the beloved Chief Magistrate was received," thought Noah Brooks.

[22] Brooks, *Washington in Lincoln's Time*, p. 250-52; N.Y. *Herald*, Apr. 11, 1865; N.Y. *Times*, Apr. 11, 1865; Sacramento *Daily Union*, May 8, 1865; Morse, ed., *Diary of Gideon Welles*, II, 278; Lincoln, *Works*, VIII, 393-94; King, *Mag. of Amer. Hist.*, XVI (Sept., 1886), 254-57. Lincoln was "radiant with happinesss" and "positively handsome" when he appeared before the crowd. William E. Doster, *Lincoln and Episodes of the Civil War* (New York and London, 1915), p. 16.

Brooks held a light as Lincoln read his carefully written out remarks. Tad scurried to pick up the sheets of paper as the President dropped them aside. The speech was longer than usual and was not what the people, listening intently, anticipated. They had expected a victory speech. Instead, Lincoln spoke of the problems ahead, complex problems that would be all the more difficult because of the residue of war-engendered feeling in both North and South; because of the "terrible enthusiasm" that was so evident to Noah Brooks, and because of the utterance of the phrase "Hang them!" in the crowd; also because of the reactions like that of a lady in Richmond who, in response to a courteous offer of assistance from a Federal officer, replied, "I wish all Yankees were in hell," or like that of the girl who was taught never to swear, but if she had to, should say "God damn all Yankees to Hell!"

When the President had finished, Senator Harlan spoke briefly. A band struck up "Rally 'Round the Flag." The mist turned to rain and the somewhat disappointed crowd melted away. Lincoln had made his last public address.[23]

While Washingtonians listened to the President's carefully planned speech some of the boys in Sherman's army were having "a great blow out." News of Lee's surrender had just reached them. The general in charge set up a punch bowl and invited all to partake, including the band.

They played once or twice, drank some, played some more, then drank some more of that never ending supply of punch, then they played again but did not keep very good time. Some of them could not wait till they got through with a tune till they had to pledge Grant and his gallant Army, also Lee and his grand fighters. Some of them seemed to think prehaps [sic] that was going a little too far but it passed. The Band finaly [sic] got so they were trying to play two or three tunes at once.

Then the music ceased. The musicians were tired. Whereupon, the general and officers relieved them:

[23] Washington *Daily Morning Chronicle*, Apr. 12, 1865; Washington *Evening Star*, Apr. 12, 1865; N.Y. *Herald*, Apr. 12, 1865; N.Y. *Times*, Apr. 12, 1865; Brooks, *Washington in Lincoln's Time*, pp. 252-57; Lincoln, *Works*, VIII, 399-405; Bill, *The Beleaguered City*, p. 282.

> He [the general] got the big drum, other officers took the
> various horns and started on a tour through the camps—
> evry [sic] fellow blowing his horn to suit himself and the
> jolly old General pounding the bass drum for all it was worth.
> Of course we all followed and some sang, or tried to sing, but
> when "Johnny Comes Marching Home Again" and "John
> Browns Body" or "Hail Columbia" and the "Star Spangled
> Banner" are all sung together they get mixed so I dont realy
> [sic] think the singing was a grand success from an artistic
> stand point at least. But it answered the purpose and let out
> a lot of pent up exuberant feeling that had to have an outlet.

Sober New Yorkers to the number of perhaps one
thousand, not being under quite such a strain, crowded
Trinity Church earlier that day for a service of thanksgiving. The minister delivered a short sermon on for-
giveness and charity and praised Abraham Lincoln as
"wise, merciful, resolute, Christian," the choir sang
"Gloria in excelsis," and the organ played the "Hallelujah
Chorus," "Hail, Columbia," and the "Star-Spangled Banner" *fortissimo.*[24]

As celebrators continued to celebrate attention was
drawn to Charleston, South Carolina, where ceremonies
of symbolic and psychological importance were scheduled
for April 14. There, after a night of band concerts and
dancing in celebration of Lee's surrender, Northern dignitaries and visitors gathered at the battery that warm,
sunny morning to be transported to Fort Sumter.

All morning small boats plied back and forth carrying
people out to the fort. Ships in the harbor were gaily
decorated for the occasion. Finally, as some three thousand people crowded into the ruined fort, the ceremonies
began. Bands played and a chorus sang "Victory at Last!"

> For many years we've waited
> To hail the day of peace,
> When our land shall be united
> And war and strife shall cease!

Amid cheers General Robert Anderson raised aloft the

---

[24] Oscar Osburn Winther, ed., *With Sherman to the Sea; The Civil War Letters,
Diaries & Reminiscences of Theodore F. Upson* (Bloomington, 1958), pp. 164-66;
Nevins, ed., *Diary of the Civil War*, pp. 580-81.

same flag that had been lowered four years before. The thrilled multitude sang the "Star-Spangled Banner" and warships and forts answered with booming cannon fire. Rev. Henry Ward Beecher made an overlong oration and the audience joined in singing the Doxology. It was a memorable occasion.

In the evening there were fireworks from the ships in the harbor. General Gillmore gave a big party at the Charleston Hotel in honor of his guests of the day. There were many speeches. When his turn came, General Anderson, a modest man, not given to lengthy talk, offered a short but sincere toast to ". . . the good, the great, the honest man, Abraham Lincoln." Abraham Lincoln was at that time enjoying "Our American Cousin" at Ford's Theatre.[25]

Laura Keene was nervous and tense; William Withers was irritated and annoyed. The leading actress in "Our American Cousin" was feeling the strain of playing before the President. She wanted to do her best and feared that she might make a slip.

Director Withers had been on the alert. When the presidential party entered the theatre about eight thirty his orchestra promptly struck up "Hail to the Chief!" The excited audience arose, applauded, and waved handkerchiefs. The President bowed. Soon everyone settled back to watch the play. Withers busied himself with preparations for the entr'acte feature:

Patriotic Song and Chorus
"Honor to Our Soldiers"
Honor to our soldiers,
Our nation's greatest pride,
Who, neath our starry Banner's folds,
Have fought, have bled and died;
They're nature's noblest handiwork—
No King so proud as they.
God bless the heroes of the land,
And cheer them on their way.

Words by H. B. Phillips; Music Composed and Arranged by Prof. William Withers, Jr.; Solos by Miss M. Hart, H. B.

[25] Philadelphia *Evening Bulletin*, Apr. 18, 1865; N.Y. *Times*, Apr. 18, 1865; Newark *Advertiser*, Apr. 18. 1865; Boston *Post*, Apr. 19, 1865; W. A. Swanberg, *First Blood; The Story of Fort Sumter* (N.Y., 1957), p. 339.

Phillips and George M. Arth, and the Ladies and Gentlemen of the Company.

The special feature was to be presented, so Withers understood, after the first act. But Miss Keene was not ready. When the second act ended, Withers was again informed that "Honor to Our Soldiers" would have to be deferred. He went out for a drink. During the third act he went backstage and found that Miss Keene was in a state of "nerves." Somewhat disgusted, he agreed that the feature would be presented at the close of the play.

On his way back to the orchestra pit Withers was startled to hear a shot. Almost immediately he was astonished and shaken as John Wilkes Booth, hobbling through the corridor toward the rear door of the theatre, lunged at him and knocked him down.

Thus it was that "Honor to Our Soldiers" was not sung that night. Lincoln did not hear it, and the piece passed into oblivion.[26]

---

[26] William Withers, Jr., came from a musical family. His father and one of his brothers were musicians. Withers was prominent in musical affairs in Washington during the war. His band and orchestra participated in musical activities, played before President Lincoln more than once, and provided the music for the dancing at the Second Inaugural Ball. He is credited with having taught Tad how to beat the drum.

Like many other orchestra and band leaders Withers also composed. His pieces included: "Canary Bird Waltz," "Livinia Waltz" and "Emma Waltz" ("Two uncommonly agreeable waltzes by a young composer whose name is seen too seldom," said *Dwight's Journal of Music*), "Cricket Polka" ("A bright, chirping little thing: introducing the notes of the Cricket at intervals," reported *Dwight's Journal*), and "Canary Bird and Jeannie—Waltz and Polka" (played at the Second Inaugural Ball).

During his years of retirement Withers lived in New York. He died in 1916.

The special feature "Honor to Our Soldiers" was added to the evening's program of April 14 when it was learned that President Lincoln was expected to be present. It was rehearsed that afternoon. According to Withers it had been done successfully several times before, but it was apparently new to Miss Keene.

The question arises, what was the last music that Lincoln heard? Did the orchestra play after the first and/or second acts while waiting for the actors to appear for "Honor to Our Soldiers?" If it did not, then Lincoln's last music was that time-honored piece that he heard at his first serenade in February, 1861, and countless times thereafter, "Hail to the Chief!"

The orchestra did play before the curtain went up, and it was customary to have music during intermissions. Withers stated many years later that when Miss Keene did not appear for the special feature the manager asked him to play his "extra act" music. N.Y. *Sun*, Feb. 11, 1917. An earlier account has Withers starting the first few measures of "Honor to Our Soldiers" and then after learning that Miss Keene was not ready, has the orchestra playing its intermission selections. [William Withers, Jr. (interview)] "The Man Who Saw Lincoln Shot," *Broadway Magazine* (May, 1904), pp. 117-22. Other accounts make no mention of it. Cf., Pawtucket (R. I.), *Evening Times*, Feb. 12, 1909, and William A. Crofutt, "Lincoln's Washington: Recollections of a Journalist Who Knew Everybody," *The Atlantic Monthly*, CXLV (Jan., 1930), 65. These accounts contain numerous inaccuracies and may be considered unreliable as to details.

No contemporary evidence has been discovered that would indicate that there was music after the first act. Withers waited in vain for Miss Keene and the cast to appear for the singing of the song. After the second act Withers, actor

As the news of Lincoln's assassination spread people everywhere were shocked and stunned. Benjamin B. French, who returned from a trip to City Point and Richmond the evening of April 14, wrote:

> We went to bed at 10, to be awakened on Saturday morning by the awful annunciation that the President was assassinated and Secy. Seward's throat 'cut from ear to ear.' Perhaps you can imagine how we felt. I thought I should suffocate, it had such an effect on me.[27]

An onlooker who chanced to see Lincoln's remains being borne from the Peterson House to the White House remarked:

> I was standing at the corner of 15th Street and Pennsylvania Avenue, near my law office, and saw the hearse pass with a white sheet and flag thrown over the body. And never before or since have I heard a crowd as that was, composed mostly of negroes, men and women, utter so loud and piercing a wail as those mourners uttered, when the body passed close to them.[28]

A famous folk-artist, Grandma Moses, recalled years later that as a little girl of four and a half years she was on a buggy trip to see her grandmother that April morning. As they came to a town her mother noticed that everything was trimmed with black and wondered why. As she remembered it—

John Dyott, and two employees of the theatre went to the restaurant next door for a drink. Testimony of Louis Carland, costumer, at the Surratt Trial. *Trial of John H. Surratt in the Criminal Court for the District of Columbia, Hon. George P. Fisher Presiding* (Washington, 1867), I, 571. Withers made no mention of this in his later statements. At the conspiracy trial he testified only that he went backstage to see the manager about the song and that he heard the shot on the way back. Benn Pitman, comp., *The Assassination of President Lincoln and the Trial of the Conspirators* (Cincinnati, 1865), pp. 79, 104; Ben: Perley Poore, *The Conspiracy Trial* (Boston, 1865), I, 198-99. Scipiano Grillo, one of the musicians, testified that he was in the orchestra between the first and second acts, but that during the third act "we had nothing to do" so he left and went to the restaurant. *Trial of John H. Surratt*, I, 177. It can hardly be inferred from this that the orchestra played after the first act, however. Further, none of the many "Recollections" thus far seen of persons who were present in the theatre that evening mentions music between the acts, but practically all mention "Hail to the Chief!" It seems unlikely that someone would not have recollected such music if it had been played, even in the excitement of the assassination.

All the evidence thus considered, it seems reasonable to conclude that there was no music during the intermissions and that "Hail to the Chief!" was the last music that Lincoln heard that night at Ford's Theatre.

[27] Benjamin B. French to Pamela French, May 21, 1865, B. B. French Papers.

[28] Doster, *Lincoln and Episodes of the Civil War*, p. 36. Secretary Welles noted that the Negroes, gathered in large numbers all that rainy day, were overwhelmed with grief, weeping and wailing the loss. Morse, ed., *Diary of Gideon Welles*, II, 288, 290, 293.

> It was war times, and we got down in the middle of Cambridge [New York], and she went into the store and asked what had happened. The pillars on the store were all wrapped in black bunting. And this man told her that President Lincoln was shot the night before. And I remember her coming back to the buggy, and she said . . . "Oh, what will become of us now?" And if she hadn't used those words, I don't suppose I would have ever remembered it.[29]

The impact of the shocking news on the town of Hillsdale, Michigan, was perhaps typical of what happened in many parts of the country. The day and evening of April 14 had been spent in celebrating the raising of the flag over Fort Sumter. Everyone was gay.

> The news of the assassination and death of President Lincoln was received here on Saturday morning by telegraph and the revlusion of feeling was sudden and terrible. Yesterday everyone was rejoicing, and last night the whole town was illuminated; today the same buildings are draped in mourning and the people go about the streets with tearful eyes, and talk in suppressed and sad voices—the bells are tolling and the flags are draped with crape.[30]

It was the same in the army. The band of the One Hundred and Fourteeth Pennsylvania Regiment was marching along toward Burkesville in Virginia when the news came. It was not believed at first, but soon was accepted as true. As the bands played dirges, gloom spread throughout the ranks. Men were sorrowful, dismayed, and the atmosphere was filled with "curses of hate and . . . hisses of scorn."[31]

At Murfreesboro a jubilation parade was in full swing. The troops were in fine spirits and everyone was feeling good. The band was playing "The Girl I Left Behind Me." Suddenly it stopped in the middle of the piece as a solemn-looking orderly rode up with a message. An officer read the news that Lincoln was dead. That ended the parade. "Without a word . . . we reversed arms and marched back, the band playing a dirge."[32]

---

[29] Otto Kallir, ed., *Grandma Moses: My Life's History* (N.Y., 1952), pp. 18-19.

[30] Detroit *Advertiser*, Apr. 18, 1865.

[31] Rauscher. *Music on the March*, p. 246.

[32] Osborn H. Oldroyd, *An Interview with Osborn H. Oldroyd* (N.Y., n.d.), pp. 4-5.

The emotional plunge from the joyous heights of victory and peace to the gloomy depths of dismay and sorrow was both manifested and reflected in an outpouring of funeral music—dirges, marches, and hymns. Composers, professional and amateur, who had already given forth hundreds of war pieces now concentrated on the single theme, the death of the martyr President.

There was no music at the White House service or at the brief ceremony at the Capitol. A singular omission, thought some. But as the funeral procession left the presidential mansion to go to the Capitol church bells were tolled and minute guns fired. The many bands in the line of march filled the air with sad melodies and dirges. Near the head of the procession marched the Marine Band and a Drum Corps led by Bandmaster Scala. The Marine Band had played for Lincoln more often than any other musical outfit. As the solemn cortege moved slowly along Pennsylvania Avenue it played a funeral march composed especially for the occasion by General J. G. Barnard.[33]

As the Lincoln funeral train moved slowly toward Springfield there was a mingling of the new and unfamiliar music with the old and familiar; music which expressed the deep-down feelings of a people in mourning. Early on the morning of April 24 the funeral train reached Jersey City. As Lincoln's remains were transferred to a ferry for the crossing of the Hudson River to New York, musical clubs two hundred strong sang hymns and dirges. Many people wept. That night one thousand singers were to chant solemn music as Lincoln lay in state in the City Hall. Far away to the southwest on the waters of the Pacific Ocean a small group of people gathered that same day in the cabin of a ship bound for San Francisco to pay tribute to the dead President. News of the assassination had been received the day before from a passing ship outward bound from San Fran-

---

[33] Sacramento *Daily Union*, May 19, 1865; Boston *Globe*, Feb. 12, 1909; Washington *Evening Star*, Apr. 20, 1865. General Barnard, a career soldier, engineer, author of many works on scientific subjects, was also a real music lover and composer.

cisco. The famous virtuoso Louis M. Gottschalk, a passenger on board, described the scene:

> The sky is blue, the sun resplendent, the sea is calm, all nature seems to smile above our heads, to render the contrast of our grief more striking with the stillness of all that surrounds us. Strange and inexplicable thing!! The woman are those who show the least regrets. Around me rude figures of the seamen leave the badly effaced traces of their tears to be seen. A judge, sitting in a corner, his head in his hands, weeps as if he had just lost a father. All the men seemed crushed, overwhelmed under the weight of an incommensurable grief. The women, after having shed some contagious tears, begin to make common conjectures about the motives of the assassin, and the means employed by him.

The memorial service was brief and simple. Some Italian singers sang the "Battle Hymn of the Republic" accompanied on the piano by Gottschalk. Adelaide Phillips, the popular operatic star, sang the "Star-Spangled Banner." Gottschalk then played his "Union."

Still pondering, Gottschalk recorded some thoughts that were both understanding and discerning:

> Where are now those frivolous judgments on the man whom we are weeping for today? His ugliness, his awkwardness, his jokes, with which we reproached him: all have disappeared in presence of the majesty of death. His greatness, his honesty, the purity of that great heart, which beats no longer, rise up to-day, and in their resplendent radiancy transfigure him whom we called the "common rail-splitter." . . . Yesterday his detractors were ridiculing his large hands without gloves, his large feet, his bluntness; to-day this type which we found grotesque appears to us on the threshold of immortality, and we understand by the universality of our grief what future generations will see in him.[34]

A week passed. The funeral train reached Chicago. Choral groups sang almost continuously while Lincoln's body lay in state. There were selections from the oratorio *St. Paul*, "Happy and blessed are they," and "Into thy hands I commit myself," and "He that shall endure to

---

[34] Washington *Evening Star*, Apr. 25, 1865; Gottschalk, *Notes of a Pianist*, pp. 359-61. Adelaide Phillips, with Isabelle Hinckley, sang the "Star-Spangled Banner" during the intermission when Lincoln attended his first opera, February 20, 1861, in New York.

the end" from *Elijah*. For the first time George F. Root's funeral tribute was heard. Just as his war songs were among the most popular, so his "Farewell Father, Friend and Guardian" became the best known of the funeral pieces.

> All our land is draped in mourning,
>   Hearts are bowed and strong men weep,
> For our loved, our noble leader
>   Sleeps his last, his dreamless sleep.
> Gone forever, gone forever,
>   Fallen by a traitor's hand,
> Though preserved, his dearest treasure,
>   Our redeemed beloved land.
>
> Chorus:
> Farewell Father, Friend and guardian,
>   Thou has joined the martyr's band;
> But thy glorious work remaineth,
>   Our redeemed, beloved land.

Leading vocalists and opera stars then in the city gave their services in the musical programs. Clara Louise Kellogg who was in Chicago at the time did not remember the music, but did recall vividly other sounds:

> But I think, of all the many diverse impressions which that spring made upon my memory, the one that I still carry with me most unforgettably, is a *sound*:—the sound of those shuffling feet, shuffle, shuffle, shuffle,—in the Court House grounds in Chicago: a sound like a great sea or forest in a wind as the people of the nation went in to look at their President whom they loved and who was dead.[35]

The final services at Springfield included some old and some new music. As the casket was brought out of the State House at noon on May 4, a chorus of 250 voices sang the eighteenth-century hymn:

> Children of the heavenly King,
> As ye journey, sweetly sing;
> Sing your Saviour's worthy praise,
> Glorious in his works and ways.

[35] *Illinois State Journal* (Springfield), May 2, 1865; Washington *Daily Morning Chronicle*, May 4, 1865; unidentified clipping, F. Lauriston Bullard Collection, Boston University; Clara Louise Kellogg, *Memoirs of an American Prima Donna* (New York and London, 1913), pp. 112, 118.

Lift your eyes, ye sons of light,
Zion's city is in sight;
There our endless home shall be,
There our Lord we soon shall see.

In the procession from the railroad station to the State House and later to the cemetery was the band of the One Hundred and Forty-Sixth Volunteer Regiment led by Captain Wilbur F. Heath. Captain Heath composed an appropriate dirge when he heard the news of the assassination. It was played on this occasion and then locked up. Only once was it brought out and used again. In observance of the death of another assassinated President, William McKinley, it was played at the Soldiers' Home in Danville, Illinois.[36]

The service at Oak Ridge Cemetery included six musical selections, opening with the "Dead March in Saul" from Handel's oratorio. After the prayer Root's "Farewell Father, Friend and Guardian" was sung. The scripture reading was followed by "To Thee, O Lord," from *St. Paul*.[37] There were dirges sung before and after Bishop Simpson's oration and a final hymn just before the benediction.[38]

No person was more eminently fitted to conclude the service than Dr. Phineas D. Gurley, minister of the New York Avenue Presbyterian Church in Washington. As minister and friend of the Lincolns Dr. Gurley was at the bedside during Lincoln's last hours. Later he comforted the distraught Mary Lincoln. The service at his church on Sunday, April 16, was impressive and appropriate. Noah Brooks who was present described it for his readers:

> The church was draped in mourning, and the well-known pew of the Lincoln family, vacant and robed in sable crape, spoke mutely to the great congregation of him that was gone. The dirge-like music, the earnest and solemn lesson inculcated by

---

[36] N.Y. *Tribune*, May 5, 1865; *Illinois State Register* (Springfield), Feb. 12, 1909; *Lincoln Lore* No. 99 (Mar. 2, 1931).

[37] The "Dead March in Saul" was widely known. "To Thee, O Lord," and "Happy and blessed are they" which was sung at Chicago, were both sung at the funeral of the composer of *St. Paul*, Felix Mendelssohn, some eighteen years earlier.

[38] *Illinois State Journal* (Springfield), May 3, 5, 1865.

the preacher, all made the service one which will be long remembered by those who heard it.[39]

Dr. Gurley gave the funeral sermon at the White House service on April 19 and offered the prayer on the morning of April 21 just before the long journey to Illinois. On the trip west Dr. Gurley wrote a hymn. It was this hymn that was sung just before the good minister pronounced the benediction over his friend in Oak Ridge Cemetery.

Rest, noble Martyr! rest in peace;
    Rest with the true and brave,
Who, like thee, fell in Freedom's cause,
    The nation's life to save.

Thy name shall live while time endures,
    And men shall say of thee,
"He saved his country from its foes,
    And bade the slave be free."

These deeds shall be thy monument,
    Better than brass or stone;
They leave thy fame in glory's light,
    Unrival'd and alone.

This consecrated spot shall be
    To Freedom ever dear;
And Freedom's son of every race
    Shall weep and worship here.

O God! before whom we, in tears,
    Our fallen Chief deplore;
Grant that the cause, for which he died,
    May live forever more.

Doxology.

To Father, Son and Holy Ghost,
    The God whom we adore,
Be glory as it was, is now,
    And shall be evermore.

---

[39] Sacramento *Daily Union*, May 17, 1865.

EPILOGUE

DURING THE FOUR LONG YEARS OF FRATRICIDAL STRIFE IN which the nation was called upon to make unprecedented effort and appalling sacrifice, music served a dual purpose. It acted as a morale builder and as an emotional outlet. Through their music the people expressed their highest hopes, their pent-up desires, and their deep-seated longings. To their music men and women often turned to relieve the tremendous emotional stresses and strains, the heartaches and heartbreaks of war.

Wherever they were—on the march or in camp, in the hell of battle or in the hush of a hospital tent, at a mighty patriotic meeting in a great city or at a neighborhood gathering on a familiar village green, in a solemn house of worship or in a quiet front parlor—there was music, music that everyone knew, everyone loved, and everyone sang.

There was the song that inspired the highest patriotism, the song that sustained the weary and strengthened the downhearted, the song that gave comfort to the sorrowing and courage to the faltering, the song of humor and the song of fun, and the song that gave hope for the future when the terrible war would be at an end.

Abraham Lincoln, like other Americans of that chaotic time, became absorbed in the music of the war that so well fitted every occasion, every mood. He heard it in the White House, throughout the city, and in many of the "hundred circling camps." He felt its strength and realized its power and influence. More than once he had been thrilled and moved to tears by it. Coming from the hearts of men and women whose lives were torn asunder by war, this music touched the heart of the wartime President time and again.

It did more. It implanted itself in the heart of the nation. Year after year as the veterans who had survived gathered in annual encampments they sang the songs of '61-'65; year after year as men, women, and children assembled on Memorial Day to honor those who had gone they listened to the music of the great conflict; year after year as the nation paused on February 12 to pay tribute to Abraham Lincoln the songs of the Civil War were played and sung once again. And year after year composers have created new music, varying from marches to symphonies, based upon the two themes of the war and the wartime President.

For there is a timelessness and a timeliness in much of the music of one hundred years ago. The ultimate triumph of justice through the ordeal of man as expressed in Julia Ward Howe's "Battle Hymn" is a hope everlasting:

> Mine eyes have seen the glory
> Of the coming of the Lord;
>
> - - - - - - - - - - -
>
> As He died to make men holy,
> Let us die to make men free.
>
> - - - - - - - - - - -
>
> His truth is marching on.

The yearning for peace and the ending of war so movingly invoked by Walter Kittredge's "Tenting Tonight" is an aspiration ever present:

> Many are the hearts that are weary tonight,
> Wishing for the war to cease;
> Many are the hearts that are looking for the right,
> To see the dawn of peace.

Deep in the hearts of men and deep in the heart of Abraham Lincoln, the music of the Civil War continues to evoke a warm and responsive note in the hearts of Americans today.

A NOTE ON SOURCES

THE SOURCES FOR THIS STUDY WERE MANY, VARIED, AND scattered, for three areas had to be explored in the search for materials—Lincolniana, the Civil War, and Music. Within these areas, the first two of which are familiar to all, but the third much less so, it was in the nooks and corners and in the byways that the specific details were to be found from which evolved the story of LINCOLN AND THE MUSIC OF THE CIVIL WAR. Such details could only be discovered "by littles," as Lincoln would say, in places widely separated.

I was fortunate in having at and near my "home base" excellent resources for basic needs. The Edward C. Stone, F. Lauriston Bullard, and Truman H. Bartlett collections of Lincolniana in the Chenery Library of Boston University provided ready access to fundamental materials and often opened up new approaches to hitherto unexplored byways. My reliance upon these collections was thus both frequent and fruitful.

The rich resources in the Music and Newspaper divisions of the Boston Public Library were systematically consulted; many hours were profitably spent at that unique haven for scholars, the Boston Athenaeum; and numerous trips were made to Brown University with its unsurpassed collection of music and its superb materials in Lincolniana.

Other libraries visited during periods of sabbatical leave and vacation were: the Library of Congress (Music, Manuscript, and Newspaper divisions); the Lincoln Library at Lincoln Memorial University, Harrogate, Tennessee; the Lincoln National Life Foundation, Fort

Wayne, Indiana; the Illinois State Historical Library, Springfield, Illinois; the Henry E. Huntington Library, San Marino, California. From the rich treasures of each of these were drawn additional important, essential, and valuable materials.

Four summers spent in Pullman, Washington, three of them while teaching at the state university there, gave me the opportunity to explore certain resources that otherwise would have been inaccessible. Briefer visits to acquire needed information on specific points were made to the National Archives, the Public Library, and the Ford's Theatre Museum, Washington, D.C., and to libraries in several other cities.

Each specific source used has been identified in the Notes, with complete bibliographical data being given with the first citation. Rather than repeat this information in a long formal bibliography, I have limited myself to making brief comments on some of the types of sources, their variety and usefulness. It is hoped that these comments will point the way for those who wish to make further use of the Notes themselves.

Newspapers proved to be the most useful single source on musical activities in Washington and on the home front generally. They also, on occasion, provided pertinent information from "the seat of the war." The papers selected represent different regions of the country from Portland, Maine, to Portland, Oregon, but with more from the East than from other areas. There are a few citations from English journals. Differing political viewpoints are also reflected in the papers used, for even musical news was sometimes slanted! This was particularly true during the presidential campaign of 1864. For day-to-day events of a musical nature the newspapers were indispensable. *Harper's Weekly* and *Frank Leslie's Illustrated Newspaper* were extremely useful supplements to the daily papers.

Of the manuscript sources used, three, all in the Library of Congress, proved especially fruitful: Benjamin B. French's letters in the B. B. French Papers, John G.

Nicolay's letters to his fiancée, Therena Bates, in the John G. Nicolay Papers, and various items in the Robert Todd Lincoln Collection. Although the remaining sources yielded but few items, those few were highly significant.

The printed writings of people who lived through the tragic years of the war—diaries, journals, letters, autobiographies, biographies, and even those often unreliable sources, reminiscences and recollections—were rewarding reservoirs of pertinent information, sometimes surprisingly so! Thus, as might be expected, the *Diary of George Templeton Strong* (Allan Nevins and Milton Halsey Thomas, eds.), contains numerous entries of a musical nature, but to find significant references to musical affairs in the *Diary of Gideon Welles* (John T. Morse, ed.), whose voluminous papers yielded nothing on music, was a pleasant surprise! Among others, Benjamin B. French, John Hay, and Orville H. Browning made reference to musical incidents and musical personages in their diaries.

Collections of letters that were useful ranged from the intensely human letters of Cornelia Hancock in *South After Gettysburg* (Henrietta Stratton Jaquette, ed.), to the formal epistles of Charles Sumner in Edward L. Pierce, *Memoir and Letters of Charles Sumner;* autobiographical works of value included those as diverse as James Freeman Clarke, *Autobiography, Diary and Correspondence* and Frederick Douglass, *Life and Times of Frederick Douglass.*

Within the wide category of recollections and reminiscences referred to were many of the familiar volumes such as Noah Brooks, *Washington in Lincoln's Time;* Francis Fisher Browne, *The Every-Day Life of Abraham Lincoln;* and F. B. Carpenter, *Six Months at the White House with Abraham Lincoln,* together with others more unusual. These latter included such varied volumes as Belle Boyd, *Belle Boyd in Camp and Prison, Written by Herself;* P. T. Barnum, *Struggles and Triumphs: or Forty Years' Recollections of P. T. Barnum,* Written by Himself; and *Grandma Moses: My Life's History* (Otto Kallir, ed.).

Military and regimental histories, together with accounts written by soldiers themselves, provided some material on musical events at the front and in camp. Among the most satisfactory of these was *The Road to Richmond: The Civil War Memoirs of Maj. Abner R. Small of the Sixteenth Maine Volunteers; with [His] Diary as a Prisoner of War* (Harold Adams Small, ed.).

Sources dealing with music, musical personages and organizations in general, included Sigmund Spaeth, *A History of Popular Music in America;* H. W. Swartz, *Bands in America;* and William Carter White, *A History of Military Music in America.* The two volumes on Civil War music, Willard A. and Porter W. Heaps, *The Singing Sixties,* and Irwin Silber, *Songs of the Civil War,* were also useful.

For the real "flavor of the times" as well as for detail, however, older books were more helpful. Typical works in this category were: Louis Albert Banks, *Immortal Songs of Camp and Field;* Charles E. Claghorn, *The Mocking Bird, The Life and Diary of Its Author, Sep Winner;* Alexander Clark, *Philip Phillips: The Story of His Life;* Louis Moreau Gottschalk, *Notes of a Pianist* (Clara Gottschalk, ed.) ; Clara Louise Kellogg, *Memoirs of an American Prima Donna;* Frank Moore, *The Civil War in Song and Story;* Philip Phillips, *Song Pilgrimages Round the World;* Frank Rauscher, *Music on the March;* and George F. Root, *The Story of a Musical Life.* Much information of interest was also found in issues of *Dwight's Journal of Music* (John S. Dwight, ed.), and of *The Musical Review and Musical World.*

Basic facts on many major musical personages and works were available in *Grove's Dictionary of Music and Musicians* (J. A. Fuller Maitland, ed.), but information on less-well-known but important figures—composers, bandleaders, singers, and instrumentalists—was not easily found. Some details were gathered from works already mentioned, some appear in *Appleton's Cyclo-*

paedia of American Biography (James Grant Wilson and John Fiske, eds.), and occasional references were found in such works as George C. D. Odell, *Annals of the New York Stage*. The musicians who contributed so much to the Civil War are a rather neglected group. George Calvin Carter's short volume *Walter Kittredge Minstrel of the Merrimack* stands almost alone in this field.

For events musical and otherwise, frequent reference was made to that unique compendium of the war years, *The Rebellion Record* (Frank Moore, ed.), and to that useful current publication, *Lincoln Lore*. From first to last, *The Collected Works of Abraham Lincoln* (Roy P. Basler, ed., Marion Dolores Pratt and Lloyd A. Dunlap, asst. eds.), and *Lincoln Day by Day* (Earl Schenck Miers, editor-in-chief), were, of course, indispensable.

A NOTE ON THE MUSIC

A VITAL PART OF THE MATERIAL FOR THIS STUDY WAS THE music itself. I wanted to see the music, to ponder the significance of titles, to go over tunes, and to read verses. I wanted to connect titles, tunes, and verses with events of the war and to associate them with the unmusical lover of music in the White House. I wanted, in short, to sense the power and force of this emotion-packed vehicle of war and peace.

Consequently, from the first, the search for materials involved the quest for music, for I hoped to locate all the pieces that would become part of the narrative itself. As I went from library to library, as I communicated with Lincolnians and collectors, more and more pieces on my "wanted" list came to light. Whenever possible I saw and studied originals, and whenever possible I secured photostats or photographic reproductions.

Although my quest was not entirely successful—there are still sought-after compositions hiding in secret places —I have seen and obtained copies of a goodly number of these musical messages of the war. It has been the deeper meaning of these messages in tune and song that I have tried to express in words in this book.

INDEX